GLOBAL LAWMAKING AND SOCIAL CHANGE

Customary international law is a widely-recognised modality of international lawmaking. It underpins all norms of international law and shapes all aspects of global society. Yet familiar approaches to customary international law struggle to answer basic questions about its role, operation, and prospects.

Pursuing an interdisciplinary approach, this book offers an alternative perspective on customary international law as a dynamic and multifaceted social phenomenon and idea. It explores customary international lawmaking in different social contexts, including the regulation of armed conflict, the treatment of the 'other', and the management of global environmental risks. Focusing on the 'varieties' of customary international law, it identifies four types of customary international law norms and explores their roles and implications.

Critically revisiting a classic topic of international law, the book provides a tool for understanding and shaping global lawmaking and social change in a rapidly changing international legal order.

Volume 95 in the series Studies in International Law

Studies in International Law

Recent titles in this series

Extraterritoriality and Climate Change Jurisdiction: Exploring EU Climate Protection under International Law
Natalie L Dobson

International Law and the War with Islamic State: Challenges for Jus ad Bellum and Jus in Bello
Saeed Bagheri

Private Actors as Participants in International Law: A Critical Analysis of Membership under the Law of the Sea
Armando Rocha

Truth and Transitional Justice: Localising the International Legal Framework in Muslim Majority Legal Systems
Alice Panepinto

State Responsibility for Non-State Actors: Past, Present and Prospects for the Future
Richard Mackenzie-Gray Scott

International Agreements between Non-State Actors as a Source of International Law
Melissa Loja

Judicial Decisions in International Law Argumentation: Between Entrapment and Creativity
Letizia Lo Giacco

South-South Migrations and the Law from Below: Case Studies on China and Nigeria
Oreva Olakpe

Territorial Status in International Law
Jure Vidmar

Marine Bioprospecting, Biodiversity and Novel Uses of Ocean Resources: New Approaches in International Law
Edited by Niels Krabbe and David Langlet

The Standard of Review Before the International Court of Justice: Between Principle and Pragmatism
Felix Fouchard

Global Lawmaking and Social Change: The Varieties of Customary International Law
Gregor Novak

For a complete list of titles in this series see www.bloomsbury.com/uk/series/studies-in-international-law/

Global Lawmaking and Social Change

The Varieties of Customary International Law

Gregor Novak

•HART•
OXFORD • LONDON • NEW YORK • NEW DELHI • SYDNEY

HART PUBLISHING

Bloomsbury Publishing Plc

Kemp House, Chawley Park, Cumnor Hill, Oxford, OX2 9PH, UK

1385 Broadway, New York, NY 10018, USA

29 Earlsfort Terrace, Dublin 2, Ireland

HART PUBLISHING, the Hart/Stag logo, BLOOMSBURY and the Diana logo are trademarks of Bloomsbury Publishing Plc

First published in Great Britain 2025

A catalogue record for this book is available from the British Library.

A catalogue record for this book is available from the Library of Congress.

Library of Congress Control Number: 2024944199

ISBN: HB: 978-1-50996-849-7
ePDF: 978-1-50996-851-0
ePub: 978-1-50996-850-3

Typeset by Compuscript Ltd, Shannon

For my mother and grandmother

Preface

At a time when many diagnose the slow death of multilateralism, decry the injustices of the international legal order, or point to the futility of law as a meaningful framework for social change, let alone justice, another book about international lawmaking, let alone of the customary international law kind, may seem naïve, if not oblivious to an increasingly broken world. This book aims to be a constructive response to the countless daily tragedies shaped by international law, only a fraction of which make headline news. There has never been a better time to reassess the contemporary state and possible trajectories of what I call, somewhat aspirationally, *global lawmaking*. Just as we witness profound frustration with the substance and ineffectiveness of international law, we are also inundated with claims about what international law requires. Just as we bemoan international law's weakness, we also acknowledge its power, even as we remain perplexed by its complexity. During the last several years, international law has increasingly permeated both expert and popular discourses across the world – beyond urgent issues of the law of armed conflict and human rights law, international law questions are raised about the make-up of the United Nations and other international organisations, the management of the global ecosystem, and the design of the global economic and financial system. Undoubtedly, there is growing dissatisfaction with the current organisation of world society underpinned by international law, and it is articulated at all levels, from civil society, academia, business, the media, politics, and the arts. At a time of a perceived aggravation of geopolitical splits, rising so-called great power competition, and countless invocations of a permanent polycrisis, many are fanning the flames of division because it promises to deliver power within the broken pieces of what will remain of the mosaic of a still fundamentally nation-state–based political order. But make no mistake. The tensions and pressures we witness every day are signs that lawmaking processes are working in overdrive. Never in human history have we seen so much transnational normative activity, involving so many people, as we do today. At least in 'free' societies, the very cacophony of normative voices today – be they from the enemies of globalism to its staunchest supporters, as well as those dreaming of an alternative world order beyond planet Earth – reflects a keen awareness of the increasingly obvious fact that there is no acceptable alternative to a world governed as one by law. No matter how we end up calling the legal order that will govern our world in the coming decades, it will inescapably be the result of global lawmaking. That is why this book focuses on customary international law, potentially the most adaptable and inclusive modality of truly global lawmaking and one underpinning many of the central doctrines, principles, and rules of contemporary international law. To be sure, my critical reader's ears might perk up at the mention of the 'global', a concept both timely and fraught, as well as of 'customary international law', a concept both timeless and seemingly outdated. Who is the 'global' and does its invocation not serve to privilege a parochial and hegemonic perspective? Is the call for global lawmaking not a contradiction in terms when global inequality makes it a pipe dream? Does the focus on customary international law not transport us back to a more parochial and primitive setting? To my mind, the promise of global lawmaking is rooted in the idea of human dignity and equality and is worth defending, especially in the face of countless attempts to undermine it. Similarly, this book's approach to customary international law emphasises its multifaceted and dynamic character, making it fully compatible with a vision of democratic global lawmaking.

As this book tries to show, contemporary customary international lawmaking can be understood by reference to at least four types of customary international law norms. This goes against the grain of prevailing conceptions of customary international law and perspectives on law in general, even if it aligns with much of interdisciplinary scholarship on international law as well as more specialised scholarship on a myriad cross-border events that are shaped also by international law. The book makes a number of general findings. First, customary international law has never been unitary but is multifaceted, varying radically in operation, role, and effect depending on the relevant context. Second, customary international law has displayed patterns that suggest recurring types of customary international law norms that can offer guidance in a seemingly infinitely complex lawmaking arena. Third, customary international lawmaking has significantly transformed due to important institutional, technological, intellectual, and social changes that have marked the last century and a half, roughly. Fourth, customary international law as a social phenomenon is affected by and itself affects a complex amalgam of ideas about the *lex non scripta*, the legal doctrine of customary international law, and international law more generally. To understand the role and operation of customary international law, including its legal doctrine, they need to be examined jointly. This book therefore develops a parsimonious framework for understanding customary international law processes and resulting norms informed by insights into customary international law as both an intellectual and doctrinal, as well as a broader social phenomenon.

All of this is in tension with basic assumptions and perspectives encountered both in legal scholarship and practice, particularly the idea that customary international law is a unitary phenomenon. That background assumption leads in practice and theorising to many additional ones – sometimes explicit, often implicit. First, the assumption that the legal doctrine of customary international law should or could approximate a broader descriptive understanding of the customary international law process. Second, the contention that customary international law as such can be useful or useless, relevant or obsolescent, democratic or undemocratic, or suitable for the regulation of new technologies or not. Third, the suggestion that the legal doctrine of customary international law should be formalised or – conversely – necessarily be informal. Ultimately, these arguments are frail because they proceed from the false descriptive premise that customary international law is susceptible to totalising assessments as a unitary phenomenon.

Received understandings of customary international law make it difficult for us to understand, let alone address, some fundamental questions. For example, in contemporary international law, seemingly elementary customary prohibitions – of refoulement, forced labour, various crimes against humanity, and genocide – often remain weak and ineffective, as compared to customary norms invoked by governments or corporations to escape responsibility, ranging from sovereign immunity, the inapplicability of customary international law to corporate conduct, or territorial sovereignty. Even purportedly peremptory legal prescriptions (*jus cogens*) are frequently not reflected in the life of the law but are thwarted by stronger competing norms. At the same time, avenues do remain to strengthen existing legal norms, develop new law, and vindicate elementary legal prescriptions, sometimes against all odds. What lies behind this perplexing normative landscape? One thing is clear: The answer lies not in a unitary conception of customary international law. To understand this lawmaking landscape means understanding how we are governed at the global level and how global lawmaking in its multifacetedness can support or stymie social change.

This book is based on my doctoral dissertation at Yale University, submitted in mid-2021. While I have tried to take into account subsequent writing on the topic of customary international law, this book is inevitably just one intervention in an ongoing conversation. My hope is that readers will go away with a more nuanced understanding of the multifaceted phenomenon of customary international law and gain a deeper appreciation of the power and limits of international law. The time when all the world's people and peoples will truly be subject to a global legal order worthy of that name presumably lies far into the future. But only our collective inaction stands in the way of a global normative order that transcends borders, the divisions of nationhood or ethnicity, and focuses on the purpose of all legal orders, namely to facilitate a dignified coexistence among diverse individuals and groups and encourage social change without succumbing to brute power or crumbling in the face of attack or adversity.

Acknowledgements

REVISITING A CLASSIC topic of international law comes with the challenge and privilege of roaming far and wide for new insights. This book grew out of my doctoral research at Yale University, which began more than a decade ago. The resulting dissertation – more than four times the length of this book – received the Yale Law School's Ambrose Gherini Prize. I am grateful to the many people who helped along the way with knowledge, advice, and encouragement and the institutions that supported my research in numerous ways.

I am especially grateful to Michael Reisman, without whose support and intellectual guidance this book would not exist. I feel extremely privileged to have had the good fortune to be his student. Hopefully, some of what I have learned from him is also reflected in this book.

In bringing this project to completion, I relied – in ways large and small – on the advice, encouragement, patience, and support of many teachers and mentors. I am very grateful to Oona Hathaway and Scott Shapiro, who served on my JSD committee, for their consistent support of my project, their availability, and for helpful pieces of advice and encouragement along the way. Numerous other scholars generously offered time, pieces of advice, and suggestions that helped me, in one way or another, to complete this book. At the earliest stages of this project, Alec Stone Sweet provided valuable comments, for which I am very grateful. I also benefited greatly from Alvin Klevorick's comments on an earlier version of a section of this book. Learning about legal historiography from John Witt as part of his seminar on 'Legal History and Historiography' proved essential as I explored the history of customary international lawmaking. While dealing with disparate literatures across various social sciences, the opportunity to serve as a Teaching Fellow in courses led by Timothy Snyder of Yale's History Department and Stephen Roach of Yale's Jackson Institute for Global Affairs provided invaluable lessons in scholarship, historiography and economics, as well as numerous opportunities to develop as a teacher. I am also grateful to Mirjan Damaška for helpful comments and advice, to Samantha Besson for helpful comments on a partial work-in-progress, to Neil Walker for his time and insights into globalisation and legal theory, to Catherine Kessedjian for a highly instructive course on 'la justice internationale', to Paul Kahn for insights into law and legal scholarship as part of a seminar he gave with Mosche Halbertal, to Tom Tyler for valuable insights during a course on law and psychology, to Samuel Moyn for pointing me to valuable research on the history of minority rights, to Harold Koh for a wise piece of advice at the earliest stage of this project, and to numerous other scholars whose contributions to this project may not be reflected in this book's references.

I am also very grateful to Michael Byers, whose work on customary international law got me interested in interdisciplinary questions of law and global politics, and Aaron Boley for their kindness and openness in graciously offering me an academic home at the Outer Space Institute at the University of British Columbia while I was working on this project in 2019–20. They gave me the opportunity to learn from some of the world's leading scientists, engineers and policymakers in the outer space field and reflect on the relationship between technology and international lawmaking. Michael Byers also kindly involved me in a stimulating undergraduate course at the UBC's Political Science Department, providing me with valuable insights into interdisciplinary research and teaching. I am also grateful to James Stewart for his openness and valuable insights into the history of international criminal law and several memorable seminar discussions.

While developing some of the ideas in this book, I had the inordinate fortune and honour to serve as a Law Clerk to several exceptional international lawyers at the International Court of Justice and to learn from them and many others, something that proved invaluable in doing research on international law. His Excellency former President Hisashi Owada provided me with deep insights into international adjudication, gave me numerous opportunities to develop as an international lawyer, and offered exceptional support, guidance and kindness. Her Excellency President Joan Donoghue provided me with generous mentoring upon my arrival at the Court, precious opportunities to experience the work of an international court from the inside, and deep insight into international judicial decision-making. I feel very lucky and am deeply grateful to both for these opportunities, which allowed me not only to develop as an international lawyer and legal scholar but also to appreciate the importance of individual decision-makers in the international legal system. I also thank His Excellency former President Peter Tomka, who served as the Court's President during my Judicial Fellowship and took a great interest in the Law Clerk cohort while never failing to remember the topic of my research. I also thank His Excellency former Registrar Philippe Couvreur, who provided valuable insights and wise guidance on several occasions during my stay at the Court. I am also very grateful to His Excellency Judge Charles Brower, who provided valuable insights into judicial decision-making and generously offered guidance and advice. Finally, I am grateful to the Court's staff and members of several cohorts of Law Clerks and Judicial Fellows, who were an integral part of my experience at the Court and my development as a legal scholar.

My interest in international law was initially sparked at the University of Vienna. I am very grateful to Gerhard Hafner, with whom I've had the privilege to work as a research assistant and associate. He shared countless insights into practically every area of public international law and provided continuous encouragement and support. His sense of humour, intelligence and kindness were instrumental in allowing me to complete this project. I am also very grateful to August Reinisch, who provided me with my first professional appointment in international law and who graciously supported me as I embarked on my graduate studies in the United States. I am grateful for his support and kindness. I am also very grateful to the many other scholars and colleagues who provided support and guidance at the University of Vienna. In addition, I am grateful to Maja Seršić of the University of Zagreb for generously welcoming me as a guest lecturer at the Faculty of Law at the earliest stage of my teaching career.

I gratefully acknowledge the generous financial and other support received from the Yale Law School and Yale University, located on the lands and waterways of what is now the state of Connecticut and which several indigenous peoples and nations have stewarded through generations. I am grateful for the generous support received from the Fox International Fellowship at Yale University's MacMillan Center, which allowed me to spend an academic year at the delightfully stimulating Green College, located on the traditional, ancestral and unceded territory of the Musqueam First Nation. I am very grateful to Mark Vessey for providing me with the opportunity to join Green College as a resident member and for the moral and intellectual support provided by the College's community. Numerous organisations and persons provided support for conference attendance and training opportunities over the last several years, including the European University Institute, the Max Planck Society, Yves Daudet, the University of Fribourg, and the Outer Space Institute. I am very grateful for the exceptional library resources and support I was lucky enough to draw on at the libraries of Yale University and its Law School, the libraries of the Hague Academy of International Law and the International Court of Justice, the library of the University of British Columbia, as well as several national and university libraries in Austria, Belgium, Croatia, France, Germany and the Netherlands.

I am grateful to Cina Santos for her kindness and encouragement. I am grateful for the kind and supportive administrators of the Yale Law School's Graduate Programs and Financial Aid Office. In particular, I am grateful to Gordon Silverstein, Maria Dino, Thais Sobzcak, Caroline Curtis and Allegra di Bonaventura for their generous availability and wise guidance on issues large and small.

At the European Union institutions and the College of Europe, I was fortunate enough to have mentors and managers who encouraged both my scholarly and practical interests in international law. I am especially grateful to Federica Mogherini, Fernando Gentilini, Maryem van den Heuvel, Fernando Castillo de la Torre, Jurij Aston, Frank Hoffmeister, Daniele Calisti, Piotr Krygiel and Katarina Tapio. Of course, the views expressed in this book, and any errors or omissions, are mine alone and in no way reflect the views of any European Union institution.

I am grateful to numerous other colleagues and fellow scholars who provided support, advice, insight and company at various times since I embarked on this project: Amnart Tangkiriphimarn, Anat Lior, Arnaldur Hjartarson, Asaf Lubin, Asier Garrido Muñoz, Azhar Tyabji, Brent Salter, Bryan DG (Bo) Tiojanco,

Canelle Trouillot, Clare Ryan, Danny Maggen, Elinathan Ohiomoba, Erlend Leonhardsen, Gershon Hasin, Gilad Abiri, Heejin Kim, Henrik Jacobsen, Hrvoje Kurelec, Ignacio Mujica Torres, Ira Fedorenko, Jane Hofbauer, Jayden Lloyd, Joachim Pierer, Johanna Lorenzo, Karolina Januszewski, Katharina Isabel Schmidt, Lena Riemer, Liiri Oja, Lucas MacClure, Marius Kothor, Mathias Walch, Max Wälde, Merryl Lawry-White, Naama Omri, Nora Stappert, Peter Bachmayer, Raeesa Vakil, Rashmi Raman, Roman Zinigrad, Samantha Godwin, Sanya Kumar, Sappho Gilbert, Sebastian Reiter, Shixue Hu, Tomas Dumbrovsky, Ying Hu, Ying Zhu, Yoon Jin Shin and Zsofia Korosy.

Parts of this book benefited from discussions of work-in-progress in various fora, including the 'Foundations of Legal Scholarship' seminar at the Yale Law School, the Doctoral Scholarship Workshop Series of the Yale Law School's Graduate Program, the 'Bilingual Colloquium on International Law and the EU' at the University of Fribourg (Switzerland), the 'ESIL Research Forum' at the European University Institute, the 'Resident Members' Series' at Green College (University of British Columbia), the 'ESIL Annual Meeting' at the University of Stockholm, the 'Virtual Round Table' of the University of Vienna's Section for International Law and International Relations, and the '8th International Four Societies (of International Law) Conference'. I am grateful to the organisers, funders, and all participants of those events for their generosity, helpful comments, and openness. I covered some of the ideas relating to international environmental law discussed in this book as a guest speaker in Michael Reisman's 'Public Order of the World Community' seminar as well as in seminars I taught in Beijing and New Haven as part of the Yale Young Global Scholars program. Some parts of this book draw on ideas also reflected in articles published in the Max Planck Encyclopedia of Comparative Constitutional Law and the Columbia Journal of Environmental Law.

I am further grateful to Sinead Moloney and her team at Hart Publishing, including Sasha Jawed, Tom Adams and Linda Goss, for taking this project on and seeing it to completion with patience, flexibility and professionalism.

Last but not least, this project relied on the friendship and moral support of many other individuals. I thank them all. In addition, I am most grateful to Misun, my wife, whose love and support were crucial in allowing me to complete this project.

Table of Contents

Introduction

UNWRITTEN FORMS OF law can illuminate central questions about the nature of law and the relationship between lawmaking, democracy, and social change because of their liminal character as law and their pervasiveness across legal orders.[1] This is also true at the international level, where unwritten forms of law are authoritatively recognised sources of international legal obligation. This book joins a vibrant scholarly debate about the role, operation, social effects, and prospects of the basic and most intriguing modality of lawmaking in the global arena: customary international law. Its core contribution is a new framework for understanding how customary international law advances and stymies social change. The framework is meant to be realistic, parsimonious, and useful to legal scholars, legal practitioners, and students of international law and other disciplines. The book tests it across a series of representative and diverse examples from the contemporary history of international law. They illustrate how norms of customary international law were sustained in different social spheres, from the regulation of war, the management of migration, and the regulation of environmental risk. Importantly, the book connects this broader study of customary international lawmaking to the legal doctrine of customary international law and other elements of its institutional design.

I. REASSESSING CUSTOMARY INTERNATIONAL LAWMAKING

In 1907, Eugen Ehrlich, who inaugurated the modern sociology of law, described the problem of customary law as one of the 'hottest and most discussed topics of our field for more than a hundred years'.[2] Today, the same could be said of customary international law. Over the last three decades, scholars have devoted enormous amounts of intellectual energy to examining, understanding, and theorising customary international law. They have juxtaposed age-old 'deductive' and 'inductive' approaches to the identification and interpretation of customary international law. Scholars have developed various approaches to customary international law by reference to distinct methods used by officials,

[1] LL Fuller, 'Human Interaction and the Law' (1969) 14(1) *American Journal of Jurisprudence* 1, reprinted in LL Fuller, *The Principles of Social Order: Selected Essays of Lon L. Fuller* (edited by KI Winston) (Durham, Duke University Press, 1981) 211.

[2] E Ehrlich, *Tatsachen des Gewohnheitsrechts, Inaugurationsrede, gehalten am 2. Dezember 1906* (Leipzig, Franz Deuticke, 1906) 3 (translation by the author). On Ehrlich, see eg M Hertogh (ed), *Living Law: Reconsidering Eugen Ehrlich* (Oxford, Hart Publishing, 2009).

judges, lawyers, or legal scholars to identify and interpret customary international law. Critiques of the formalism of the legal doctrine of customary international law doctrine are also hardly new. As early as 1939, Hans Kelsen noted that '[t]he two-element theory [of customary international law] has no other function but to hide the … dominant role that the will of the competent law-applying organ plays in the formation of customary law'.[3] In 1969, in an insightful study of unwritten law with important implications for customary international law, Lon Fuller argued that '[w]e cannot understand 'ordinary' law (that is, officially declared or enacted law) unless we first obtain an understanding of what is called customary law'.[4] In the same year, Alfred Verdross made valuable inroads into identifying different types of customary international law, albeit from a doctrinal perspective.[5] In 1998, Maurice Mendelson emphasised that '[t]o speak of the formal rules about how custom is made and unmade is … in a way to miss the whole point'.[6] In 1999, two sets of influential accounts of customary international law, by Michael Byers from the political science angle and by Jack Goldsmith and Eric Posner from the law and economics perspective, opened the door to a continuing stream of interdisciplinary scholarship about customary international law.[7] In 2010, Daniel Bodansky cautioned that '[i]f we view customary international law as a single phenomenon, the tendency is to develop a single explanatory account'.[8] In 2020, Monica Hakimi suggested that scholars should 'retire the rulebook conception and recognize that [customary international law] is an inherently contingent and variable kind of law'.[9] In parallel, scholars have proposed or discussed more refined descriptive or explanatory theories of lawmaking in the international context, including by reference to customary international law. At the same time, due to its cross-cutting nature, nearly every scholar or lawyer facing an issue of international law, be it practical or academic, has needed to grapple with customary international law, directly or indirectly.[10]

[3] H Kelsen, *Écrits français de droit international* (edited by C Leben) (Paris, Presses universitaires de France, 2001) 75 (translation by the author).

[4] Fuller, 'Human Interaction and the Law' (n 1) 2.

[5] See A Verdross, 'Entstehungsweisen und Geltungsgrund des universellen völkerrechtlichen Gewohnheitsrechts' (1969) 29 *Zeitschrift für ausländisches öffentliches Recht und Völkerrecht* 635; see also R Kolb, 'Selected Problems in the Theory of Customary International Law' (2003) 50(2) *Netherlands International Law Review* 119, 128–30.

[6] M Mendelson, 'The Formation of Customary International Law' (1998) 272 *Collected Courses of the Hague Academy of International Law* 155, 172–3.

[7] M Byers, *Custom, Power and the Power of Rules: International Relations and Customary International Law* (Cambridge, Cambridge University Press, 1999); JL Goldsmith and EA Posner, 'A Theory of Customary International Law' (1999) 66 *University of Chicago Law Review* 1113.

[8] D Bodansky, 'Prologue to a Theory of Non-Treaty Norms' in MH Arsanjani et al (eds), *Looking to the Future: Essays on International Law in Honor of W. Michael Reisman* (Leiden, Martinus Nijhoff, 2010) 124, 133.

[9] M Hakimi, 'Making Sense of Customary International Law' (2020) 118 *Michigan Law Review* 1487, 1491.

[10] Among a wide variety of contributions to the study of customary international law, there are many specialised and partial takes, discussions assembling a myriad random thoughts,

International law shapes most aspects of contemporary world society and influences the lives of billions. Understanding how the design of customary international lawmaking, an important part of international law, affects substantive outcomes is important because such outcomes, in the form of norms, decisions, as well as social entailments, shape the protection of persecuted or vulnerable individuals and groups, the access to and distribution of valued resources, the management of global and regional environmental risks, the prevention and regulation of armed conflict, and the sustainable uses of shared resources, among others. Explaining what sustains customary international law helps reveal how global-level norms affect world society and how meaningful social change can be better supported and nourished at this seemingly vertiginous level. It is also essential to gain a better understanding of customary international lawmaking at a time when international law appears to be under unprecedented pressure and dim prospects of closer multilateral cooperation pose existential risks to human safety, welfare, and life.

Nonetheless, we lack a comprehensive and contextual framework for understanding of how international law is made and changed. This is true also in respect of customary international law, a basic and widely accepted modality of international lawmaking that many contemporary legal scholars conceive of as a unitary 'source of law' derived from a combination of state practice and so-called *opinio iuris*.[11] This book focuses on customary international law as a social phenomenon and set of ideas, two sides of an indissociable coin. In the most general sense, customary international law refers to a slice of the unwritten parts of international law – famously, the ICJ is directed to apply it in Article 38 of its Statute.[12] As noted, while discussions centred on the legal doctrine of customary international law are legion,[13] and many valuable interdisciplinary studies of customary international law exist,[14] comprehensive and contextual studies of the phenomenon are rare. To be sure, several scholars have tried to

unexplored hunches, and untested hypotheses about customary international law. A good example is NG Onuf (ed), *Law-Making in the Global Community* (Durham, Carolina Academic Press, 1982). In Mendelson's words, for example, 'the ideas expressed [about customary international law] are perhaps too complex and numerous to be easily summed up'. See Mendelson, 'The Formation of Customary International Law' (n 6) 172–3.

[11] See eg the references at n 20.

[12] See *North Sea Continental Shelf Cases (Germany v Denmark, Germany v Netherlands)* (Judgment) [1969] ICJ Rep 3, para 77. See also ILC, 'Draft Conclusions on Identification of Customary International Law, With Commentaries' (2018) UN Doc A/73/10 122; International Law Association, *Final Report of the Committee on Formation of Customary (General) International Law* (London, ILA, 2000); see also P Haggenmacher, 'An Archaeological Look at "International Custom as Evidence of a General Practice Accepted as Law" and Article 38 of the World Court's Statute' (2021) 34(3) *Leiden Journal of International Law* 1, 4–5.

[13] See on the legal doctrine of customary international law, with further references, Chapter 6.

[14] Both the literature dealing explicitly and implicitly with customary international are enormous. See, eg, in addition to the works already cited and limited to the last three decades, DP Fidler, 'Challenging the Classical Concept of Custom: Perspectives on the Future of Customary International Law' (1996) 39 *German Yearbook of International Law* 198; JP Trachtman, *The Economic*

develop more nuanced and realistic approaches to customary international law.[15] Scholars have also examined the different substantive and institutional contexts in which customary international law is identified and applied. However, with some exceptions, even social scientists studying international law have too often taken at face value an image of customary international law that has little purchase on how customary international law is crafted 'in the wild', or how it is wielded by lawyers and policymakers. This affects our ability to arbitrate between various proposals for social change through legal reform, regardless of whether they focus on the redesign of lawmaking institutions, the prescription of particular substantive norms, the codification of the meta-norms governing

Structure of International Law (Cambridge, Harvard University Press, 2008); AT Guzman, *How International Law Works: A Rational Choice Theory* (Oxford, Oxford University Press, 2008); BD Lepard, *Customary International Law: A New Theory with Practical Applications* (Cambridge, Cambridge University Press, 2010); RB Baker, 'Customary International Law in the 21st Century: Old Challenges and New Debates' (2010) 21(1) *European Journal of International Law* 173; BD Lepard (ed), *Reexamining Customary International Law* (Cambridge, Cambridge University Press, 2017); J Brunnée and SJ Toope, *Legitimacy and Legality in International Law: An Interactional Account* (Oxford, Oxford University Press, 2010); M Koskenniemi, *From Apology to Utopia: The Structure of International Legal Argument* (reissue with a new Epilogue) (Cambridge, Cambridge University Press, 2006) 388–473; N Arajärvi, *The Changing Nature of Customary International Law: Methods of Interpreting the Concept of Custom in International Criminal Tribunals* (Abingdon, Routledge, 2014); JB Murphy, *The Philosophy of Customary Law* (Oxford, Oxford University Press, 2014); SC Neff, *Justice Among Nations* (Cambridge, Harvard University Press, 2014); CA Bradley (ed), *Custom's Future: International Law in a Changing World* (Cambridge, Cambridge University Press, 2016); S Droubi and J d'Aspremont (eds), *International Organisations, Non-State Actors, and the Formation of Customary International Law* (Manchester, Manchester University Press, 2020); P Dumberry, *The Formation and Identification of Rules of Customary International Law in International Investment Law* (Cambridge, Cambridge University Press, 2018); J d'Aspremont, *The Discourse on Customary International Law* (Oxford, Oxford University Press, 2021); P Merkouris et al (eds), *Custom and its Interpretation in International Investment Law* (Cambridge, Cambridge University Press, 2024); P Merkouris, J Kammerhofer, and N Arajärvi (eds), *The Theory, Practice, and Interpretation of Customary International Law* (Cambridge, Cambridge University Press, 2022); PM Dupuy (ed), *Customary International Law* (Cheltenham, Edward Elgar, 2021); J Brunnée and S Toope, 'Interactional International Law: An Introduction' (2011) 3(2) *International Theory* 307; PH Verdier and E Voeten, 'How Does Customary International Law Change? The Case of State Immunity' (2015) 59 (2) *International Studies Quarterly* 209; JA Green, *The Persistent Objector Rule in International Law* (Oxford, Oxford University Press, 2016); PH Verdier and E Voeten, 'Precedent, Compliance, and Change in Customary International Law: An Explanatory Theory' (2014) 108(3) *The American Journal of International Law* 389; S Talmon, 'Determining Customary International Law: The ICJ's Methodology between Induction, Deduction and Assertion' (2015) 26(2) *European Journal of International Law* 417; N Petersen, 'The International Court of Justice and the Judicial Politics of Identifying Customary International Law' (2017) 28(2) *European Journal of International Law* 357; see also generally CJ Tams and James Sloan (eds), *The Development of International Law by the International Court of Justice* (Oxford, Oxford University Press, 2013).

[15] ibid and see also R Kolb, 'Selected Problems in the Theory of Customary International Law' (2003) 50 *Netherlands International Law Review* 119; HG Cohen, 'Finding International Law, Part II: Our Fragmenting Legal Community' (2012) 44(4) *New York University Journal of International Law and Politics* 1049; HG Cohen, 'Finding International Law: Rethinking the Doctrine of Sources' (2007) 93 *Iowa Law Review* 65; HG Cohen, 'The Plural Sources of Customary International Law' (2023) 1 *University of Georgia School of Law Research Paper Series* 1; N Krisch and E Yildiz (eds), *The Many Paths of Change in International Law* (Oxford, Oxford University Press, 2023) (focusing on processes of international lawmaking generally).

customary international lawmaking, or the very place of customary international law in international law's list of authoritative 'sources'.[16]

By postulating that customary international law is a unitary 'source of law' made and sustained similarly across different social contexts, contemporary legal scholarship has produced a distorted and partial picture of the international 'law in action' that stifles the possibility of social change through international law. In parallel, scholars have called for changes to the legal doctrine of customary international law, be it through the formalisation of its doctrine or its wholesale redefinition. All the while, others have called for custom's abandonment – arguing that it is ineffective, defective, or leads to morally questionable outcomes. Legal scholars have also proposed numerous critiques of and attempts at reconceptualising customary international law.[17] Some scholars have resisted calls for the formalisation of customary international law, arguing that these are based on mistaken descriptive assumptions,[18] or urged scholars to abandon the 'rulebook conception' of customary international law.[19] As important as these efforts have been, they have only started to open the field up to alternative, more realistic, and comprehensive understandings of customary international law. In other words, over the last several decades, diverse normative arguments have been built on top of a largely underdeveloped descriptive understanding of customary international lawmaking. In short, few topics have garnered as much sustained attention from international legal scholars as customary international law. However, several basic questions remain unanswered because of the persistence of a unitary understanding of customary international law.[20]

[16] This seems especially relevant in a field characterised by a tension between 'commitment' and 'cynicism'. See also M Koskenniemi, 'Between Commitment and Cynicism: Outline for a Theory of International Law as Practice' in J d'Aspremont et al (eds), *International Law as a Profession* (Cambridge, Cambridge University Press, 2017) 40.

[17] See above and also eg BS Chimni, 'Customary International Law: A Third World Perspective' (2018) 112 *American Journal of International Law* 1; DH Joyner, 'Why I Stopped Believing in Customary International Law' (2019) 9(1) *Asian Journal of International Law* 31, 33; WM Reisman, 'The Cult of Custom in the late 20th Century' (1987) 17 *California Western International Law Journal* 133, 142–3; H Charlesworth and C Chinkin, *The Boundaries of International Law: A Feminist Analysis* (Manchester, Manchester University Press, 2000) 67–95.

[18] See eg TL Meyer, 'Towards a Communicative Theory of International Law' (2012) 13 *Melbourne Journal of International Law* 1, 13.

[19] Hakimi, 'Making Sense of Customary International Law' (n 9) 1491.

[20] The mainstream view of customary international law among international law scholars is presented persuasively in the latest edition of Malcolm Evans' textbook on international law. See AE Roberts and S Sivakumaran, 'The Theory and Reality of the Sources of International Law' in MD Evans (ed), *International Law*, 5th edn (Oxford, Oxford University Press, 2014) 89 (on the basis of the earlier text by Hugh Thirlway). While this account is largely internal to the legal enterprise, it is grounded in varied doctrinal interpretations of the practices of courts and legal officials, as tentative or contextual as these may be. At the same time, the account only hints at ways in which the legal doctrine of sources is related to international lawmaking more broadly. See also Roberts' influential contribution to the study of customary international law doctrine in AE Roberts, 'Traditional and Modern Approaches to Customary International Law: A Reconciliation' (2001) 95(4) *American Journal of International Law* 757. See also James Crawford, *Brownlie's Principles of Public International Law*, 9th edn (Oxford, Oxford University Press, 2019) 21–8.

From the most general perspective, customary international law refers both to a multifaceted social phenomenon and a set of ideas. It shares this dual character with law 'in general' and other comparable social phenomena.[21] As a social phenomenon, customary international law appears in a variety of lawmaking processes and resulting norms. As an idea, it can be conceived of as an intellectual amalgam of ideas about the *lex non scripta* in general and particular legal doctrines and ideas that pertain to it as a relatively recent and contingent form of unwritten international law. These two aspects of customary international law are ever-changing and continuously affect one another.[22] Before proceeding further, some attention should be paid to what I mean by customary international law processes and norms. Legal norms[23] can be observed in a variety of contexts: For example, domestic courts can announce norms, treaties can spell them out, expert reports can codify them, a midair collision can embody them, and domestic implementation can try to effectuate them. All these can be understood as communicative acts – claims, counter-claims, and so on – that give us an initial indication of what the governing law on some particular matter is. Whether and to what extent a particular norm is effective in a particular community needs, however, to be investigated from a more fine-grained perspective. The outcomes of various customary international law processes, that is, legal norms, can be defined as shared and effective expectations about relevant social facts (such as conduct) of relevant actors in any particular social interaction (or more generally) that are understood – implicitly or explicitly – as customary international law by those actors. Whether or not a customary international law norm exists in a particular instance (i.e., is accompanied by shared and effective legal expectations) requires a broader investigation. Notwithstanding this general definition of legal norms, however, I will later explain why different types of customary international law norms need to be distinguished on account of their particular characteristics.

This book proposes a new framework for understanding a central phenomenon of contemporary international law focused on the 'varieties' of customary international law norms. It seeks to complement existing accounts of customary international law, leaning on the rich tradition of research going under the name of socio-legal studies and legal pluralism. However, its aim is

[21] See eg K Tuori, *Ratio and Voluntas: The Tension Between Reason and Will in Law* (Farnham, Ashgate, 2013); F Pirie, *The Anthropology of Law* (Oxford, Oxford University Press, 2013); see also, on the concept of the social, social phenomena, and social science, B Latour, *Reassembling the Social: An Introduction to Actor-Network-Theory* (Oxford, Oxford University Press, 2005) 7; M Koskenniemi, *The Gentle Civilizer of Nations: The Rise and Fall of International Law 1870–1960* (Cambridge, Cambridge University Press, 2001) 7.

[22] See also K Tuori, *Ratio and Voluntas: The Tension Between Reason and Will in Law* (Farnham, Ashgate, 2013) ix.

[23] See Chapter 1, Section IV.

decidedly not to enlarge the scope of what legal scholars and legal practitioners already refer to as customary international law. Instead, its contribution is chiefly perspectival, seeking to advance our understanding of a basic category of legal scholarship and practice. In short, this book's main novel contribution lies in proposing an analytical and explanatory framework of the 'varieties' of contemporary customary international lawmaking and corresponding types of customary international law norms. It identifies four types of contemporary customary international law norms by reference to distinct configurations of sustaining factors that render them effective in particular contexts. It develops this framework based on an examination of the phenomenon of customary international law from both its intellectual first principles and through a series of 'normative episodes' of the customary international law 'in action' from around the nineteenth century to the present.

A contextual and multifaceted understanding of customary international law as an idea and social phenomenon[24] helps reveal its limits and potential at a time when rising expectations placed on international law meet growing exasperation with its ability to mirror, let alone advance, social change. The last several years have been marked by attempts by authoritarian movements at eroding the rule of law and norms associated with good governance, as well as rising nationalism and a partial retreat from multilateral lawmaking, in particular treaty-making and independent third-party adjudication. A better understanding of contemporary customary international lawmaking in its broader socio-legal context will allow scholars and policymakers, as well as all interested observers, to recognise and leverage avenues for social change through law in the face of environmental degradation, global socio-economic inequality, devastating armed conflicts, and generally declining global cooperation. We also need a better understanding of what holds the international legal order together during times of crisis and instability, if only to recognise the fragile legal foundation on which the current world order ultimately rests.

The judge and other third-party decision-makers play important roles in most legal systems. Courts sometimes play a significant role in international law, albeit a distinctive one given the non-hierarchical and pluralistic architecture of the international legal order.[25] In particular, domestic and international courts

[24] See eg BZ Tamanaha, *Sociological Approaches to Theories of Law, Cambridge Elements in Philosophy of Law* (Cambridge, Cambridge University Press, 2022); R Cotterrell, *Law's Community: Legal Theory in Sociological Perspective* (Oxford, Oxford University Press, 1997).

[25] The role of the judge in the identification of customary international law is closely connected also to what Michael Reisman has described as the 'problem of enforcement', or 'the core problem [in international law]'. See WM Reisman, *Nullity and Revision: The Review and Enforcement of International Judgments and Awards* (New Haven, Yale University Press, 1971) 639 and 641–4. See also, with further references, LL Giacco, *Judicial Decisions in International Law Argumentation: Between Entrapment and Creativity* (Oxford, Hart Publishing, 2022) 9–12.

and tribunals uphold the legal fiction of a unitary customary international law, as do many jurists when they engage in doctrinal discourse. That will not come as a surprise to lawyers – after all, courts in many legal systems engage in forms of performance and deploy legal fictions to rationalise the past and reaffirm the legal order.[26] While such behaviour can seem puzzling, it serves an important role in integrating, stabilising, and developing the international legal order. It also serves to channel and legitimate judicial decision-making.[27] However, this fiction is severely limiting as we seek to understand customary international law from a broader scholarly perspective.

Notably, I suggest that international courts and tribunals have a relationship to custom that is more complicated than commonly realised and differs from that of domestic judicial institutions (in relation to domestic forms of 'customary law'). When international courts refer to customary international law, they tend to refer to one of the types of customary international law identified in this book. Of course, courts do not distinguish between or label different types of customary international law since they operate within the framework of a legal fiction reflected in the (unitary) legal doctrine of customary international law, which has its own role and function.[28] In that sense, my finding goes beyond accounts that try to analogise customary international law to the common law or that focus on 'how courts do custom', that is, how they claim to identify or interpret custom. That analogy fails because international courts are generally neither positioned hierarchically to each other nor have they monopolised the authoritative identification and interpretation of international law to the extent this is the case in many domestic legal orders. To be sure, scholars have found courts to 'do custom' in a particular way,[29] suggesting that there is a distinctive (if complex) way in which courts – including international courts – find customary international law. Some of these accounts are, in fact, compatible with mine to the extent that they suggest that 'a mixture of … methods … is characteristic' of their approach.[30] However, such accounts tend to abstract the various findings of custom by international courts (or one particular court) from the social context that renders customary international law norms effective.

Aside from the important but limited role of courts in international law, my approach focuses on customary international law as a comprehensive process in

[26] See eg C Kessedjian, 'Le tiers impartial et indépendant en droit international: juge, arbitre, médiateur, conciliateur: cours général de droit international' (2019) 403 *Collected Courses of the Hague Academy of International Law* 49, 501–10.

[27] See eg Reisman, *Nullity and Revision: The Review and Enforcement of International Judgments and Awards* (n 25) 641–4.

[28] To emphasise, by no means do I suggest that courts *should* distinguish between types of customary international law.

[29] See eg SJ Choi and M Gulati, 'Customary International Law: How do Courts Do It?' in Bradley (ed), *Custom's Future* (n 14) 117; N Petersen, 'The International Court of Justice and the Judicial Politics of Identifying Customary International Law' (n 14) 357.

[30] S Talmon, 'Determining Customary International Law: The ICJ's Methodology between Induction, Deduction and Assertion' (n 14) 441.

which courts are significant, but not the only relevant, actors. At any rate, for each type of customary international law norm, my typology suggests a characteristic configuration of sustaining factors. These factors describe ways in which various forms of power in international society are channeled, transformed, and indeed augmented. One type is not better than the other; that much can be said for now, even if they can of course be evaluated normatively. They simply represent different types of customary international law norms that have emerged and play distinct roles in international society.

As I argue in this book, normative proposals and descriptive accounts of customary international law that posit a unitary form of customary international law should be resisted. Descriptively, they tend to be based on a faulty and limited empirical understanding of customary international law, which is a multifaceted social phenomenon and idea. Normatively, they would impoverish international law's multifaceted set of lawmaking modalities in favour of an unimaginative analogy that borrows from idealised or particular domestic legal precedents that are themselves mythical. Finally, little supports the assumption that customary international law as such would be less democratic than other modalities of international lawmaking. In fact, strong arguments point in the opposite direction.

II. STABILITY AND CHANGE IN GLOBAL LAWMAKING

Customary international law is a significant modality of international lawmaking and understanding how it works has far-reaching intellectual and potential social payoffs: Despite the hope, blame, or indifference that international law can elicit both in public debates and in scholarship, the links between processes of international lawmaking and outcomes on the ground remain as important as they are insufficiently examined and poorly understood. It is crucial to understand how the design of customary international lawmaking relates to substantive outcomes because international law shapes our lives in profound but not always apparent ways. From norms entrenching territorial sovereignty, regulating cross-border pollution and trade, dividing up valuable maritime zones, and preventing or enabling movement and migration: Are all based on customary international law or a variety of other global lawmaking processes that are undergirded by customary international law. As such, customary international law shapes most aspects of contemporary world society and influences the lives of billions. Explaining what sustains it can therefore help us understand how meaningful social change can be better supported and nourished using customary international law. Without a thorough understanding of customary international lawmaking, we lack the ability to arbitrate between the varying proposals for social change through legal reform, be it by redesigning lawmaking institutions, prescribing particular substantive norms, or removing customary international law from the equation altogether. Crucially, an understanding of the varieties and dynamics of customary international lawmaking can shed light on how international law performs and could perform better in terms of the imperative of any legal order: To support social change without becoming indistinguishable from untrammelled power or crumbling in the face of challenges.

In most legal orders, legal norms vary in terms of how they are created, sustained, and changed and in the degree of their importance and stability. This is true both when certain groups of legal norms enjoy a higher status and when a central adjudicator can authoritatively balance the priority of competing claims in individual cases. In general, the diversity of normative arrangements across legal orders helps organise and structure social change. As mentioned, ideally, lawmaking processes and legal norms should on the whole be flexible enough to allow social change to be realised without becoming indistinguishable from untrammelled power or crumbling in the face of challenges.[31] This is also true in the field of international law, even if its characteristic features of decentralisation, normative polyphony, and dynamism work together to produce a distinctive lawmaking arena with more porous hierarchies and a deficit of authoritative and effective third-party decision-makers.

Customary international law is a compelling context in which to study the ubiquitous tension between legal stability and dynamism visible across legal orders, as well as the relationship between the design of international lawmaking and social outcomes. As I try to show, this is because customary international law's multifaceted nature offers a variety of opportunities for normative change, both on the level of substantive norms and customary international lawmaking itself. This book tries to illustrate this central insight by challenging the common understanding of customary international law as a unitary phenomenon and idea. It does this by exploring how and why customary international law norms emerge, are sustained, change, and wither away. It also highlights the role of the legal doctrine of customary international law, which is also a legal fiction allowing third-party decision-makers to leverage a wide range of normatively relevant information to rationalise the past and shape the future. However, beneath this veneer, customary international law is a multifaceted type of unwritten international law (the *lex non scripta*) whose norms derive from a variety of lawmaking processes.

At a time when the 'global' appears increasingly questioned, is it still justified to refer to 'global lawmaking' when describing the present or projecting possible futures of international law? My answer is an unequivocal yes because the last few years, far from signalling a demise of the global, in fact, confirm that we live in a global world, and one increasingly characterised by truly 'global lawmaking', as much as some seek to retreat to a world of walls and barbed wire fences.

[31] On stability and change in international law, see also N Krisch, 'The Dynamics of International Law Redux' (2021) 74 *Current Legal Problems* 269.

Paradoxically, just as we hear more about multipolarity, anti-globalism, and growing tensions among states and various groups, the world is more global than ever, considering nearly every conceivable metric. More people than ever are connected to the global internet, albeit with local and regional limitations, and a wider range of countries is connected by networks of cross-border regulation, but also education, research, and activisms. Attempts by many governments to buttress 'sovereignty' and 'security' or to uphold barriers to the free movement of goods, services, persons, information, or capital thus do not negate the continuing pull of the 'global' and 'global law'.

III. THE VARIETIES OF CUSTOMARY INTERNATIONAL LAW

This book makes two main contributions, beyond a set of accounts of the law in action and studies of the intellectual context of the international *lex non scripta*.

First, it argues that customary international law is a multifaceted phenomenon. As a social phenomenon, it has a complex and dynamic relationship to its intellectual context. Rather than necessarily a 'primitive' or obsolete form of law, it can display strengths that make it a particularly apt modality of international lawmaking. At the same time, our understanding of the phenomenon is severely limited by the conventional view of customary international law, which mistakes myth and legal fiction for social reality. This often leads to a mischaracterisation of customary international law as an idea and a social phenomenon, a misdiagnosis of its defects, and the tabling of questionable remedies (such as wholesale formalisation), thereby stifling either feasible or desirable changes to its institutional design, that is, its legal doctrine coupled with the institutional elements affecting its creation, maintenance, and change.

Second, this book develops an analytical and explanatory framework for understanding customary international law. That framework highlights what sustains different types of contemporary customary international law norms by reference to distinct configurations of factors that render them effective in particular contexts. My framework draws on insights from the study of related topics, including the idea of the international *lex non scripta* (unwritten law), the history of the legal doctrine of customary international law, particular episodes from the life of customary international law across a variety of social areas, and insights into the relationship between ideas and legal doctrines of customary international law and customary international lawmaking more broadly. In other words, this book aims to uncover a catalogue of factors characteristic of customary international lawmaking that channel, transform, and indeed augment various forms of power in international society.

Structural features of the international legal order that can be traced to at least the nineteenth century contributed to the development of distinct forms of the *lex non scripta* in the international domain that differ markedly from those familiar from domestic legal settings, such as the common law, various types of local customary law, or other kinds of unwritten law. These structural features include – among others – the absence of any general legal hierarchy and judicial centralisation, the development of a complex institutional infrastructure for the development, application, and enforcement of international law, the presence of multiple sources of power in a pool of many formally independent but vastly unequal polities, a fount of exposure to and thinking about different forms of unwritten law, a panoply of actors striving to shape legal expectations in global society, and finally the presence of customary international law as a recognised formal 'source' of international law.

This book argues that customary international lawmaking is best described by reference to particular configurations of factors that sustain norms of customary international law, rather than by an account of the underlying 'processes' themselves.[32] Effective customary international law norms that result from various processes are not all alike. They are sustained by different configurations of factors, leading to a limited set of representative types of customary international law norms. These types of customary international norms are characterised by distinct sets of sustaining factors, causes, explanations, roles, and effects. Notably, in their particular manifestations, customary international law norms are sustained by factors that can be characterised as *institutional*, participatory or *democratic*, substantive or *teleological*, and *procedural*. In developing a parsimonious account, I identify four paradigmatic configurations of factors that correspond to four types of customary international law norms. I propose that depending on characteristic configurations of factors that sustain customary international law norms, we can speak of different *ideal types* of customary international law norms. An ideal type (more on the concept below) refers to an abstract representation and not a normative evaluation, at least not initially. It simply reflects the observation that there are distinct types of customary international law norms characterised by particular features and implications. I offer some suggestions as to why these ideal types are characteristic of present-day international law, how this set of ideal types might evolve in the near future, how they are interrelated, and how we should assess them prescriptively.

The core of *Global Lawmaking and Social Change* is a new framework to help us better understand how the design of global lawmaking, and customary international lawmaking in particular, both advances and stymies social change. This framework – which aims to foreground the varieties and dynamics of customary international law – consists of i) the mentioned four-fold typology of customary international law norms, ii) an explanation of the characteristic factors that sustain each type of customary international law norm;

[32] I follow Ullmann-Margalit's suggestion (by reference to Raz) to look to the 'conditions of existence' of norms rather than to 'how they come about'. See, by reference to Raz, E Ullmann-Margalit, *The Emergence of Norms* (Oxford, Clarendon Press, 1977) 7–8.

iii) an account of how the four types of customary international law norms relate to one another to promote or stymie social change; and iv) an analysis of the implications of this analysis for the design of the legal doctrine of customary international law and the processes involved in global lawmaking. The book tests this framework through a set of thematically wide-ranging 'normative episodes' that illustrate how the international 'law in action' emerges and is sustained and how it is connected to evolving ideas and legal doctrines of customary international law. These thematic examples cover the breadth of contemporary international lawmaking, from the plight of refugees to global public health. Once we look at contemporary international lawmaking through the lens of this framework, features of customary international law that have long puzzled legal scholars and students become more intelligible. Adopting the framework as a lens for understanding customary international law also allows us to reevaluate normative proposals concerning customary international law. The framework thus provides a new way to understand and seek to improve customary international law and thereby, indirectly, advance social change. More concretely, by providing a more realistic account of customary international lawmaking, the framework allows us to identify those factors shaping customary international lawmaking that stymie or support lawmaking on key issues of global concern. In this way, I try to provide a key argument and piece of evidence in an ongoing scholarly debate about the role, operation, social effects, and prospects of customary international law. Ultimately, a better descriptive account of international lawmaking offers the necessary basis for improving international lawmaking outcomes[33] and advancing our understanding of normative phenomena more generally.[34] This book seeks to provide such an account through a wide-ranging study culminating in a framework meant to be realistic, parsimonious, and useful to legal scholars, legal practitioners, and students of international law and other disciplines.

As noted, the framework developed in the book centres around four types of customary international law norms and draws descriptive and normative implications from their characteristics and interrelationships. These four types of customary international law norms are: First, *entrenched background custom*: This is a widely shared and deeply rooted type of custom underlying basic principles of contemporary international law, from sovereignty to non-discrimination. Second, *analogical custom*: This is a type of law both derivative and novel; it 'coasts' on deeply entrenched background custom, often addressing newly emerging legal questions, and commonly arising in the field of rapid

[33] To be sure, evaluating social progress on the macro level and comparing it across time is an extremely difficult and contested exercise. See in this context eg P Singer, *Ethics in the Real World: 82 Brief Essays on Things That Matter* (Princeton, Princeton University Press, 2017) 11; S Moyn, *Not Enough: Human Rights in an Unequal World* (Cambridge, Harvard University Press, 2018) 40.

[34] See eg JP Trachtman, *The Economic Structure of International Law* (n 14) 21–2.

technological or socio-economic change. Third, *dynamic custom*: This is the wild beast among the framework's quartet of norm types and the least law-like type of custom. It allows powerful actors to set controlling but brittle equilibria in key areas of global law and politics. Fourth, *pure judicial custom*: This is roughly the 'common law' equivalent of law on the international plane. This type of custom is initially fragile and institutionally circumscribed. However, it is a potentially powerful and highly authoritative type of custom with profound effects on broader international lawmaking. Each member of this quartet of customary international law norms has different characteristics, origins, and degrees of stability. Each type of custom is the product of a particular configuration of underlying lawmaking factors that coalesce to sustain a norm of customary international law. These four types of custom can be observed across virtually all fields of international law. Understanding them and how they relate to each other can allow the legal scholar or policymaker to make better sense of the possibilities of and obstacles to social change through international law. As noted, it can also inform normative proposals for the redesign of customary international lawmaking and thus for improving social outcomes.

The legal fiction of a unitary customary international law proclaimed by courts and legal scholars has an important role and function.[35] But it should not be taken at face value by legal scholars interested in advancing our understanding of international lawmaking as a comprehensive process. Lawmaking processes on the international plane are varied and malleable and, in some cases, more democratic, dynamic, and amenable to change than those found in many domestic legal systems. At the same time, customary international lawmaking processes and resulting norms reflect both differences in power and the limits of law to achieve certain ideals of justice – be it formal, procedural, or substantive. In that sense, much like lawmaking processes in other settings, those of the customary international law variety – to various extents and in different ways – work to legitimate power, for good or ill, simultaneously enabling and restraining the untrammelled exercise of power.

IV. CUSTOMARY INTERNATIONAL LAW, IDEOLOGY, GLOBALISATION, AND SOCIAL CHANGE

Because international law, like law generally, often enables forms of domination and can undergird a host of persistent injustices, the design of legal institutions is a central site of distributional and ideological contestation. This explains why the idea that customary international law could be a meaningful, let alone

[35] See eg JB Murphy, *The Philosophy of Customary Law* (Oxford, Oxford University Press, 2014) 67–8. As I note below, there appears to be a non-trivial relationship between the function of legal fictions and forms of rationalization that are the subject of more recent research in the cognitive and behavioural sciences.

progressive, modality of lawmaking on the global plane often confronts scepticism. After all, forms of custom and customary law are often associated with the status quo or traditional social arrangements. Normative arguments in favour of custom and customary law are therefore often allied with conservative political ideologies.[36] As a result, those who advocate something resembling 'customary law' on the domestic level in societies characterised by social, economic, and status inequalities tend to adhere to either conservative, anarcho-capitalist, libertarian, or 'market fundamentalist' ideologies.[37] In short, on the one hand, many observers doubt that addressing important political, social, economic, and environmental challenges could be paved by something resembling customary law.[38] On the other hand, forms of lawmaking that are more decentralised and participatory in nature, including some forms of customary law, are often embraced by those committed to fighting persistent inequalities, domination, and social hierarchies.

As I will show in this book, while the design of lawmaking institutions profoundly affects social outcomes, it is a category error to equate a generic modality of lawmaking with particular social outcomes or ideologies. A normative assessment of customary international law's role in contemporary international law requires a nuanced inquiry. Customary forms of lawmaking *as such* may have different intellectual genealogies but many of them do not have a necessary ideological flavour at all. Suffice it here to anticipate that the connection between ideologies such as conservativism or libertarianism, on the one hand, and unwritten law, on the other, is more complicated and tenuous than might at first appear. Importantly, as I argue in this book, there is no such thing as a unitary customary international law – instead, different types of custom must be distinguished and evaluated on their own terms. Moreover, analogies between customary international law and domestic types of unwritten law need to be treated cautiously because they arise in distinct legal and political contexts. The reasons why one might advocate for a continued or even growing place of customary international law in world society do not have a necessary connection to any particular ideology, nor do they map onto categories familiar from domestic contexts. Moreover, while some varieties of customary international law tend to decentre the state, other conceptions

[36] See eg in relation to the common law as a type of 'customary law', KI Kersch, 'Constitutive Stories about the Common Law in Modern American Conservativism' (2016) 56 *Nomos* 211. See also L Petrazycki, *Law and Morality* (translated by HW Babb) (Cambridge, Cambridge University Press, 1955) 262–71.

[37] I borrow these distinctions from JC Scott, *Two Cheers for Anarchism: Six Easy Pieces on Autonomy, Dignity, and Meaningful Work and Play* (Princeton, Princeton University Press, 2012) xii–vi; see also, on various variations within anarchist thought, A Fiala, 'Anarchism' in *Stanford Encyclopedia of Philosophy* (latest version 26 October 2021).

[38] See eg F Schauer, *Thinking Like a Lawyer: A New Introduction to Legal Reasoning* (Cambridge, Harvard University Press, 2009) 105–6; JR Maxeiner, *Failures of American Methods of Lawmaking in Historical and Comparative Perspectives* (Cambridge, Cambridge University Press, 2018) 15–22.

of customary international law are far from anti-statist. In this book, I foreground a multifaceted conception of customary international lawmaking emphasising that customary international law is not only multifaceted but also part of a broader international legal order made up of a myriad other modalities of lawmaking. Customary international law is an important part of that legal totality, but cannot be seen in isolation from it. This totality resembles in many ways what we understand as a 'state' legal order, in the sense of a set of institutions on the international level that could – under the right conditions – ensure cooperation, democratic government, and the rule of law in a decentralised system organised around legitimate states and international institutions. Problems facing world society today require a legal order on the international and local levels that ensures social justice and a high degree of relative equality among individuals and groups. This sort of legal order can be built around states while being democratically responsive and adaptable to changing circumstances without the need either for a hierarchical world-state or a radically anti-statist international legal order.[39] As such, emphasising customary international law as an important modality of international lawmaking is prima facie ideologically neutral and also fully compatible with various democratic conceptions of statehood or governance.

Nonetheless, I contend that there is a correlation between a multifaceted conception of customary international law and progressive social change. This argument proceeds from an awareness of the fact of persistent global injustice. As many scholars have argued – and as is becoming more widely recognised in the public sphere – global injustices have structural and systemic causes. Structures and systems of governance, and these include contemporary international law, help perpetuate, in what one scholar has described as an 'authoritarian' way, a host of injustices.[40] If such structures and systems are unitary, it is more difficult to change them. This puts a premium on lawmaking approaches that are multifaceted and democratic in the sense of allowing a wider range of persons and groups to participate in lawmaking processes and take ownership of the international legal order. I argue in this book that customary international law should be distinguished by reference to distinct types of norms, deriving from a variety of different normative processes, some of which embody an inclusive and democratic form of lawmaking. This is not to say that other processes of lawmaking are not also relevant. It simply emphasises the often-underappreciated role of customary international law in social change.

As we consider the role of global lawmaking for social change we must also contend with modern international law's rise in the 'shadow of empire',

[39] See, by analogy, Scott, *Two Cheers for Anarchism* (n 37) xxii.

[40] See eg TJ Donahue-Ochoa, *Unfreedom for All: How the World's Injustices Harm You* (Oxford, Oxford University Press, 2019) 12.

a legacy with persistent links to the contemporary international legal order.[41] Such links are manifest in various contexts in customary international law, too. For example, customary international law is often considered as binding on new states automatically upon independence. International law thus posits a continuity of customary international law norms regardless of decolonisation.[42] Although there is a rich discussion about the conceptual links between the legal doctrine of customary international law and capitalism and imperialism,[43] contemporary international lawmaking is more complex and adaptable than the idea of a dead hand of the past would suggest. This is true especially for unwritten forms of law since the origin of an unwritten legal norm does not tell us much about its role in a new environment. To be sure, contemporary international law reflects and helps sustain particular values and ideologies, but the role of customary international law varies by context and is closely linked to different forms of power characterising world society.[44] International law's imperial legacy and economic background should have implications for any study of customary international law. However, like all law, customary international law is closely related to power but also a dynamic process that can continuously be shaped anew. Given that international law shapes many aspects of world society that are rightly rejected as fundamentally unjust, this book shows the extent to and ways in which customary international law has served and could serve as an engine of normative and social change in international society. Nothing in this book should, therefore, be seen to suggest that how international law is made cannot be improved. On the contrary – failings in customary international lawmaking have frequently led to negative legal and social outcomes in a range of areas. However, any reform of customary international lawmaking requires a solid descriptive understanding of it, sensitive to the actual operation of customary international law as a multifaceted phenomenon and the different ways in which the past remains entangled with the present.

[41] See eg O Yasuaki, *International Law in a Transcivilizational World* (Cambridge, Cambridge University Press, 2017) 103–85; A Anghie, *Imperialism, Sovereignty and the Making of International Law* (Cambridge, Cambridge University Press, 2004); JT Gathii, 'Review Essay: International Law and Eurocentricity' (1998) 9 *European Journal of International Law* 184; SP Sinha, *Legal Polycentricity and International Law* (Durham, Carolina Academic Press, 1996); S Pahuja, *Decolonising International Law: Development, Economic Growth and the Politics of Universality* (Cambridge, Cambridge University Press, 2011).

[42] See M Craven, *The Decolonization of International Law: State Succession and the Law of Treaties* (Cambridge, Cambridge University Press, 2007); M Koskenniemi and PM Eisemann (eds), *State Sucession: Codification Tested against the Facts* (The Hague, Martinus Nijhoff, 2000); on the earlier origins of state succession in Central Europe, see N Wheatley, *The Life and Death of States: Central Europe and the Transformation of Modern Sovereignty* (Princeton, Princeton University Press, 2023); see also generally G Hafner and G Novak, 'State Sucession in Respect of Treaty Relationships' in DB Hollis, *The Oxford Guide to Treaties*, 2nd edn (Oxford, Oxford University Press, 2020) 383.

[43] See Chimni, 'Customary International Law: A Third World Perspective' (n 17).

[44] See eg by reference to Gramsci, WM Reisman, 'The Shadows Looming over International Law' (2006) 6(1) *Baltic Yearbook of International Law* 7, 19.

V. SCOPE AND LIMITS OF THE BOOK

This book examines how customary international law's institutional design shapes social change, contributing to a rich scholarly conversation about its role, operation, social effects, and prospects. While it draws on much of the existing literature on customary international law, it tries to connect disparate streams of scholarship and reorient the field's research agenda. It also proposes an analytical and explanatory framework centred on four types of customary international law norms, seen in their broader context. The book tries to highlight the variety, dynamism, and malleability of both customary international lawmaking and its resulting norms. At the same time, customary international law also reflects vast differences in power, which points to the limits of customary international lawmaking's ability to achieve certain ideals of justice, be they formal, procedural, or substantive. The book thus shows how multiple types of customary international law can complement, or even block each other to enable or stymie legal and social change. It also highlights the interrelationships between different types of customary international law norms as well as their links to the idea and legal doctrine of customary international law. As such, the book necessarily draws on insights from a wide range of disciplines and historical contexts, seeking to weave them into a parsimonious analytical and explanatory framework, all to foreground the question of the relationship between customary international law and social change.

As I argue in this book, to speak about a particular norm of customary international law requires us to identify the particular configuration of factors sustaining that particular customary norm.[45] The framework I use to categorise customary international law norms is not meant to map the complex reality of lawmaking one-to-one. Nor is it meant to be a contribution to debates about the legal doctrine of customary international law or the different approaches to the identification or interpretation of customary international law norms. Indeed, international legal scholars have already proposed typologies for better understanding the multifaceted nature of customary international law from doctrinal and hermeneutic perspectives.[46] Nor do I simply propose that the legal doctrine of customary international law does not reflect the contextual reality of the way customary international law arises and is identified or interpreted.[47] Instead, my book tries to offer a framework for understanding customary international law processes and resulting norms that integrates various approaches to the study of international law.

[45] In that sense, my approach is close to studies by socio-legal scholars who emphasise the multifaceted nature of law. See eg Pirie, *The Anthropology of Law* (n 21) 7–8.

[46] See eg Verdross, 'Entstehungsweisen und Geltungsgrund des universellen völkerrechtlichen Gewohnheitsrechts' (n 5) 635. Verdross' work has been drawn on by others, including Koskenniemi, to study the so-called problem of fragmentation of international law. See Koskenniemi, *From Apology to Utopia: The Structure of International Legal Argument* (n 14) 392.

[47] Hakimi, 'Making Sense of Customary International Law' (n 9).

While this book takes into account a plethora of scholarly sources and literatures, it does not seek to contribute to all of them. Rather, its main aim is to contribute to a tiny sliver of international legal scholarship dealing with the relationship between customary international law as both an idea and legal doctrine and as a broader social phenomenon. For example, while this book is informed by other manifestations of unwritten law, including customary law in other contexts, it does not itself seek to contribute to the legal theory of unwritten law as such. Similarly, while this book engages with a variety of substantive areas of international law especially in Chapters 2 to 5, it does not purport to contribute to the literature on the laws of war or international environmental law as such. Moreover, this book does not seek to broaden the scope of customary international law norms to include those that the relevant communities, including legal scholars and practising lawyers, do not consider to be ones of custom. It also does not seek to amend or challenge any existing doctrinal definition of customary international law, but rather to explicate its role in the broader context of customary international law. Where the book parts ways with conventional descriptive accounts of customary international law is in its perspective on customary international lawmaking and its resulting norms. More generally, this book should be seen as just one intervention in an ongoing conversation about customary international law. I hope that readers will go away with a more nuanced understanding of the multifaceted phenomenon that is customary international law and thereby gain a deeper appreciation of the power and limits of international law.

Because almost all international legal scholars have either explicitly or implicitly said something about customary international law, nearly everyone has planted their intellectual flag and, occasionally, expressed strong views on the topic. Some legal scholars take the relevance of customary international law for granted, others argue vehemently against its status as law, while others have proposed more or less complex theories to explain various aspects of the phenomenon. In other words, contrary to what one may suppose, scholarship on customary international law is rich with passion. This makes it both a fruitful but also potentially strongly opinionated area of legal scholarship. I inevitably bring particular assumptions, biases, and opinions to this book. While it goes without saying, I have tried to be as open-minded and balanced as possible in my analysis and assessment of others' contributions, especially those I disagree with.

VI. OUTLINE OF THE BOOK

This book seeks to provide an empirically and theoretically grounded account of the polyphonous landscape of global lawmaking centred around four types of customary international law norms, viewed in their broader intellectual and social context. As a general matter, this book proceeds from the recognition that customary international law is both a social phenomenon and a set of ideas, two sides of an indissociable coin. Chapter 1 highlights the book's basic approach and methodology, surveys the main strands of legal scholarship it seeks to engage with, and highlights the need to see customary international law as a form of unwritten law. Chapter 2 develops the book's core contribution: a framework centred around four types of customary international law norms. Chapters 3 to 5 undertake a thematically wide-ranging examination of customary international lawmaking since the late nineteenth century. Thematically, the examples in this part of the book illustrate the varieties of global lawmaking across different social contexts and provide a basis for the principal contribution of this book. Importantly, they illustrate the presence of all four types of customary international law norms and thus demonstrate the power of the book's framework across a diverse and representative set of themes and the entire span of modern international law. These chapters focus on how major international or cross-border problems came to be discussed, addressed, or regulated in legal ways and sometimes by reference to customary international law. These include humanity's uses of various technologies, growing interactions between humans and their natural environment, and the long-standing question of the treatment of the 'other' in a world society structured around territorial states amid ever-increasing interconnectedness. Crucially, the book goes on in Chapter 6 to discuss how the legal doctrine of customary international law is related to, but not to be confused with, the comprehensive process of customary international lawmaking and its resulting norms. In its Conclusion, the book highlights the intellectual and practical payoffs of its findings.

1

Studying Global Lawmaking and Social Change

I. UNDERSTANDING CUSTOMARY INTERNATIONAL LAWMAKING

A WEALTH OF existing theories and tools helps us make sense of the way we are governed at the global level, including through customary international law. At the same time, like contemporary international law more generally, customary international law is transforming in tandem with global geopolitical, socio-economic, and cultural shifts. A realistic, parsimonious, and useful account of customary international law should provide new answers to two basic questions. First, how and why do customary international law norms emerge, stabilise, change, and wither away? Second, how do the institutions that undergird customary international lawmaking, such as the legal doctrine of custom and various institutions that structure contemporary global lawmaking, relate to customary international law as a broader social phenomenon? Answering both questions requires a comprehensive and historically informed view of customary international law from the time when many sites and institutions of contemporary international lawmaking emerged, albeit in a very different global context, to the present. It also requires us to adopt a combination of the so-called internal, external, and intermediate points of view on international law.[1]

This book's approach to customary international law focuses on factors that sustain norms and does not attempt a systematic account of the myriad ways in which norms are created and changed, although I frequently point the reader to relevant examples. I thereby follow the suggestion of Edna Ullmann-Margalit, who noted by reference to Joseph Raz that one should 'give up the question of how norms come about and ask instead what are their conditions of existence' because '[n]orms do not as a rule come into existence at a definite point in time, nor are they the result of a manageable number of identifiable acts'.[2] This does not mean that how a particular norm comes about is unimportant or that distinguishing between different types of norms is not meaningful. However, the

[1] See eg BZ Tamanaha, *A General Jurisprudence of Law and Society* (Cambridge, Cambridge University Press, 2001) 226–7.

[2] E Ullmann-Margalit, *The Emergence of Norms* (Oxford, Oxford University Press, 2015) 7–8.

questions of interest to me here can be answered by focusing on how customary international law norms are typically sustained and, by implication, created, changed, and dissolved.

II. THE RECENT SURGE OF INTEREST IN CUSTOMARY INTERNATIONAL LAW

International legal scholars have engaged with customary international law regularly for more than a century,[3] but three contemporary developments explain the most recent wave of scholarly interest in the topic. Prescriptive questions about international lawmaking have become acute in recent years. It is increasingly understood that major social questions, ranging from armed conflict, inequality, environmental degradation, and climate change, are shaped if not determined by global-level norms. The awareness that humanity's greatest challenges should be addressed on the global level is no longer an acquired taste of a narrow class of cosmopolitan intellectuals or globalist entrepreneurs but increasingly apparent to and shared by a growing share of the world's population, just as communications and transportation technologies continue to accelerate global interconnection. At the same time, while international law is one means for addressing global challenges, it is uncertain whether international lawmaking, including customary international lawmaking, in its contemporary form is capable of helping humanity address them in the course of the twenty-first century and to what extent is it legitimate, participatory, and capable of adapting to changing circumstances.

Over the last decades, both formal and informal international lawmaking has transformed and expanded, even if not as radically as some have suggested.[4] An increasingly diverse set of actors (beyond state governments) – international organisations, non-governmental organisations, individuals, and various sub-state governments – visibly participate in international lawmaking processes.[5] It is ever more widely understood that contemporary modalities

[3] G Gianni, *La coutume en droit international* (Paris, Pedone, 1931); NM Matte, *La coutume dans les cycles juridiques internationaux* (Paris, Pedone, 1947); B Simma, *Das Reziprozitätselement in der Entstehung des Völkergewohnheitsrechts* (Berlin, Duncker & Humblot, 1970); H Günther, *Zur Entstehung von Völkergewohnheitsrecht* (Berlin, Duncker & Humblot, 1970); AA D'Amato, *The Concept of Custom in International Law* (Ithaca, Cornell University Press, 1971); SA Schwarztrauber, *The Three-mile Limit of Territorial Seas* (Annapolis, Naval Institute Press, 1972). For a selection of more recent contributions, see the references included in the Introduction.

[4] The literature that in some way comments or analyzes this development is vast. See eg C Brölmann and Y Radi (eds), *Research Handbook on the Theory and Practice of International Lawmaking* (Cheltenham, Edward Elgar, 2016); J Pauwelyn, R Wessel, and J Wouters (eds), *Informal International Lawmaking* (Oxford, Oxford University Press, 2012); JE Alvarez, *International Organizations as Law-makers* (Oxford, Oxford University Press 2006).

[5] See eg D Kennedy, 'The Mystery of Global Governance' in J Dunoff and J Trachtman (eds), *Ruling the World? Constitutionalism, International Law, and Global Governance* (Cambridge, Cambridge University Press, 2009) 37, 38–9.

of lawmaking straddle the conceptual and institutional boundaries between the domestic, international, and other planes.[6] These factual and epistemic developments have called into question existing accounts of international lawmaking. They have raised questions about how the legal doctrine of customary international law, and associated legal institutions and practices, should adapt (if at all) to this changing environment.[7] At the same time, scholars have tried to reconceptualise international law and lawmaking on the global level from more pluralistic, multi-level, and indeed comprehensive perspectives.[8]

In parallel, international legal scholarship is characterised by growing cross-disciplinary engagement. In recent decades, scholars with a range of interests and backgrounds (in sociology, political science, anthropology, the humanities, or economics) have turned their attention to international law, including international lawmaking. To be sure, the interdisciplinary (and multidisciplinary) study of law has a long history. In some sense, law can be understood as the quintessentially interdisciplinary field.[9] Yet, in the field of international law, interdisciplinarity has had a distinct flavour. This is due to two principal factors. On the one hand, the degree to which law is viewed as an autonomous discipline and closely related to the practice of law still varies widely across legal cultures and systems. As a result, the role of law and legal scholarship across the world often reflects particular historical experiences and values, something that affects the degree of interdisciplinarity's relative acceptance. On the other hand, international legal scholars' object is by definition, if not always in practice, a global one. This dichotomy in a field that is closely tied to national and regional contexts but also oriented towards research questions that are quintessentially global creates significant tensions. Unlike fields that are more localised, the disciplinary direction of international law on the global level, therefore, remains highly contested. The result is that international legal scholarship is relatively more open than other fields to eclectic forms of research and to the testing of new theoretical, empirical, and normative questions about international lawmaking, including customary international law.[10] Moreover, both the rise of prescriptive questions and

[6] See eg D Zaring, *The Globalized Governance of Finance* (Cambridge, Cambridge University Press, 2019) 4–5; TC Halliday and G Shaffer (eds), *Transnational Legal Orders* (Cambridge, Cambridge University Press, 2014).

[7] See eg E Heffes, 'Some Reflections on the Theory of Sources of International Law: Re-examining Customary International Law' (2018) 51(3) *Israel Law Review* 485, 486.

[8] Eg BZ Tamanaha, *A Realistic Theory of Law* (Cambridge, Cambridge University Press, 2017) 191.

[9] See for a critical discussion of the powers and limits of interdisciplinarity as practised in the (US) American legal academy, DL Rhode, 'Legal Scholarship' (2002) 115 (5) *Harvard Law Review* 1327, 1329; see also G Calabresi, *The Future of Law and Economics: Essays in Reform and Recollection* (New Haven, Yale University Press, 2016) 6.

[10] On the role of interdisciplinarity in international law, see eg S Besson, 'Moral Philosophy and International Law' in A Orford and F Hoffmann (eds), *The Oxford Handbook of the Theory of International Law* (Oxford, Oxford University Press, 2016) 385, 388; see also J Klabbers, 'The Relative Autonomy of International Law or the Forgotten Politics of Interdisciplinary' (2004) 1

the rise of cross-disciplinary engagement are related to relatively recent but still uneven shifts in the nature of legal education across the world, displaying a movement from traditional doctrinal teaching to more critical, contextual, and normative ways of studying the law.

To be sure, these three drivers of the latest wave of interest in customary international lawmaking are not unprecedented. More than a century ago, the world witnessed influential theoretical and methodological innovations in legal scholarship, relatively expanded participation in international lawmaking, and new normative concerns brought to bear on legal aspects of (also international) governance. However, these more recent developments and the ways in which they coalesce in the contemporary period have resulted in a distinctive scholarly landscape.

III. WAYS OF SEEING CUSTOMARY INTERNATIONAL LAW

Even a survey of the most important *contemporary* contributions to the study of customary international law would by far exceed the constraints of a monograph.[11] Some of them refer explicitly to customary international law, but much of them have a broader ambit, concerned with how international law in general (or in its various manifestations) is made, maintained, and changed. Ultimately, all accounts of customary international law tell us something, even if inadvertently, about how we are and how we ought to be governed on the global level. Given the breadth of approaches and answers to those questions, it is important to clarify the shape of the scholarly literature that this book tries to enter into conversation with.

Although international law purports to be a shared object of study across the globe,[12] scholarly approaches to international law differ widely not only along disciplinary, methodological,[13] and even ideological lines[14] but more broadly (and sometimes relatedly) along cultural and national ones.[15] The diversity of

Journal of International Law & International Relations 35, 36; J Klabbers, 'The Bridge Crack'd: A Critical Look at Interdisciplinary Relations' (2009) 23(1) *International Relations* 119.

[11] For a selection of more recent contributions, see the references included in the Introduction.

[12] A Anghie, 'Finding the Peripheries: Soveriegnty and Colonialism in Nineteenth-Century International Law' (1999) 40 *Harvard International Law Journal* 1.

[13] R van Gestel, HW Micklitz, and EL Rubin (eds), *Rethinking Legal Scholarship: A Transatlantic Dialogue* (Cambridge, Cambridge University Press, 2017).

[14] See J Hanson, *Ideology, Psychology, and Law* (Oxford, Oxford University Press, 2012); see also JB Fischman and DS Law, 'What Is Judicial Ideology, and How Should We Measure It?' (2009) 29 *Washington University Journal of Law & Policy* 133.

[15] See eg A Roberts et al (eds), *Comparative International Law* (Oxford, Oxford University Press, 2018); A Roberts, *Is International Law International?* (Oxford, Oxford University Press, 2017); BN Mamlyuk and U Mattei, 'Comparative International Law' (2011) 36 *Brooklyn Journal of International Law 385*; A Roberts, PB Stephan, PH Verdier, and M Versteeg, 'Comparative International Law: Framing the Field' (2015) 109(3) *The American Journal of International Law* 467. For a

approaches to international law[16] is due to forces deeper than the habits of international legal scholars, notably the growing reach of international law, which has attracted the attention of scholars from a variety of disciplines, the particular strengths and limits of various approaches, the eclectic nature of socio-legal theories more broadly, and the unavoidable fact that scholars can hardly ever completely transcend their social and other backgrounds and biases (regardless of the 'observational standpoint' they may adopt as scholars).[17] At the same time, despite occasional conversations between scholars of international law and other disciplines,[18] there is considerable room for more interdisciplinary engagement.

From a bird's eye view, contemporary thinking about customary international law can be split into several basic approaches,[19] each placing emphasis

historical account, see M Koskenniemi, *The Gentle Civilizer of Nations: The Rise and Fall of International Law* 1870–1960 (Cambridge, Cambridge University Press, 2001).

[16] See eg the contributions in 'Diversity or Cacophony? New Sources of Norms in International Law: Symposium' (2004) 25(4) *Michigan Journal of International Law* 845.

[17] See eg JL Dunoff and MA Pollack (eds), *International Legal Theory: Foundations and Frontiers* (Cambridge, Cambridge University Press, 2022); see also A Bianchi, *International Law Theories: An Inquiry into Different Ways of Thinking* (Oxford, Oxford University Press, 2016).

[18] See for an earlier (2000s) assessment eg SJ Toope, 'Emerging Patterns of Governance and International Law' in M Byers (ed), *The Role of Law in International Politics: Essays in International Relations and International Law* (Oxford, Oxford University Press, 2001) 91, 91–3.

[19] Many excellent surveys and (explicit or implicit) attempts at a classification of (also) international legal scholarship already exist. See eg Dunoff and Pollack (eds) (n 17); Kennedy, 'The Mystery of Global Governance' (n 5) 43–54; D Kennedy, 'Three Globalizations of Law and Legal Thought: 1850–2000' in DM Trubek and A Santos, *The New Law and Economic Development: A Critical Appraisal* (Cambridge, Cambridge University Press, 2006) 19; PM Dupuy (ed), *Customary International Law* (Cheltenham, Edward Elgar, 2021); B Bix, *Jurisprudence: Theory and Context*, 9th edn (London, Sweet & Maxwell, 2023); W Twining, *General Jurisprudence: Understanding Law from a Global Perspective* (Cambridge, Cambridge University Press, 2009); HH Koh, 'The 1994 Roscoe Pound Lecture: Transnational Legal Process' (1996) 75 *Nebraska Law Review* 181; S Wiessner (ed), *General Theory of International Law, Volume 1, American Classics of International Law* (Leiden, Martinus Nijhoff, 2017); Bianchi, *International Law Theories* (n 17); BS Chimni, *International Law and World Order: A Critique of Contemporary Approaches*, 2nd edn (Cambridge, Cambridge University Press, 2017); AM Slaughter, AS Tulumello, and S Wood, 'International Law and International Relations Theory: A New Generation of Interdisciplinary Scholarship' (1998) 92(3) *The American Journal of International Law* 367; SR Ratner and AM Slaughter, 'Appraising the Methods of International Law: A Prospectus for Readers' (1999) 93(2) *The American Journal of International Law* 291; JL Dunoff and MA Pollack, 'International Law and International Relations' in JL Dunoff and MA Pollack (eds), *Interdisciplinary Perspectives on International Law and International Relations: The State of the Art* (Cambridge, Cambridge University Press, 2012) 3; DJ Bederman, 'Constructivism, Positivism, and Empiricism in International Law' (2001) 89(2) *Georgetown Law Journal* 469; E Jouannet, *The Liberal-Welfarist Law of Nations: A History of International Law* (Cambridge, Cambridge University Press, 2012); E Jouannet, *A Short Introduction to International Law* (Cambridge, Cambridge University Press, 2014); O Corten, *Le Discours du Droit International: Pour un Positivisme Critique* (Paris, Pedone, 2009); A Nissel and J Weiler (eds), *International Law* (6 Volumes) (New York, Routledge, 2011); A Roberts, *Is International Law International?* (n 15); R Posner, *Frontiers of Legal Theory*, 4th edn (Cambridge, Harvard University Press, 2001); DZ Cass, 'Navigating the Newstream: Recent Critical Scholarship in International Law' (1996) 65 *Nordic Journal of International Law* 341.

on a distinct facet of customary international law as both a social phenomenon and a related set of ideas or doctrines. These basic approaches differ mainly by virtue of their focus or question, rather than their method or disciplinary perspective, which can include descriptive, normative, theoretical, or empirical ones, some more interdisciplinary than others. At the same time, across all approaches, scholars further divide along disciplinary and methodological lines. As a result, scholars with the same focus or question but distinct disciplinary perspectives and methodologies may not interact much, if at all. This can have significant consequences for collective research outcomes.

One set of approaches addresses customary international law as a complex social phenomenon, be it as an institution, process, practice (for example, a 'communicative practice'[20]), field, system, culture, or similar.[21] Within this first category, an enormous variety of approaches coexist, in parallel with similar approaches to the study of law in other contexts.[22] Scholars who come to the study of customary international law from the perspective of the social sciences, including political science, economics, sociology, social psychology, anthropology, and some strands of interdisciplinary legal scholarship,[23] tend to focus on two main descriptive questions, even if both have significant normative implications. The first asks about the effects of customary international law (or international law more broadly) on individual or collective behaviour or action.[24] The second asks about the factors that explain or 'cause' customary international law either in general or in particular contexts. In other words, it asks about the factors that help explain how customary international law processes work and how customary international norms are sustained.[25] These two questions are central to this book, too, even if I attempt to approach them

[20] I Venzke, 'Contemporary Theories and International Lawmaking' in Brölmann and Radi (eds), *Research Handbook on the Theory and Practice of International Lawmaking* (n 4) 66.

[21] RE Goodin, 'Institutions and Their Design' in RE Goodin (ed), *The Theory of Institutional Design* (Cambridge, Cambridge University Press, 1996) 1.

[22] See eg A Sarat and TR Kearns (eds), *Law in Everyday Life* (Ann Arbor, University of Michigan Press, 1995) 21–2.

[23] To be sure, none of the social sciences referred to in this book are internally homogeneous. See eg WL Gould and M Barkun, *International Law and the Social Sciences* (Princeton, Princeton University Press, 1970); J Coleman, *Foundations of Social Theory* (Cambridge, Harvard University Press, 1994) 2; see also E Durkheim, *The Rules of Sociological Method and Selected Texts on Sociology and its Method* (edited by S Lukes and translated by WD Halls) (New York, Free Press, 2013[1982]); P Manicas, 'The Social Sciences Since World War II: The Rise and Fall of Scientism' in W Outhwaite and S Turner (eds), *The SAGE Handbook of Social Science Methodology* (Thousand Oaks, Sage Publishing, 2007) 7; M Martin and LC McIntyre (eds), *Readings in the Philosophy of Social Science* (Cambridge, MIT Press, 1994); D Ross, *The Origins of American Social Science* (Cambridge, Cambridge University Press, 1991); TM Porter and D Ross (eds), *The Cambridge History of Science, Volume 7, The Modern Social Sciences* (Cambridge, Cambridge University Press, 2003).

[24] See JP Trachtman, *The Economic Structure of International Law* (Cambridge, Harvard University Press, 2009) 2. Beyond international law, see also RC Ellickson, *Order Without Law: How Neighbors Settle Disputes* (Cambridge, Harvard University Press, 1991).

[25] See eg W Sandholtz, *Prohibiting Plunder: How Norms Change* (Oxford, Oxford University Press, 2007).

in a distinctive way. Recent social scientific approaches to the study of customary international law arguably represent the most significant advance in the study of international lawmaking since, at least, the New Haven School, itself a precursor given its explicitly interdisciplinary and policy-oriented approach. The various social scientific approaches to the study of customary international law, either individually or collectively, are significant because they provide insights into international lawmaking that go beyond received legal knowledge and even the practical knowledge available to professional lawyers. By trying to open up the legal 'black box', they can profoundly shape the practice of international law and the extent to which interested groups can engage with it effectively. At the same time, many social scientific approaches to the study of customary international law have serious limitations. In particular, they tend to avoid integrated or comprehensive approaches to the phenomenon. Most try to be interdisciplinary but oftentimes cannot help but be bi- if not uni-disciplinary, noticeably privileging a particular perspective and minimising another. Moreover, many social scientific approaches to customary international law focus on processes but tend to underestimate or ignore how the design of legal institutions, including legal doctrines, affects such processes. Relatedly, many social scientific accounts of customary international law tend to adopt a unitary understanding of the phenomenon in a misplaced show of deference to 'legal' expertise. Many social scientific approaches to customary international law also tend to adopt an atemporal and ahistorical perspective, treating normative phenomena in different contexts as if they were identical, without justifying far-reaching assumptions about the stability of customary international lawmaking over time. Finally, the role of social scientific approaches for the study of customary international law is highly uneven globally due to entrenched differences across legal academies, despite a trend towards global convergence.

Another set of approaches examines customary international law primarily as an idea, be it as a legal-doctrinal concept, an intellectual category, a discourse, or a comparative notion. Great variation exists within this family of approaches, some of which have important links to social scientific approaches to the study of customary international law. Indeed, it is practically impossible for a study of customary international law from a social scientific perspective to avoid touching upon both social and intellectual factors, and vice versa – be it explicitly or implicitly. After all, customary international law is, like similar phenomena, both an intellectual and social one. However, for disciplinary and methodological reasons that tend to have little to do with important questions raised by customary international lawmaking itself, some approaches focus more strongly on social phenomena and behaviour, while others focus more strongly, and sometimes exclusively, on ideas, doctrines, or ideologies. Among this set of approaches we can find a huge variety, some of which are purely doctrinal, some focused on intellectual history, and others coming very close to social scientific approaches to customary international law.

A third set of approaches to customary international law is best described as meta-theoretical or 'jurisprudential'. These address customary international law from a conceptual and legal-philosophical perspective. Their *meta*-theoretical angle lies in their explicit aim to link and integrate understandings of customary international law as a dynamic and complex intellectual and social phenomenon.[26] Overall, legal-philosophical or jurisprudential approaches to customary international lawmaking differ widely in how they approach the study of customary international law. This makes them relatively difficult to evaluate as a group. However, they tend to be comprehensive and provide insights into customary international law as both a social and intellectual phenomenon. Moreover, their emphasis on legal theory (or jurisprudence) makes them particularly suitable for the study of types of law at the boundaries of conventional legality, such as customary international law. At the same time, such approaches have two main limitations. First, they tend to adopt an ahistorical perspective on an inherently dynamic legal phenomenon such as customary international law. Second, they tend to reflect the widely shared understanding of customary international law as a unitary phenomenon. Even jurisprudential approaches adopting a relatively narrow temporal scope tend to overlook the multifaceted and contextual nature of customary international law processes and norms. This is partly due to the limited use of empirical detail in most legal-philosophical or jurisprudential accounts of customary international law.

So-called 'critical' and 'normative' approaches can be seen as belonging to the meta-theoretical category because they often adopt strong views about the relationship between law as an idea and a social phenomenon. Normative and critical takes on customary international law are useful tools for questioning existing approaches to customary international law and developing a better and more nuanced understanding of the phenomenon. They sometimes highlight or exaggerate points of disagreement (as well as agreement) with respect to dominant descriptive assumptions, frameworks, approaches, and even vocabularies. Moreover, they tend to reveal unstated normative assumptions or commitments, as well as ideological biases, reflected in both international law and legal scholarship. As a matter of intellectual history, critical accounts of customary international law are also valuable because they indicate the range of views about international law that hold sway within the legal community. They reveal the concerns, interests, and common limitations to the imagination of international lawyers and legal scholars in particular times and places and suggest how ideas can affect the customary international law in action. A major limitation of normative and critical approaches to customary international law is that they tend to assume that customary international law is a unitary

[26] See eg JB Murphy, *The Philosophy of Customary Law* (Oxford, Oxford University Press, 2014); GJ Postema, 'Custom, Normative Practice, and the Law' (2012) 62 *Duke Law Journal* 707.

category, that it lacks dynamism, or that it remains relatively static, despite important shifts in context. Many normative and critical approaches tend to be less persuasive than they could be since they produce critiques not of customary international law, but of its context or some of its particular manifestations. Another limitation of normative and critical approaches is that they tend to reject the possibility of a comprehensive account of the social and intellectual phenomenon called customary international law as an unjustified cop out. As a result, their critical bite often needs to be traded off against their immediate constructive potential.

Finally, it is worth pointing to a set of approaches to customary international law that are best described as 'partial'. Customary international lawmaking is powerfully affected by its relevant (institutional, substantive, temporal) context. That context can be leveraged by legal scholars when they focus on how customary international law operates across a variety of specialised fields and institutions. 'Partial' perspectives on the phenomenon are therefore popular and potentially fruitful. A perspective on customary international law is partial when it is limited substantively (such as to the law of the sea, international investment law, or international criminal law), geographically, culturally, or temporally, or in respect of particular actors or institutions. Such partial perspectives can be highly impactful since they are often of interest to practising lawyers who tend to occupy important functions in the legal machine. However, most partial approaches to customary international law are not aimed at providing a comprehensive account of customary international lawmaking. They tend to avoid broader questions about the reasons why customary international law processes or norms differ across contexts, even if they often point to important research questions. In short, such approaches leverage the benefits of focus and specialisation but forgo a comprehensive approach to customary international law.

Much of contemporary international legal scholarship contributes, directly or indirectly, also to some of the questions of interest to me here. Despite their lacunae, social scientific, meta-theoretical, and so-called 'critical' and normative approaches to customary international law offer the greatest promise for a better understanding of the phenomenon, even if their global reach still remains limited. This book is informed by this high-level map of the relevant literature on customary international law. While proposing a novel approach, it tries to enter into conversation with all of these basic approaches to the study of customary international law.

IV. CUSTOMARY INTERNATIONAL LAW AS UNWRITTEN LAW

While this book is informed by thinking about unwritten law in various contexts, it focuses squarely on customary international law. Nonetheless, it is worth emphasising that unwritten forms of law, and customary law in particular, have attracted the interest of scholars for centuries.[27] Indeed, influential lines of thinking about the relationship between legislation, adjudication, and custom can be traced to ancient times.[28] Valuable insights can be gained by comparing customary international law to other manifestations of unwritten law. At the same time, it is important to be cautious in drawing facile analogies. When discussing the role of customary law and its relationship to 'written' law, it is also worth pointing to the work of the towering legal scholar Hans Kelsen. Kelsen, whose interests were wide-ranging but who may be largely known for his 'pure theory of law',[29] understood that customary international law was compatible with modern lawmaking, though it was for him a 'decentralized' modality of lawmaking.[30] Indeed, Kelsen also articulated the idea that customary international lawmaking differed depending on the specific context in which it was created, emphasising the role of third-party decision makers for its development.

During the last decades, unwritten forms of law have consistently attracted the attention of legal scholars and social scientists, many of whom have studied the origins, creation, maintenance, and disappearance of the *lex non scripta* in varied settings and from different angles.[31] Scholarship relating to unwritten law reflects the diversity of jurisprudential conceptions of law and the diversity of law-governed societies across the world.[32] But questions about socio-legal phenomena as dynamic as various forms of unwritten law can always productively be asked anew using new approaches,[33] something that extends to the

[27] CCW Klötzer, *Versuch eines Beytrags zur Revision der Theorie vom Gewohnheitsrecht* (Jena, Mauke und Söhne, 1813); NM Korkunov, *General Theory of Law* (translated by WG Hastings) (Boston, Boston Book Company 1909); A Dundes Renteln and A Dundes (eds), *Folk Law: Essays in the Theory and Practice of Lex Non Scripta* (2 Volumes) (Madison, University of Wisconsin Press, 1994); A Watson, *The Evolution of Western Private Law* (Baltimore, Johns Hopkins University Press, 1985).

[28] See eg the discussion of various types of order, with numerous references, in FA Hayek, *Law, Legislation and Liberty, Volume I: Rules and Order* (Chicago, University of Chicago Press, 1973) 35–46.

[29] See generally eg Jochen von Bernstorff, *The Public International Law Theory of Hans Kelsen: Believing in Universal Law* (Cambridge, Cambridge University Press, 2010).

[30] See H Kelsen, *Écrits français de droit international* (edited by C Leben) (Paris, Presses universitaires de France, 2001) 76–8.

[31] See eg WM Reisman, *Law in Brief Encounters* (New Haven, Yale University Press, 1999); Neil MacCormick, *Institutions of Law: An Essay in Legal Theory* (Oxford, Oxford University Press, 2007).

[32] See eg N MacCormick, 'Four quadrants of jurisprudence' in W Krawietz et al (eds), *Prescriptive Formality and Normative Rationality in Modern Legal Systems: Festschrift for Robert S. Summers* (Berlin, Duncker & Humblot, 1994) 53.

[33] The multidisciplinary study of various normative phenomena, including customary law, drawing on theories and methods developed by economists, sociologists, political scientists, or psychologists, is a rich and growing field of research. See eg Ellickson, *Order Without Law* (n 24); Ullmann-Margalit, *The Emergence of Norms* (n 2); T Skocpol, *States and Social Revolutions: A Comparative Analysis of France, Russia and China* (Cambridge, Cambridge University Press, 1979); see also G Brennan, L Eriksson, RE Goodin, and N Southwood, *Explaining Norms* (Oxford, Oxford University Press, 2013); C Bicchieri, *Norms in the Wild: How to Diagnose, Measure, and Change Social Norms*

study of customary international law.[34] However, it is important to emphasise several points about the nature and scope of the relationship between customary international law and customary law generally. *First*, ideas about customary law and customary international law sit on different planes. Customary, or unwritten law, is a general category of law (as a jurisprudential concept).[35] In contrast, customary international law is a specific member of that category, just like the customary law of the Indigenous Australian peoples or Andorran customary law.[36] At the same time, although 'customary law' can refer to a wide variety of phenomena, certain well-known types of customary law have shaped dominant assumptions about unwritten law as a general category. Therefore, whenever we try to connect the idea of customary international law to the idea of unwritten law more generally, there is a risk of indirectly superimposing a particular idea of unwritten or customary law onto something contingent.[37] That risk counsels us to keep in mind that particular types of customary law are not only internally multifaceted but also might only have a tenuous relationship to any general category of unwritten law deemed 'typical'. *Second*, and relatedly, the idea of customary international law does not necessarily correspond to the idea of unwritten or customary law in other contexts, other than perhaps in the shape of a family resemblance. This is observed by some scholars who have studied the relationship between customary law on the local level and customary international law.[38] Nonetheless, despite apparent differences between various forms of customary law, there is arguably a non-trivial – that is, a more than etymological – relationship between customary law as a set of ideas, on the one hand, and ideas about customary international law, on the other, in the shape of a family resemblance. At the same time, while comparative studies of unwritten law appear promising and have often been suggested, it is possible and indeed likely that 'customary law' has a unique, especially relevant,

(Oxford, Oxford University Press, 2017); RXD Hawkins, ND Goodman, and RL Goldstone, 'The Emergence of Social Norms and Conventions' (2019) 23(2) *Trends in Cognitive Sciences* 158, 162.

[34] See eg AE Roberts, 'Traditional and Modern Approaches to Customary International Law: A Reconciliation' (2001) 95(4) *American Journal of International Law* (2001) 757; J d'Aspremont, *The Discourse on Customary International Law* (Oxford, Oxford University Press, 2021); BD Lepard, *Customary International Law: A New Theory with Practical Applications* (Cambridge, Cambridge University Press, 2010); BD Lepard (ed), *Reexamining Customary International Law* (Cambridge, Cambridge University Press, 2017); CA Bradley (ed), *Custom's Future: International Law in a Changing World* (Cambridge, Cambridge University Press, 2016); S Droubi and J d'Aspremont (eds), *International Organisations, Non-State Actors, and the Formation of Customary International Law* (Manchester, Manchester University Press, 2020).

[35] See generally RA Shiner, *Legal Institutions and the Sources of Law*, Volume 3 of the *Treatise of Legal Philosophy and General Jurisprudence* (Dordrecht, Springer, 2005) (Chapter 4 on 'Custom').

[36] Tamanaha, *A Realistic Theory of Law* (n 8) 178–9.

[37] See also B Dupret, 'Legal Traditions and State-Centered Law: Drawing from Tribal and Customary Law Cases of Yemen and Egypt' in D Chatty (ed), *Nomadic Societies in the Middle East and North Africa: Entering the 21st Century* (Leiden, Brill, 2006) 280, 281–2.

[38] Seeeg P Ørebech and M Chanock, 'Towards Sustainability: The Basis in International Law' in P Ørebech et al (eds), *The Role of Customary Law in Sustainable Development* (Cambridge, Cambridge University Press, 2009) 385.

or other qualitatively different role to play in international settings. But that simply suggests that comparative studies of unwritten forms of law need to be mindful of their context. *Third*, the idea of customary international law does not exhaust the forms of unwritten law that are relevant in international law. At the same time, customary international law is an exemplary and arguably the most relevant form of unwritten international law. Moreover, it is not always easy to precisely distinguish various kinds of unwritten international law. The existence of blurred boundaries between various forms of unwritten law is not, however, unique to international law. In short, the recurrent merging of concepts like custom, customary law, and unwritten law in the history of legal thought and practice is a valuable reminder of the difficulty of any attempt to delimit customary law neatly from other kinds of unwritten law. However, to the extent that international legal thought has been shaped by ideas about the *lex non scripta*, it is to a large degree also reflected in thinking about and in the legal doctrine of customary international law.

In both secular and religious contexts, the idea of law tends to be intimately bound up with a constitutive act of, usually written,[39] lawmaking.[40] We see this with the revered US Constitution,[41] in several Latin American countries since the nineteenth century, as well as in Post-War Germany and Japan, South Africa, India, or the Philippines.[42] In the field of EU law, the Treaty of Maastricht is seen as representing a decisive constitutive moment for the supranational EU,[43] just as the subsequently failed draft Treaty Establishing a Constitution for Europe, which was animated by federalist desires to place the EU on a more solid legal-ideational basis.[44] In the field of international law,[45] some scholars treat the adoption of the UN Charter as a quasi-constitutional moment and the Charter as a quasi-constitution of the international community.[46] Even if that analogy may be a minority view today, it is not difficult to appreciate the seductiveness

[39] See, discussing the distinction between written and unwritten constitutions in the UK context, J Waldron, *The Law* (New York, Routledge, 1990) 85.

[40] See generally R Albert, M Guruswamy, and N Basnyat (eds), *Founding Moments in Constitutionalism* (Oxford, Hart Publishing, 2019).

[41] See A Rana, *The Constitutional Bind: How Americans Came to Idolize a Document That Fails Them* (Chicago, Chicago University Press, 2024); however, on the complex interaction between the written and 'unwritten' constitution, see AR Amar, *America's Unwritten Constitution: The Precedents and Principles We Live By* (New York, Basic Books, 2012); see also generally B Ackerman, *We the People, Volume 2: Transformations* (Cambridge, Harvard University Press, 1991).

[42] See R De, *A People's Constitution: The Everyday Life of Law in the Indian Republic* (Princeton, Princeton University Press, 2018) 2.

[43] JHH Weiler, *The Constitution of Europe: 'Do the New Clothes Have an Emperor?' and Other Essays on European Integration* (Cambridge, Cambridge University Press, 1999) 4.

[44] N Walker, 'Europe's Constitutional Overture' in N Barber, M Cahill, and R Ekins (eds), *The Rise and Fall of the European Constitution* (Oxford, Hart Publishing, 2018) 177.

[45] The 'constitutional' interpretation of international law can be traced to the pre-UN period. In particular, see A Verdross, *Die Verfassung der Völkerrechtsgemeinschaft* (Vienna, Springer Verlag, 1926).

[46] See B Fassbender, *The United Nations Charter as the Constitution of the International Community* (Leiden, Martinus Nijhoff, 2009) 170–1.

and constructive implications of such a constitutional analogy for international lawyers.[47] However, the degree to which the myth of a constitutive moment embodied in a written document is shared across societies varies enormously. With some exceptions (such as the United Kingdom or Israel, which have unwritten constitutions),[48] a supreme constitutional document is central to many of the world's legal orders. At the same time, to say that the written character of a constitution is mythical is not to say it is not meaningful. To the contrary, the embodied form of a society's law can be highly influential simply because it serves as a focal point for a particular population's constitution through law. Moreover, from a longer historical perspective, transitions from unwritten to written forms of law (and indeed from orality to writing) were highly significant, as the example of ancient Greece shows.[49] Moreover, in the major monotheistic religious traditions, including those of Judaism, Christianity, and Islam, high importance was traditionally accorded to the enactment of written law.[50]

And yet, here as in similar contexts, such narratives of legal enactment – of a first, constitutive lawmaking moment – are known to overshadow the more nuanced reality of earlier, parallel, and constantly changing unwritten laws.[51] A comparable point also applies in relation to other exemplars of the *lex scripta*: from 'living documents' like the US Constitution,[52] contracts structuring innumerable business transactions, to founding agreements of international organisations. While the exaltation of written law has an important function in many legal systems and societies, it is a type of myth, not in any pejorative sense but simply in the sense of serving a symbolic function without giving a complete picture of a legal system's operation. Beyond the constitutional or international law context, unwritten forms of law are seen as fundamental also in the area of private law.[53] In short, the often supposed dichotomy between customary law and modernity sits on weak foundations, and unwritten law, rather than displacing written or promulgated law, has a close and mutually constitutive relationship to written law.

Philosophical accounts of customary law are also helpful in underlining the close relationship between written and unwritten law. One intellectual strategy

[47] See eg A Verdross, *Die Verfassung der Völkerrechtsgemeinschaft* (n 45).

[48] For background and contemporary arguments for a written UK constitution, see eg B Dickson, *Writing the United Kingdom Constitution* (Manchester, Manchester University Press, 2019) 16.

[49] M Gagarin, *Writing Greek Law* (Cambridge, Cambridge University Press 2009) 33.

[50] For example, in Jewish law, the transmission of the law to Moses, as recounted in the Torah's Book of Exodus, marks a point of rupture in the community's (legal) traditional narrative and represents a founding moment for the community. See eg Volumes I and II of M Elon, *Jewish Law: History, Sources, Principles*, 1st English edn (Philadelphia, Jewish Publication Society, 1994).

[51] See eg S Wilf, *The Law Before the Law* (Lanham, Lexington Books, 2008) xiii.

[52] See eg PW Kahn, 'Reason and Will in the Origins of American Constitutionalism' (1989) 98(2) *Yale Law Journal* 449.

[53] See S Meder, *Ius non scriptum – Traditionen privater Rechtsetzung*, 2nd edn (Tübingen, Mohr Siebeck, 2009).

pursued by legal philosophers who study customary law (as a generic or particular phenomenon) entails splitting it up into its essential or necessary components. This approach is meant to provide an account of the distinctive features of customary law, as compared to other forms of law. One prominent approach in this vein is offered by James Bernard Murphy, who draws on the concepts of habit and convention to develop a philosophical account of both custom and customary law.[54] Murphy points to the fact that philosophers have had a long-standing preoccupation with habit and convention, two of the components or fundamental elements that he views as helpful, if not necessary, for understanding the nature and relevance of custom, and relatedly, customary law. He thus places habit and convention at the core of both custom and customary law. Murphy's central point is that rather than leading to the displacement of custom or customary law, law as legislation, custom, and customary law are all intimately related. This suggests that customary law, rather than being an opposite of written law, already contains within it the duality between 'will' and 'reason' that is often reflected in all kinds of legal norms. Of the two 'components' of custom highlighted by Murphy, habit has long been the object of a remarkably rich engagement by a variety of thinkers.[55] Crucially, age-old debates over habit can be interpreted at heart as concerning the evaluation of habit along two opposed but ultimately complementary poles: constraint and freedom.[56] Another way to get at the concept of habit is by juxtaposing it to reason (although this dichotomy is contested by some thinkers, Murphy in particular).[57] Another source of thinking about the relationship between unwritten and written law is reflected in the writings of Hannah Arendt. In 'On Revolution,' Arendt discussed the relationship between law and power by reference to the experiences of the French and American revolutions. Arendt refers to the 'enormous difference in power and authority that exists between a constitution imposed by a government upon a people and the constitution by which a people constitutes its own government.'[58] Thus, the contrast between 'imposed' and 'constituted' law is identified as a central element of power and authority. This idea can be extended to legal thought more generally, suggesting that law imposed versus law constituted from below (much like some types of customary law) would tend to enjoy a lesser degree of 'power and authority.' In his study of the history of the theory of the common law, Gerald Postema has further highlighted

[54] JB Murphy, *The Philosophy of Customary Law* (Oxford, Oxford University Press, 2014).

[55] See eg AM Graybiel, 'Habits, Rituals, and the Evaluative Brain' (2008) 31 *Annual Review of Neuroscience* 359. As Clare Carlisle explains, 'habit' can plausibly be seen as a recurrent theme of Western philosophical thought since European Antiquity. See C Carlisle, *On Habit* (New York, Routledge, 2014).

[56] ibid 3–4. Carlisle highlights the dual, only seemingly contradictory, character of habit as both an inhibitor and an enabler of human freedom and flourishing.

[57] See AT Kronman, 'The Value of Moral Philosophy' (1998) 111(7) *Harvard Law Review* 1751, 1760 (noting that habit can indeed be seen as a moral virtue, but that occasionally, it must be supplemented by 'reason').

[58] H Arendt, *On Revolution* (New York, Penguin Press, 1963) 144.

the complex relationship between unwritten law, written law, and law more generally. As Postema notes, according to one of the most well-known theorists of the common law, Matthew Hale, both 'judicial decisions' and 'enacted law' are initially without consequence. Both of these types of law only '*become law* by eventually *becoming custom*.'[59] Indeed, the absence of unwritten or customary law would, in effect, frustrate the effective operation of most legal systems.

In short, law is often conceived by lawyers and legal scholars as being divided into several related types, parts, kinds, or forms.[60] The same is true in the field of international law, where customary international law is generally understood as supplementing the characteristic rigidities and lacunae that a written and preconceived legal code necessarily creates.[61] In general, it embodies the complementary, unwritten, and dynamic part of the international lawmaking universe. The idea that law is a composite is also linked to debates traditionally pitting legal positivism against the natural law tradition.[62] Customary law has been of special interest to legal scholars who study non-positive forms of lawmaking because it appears harder to square with positivist approaches to law.[63] Indeed, the most plausible way of interpreting the rise of customary international law in the nineteenth and early twentieth century is by reference to its displacement of natural law, notwithstanding that it was formally declared to be a source of 'positive law', akin to treaties – in reality, its tenuous link to state consent was apparent.[64] Arguably, with natural law's decline in relevance in legal thought by the nineteenth century, customary law functionally assumed the latter's role and place. In a similar sense, customary international law, especially as understood in international legal doctrine, became a functional placeholder for the earlier natural law.[65]

[59] GJ Postema, *Bentham and the Common Law Tradition* (Oxford, Clarendon Press, 1986) 25–6.

[60] This sort of division can take multiple forms, for example, procedural and substantive, written and unwritten, principles versus rules of law, constitutional and ordinary, individual and general, and many more.

[61] The specific manifestation of this duality and its functional relevance is eloquently described in R Kolb, *Theory of International Law* (Oxford, Hart Publishing, 2016) 123.

[62] For example, as Robert Alexy notes, 'the dual-nature thesis [of law], in setting out the claim that law necessarily comprises both a real and ideal dimension, implies non-positivism'. R Alexy, 'The Ideal Dimension of Law' in G Duke and RP George, *The Cambridge Companion to Natural Law Jurisdprudence* (Cambridge, Cambridge University Press, 2017) 314.

[63] See eg J Finnis, *Natural Law and Natural Rights*, 2nd edn (Oxford, Clarendon Press) 238–45. For a review of the latter, see in particular N Maccormick, 'Natural Law and the Separation of Law and Morals' in RP George (ed), *Natural Law Theory: Contemporary Essays* (Oxford, Oxford University press, 1994) 105.

[64] While Haggenmacher emphasises that custom was seen at the time as a positive source of law, even the context of the Committee of Jurists' debates shows that it was in fact understood to have a rather tenuous connection to state consent. See P Haggenmacher, 'An Archaeological Look at "International Custom as Evidence of a General Practice Accepted as Law" and Article 38 of the World Court's Statute' (2021) 34(3) *Leiden Journal of International Law* 1, 16.

[65] See eg SC Neff, *Justice Among Nations* (Cambridge, Harvard University Press, 2014) 261; see also F Iurlaro, *The Invention of Custom: Natural Law and the Law of Nations, ca. 1550–1750* (Oxford, Oxford University Press, 2021).

V. KEY SUBSTANTIVE THEMES AND NORMATIVE EPISODES

To obtain a more realistic and fine-grained understanding of international law, in recent decades, many scholars have devoted themselves to the study of particular incidents or cases, using a variety of methods and approaches.[66] Especially in the case of customary international law, given its close link to 'practice', this approach seems especially promising. Chapters 3 to 5 therefore assemble a series of representative and diverse 'normative episodes' meant to illustrate the operation of customary international law across different social arenas and periods, even if many of them inevitably have numerous points of connection.[67] They examine customary international law as an instance of the law 'in action', a feature of experience and behaviour rather than merely of doctrine or rhetoric.[68] At the same time, they acknowledge that customary international law, even in its particular and contingent manifestations, remains closely connected to the prevailing legal doctrine of customary international law, something discussed later in this book. From a chronological perspective, each chapter begins during a period widely understood as initiating the defining features of contemporary international society and law, even if links to the deeper past are highlighted.[69] Each chapter also covers the highly impactful reordering of international society

[66] See eg WM Reisman and AR Willard (eds), *International Incidents: The Law That Counts in World Politics* (Princeton University Press, 1988); WM Reisman, 'International Incidents: Introduction to a New Genre in the Study of International Law' (1984) 10 *Yale Journal of International Law* 1; T Ruys, O Corten, and A Hofer (eds), *The Use of Force in International Law: A Case-Based Approach* (Oxford, Oxford University Press, 2018); see also N Tannenwald, 'Stigmatizing the Bomb: Origins of the Nuclear Taboo' (2005) 29(4) *International Security* 5; JE Noyes, LA Dickinson, and MW Janis (eds), *International Law Stories* (New York, Foundation Press, 2007); V Lowe, 'The Politics of Law-Making: Are the Method and Character of Norm Creation Changing?' in M Byers, *The Role of Law in International Politics: Essays in International Relations and International Law* (Oxford, Oxford University Press, 2001) 207, 223 (noting that traditionally '[t]he incident embodies the norm'); A Carty, 'The Practice of International Law' in D Armstrong (ed), *Routledge Handbook of International Law* (London, Routledge, 2009) 81; D Kennedy, *A World of Struggle: How Power, Law, and Expertise Shape Global Political Economy* (Princeton, Princeton University Press, 2016); see also generally P Blokker and C Thornhill (eds), *Sociological Constitutionalism* (Cambridge, Cambridge University Press, 2017).

[67] See generally J Gerring, *Case Study Research Principles and Practices*, 2nd edn (Cambridge, Cambridge University Press, 2016) 86–150.

[68] For an account of the 'law in action' across a number of fields, see also DM Johnston, *The Historical Foundations of World Order: The Tower and the Arena* (Leiden, Martinus Nijhoff, 2008) 3–103. On Holmes' juxtaposition of 'experience' and 'logic', see eg B Leiter, 'Holmes, Economics, and Classical Realism' in SJ Burton (ed), *The Path of the Law and its Influence: The Legacy of Oliver Wendell Holmes, Jr* (Cambridge, Cambridge University Press, 2000) 285, 312.

[69] On nineteenth century social thought, see eg WW Breckman and P Gordon, 'Introduction' in WW Breckman and P Gordon (eds), *The Cambridge History of Modern European Thought, Volume I (Cambridge, Cambridge University Press, 2019)* 1. On earlier examples of 'interpolity' law, see eg L Benton and A Clulow, 'Legal Encounters and the Origins of Global Law' in JH Bentley et al (eds), *The Cambridge World History: Volume 6: The Construction of a Global World, 1400–1800 CE, Part 2* (Cambridge, Cambridge University Press, 2015) 80.

in the wake of World War II, which saw the consolidation of the most distinctive ideas and trends of the contemporary era, with important consequences for international law.[70] Finally, the narrative focuses on customary international lawmaking during the last three decades, which were shaped by the tension between globalisation, on the one hand, and rising multipolarity or pluralism, on the other.

[70] See CS Maier, 'The World Economy and the Cold War in the Middle of the Twentieth Century' in MP Leffler and OA Westad (eds), *The Cambridge History of the Cold War, Volume I* (Cambridge, Cambridge University Press, 2010) 44, 46.

2

Four Types of Customary International Law

THE FRAMEWORK DEVELOPED in this chapter is based on a comprehensive approach to customary international law as a complex system of social order and control. We can trace the idea of law as a system of social order and control to sociological theories that first gained currency in the late nineteenth century in multiple intellectual centres.[1] Since then, many socio-legal scholars have relied on this versatile proposition to develop approaches for understanding different socio-legal phenomena.[2] Essentially, it suggests that the operation of socio-legal phenomena tends to be related to both legal and non-legal norms and institutions, to a range of organisations, and to various other relationships among socio-legal actors, norms, and institutions. Therefore, a productive way of beginning to describe a complex socio-legal phenomenon is by identifying its components, with a focus on their respective roles, composition, and relationships.[3] Customary international lawmaking appears to take place within variety of settings and is affected by different institutional, participatory, procedural, and normative factors. A description of customary international law as a system of

[1] See eg JJ Chriss, 'Social Control: History of the Concept' in M Deflem (ed), *The Handbook of Social Control* (Oxford, Wiley, 2019) 9; see also RC Ellickson, 'A Critique of Economic and Sociological Theories of Social Control' (January 1987) XVI *Journal of Legal Studies* 67; J Griffiths, 'What is Sociology of Law? (On law, rules, social control and sociology)' (2017) 49(2) *The Journal of Legal Pluralism and Unofficial Law* 93. See for a discussion of Brian Tamanaha's critique of the 'social order function' of law, W Twining, *General Jurisprudence: Understanding Law from a Global Perspective* (Cambridge, Cambridge University Press, 2009) 97–9. I adopt a similar framing, albeit in a different context, in G Novak, 'Reading the Waves: Continuity and Change in Ocean Lawmaking' (2022) 47(2) *Columbia Journal of Environmental Law* 359, 455.

[2] See RC Ellickson, *Order Without Law: How Neighbors Settle Disputes* (Cambridge, Harvard University Press, 1991) 127 (referring to Max Weber as 'surely one of the most impressive theorists of social control'). Ellickson draws on D Black's multi-volume *Toward a General Theory of Social Control* (1984). See also F Grisel, *The Limits of Private Governance: Norms and Rules in a Mediterranean Fishery* (Oxford, Hart Publishing, 2021); WM Reisman, 'The Breakdown of the Control Mechanism in ICSID Arbitration' (1989) 1989(4) *Duke Law Journal* 739, 741.

[3] A focus on relationships is also reflected in newer research into the practice of diplomacy and international affairs. See eg R Adler-Nissen, 'Conclusion: Relationalism or Why Diplomats Find International Relations Theory Strange' in OJ Sending, V Pouliot, and IB Neumann (eds), *Diplomacy and the Making of World Politics* (Cambridge, Cambridge University Press, 2015) 284, 286.

social order and control therefore needs to address questions such as: Who are the relevant actors engaged in customary international lawmaking and what explains their behaviour? How do they relate to each other and, if they are groups of individuals or entities, how are they organized internally? How are they embedded in various legal and non-legal institutions? To what extent are they representative of global society or its constituent groups?

As noted in the Introduction, the framework developed in this chapter is centred around four representative types of customary international law norms. Their interrelationships have important implications both for our understanding of customary international law and the myriad normative questions that follow from it. These four types of customary international law norms are: First, *entrenched background custom*: This is a widely shared and deeply rooted type of custom underlying basic principles of contemporary international law, from the norm of sovereignty to the principle of non-discrimination. Second, *analogical custom*: This is a type of law both derivative and novel; it 'coasts' on deeply entrenched background custom, often addressing newly emerging legal questions, and commonly arising in the field of rapid technological or socio-economic change. Third, *dynamic custom*: This is the wild beast among the framework's quartet of norm types and the least law-like type of custom. It allows powerful actors to set controlling but brittle equilibria in key areas of global law and politics. Fourth, *pure judicial custom*: This is roughly the 'common law' equivalent of law on the international plane. This type of custom is initially fragile and institutionally circumscribed. However, it is a potentially powerful and highly authoritative type of custom with profound effects on broader international lawmaking. Each member of this quartet of customary international law norms has different characteristics, origins, and degrees of stability. Each type of custom is the product of a particular configuration of underlying lawmaking factors that coalesce to sustain a norm of customary international law. These four types of custom can be observed across virtually all fields of international law. Understanding them and how they relate to each other can allow the legal scholar or policymaker to make better sense of the possibilities of and obstacles to social change through international law. It can also inform normative proposals for the redesign of customary international lawmaking and thus improving downstream social outcomes.

As noted, each of these 'four types of custom' has different characteristics, origins, and degrees of stability. Such variations are related to characteristic lawmaking factors (institutional, participatory, normative, and procedural) and other contextual (political, technological, socio-economic) circumstances that undergird and sustain different types of customary international law norms. These underlying factors are universal in the sense that they are part of many lawmaking processes and norms in local and other settings.

It is important to note that the underlying factors that shape lawmaking processes and their respective outcomes can be closely related but also appear individually. Moreover, these factors do not express themselves in a binary fashion. Instead, their presence is a matter of both kind and degree. This leads to a *theoretically* infinite number of potential types of customary international law norms. In other words, customary international law processes are extremely multifaceted, and the types of customary international law norms identified in this chapter are constructed by drawing on certain characteristic lawmaking factors whose presence in any particular scenario is a matter of both kind and degree. However, I single out four *representative* patterns, resulting in four types of customary international law norms. The four types are thus ideal types, rather than 1:1 representations of an inherently complex lawmaking landscape. Ideal types are high-level abstractions of social patterns.[4] Weber calls them *Utopien* ('utopias') and they are usually schematic and simplified representations of an infinitely complex reality.[5] As with Weber's ideal types (*Idealtypen*), the ideal typology introduced in this chapter is meant to offer what Michael Reisman has described as 'a conceptual tool for understanding, collecting and processing relevant data about the lawmaking which occurs in the widely varying circumstances of international law'.[6] It is meant to complement and try to inform, rather than substitute, other descriptive accounts of customary international law – be they doctrinal, historical, social scientific, or other.

Temporally, this framework focuses on contemporary customary international law. Earlier periods may have seen different configurations of factors shaping customary international lawmaking and thus may have featured different customary international lawmaking processes and resulting norms. Conversely, subtle or radical shifts in global lawmaking may well occur in the future, including to customary international lawmaking. To be sure, the operation of customary international law over the last century is marked by both continuities and discontinuities, both of which I highlight below. Nonetheless, I am ultimately most interested in what we can learn from the past about ourselves and customary international lawmaking today given growing calls for a global legal order better able to meet the imperative of allowing social change to be realised without becoming indistinguishable from untrammelled power or crumbling in the face of challenges.

[4] M Weber, 'Die „Objektivität" sozialwissenschaftlicher und sozialpolitischer Erkenntnis' (1904) 19 *Archiv für Sozialwissenschaft und Sozialpolitik* 22, 65.

[5] Examples of legal scholars deploying ideal typologies are myriad. See eg MR Damaška, *The Faces of Justice and State Authority: A Comparative Approach to the Legal Process* (New Haven, Yale University Press, 1986).

[6] WM Reisman, 'The Quest for World Order and Human Dignity in the Twenty-First Century: Constitutive Process and Individual Commitment: General Course on Public International Law' (2013) 135 *Collected Courses of the Hague Academy of International Law* 9, 120.

A basic objection to my approach from the perspective of the legal doctrine of customary international law is that such a typology is insensitive to the fact that customary international law has a particular, albeit not uncontentious, doctrinal definition. After all, customary international law is conceived by legal professionals and many legal scholars as a unitary phenomenon, and differences in its application may be explained by different approaches to the identification and interpretation of customary international law. What use could an expanded scholarly focus on a purported typology of customary international law norms have? The answer is that the legal doctrine of customary international law and different approaches to the identification and interpretation of customary international law are important, but hardly the only, elements of customary international law as a broader social phenomenon. To understand how customary international law is 'made' and how it shapes social life, it is essential to understand the relationship between the legal doctrine of customary international law and its broader social context. Legal scholars are most suited to this task because their interdisciplinary training allows them to integrate an internal perspective on the law with cross-disciplinary insights into the operation of various normative phenomena, including international law.

By proposing an ideal typology, this chapter weaves a wealth of insights from the life of international law into a parsimonious account of the diversity of contemporary customary international lawmaking processes and resulting norms. Essentially, I argue that contemporary customary international law norms can be represented as arising in four basic ideal types. Each is characterised by the extent to which it reflects certain features of customary international lawmaking processes more generally. These ideal types are meant to synthesise patterns that reappear across a variety of contemporary manifestations of customary international law. To reiterate, each ideal type represents a particular configuration of factors determining or shaping customary international lawmaking processes and their respective outcomes, norms of customary international law.[7] It results from an iterative intellectual process that moves between two poles. On the one hand, it draws on patterns emerging from a range of representative and diverse episodes of customary international lawmaking. On the other hand, it derives from insights into unwritten types of law in general, the legal doctrine of customary international law, and the latter's role in customary international lawmaking as a broader social phenomenon.

[7] As noted, I posit that customary international lawmaking processes are best described by reference to particular configurations of factors that sustain norms of customary international law, rather than by an account of such 'processes' themselves. I follow here Ullmann-Margalit's admonition (by reference to Raz) to look to the 'conditions of existence' of norms rather than to 'how they come about'. See E Ullmann-Margalit, *The Emergence of Norms* (Oxford, Oxford University Press, 2015) 7–8.

I. CHARACTERISTICS OF LAWMAKING PROCESSES

Each of the four ideal types introduced below refers to a particular configuration of factors determining or shaping customary international lawmaking processes and their respective outcomes: norms of customary international law. This four-fold typology is meant to supplement the legal fiction reflected in the legal doctrine of customary international law, which serves an important function but tends to obscure our understanding of customary international law as a broader social phenomenon. The factors that inform and support this four-fold ideal typology relate to the *institutional*, participatory or *democratic*, '*normative*' or teleological, and *procedural* characteristics of lawmaking processes; these factors sometimes attach also to their outcomes, customary international law norms. As noted, these factors are universal in the sense that they are part of many lawmaking processes and norms in local and other settings; at the same time, they assume a particular and contingent form and relevance in the context of international lawmaking.

A. Institutional Factors

Formal institutions help structure or are involved in a plethora of international lawmaking processes. As a result, they shape – sometimes marginally and sometimes significantly – the nature and quality of various lawmaking processes and the stability of their outcomes, norms of international law.[8] Today, an immense number and variety of formal institutions affect international lawmaking processes, leading to an increasingly complex and multilayered institutional landscape. To some extent, formal international institutions have radically transformed the very nature of contemporary global affairs. In particular, as a result of improvements in communication, transportation, and other socio-economic factors, domestic, transnational, and international lawmaking processes have become so closely institutionally enmeshed that it is becoming hard to compare the contemporary era of global lawmaking to earlier epochs characterised by an effectively more structured separation between different levels of regulation.

The concept of an 'institution' is used in different ways across the social sciences and in legal scholarship, alternatively referring to doctrines, norms, customary practices, organisations in the sociological sense, or all of the above.[9]

[8] This includes the number and arrangement of available institutions, the presence of third-party decision makers of various sorts, and the nature of the relationship between international and domestic institutions.

[9] See generally RE Goodin, 'Institutions and Their Design' in RE Goodin (ed), *The Theory of Institutional Design* (Cambridge, Cambridge University Press, 1996) 1; see also DC North, *Institutions, Institutional Change and Economic Performance* (Cambridge, Cambridge University Press, 1990).

I refer to formal institutions and institutional factors here in a narrow legal-sociological sense, meaning organisations or organised networks of people characterised by at least some stability and involved in lawmaking processes of various kinds. This would include, for example, domestic courts, international courts or tribunals of various sorts (the ICJ, ad hoc arbitral tribunals), international organisations (like the WHO or the ITU), structured consultation networks between various authorities, or meetings of various degrees of informality (G20 meetings, UN treaty conferences, and so on). All of these institutions serve to connect a range of actors, including public authorities and officials, non-governmental organisations, businesses, and various other individuals. In an age of growing electronic communication, formal institutions rely to an important extent on information and communication technologies, with important implications for the character of lawmaking processes.

Formal international institutions provide a range of valuable public goods and are so prevalent that it is easy to take them for granted. They often serve a range of actors as intermediaries or fora but can also fulfil various incidental roles. For example, they can provide the infrastructure and technical and expert support required for both one-off and especially regular meetings by different actors. They can serve as information conduits by helping organise and transmit various kinds of information about facts and expectations across large networks of persons and organisations. Institutions can serve the important function of third-party dispute settlement, as in the case of mediation, arbitration, and adjudication. In some cases, institutions can possess delegated powers to take decisions binding on their members or other parties, as in the case of several specialised organisations or bodies that regularly exercise administrative or quasi-legislative powers, such as the UN Security Council. Such decisions can vary immensely in nature and effect. In addition, institutions can serve as public fora, places of ritual performance and reaffirmation of social or legal norms, and as venues used for the public dissemination of various kinds of information. At the same time, institutions can also serve as sites for secret or closed-door decision-making processes of various kinds, as well as multi-track diplomacy.

While formal international institutions play an important role in international lawmaking, in the case of customary international law, many domestic and transnational institutions – individually or collectively – also play a significant role. In many ways, the extent to which international law is effective in fact depends largely on the extent to which domestic institutions choose to recognise and enforce international legal norms. Moreover, norms of customary international law often develop through bottom-up processes, in which domestic institutions first engage in practices that spread and only later become codified, applied, or enforced at the international level, often in conjunction and coordination with international institutions and transnational actors.

In all these ways, formal institutions are diverse (in kind and in terms of their internal organisation) and can be involved in coordination, cooperation, and conflict both horizontally and hierarchically. Importantly, this factor of international lawmaking was essentially invented in the nineteenth century but has exploded on the global level chiefly since the second half of the twentieth century.

B. Participatory or Democratic Factors

The relationship between democracy and lawmaking, in general, raises difficult descriptive and normative questions.[10] The normative arguments for global democracy are persuasive, but how democratic precepts should be applied to the regional, let alone international, level remains hotly debated.[11] For one, there are multiple conceptions of democracy and myriad ways in which they can be reflected in international lawmaking. Moreover, a variety of actors or political units are conceivably relevant for democratising international lawmaking.[12] Given ongoing contestation about the shape and extent of democratic governance on the local level, talk of global democracy may thus seem unproductive. However, it is meaningful to ask whether, under what conditions, and to what extent international law in general, and customary international law in its various manifestations, is likely to be more inclusive, more responsive to changing circumstances or majoritarian preferences, or more likely to give a voice to a diverse set of populations and groups, as compared to alternative modalities of lawmaking. At this stage, I cannot provide any definitive answer to whether 'customary international law' in its various manifestation can be more 'democratic' than

[10] The literature on this topic is very extensive. Generally see eg C Tilly, *Democracy* (Cambridge, Cambridge University Press, 2007) 1–24; see also J Elster, 'Introduction' in J Elster (ed), *Deliberative Democracy* (Cambridge, Cambridge University Press, 1998) 8; see also D Stasavage, *The Decline and Rise of Democracy: A Global History from Antiquity to Today* (Princeton, Princeton University Press, 2020).

[11] See eg H Landemore, *Open Democracy* (Princeton, Princeton University Press, 2020) 211; contributions by RA Falk, R Christiano, A Follesdal, BS Frey, K Macdonald, and BS Chimni in D Archibugi et al (eds), *Global Democracy: Normative and Empirical Perspectives* (Cambridge, Cambridge University Press, 2011); D Otto, 'Subalternity and International Law: The Problems of Global Community and the Incommensurability of Difference' (1996) 5(3) *Social & Legal Studies* 337; L Bernholz, H Landemore, and R Reich (eds), *Digital Technology and Democratic Theory* (Chicago, University of Chicago Press, 2021); S Wheatley, *The Democratic Legitimacy of International Law* (Oxford, Oxford University Press, 2010); S Wheatley, 'A Democratic Rule of International Law' (2011) 22(2) *European Journal of International Law* 525; contributions by A Peters, A Boyle, and P Alston in A Cassese (ed), *Realizing Utopia: The Future of International Law* (Oxford, Oxford University Press, 2012); S Marks, *The Riddle of All Constitutions: International Law, Democracy, and the Critique of Ideology* (Oxford, Oxford University Press, 2003); JA Scholte (ed), *Building Global Democracy: Civil Society and Accountable Global Governance* (Cambridge, Cambridge University Press, 2011).

[12] See eg J Lin, *Governing Climate Change: Global Cities and Transnational Lawmaking* (Cambridge, Cambridge University Press, 2018); S Tully, *Corporations and International Lawmaking* (Leiden, Martinus Nijhoff, 2007); Barbara K. Woodward, *Global Civil Society in International Lawmaking and Global Governance: Theory and Practice* (Leiden, Martinus Nijhoff, 2010).

other modalities of lawmaking. After all, a satisfactory answer to that question would need to rely on many additional descriptive insights, in addition to a well-reasoned normative vantage point, awareness of the specific type of customary law at issue, and the relevant institutional and substantive context.

To varying degrees, international lawmaking processes display participatory and democratic characteristics. They assume a wide variety of forms, but broadly refer to two distinct but related dimensions. On the one hand, participatory or democratic factors of lawmaking processes concern the extent to and the ways in which different relevant actors can become directly involved in and affect international lawmaking. In that sense, lawmaking processes are fully participatory (or inclusive) if they directly involve members of the broadest possible range of different groups of people. If they are essentially dictatorial or involve only a small number of individuals representing one or only a few groups, they are instead exclusionary. A broad spectrum stretches between these two poles. Because customary international lawmaking is often decentralised, one needs to consider not only the international but also the local, national, and regional levels together in order to evaluate its participatory nature. Since lawmaking relies heavily on and could even be defined as a process of communication, the quality of participation depends not only on the formal design of lawmaking processes but also on adjacent elements that affect communication, such as the accessibility of communication, its quality, language-related factors, and similar. In that sense, participation depends on communication and the technologies that enable it, which can profoundly shape international lawmaking processes and their outcomes.

On the other hand, participatory or democratic factors of lawmaking also concern the degree to which the broader public is involved in or aware of lawmaking processes. In other words, they refer to the various ways in which the broader public can indirectly become part of lawmaking processes and how information about lawmaking processes and their outcomes are communicated and debated in society more generally.[13] Such involvement can occur in a variety of ways – through consultation, polling, deliberation, transparency-oriented measures, or through the mediation of scientists, experts, and civil society organisations, for example.[14] But such involvement can also be direct, immediate, or 'physical', as when a large number of people are involved in a particular

[13] See, for a brief and accessible, but nuanced, account of the value of 'social media', broadly understood, C Shirky, 'The Political Power of Social Media: Technology, the Public Sphere, and Political Change' (January/February 2011) *Foreign Affairs*.

[14] Various democratic dimensions of lawmaking play a key role in fostering publicity about the respective lawmaking process – they highlight that publicity is not simply about freedom of information, but other attributes of a vibrant public sphere, such as accessibility and discourse quality. The open, inclusive, and discourse-supported dissemination of information indirectly supports the quality of lawmaking because it signals to lawmakers the possibility of accountability. Additionally, it enhances the ability of individuals and groups, as well as civil society organisations of various sorts, to rally public support or adjust behaviour. All this furthers the democratisation of international lawmaking and influences the stability and quality of its outcomes.

law-governed practice, like wearing medical masks or using connected digital devices.

Any lawmaking process (be it inclusive or exclusionary) will be of interest to many more people than can likely ever reasonably be expected to participate in it. This is particularly true in relation to customary international law, which (usually) claims universal applicability but is (commonly) relatively removed from formalised institutions of lawmaking or, at least, often tends to be more diffuse than other modalities of lawmaking. These features of unwritten law make wider social participation important in anchoring customary international law in the expectations of all relevant actors in an effective and durable way. A norm that emerges from a highly participatory process will therefore tend to be more stable but not necessarily normatively preferable to its alternative. For example, the involvement of domestic audiences in international disputes can influence outcomes in pathological ways, notably by making governments more belligerent and uncompromising in the context of a dispute than they would otherwise be, which can lead not only to a lack of agreement but to the deterioration of cooperation and the erosion of norms on the international level.[15] Nonetheless, a norm resulting from a highly participatory process will tend to be more stable than one without any form of societal rootedness. As with forms of direct participation, a proper evaluation of indirect participation in a lawmaking process also needs to consider the quality of participation. And just like in the case of direct forms of participation, adjacent elements such as the quality and accessibility of communication and language-related factors all play important roles also for indirect participatory and democratic factors of a lawmaking process.

C. Perceptions of Normative Justice (Procedural, Formal, and Substantive)

Across different legal systems, generations of scholars have observed a close relationship between the substance, legitimacy, and effectiveness of law. A major insight of studies of lawmaking informed especially by sociological, psychological, and cultural approaches is that normative factors – and not only instrumental ones – play a key role in explaining the effectiveness and indeed the purpose of law and legal institutions.[16] While this basic insight is not new,[17] the newer literature in this vein has tried to demonstrate claims of this sort empirically by reference to a broad range of legal contexts. Notably, in his influential 'Why People Obey Law' and other contributions, Tom Tyler

[15] E Root, 'The Need of Popular Understanding of International Law' (1907) 1 *The American Journal of International Law* 1 (already making this point in the early twentieth century).

[16] See eg SJ Shapiro, *Legality* (Cambridge, Belknap Press, 2011) 392.

[17] See eg NS Timasheff, *An Introduction to the Sociology of Law* (Cambridge, Harvard University Committee on Research in the Social Sciences, 1939) 248.

empirically examined the central role and operation of certain normative factors in a variety of legal contexts.[18] Tyler treats 'legitimacy' as a factor distinct from both 'instrumentalism' and approaches that focus on 'social norms, moral values or ideologies'.[19] In 'The Power of Legitimacy among Nations',[20] Thomas Franck similarly emphasised the relationship between legitimacy and compliance with international law. As an early adopter of this idea in the field of international law, Franck explicitly drew on Tyler's work to develop an account of the legitimacy of norms of international law.[21] To be sure, it may not always be clear to what extent insights deriving from this literature can be expanded to cross-cultural contexts such as those of interest here.[22] At the same time, a number of other legal scholars have tried to extend this basic insight to international law,[23] while some have contested that it applies by analogy on the international plane.[24]

There are many ways of defining legitimacy in the legal context and normative factors that can shape perceptions of normative justice. Some of the factors that appear to affect the 'legitimacy' of customary international lawmaking processes or resulting norms are linked to moral values, including utilitarian considerations (as in the case of norms that are 'general' or community-oriented, in contrast to particularistic or interest group-oriented ones). In general, normative factors that matter in the context of customary international lawmaking seem to include various elements of procedural, formal, and substantive justice valued by those

[18] TR Tyler, *Why People Obey the Law* (Princeton, Princeton University Press, 1990). See also for a retrospective TR Tyler, 'Whither Legitimacy? Legal Authority in the Twenty-First Century' (2023) 19 *Annual Review of Law and Social Science* 1.

[19] ibid.

[20] See TM Franck, *The Power of Legitimacy among Nations* (Oxford, Oxford University Press, 1990) 26.

[21] TM Franck, *Fairness in International Law and Institutions* (Oxford, Oxford University Press, 1995) 30.

[22] TR Tyler, 'Procedural Justice' in A Sarat (ed), *The Blackwell Companion to Law and Society* (2004) 435, 436.

[23] See eg HH Koh, 'Review Essay: Why Do Nations Obey International Law?' (1997) 106(8) *Yale Law Journal* 2599, 2603; HH Koh, 'The 1998 Frankel Lecture: Bringing International Law Home' (1998) 35 *Houston Law Review* 623, 628–9; JP Kelly, 'The Twilight of Customary International Law' (2000) 40 *Virginia Journal of International Law* 449, 531; D Bodansky, 'Customary (and Not So Customary) International Environmental Law' (1995) 3(1) *Indiana Journal of Global Legal Studies* 105, 118; J Goldsmith and D Levinson, 'Law for States: International Law, Constitutional Law, Public Law' (2009) 122 *Harvard Law Review* 1791, 1841–2; B Kingsbury, 'The Concept of Compliance as a Function of Competing Conceptions of International Law' (1998) 19 *Michigan Journal of International Law* 345, 354–6; O Hathaway and SJ Shapiro, 'Outcasting: Enforcement in Domestic and International Law' (2011) 121 *Yale Law Journal* 252, 323; see also R Howse and R Teitel, 'Beyond Compliance: Rethinking Why International Law Really Matters' (2010) 1(2) *Global Policy* 127; A van Aaken, 'Behavioral International Law and Economics' (2014) 55 Harvard International Law Journal 421, 471.

[24] See eg, EA Posner and AO Sykes, 'Efficient Breach of International Law: Optimal Remedies, "Legalized Noncompliance," and Related Issues' (2011) 110(2) *Michigan Law Review* 243, 271 (noting that the argument developed by Tom Tyler 'does not work well with international law'); see also EA Posner, 'International Law and the Disaggregated State' (2005) 32 *Florida State University Law Review* 797, 811 (questioning whether normative factors explain compliance with international law).

who interact with the law. In practice, this can include procedures, rituals, and other forms of participation, but also formal or even substantive characteristics of the respective norms, such as their generality or community-orientation. My approach tries to single out different factors related to perceptions of normative justice attaching to lawmaking processes or the resulting norms. It adopts a minimal conception of morality or utilitarianism that comes close to a slightly more substantive version of the legitimacy that Tyler advocates in local settings. Drawing on representative examples surveyed in the rest of this book, I argue that also in the case of customary international law, the effectiveness of norms is supported by perceptions of procedural, formal, and substantive justice. However, given my finding that customary international law is best understood as a multifaceted phenomenon, the relevance of such normative factors varies by context.

Because the notion of normativity is so polyvalent, a clarification is in order: 'Normative' factors are referred to here in a subjective sense. For example, a rule that is 'general' or that has passed through a more deliberative procedural mechanism will seem more legitimate to the participants of the relevant legal order even if it may offend us from a particular moral standpoint. The point here is simply that in a variety of contexts, normative judgments or perceptions about both customary international lawmaking processes and resulting norms by both legal and policy experts and the general public can affect compliance, or more generally, the effectiveness of customary international law norms.

Two basic questions arise when we consider the relationship between perceptions of procedural, formal, or substantive justice and a norm's effectiveness. The first concerns particular examples of perceptions of procedural, formal, or substantive fairness or justice that affect or relate to a norm's perceived legitimacy and effectiveness. The second concerns the question of the mechanism by which such perceptions support the legitimacy as well as the effectiveness or a norm. What kinds of procedural, substantive, or formal factors can affect perceptions of legitimacy and the effectiveness of various types of customary international law norms, and how? With respect to substantive and formal characteristics of norms, norms that are general versus specific, community-oriented versus particularistic, and the product of analogical reasoning rather than completely novel will tend to be perceived as more legitimate and will therefore tend to be relatively more effective.

Generality as a characteristic of norms allows a decision-maker who applies them to use relatively broad discretion and to consider evolving practices. In contrast, a very specific rule requires a binary decision.[25] However, generality does not necessarily correlate with hierarchy because a hierarchically superior

[25] The distinction between general and specific chimes with the contrast between 'evaluation' and 'verification' rules discussed by Michael Reisman in an article dealing with the identification of customary international law by international investment tribunals. See WM Reisman, 'Canute Confronts the Tide: States vs. Tribunals and the Evolution of the Minimum Standard in Customary International Law' (2015) 30(3) *ICSID Review—Foreign Investment Law Journal* 616.

norm can be very specific. *Community orientation* is another characteristic of norms that can affect their legitimacy and effectiveness. In this context, community orientation refers to the degree to which the substance of a norm is perceived as having community-oriented goals, as opposed to advancing the goals of a particular individual, group, or special interest. An intermediate category is possible where a norm achieves some sort of balance between the two.[26] *Novelty* concerns the degree to which a norm is completely new rather than derivative, as a product of analogical reasoning. A norm derived from analogical reasoning is, in some sense and to a large extent, already 'there' and thus tentatively effective. For example, we often observe that new factual situations can be effectively regulated by the analogous application of a preexisting rule. In contrast, some situations will be so unprecedented that no analogy will be readily available or apposite and a new norm will need to emerge. At the same time, intermediate categories can be imagined.

The role of perceptions of normative justice can vary considerably according to the relevant institutional context. For example, when it comes to highly institutionalised settings, deliberative and participatory lawmaking processes will be perceived as relatively more legitimate and thus help stabilise a resulting norm. In less institutionalised settings, issues of procedural justice will play less of a role in affecting the stability of a customary law norm while other normative considerations might nonetheless be significant.

In this context, courts are the paradigmatic legal institutions. When courts seek to identify or interpret customary international law, they are often faulted by legal scholars for not articulating the precise method used to find norms of customary international law. However, the legal doctrine of customary international law is, to a large extent, a legal fiction. From the perspective of the legitimacy and effectiveness of norms, for a court to follow a particular 'method' for the identification or interpretation of customary international law may be less important than the deliberative nature of the judicial process itself, the representativeness of the respective decision-making body, and the extent to which the decision-makers were able to carefully consider a wide array of practices. To be sure, the question of whether justice must not only be done but also be seen to be done arises in this context. Nonetheless, what ultimately matters to a court in the international arena and from the perspective of legal effectiveness is to accurately anticipate which legal norm will be widely accepted or has the potential to become effective.[27] From that perspective, it matters less whether or not a court has faithfully applied any legal doctrine of customary international law.

[26] To clarify, the various characteristics discussed here can be, but are not necessarily, related. For example, a non-inclusive process of lawmaking can nonetheless produce a community-oriented norm, and inversely, an inclusive process of lawmaking can develop a special interest group-oriented norm.

[27] See on this point eg Eyal Benvenisti's argument relating to the ICJ's role in the context of the law of international watercourses. E Benvenisti, *Sharing Transboundary Resources: International Law and Optimal Resource Use* (Cambridge, Cambridge University Press, 2009) 201–31.

Following any strict 'method' for custom identification may in fact be counterproductive, at least if the aim is to ensure the legitimacy and effectiveness of a legal norm.

This raises the question of the role of the legal fiction as reflected in the legal doctrine of customary international law. One answer that can be inferred by analogy from relevant findings in social psychology is that a legal fiction helps decision-makers integrate a host of socially relevant information into future-oriented decisions in the form of a 'rationalization'.[28] More concretely, it can serve as a signal to dispersed lower-level actors to engage in practices that a third-party decision-maker can take into account if and when it is called on to identify or interpret a norm of customary international law. In the case of a court, this legal fiction gives its members the leeway to make new law when it has the chance of becoming effective. More broadly, it serves as an incentive or engine for bottom-up lawmaking for a wide variety of social actors. In that sense, customary international lawmaking neither starts nor ends with the pronouncement of a court – instead, one can view the role of courts and the legal doctrine they purport to apply as tools that enable customary international lawmaking processes to operate. From that perspective, arguments that envisage a formalization – or freezing – of any particular legal doctrine of customary international law appear highly risky without having any obvious upside from a normative perspective (such as, for example, of procedural justice).

D. Procedural Factors

Legal scholarship on the types of procedural traditions and practices in law is vast and diverse.[29] Emphasising the role of procedure for lawmaking processes and their outcomes draws on a rich legal theory literature that links the quality or stability of a norm to the procedures from which it derives. However, while 'procedure' has a particular connotation in legal scholarship, I refer to it in this subsection mostly in a technical sense. Notably, every social interaction – including international negotiations, arbitration proceedings, mid-air aircraft scrambles, and the conduct of military commanders or soldiers in war – can be understood as embodying a kind of 'procedure' (while also being governed by a host of legal and other procedures). Thus 'procedure' is used here in a particular, technical sense, referring to a certain kind of ordering of interactions between agents in time and space. In particular, I observe that in the context

[28] I raise this point here merely to illustrate one possible direction for scholarship in this area. See eg F Cushman, 'Rationalization is Rational' (2020) 43 (e28) *Behavioral and Brain Sciences* 1, 3.

[29] See eg MR Damaška, *The Faces of Justice and State Authority* (n 5); J Zekoll, 'Comparative Civil Procedure' in M Reimann and R Zimmermann (eds), *The Oxford Handbook of Comparative Law*, 2nd edn (Oxford, Oxford University Press, 2019) 1306.

of customary international law, distinctions among different procedures arise along three characteristic dimensions.

One dimension affecting procedure is the basic architecture of the respective lawmaking process. As a general matter, lawmaking processes can be pluralistic, decentralised, or centralised. A pluralistic structure (alternatively, we can refer to it as a federalised one) has elements of both centralisation and decentralisation. The classic case involves a scenario where an international court has jurisdiction while no international organ with effective enforcement powers exists. A pluralistic structure can also involve an appellate court empowered to review lower court decisions. On the opposite side of a perfectly centralised model (which today does not exist anywhere in the international law arena) is a decentralised structure that is essentially anarchic, with all relationships being ad hoc. The basic architectural setup of a lawmaking process has distinct implications for the types and numbers of interactions that occur within it.

A related procedural dimension of lawmaking processes concerns the relevant number of stages to a procedure. The basic architecture of a lawmaking process and the number of stages it involves are frequently correlated: A decentralised structure will tend to involve multiple stages, and thus a more complex and potentially more inclusive lawmaking process. Especially in the context of customary international law, the relevant lawmaking processes rarely occur in a single stage, although it is not inconceivable that they may. For example, one can sometimes observe extremely high-stakes, rare decisions or situations where the law changes so rapidly that it only ever applies to one incident; in these cases, we arrive at the edge of any meaningful concept of law, however. At any rate, most instances of customary international lawmaking can be described as either two-stage or multiple-stage processes. Of course, for the number of stages to be relevant, they need to be linked to each other in some way, for example through their precedential value.

Another related dimension of procedure concerns the speed and quality of interactions among actors within a lawmaking process, which is affected by and also affects both the architecture and organisation of lawmaking processes. This factor is strongly influenced by information and communication technologies. However, the speed and quality of interactions affect some processes more than others. Especially decentralised processes – such as those sometimes observed in the field of customary international lawmaking – tend to be more strongly affected by technologies of information and communication than centralised ones. This has important implications in an era characterised by rapid advances in information and communication technologies. As technological developments make some customary international law processes and resulting norms more relevant, their relative importance in international law may grow. Moreover, we can also imagine procedures involving only non-human agents, a scenario that is becoming increasingly relevant in the context of cyber warfare, for example.

Finally, if we consider 'procedure' in the narrow juridical sense, we also observe that procedures can take distinct shapes – from highly legalistic and formal procedures to largely unscripted ones. For example, a court deliberation (say, before the ICJ) will tend to follow a more or less legalistic script. In contrast, a military manoeuvre on the high seas will hardly be legalised at all – at most, it will be legalised in particular ways. For example, the decision-making processes within each of the relevant military structures may be legalised to some extent. But this will vary and depend on the situation and differ starkly from the kind of legalised procedure familiar from international adjudication. These procedural differences across lawmaking processes can all affect the nature and speed of interactions that occur in different lawmaking arenas, and consequently the resulting customary international law norms.

E. Cross-Cutting Points

A key implication of this chapter's typological framework concerns differences in the extent to which the various factors sustaining customary international law norms are amenable to change over (relatively) short periods of time. For example, the quality of communication between participants to a negotiation, the types of actors that can make submissions to international courts and tribunals, or the substance of a legal codification are all – at least in principle – relatively dynamic. In other words, they can be altered relatively easily and at low cost. In contrast, other factors operate on a deeper level and are more static, less liable to change by fiat, and more costly to redesign. This concerns the availability of public information, institutional aspects of customary lawmaking processes, and similar.

An awareness of those aspects of customary international lawmaking processes that can be modified more easily than others is extremely valuable. Not only does it improve our ability to shape customary international law or our attempts at improving or otherwise changing customary international lawmaking. It also suggests, ceteris paribus, that control over international lawmaking is hard to monopolise, even in the presence of highly centralised and undemocratic actors because customary international lawmaking can be shaped through a variety of factors and a multitude of actors at various levels. At least, this is true for contemporary customary international lawmaking. This should make us hopeful about the potential for advancing the democratisation of international lawmaking in the long term. It also points to an enduring strength of customary international law, as compared to other modalities of international lawmaking – notably the treaty form, which could, in theory, be co-opted more easily by a group of authoritarian states.

As noted above, customary international lawmaking processes are extremely multifaceted, and the types of customary international law norms identified in this chapter are constructed by drawing on certain characteristic lawmaking factors whose presence in any particular scenario is a matter of both kind and degree. I single out four *representative* patterns, resulting in four types of customary international law norms. The following four types are thus ideal types, rather than 1:1 representations of an inherently complex lawmaking landscape.

II. FOUR TYPES OF CUSTOMARY INTERNATIONAL LAW

Having outlined the sets of factors that feed into any characterization of customary international law processes and resulting norms (as noted, the presence of these factors is a matter of both kind and degree), I draw on a set of representative and diverse examples to identify certain typical configurations of factors that produce a set of recurring customary international law norm types. As noted above, I distinguish four ideal types of customary international law norms: First, *entrenched background custom*. Second, *analogical custom*. Third, *dynamic custom*. Fourth, *pure judicial custom*. It should be stressed that I distinguish between judicial custom and *pure* judicial custom for the sake of clarity. Generally, judicial custom does not refer to a type of customary international norm. Rather, it refers to any pronouncement of a court (for convenience, but technically, any quasi-independent institution) relating to a purported customary international law norm. In other words, judicial custom can relate to any of the four types of custom discussed. In contrast, pure judicial custom is a distinctive type of customary international law norm that is relevant and effective only in the judicial context. Pure judicial custom is judge-made law or a common law-type of customary international law norm. While it can morph into or be mirrored in other types of customary international law, it represents a distinct category in this framework.

A. Entrenched Background Custom

What I call 'entrenched background custom' here is, in some ways, the 'strongest' and most stable type of customary international law norm.[30] Examples are many – the norm of territorial and aerial sovereignty, the prohibition of the use of force, certain jurisdictional immunities of states,

[30] The notion of 'background norms' has been used by legal scholars in various contexts. It usually refers to norms that are relatively more general or that serve to resolve conflicts among more specific norms. See eg S Banner, *Who Owns the Sky? The Struggle to Control Airspace from the Wright Brothers On* (Cambridge, Harvard University Press, 2008) 62; CR Sunstein, *After the Rights Revolution: Reconceiving the Regulatory State* (Cambridge, Harvard University Press, 1993) 160. Here, I use the term somewhat idiosyncratically, defining it in terms of its sustaining factors and placing it into a typology of customary international law norms.

the right of diplomatic protection, the principle of non-discrimination, and some others. Such norms, although they emerge from a wide range of processes, tend to be the products of a distinct configuration of sustaining factors. In particular, they tend to be supported by processes with a high degree of institutionalisation and broad participation among states and other actors, including individuals, groups, and associations. They tend to be rooted in popular understandings and reflected in public discourse, all of which helps sustain such norms. They tend to be the product of innumerable individual incidents, are sometimes characterised by strong legalization, and often feature domestic-level rootedness. While there is considerable controversy around the precise contours of and exceptions to such norms,[31] they are general and largely community-oriented in substance (which, as noted, is not meant here as a prescriptive statement). For example, on the margins of the aerial sovereignty norm, powerful states often engage in processes of customary international lawmaking to determine the precise limits of the norm. Rather than being analogical itself, entrenched background custom tends to be drawn on in support of other types of customary international law.

To say that entrenched background custom is perceived as legitimate, is effective, or is the product of a particularly dense set of factors that can characterise customary international law processes and resulting norms is not, initially, a prescriptive statement.[32] To be sure, there might be a frequent correlation between such types of custom and particular normative precepts. But we should not necessarily assume a connection. For there is no inherent reason why deeply entrenched background custom cannot also be pernicious or have serious negative effects. This is apparent when we consider the effects of some of the above-mentioned norms for the enforcement of human rights law (say, jurisdictional immunities) or in relation to the management of transboundary harm (in the case of territorial and aerial sovereignty).

One further important feature of entrenched background custom is its frequently trans-substantive nature, meaning that such norms get reinforced more strongly because they are more widely applicable. For example, widely accepted human rights norms, or norms concerning territorial sovereignty, are not simply deeply enshrined expectations. Rather, they tend to affect lawmaking across various other more specific issue areas. For instance, when experts develop 'soft-law' instruments concerning topics as disparate as epidemics, climate change, or personal data protection, such norms tend to become incorporated into

[31] See eg M Saul, 'The Normative Status of Self-Determination in International Law: A Formula for Uncertainty in the Scope and Content of the Right?' (2011) 11(4) *Human Rights Law Review* 609, 643; KA Johnston, 'Identifying the *jus cogens* Norm in the *jus ad bellum*' (2021) 70 *International and Comparative Law Quarterly* 29, 34 and 57.

[32] On the distinction between normative and empirical claims in relation to global governance, see for example JN Rosenau, 'Governance, Order, and Change in World Politics' in JN Rosenau and EO Czempiel (eds), *Governance without Government: Order and Change in World Politics* (Cambridge, Cambridge University Press, 1992) 1, 10.

them. Through this application and dissemination, they are further entrenched more broadly than before. In that sense, certain types of norms, but not others, are accompanied or characterised by self-reinforcing mechanisms that can be described as a kind of network effect.

B. Analogical Custom

What I call analogical custom here is a type of customary international law that is both new (by explicitly regulating a new situation and positing a new effective norm) and derivative (by relying heavily on existing norms of customary international law or similar types of unwritten law that support it, including customary international law codified in treaties or other instruments). A number of examples fall in this category, including certain norms of the law of treaties, the law of state responsibility, norms of international environmental law, or norms regulating the conduct of war. The effectiveness of such norms often appears mysterious until one takes into account that they are normative analogies that can be effective without having to become deeply entrenched like the norms on which they draw. The norms in this category tend to be more specific and particular than norms of entrenched background custom. They can also emerge from processes that are poorly institutionalised as well as in a centralised fashion as long as they are understood as analogical derivations of entrenched background custom.

For example, the use of analogies was an important way in which new norms were proposed and justified to regulate new activities like balloon reconnaissance in the late nineteenth century. Using precedents and existing definitions allowed lawyers to thwart attempts by one party to dictate a new rule under novel factual circumstances merely on the basis of military capacity. In other words, analogical reasoning provided an important basis for effectively regulating new types of activities and for modulating the effect of sheer power on lawmaking. This was not necessarily because such analogies were appropriate but because analogical reasoning effectively transferred the lawmaking process onto a more deliberative plane, where it could be associated with a particular deeply entrenched background custom. Importantly, while analogical custom may well appear also in the courtroom, it needs to be distinguished from pure judicial custom. The latter is exclusively a product of judicial decision-making, even if pure judicial custom sometimes resembles analogical custom given that legal interpretation often relies on analogical as well as deductive reasoning.

C. Dynamic Custom

Dynamic custom is a very different beast from the first two types of customary international law examined above. Indeed, it is hard to speak of dynamic custom as law in any but the most general sense because it tends to lack features of generality and stability that law tends to possess in domestic settings and that some legal theorists tend to demand of law as a normative matter (for example, in the form of certain formal or procedural criteria of legality).[33] This is not, however, a critique of dynamic custom but rather a prescriptively neutral statement. In practice, the dynamism and lack of participation that characterises this type of custom can be both its virtue and defect. There might be good reasons why dynamic custom exists in some areas: It may be the only type of law we can expect to arise in some contexts given the absence of any forms of institutionalisation. Moreover, this type of custom's dynamism means that as pernicious as it may be, it can rapidly disappear or change. In that sense, dynamic custom distills the presence of power in lawmaking when most other factors that shape lawmaking processes are in short supply.

Examples of dynamic custom tend to concern particular norms affecting specific situations (such as geographical areas) and are often observed in bilateral, plurilateral, or non-participatory contexts. In fact, they can arise outside any public or institutional scrutiny. Thus, they tend to emerge in poorly institutionalised settings or what have been called the 'offshore zones' of international law. In terms of procedure, while they can involve a few or many stages and develop rapidly, they are always poorly legalised. One example includes norms about population exchanges, which were part of a larger normative universe concerning the situation of minorities and refugees. As the historical record suggests, while the practice of population transfers was accepted by key actors during the mid-twentieth century, this permissive norm was very weakly embedded and, as a result, highly unstable. Shared expectations about the acceptability of population exchanges shifted rapidly depending on the existence of a consensus among the relevant powers.

Dynamic custom's stability and potentially our normative assessment of it can show remarkable differences on a case-by-case basis. After all, when lawmaking occurs in relatively non-participatory arenas and in bilateral settings, the actors involved can still perform better or worse along various dimensions. The choices they make in that respect can affect the nature of the lawmaking process and, importantly, its outcomes. For example, military commanders can be guided by rules and principles from across the international legal system when seeking to establish norms of dynamic custom, or they can ignore them.[34] From that perspective, it is especially in such contexts that

[33] See eg LL Fuller, *The Morality of Law* (New Haven, Yale University Press, 1964). I use the term 'dynamic' to mean susceptible to change. For an intellectual history of 'dynamism' in law in Germany between 1918 and 1945, see LM Keppeler, *Oswald Spengler und die Jurisprudenz: Die Spenglerrezeption in der Rechtswissenschaft zwischen 1918 und 1945, insbesondere innerhalb der «dynamischen Rechtslehre», der Rechtshistoriographie und der Staatsrechtswissenschaft* (Tübingen, Mohr Siebeck, 2014).

[34] See eg M Kelly, 'The Role of the Military in Globalizing the Rule of Law' in S Zifcak (ed), *Globalisation and the Rule of Law* (New York, Routledge, 2004) 184, 185.

the performance of international lawmaking ultimately depends also on the effective personal qualities, including ethical values, of the individuals tasked with the exercise of power.

D. Pure Judicial Custom

What I call 'pure judicial custom' refers, in the main, to something akin to the common law or straightforward judicial lawmaking. However, that analogy needs to be treated with caution because international courts (and domestic courts as a decentralised collectivity of international 'lawmakers') tend to have a far more limited degree of authority than their domestic counterparts, despite important nuances and exceptions. Pure judicial custom is initially purely the invention of jurists. While it sometimes resembles both analogical and dynamic custom, it is more accurately seen as a separate type because of the specific institutional and procedural context in which it occurs. Like judicial custom generally (see for the distinction above), pure judicial custom tends to be accompanied by formal invocations of the legal doctrine of customary international law, even if courts almost never faithfully apply it (if that were even possible or desirable). In terms of institutionalisation, pure judicial custom is moderately institutionalised since it derives initially only from courts or tribunals. When it is reflected in a series of domestic court decisions or the decisions of multiple arbitral tribunals, pure judicial custom arises in a decentralised way through mimicry. However, it can also arise centrally, or by fiat, such as through the pronouncement of an influential international court.

Pure judicial custom is to some extent participatory in that international courts are in a position to process and consider a wide variety of submissions. International courts also tend to operate in the public eye. Their pronouncements, even if methodologically questionable, tend to benefit from a perception of procedural and substantive justice – although this depends on their composition, deliberation method, and the quality of their output and reasoning. The effectiveness of pure judicial custom depends on a number of factors. Because international courts operate in a fundamentally non-hierarchical system, pure judicial custom relies on the extent to which it is supported by lower-level actors. Pure judicial custom is, in contemporary international law, potentially highly fragile. Support for it, as noted, can result from factors such as a legalised procedure, decentralisation, a participatory process, and positive perceptions of procedural, formal, and substantive justice relating to the relevant lawmaking process or its outcome. Finally, it is conceivable that in a world in which international courts have much greater authority than they do at present, pure judicial custom could turn into the international equivalent of the common law. At present, however, it remains the common law's little sibling.

Readers might now be asking themselves how something like pure judicial custom is relevant for a broader study of customary international law. Take the example of a norm of customary international law that is applied to a situation both by an international or regional court and 'on the ground' by the governments directly involved. It is possible for the court to adopt a decision based on what I call pure judicial custom, while the relevant governments follow quite a different norm in respect of the same situation. How is it possible for the same 'norm' to appear in distinct contexts, where, as a result of a particular configuration of 'sustaining factors', it is in each case distinguishable? The response to this question is rather straightforward: First, a relevant legal norm (as defined here by reference to effective legal expectations) needs to possess a certain degree of effectiveness. In the case of pure judicial custom, the effectiveness of the relevant norm tends initially to be quite limited in scope, at least in most areas of contemporary international law. However, a pure judicial custom can have a broader impact. When it is supported by other lawmaking factors, it can become a generally effective type of customary international law norm, either because of the legal status of the respective court or tribunal (an unlikely scenario in the contemporary context) or because the pure judicial custom becomes deeply entrenched, for example. To be sure, in domestic legal contexts, a judicially created norm can often be immediately effective (though there too, effectiveness is rarely guaranteed). The context is, however, fundamentally different in the global arena, where there is far less coherence within the relevant legal community and in which enforcement occurs in a fundamentally decentralised manner, in most cases. In short, it is possible for different norms concerning the same subject matter to be both pure judicial custom and another type of customary international law at the same time.

III. CUSTOMARY INTERNATIONAL LAWMAKING AND SOCIAL CHANGE

It is widely understood that customary international law norms are more amenable to change than, say, treaty norms. But customary international lawmaking itself is also more amenable to change than other modalities of lawmaking, even if the legal doctrine of customary international law seems solidly entrenched. Indeed, because the processes by which customary international law is developed and identified are poorly formalised, they themselves (as a type of 'meta-law') are more susceptible to change as a result of socio-legal developments than other modalities of international lawmaking. Importantly, the varieties of customary international lawmaking identified in this chapter are all capable of change, but to different degrees. There is also movement across the types of customary international law norms; in other words, a norm of one type can morph into that of another. Norms of customary international law can thus not only change in substance, which is unsurprising, but also in kind, over time.

While the four-fold structure I develop in this book is relatively stable, in the sense that it is itself an example of a deeply entrenched background norm, it remains malleable and subject to change too. As a more high-level conclusion, the co-existence of continuities and discontinuities across the basic factors characterising customary international lawmaking suggests that the factors shaping each type of customary international norm play an important role for both social and legal change.

IV. THE WAY FORWARD

This chapter developed an analytical and explanatory framework that offers a novel perspective on the inherently complex and dynamic phenomenon of customary international law. Understanding typical patterns of customary international lawmaking processes and resulting norms in contemporary international society can help us reassess existing descriptive accounts of customary international law and the normative proposals that have been built on top of them. The resulting framework can be used not only to assess events implicating customary international law but also to normatively evaluate the latter's various possible futures. At the same time, this chapter has mostly tried to reframe the contemporary debate about customary international lawmaking. It also pointed to the need for further empirical and theoretical engagement with customary international law – one that takes seriously the mutual relationship between customary international law as a broader social phenomenon and its legal doctrine. It also raised many deeper questions about customary international law, including how and why this distinctive and multifaceted lawmaking landscape developed on the international plane and how it may evolve in the future. In the following chapters, I take up some of these questions by examining the customary international law 'in action' across several areas of social life. This is followed by a discussion of the relationship between customary international law as a broader social phenomenon and the legal doctrine of customary international law. Finally, the book elaborates on how the proposed framework can concretely contribute to both the scholarly and practical engagement with customary international law.

3

Technology and Globalisation as Motors of Global Lawmaking

TECHNOLOGY CHANGES, SOMETIMES radically and often unpredictably, human capabilities, with profound implications for all social institutions, including those central to customary international lawmaking. Compare a world in which humans can observe the planet from orbit, traverse thousands of kilometres in a matter of hours, communicate across continents simultaneously, make use of exponential advances in computer processing power, release weapons of mass destruction from an airplane, or ship perishable goods across continents to one where none of this were possible. The two worlds are profoundly different in terms of the capabilities of individuals, groups, and societies. These shifts in human capabilities raise important regulatory questions but are also consequential for lawmaking processes themselves. Notably, certain forms of communication and decision-making are only possible due to the emergence and dissemination of particular transportation, communication, and information technologies, which occurred in the historical blink of an eye. At the same time, new technologies are always embedded in a particular social and legal context, where they often raise important distributional and ethical concerns. Existing norms can also prove inadequate for the regulation of new technologies,[1] leading to additional challenges linked to state capacity, regulatory capture, and innovation.[2] As such, many technological changes of the last centuries have made cross-border and global forms of regulation both more feasible and more necessary. At the same time, largely contingent geographical, political, social, and technological factors were often decisive in motivating, timing, and shaping both the issues deemed important by contemporaries and how they would be addressed by law. For example, in

[1] See eg W Thomas, *The Ethics of Destruction: Norms and Force in International Relations* (Ithaca, Cornell University Press, 2014) 42.

[2] See eg R Brownsword and M Goodwin, *Law and the Technologies of the Twenty-First Century: Text and Materials* (Cambridge, Cambridge University Press, 2012) 46–71; C Juma, *Innovation and Its Enemies: Why People Resist New Technologies* (Oxford, Oxford University Press, 2016) 5; P Chakrabarti and M Worboys, 'Science and Imperialism since 1870' in *The Cambridge History of Science, Volume 8* (Cambridge, Cambridge University Press, 2020) 9; KD Acemoglu and S Johnson, *Power and Progress: Our Thousand-Year Struggle Over Technology and Prosperity* (London, Basic Books, 2023).

its earliest history, incipient forms of aviation were dominated by France and other European imperial powers of the era. Although aviation would spread globally, it emerged in the small but politically fragmented and globally dominant European subcontinent, a propitious setting in which aviation become a problem addressed also by international law. In parallel, with growing popular engagement with both science and technology, ever larger groups of the population were in some form roped into the relevant lawmaking processes.[3] At the same time, the then-developing field of public international law, with all its particularities, biases, and limitations, became the most proximate modality for the regulation of aviation, as opposed to domestic law or some other form of legal or quasi-level ordering. Although seemingly peripheral, this basic fact provides an important insight into international lawmaking since it shows that geographic and other contingent factors can determine the paths along which legal regulation proceeds, with potentially significant and rarely predictable long-term consequences.

This chapter examines several episodes of customary international lawmaking related to the scientific and technological developments that shaped the rise of both globalization and international law. Illustrating different types of customary international law 'in action', it also shows that science and technology have directly and indirectly reshaped all spheres of social life, including those closely connected to customary international lawmaking itself, such as transportation, communication, and warfare. This is true despite the inevitable contingency and situatedness of both scientific and technological developments and their socio-economic context, as reflected in inequalities of access to, control over, and influence on the regulation of science and technology.

I. PRISONERS OF WAR, SPIES, AND THE EARLY LAWS OF WAR

Although balloon reconnaissance may appear quaint considering contemporary forms of pervasive high-tech surveillance, it was of considerable interest to international lawyers during the late nineteenth century. Because wartime military reconnaissance emerged as one of aviation's earliest and most practical applications, questions concerning the treatment of aircraft and their operators (be it balloonists, aeronauts, or pilots) when engaged in reconnaissance quickly followed. One question that came on the agenda as early as the American Civil War and later became acute again in the context of the Franco-Prussian War was whether such operators should be treated as spies, with the effect of making them ineligible for prisoner of war status. The legal treatment of captured balloonists offers an early illustration of how international law was made in the context of

[3] See eg MR Lynn, *Popular Science and Public Opinion in Eighteenth-Century France* (Manchester, Manchester University Press, 2006) 2–3.

a changing technological and socio-political context. Its regulation involved a variety of actors, historical events, and sites of lawmaking, from the domestic to the international levels. As such, it provides insights into international lawmaking in the context of an important era in the history of the laws of war.[4]

During the American Civil War, both the Union and, to a lesser extent, the Confederate armies, integrated balloon reconnaissance capabilities into their operations, even as these efforts remained short-lived.[5] After several of the most prominent American aeronauts had competed to provide balloon reconnaissance services to the Union Army, Thaddeus S.C. Lowe, an adventurous, ambitious, and self-taught American inventor and entrepreneur convinced President Lincoln to charge him with leading a newly created balloon force.[6] Eye-witness accounts of the American Civil War, including letters and diary entries of soldiers and an army surgeon, testify to the use, utility, and limits of aerial vehicles for purposes of reconnaissance, conveying the novelty and utility of the new technology, as well as a degree of scepticism towards it.[7] As noted, the use of balloon reconnaissance raised questions about the treatment of captured balloonists: Were they spies or prisoners of war? That distinction was legally significant because, under the laws of war, a captured spy could be treated differently than a regular captured combatant or civilian. To be sure, the practical significance of this distinction became acute only when relatively effective limitations on the treatment of prisoners of war were introduced and implemented. While the legal protection given to captured combatants in the late nineteenth century was hardly perfect,[8] mortality estimates suggest that captured combatants enjoyed greater protections than irregular combatants or spies.[9] At any rate, treating aeronauts captured in the course of a reconnaissance mission as prisoners of war would have effectively made their activity more permissible in the eyes of the laws of war. To be sure, treating captured aeronauts as prisoners

[4] On the transformation of warfare since the 1860s, see eg JQ Whitman, *The Verdict of Battle: The Law of Victory and the Making of Modern War* (Cambridge, Harvard University Press, 2012) 7.

[5] See CM Evans, *The War of the Aeronauts: A History of Ballooning During the Civil War* (Harrisburg, Stackpole Books, 2002); SD Culpepper, LCDR, USN, 'Balloons of the Civil War', Master (of Military Art and Science) Thesis, US Army Command and General Staff College, Fort Leavenworth, Kansas (1994).

[6] See eg R Holmes, *Falling Upwards: How We Took to the Air* (London, William Collins, 2013) 127–28; R Hallion, *Taking Flight: Inventing the Aerial Age from Antiquity Through the First World War* (Oxford, Oxford University Press, 2003) 68.

[7] See 'Diary of Thomas T. Ellis, June, 1862' in TT Ellis, *Leaves from the Diary of an Army Surgeon: or, Incidents of Field, Camp, and Hospital Life* (New York, John Bradburn, 1863) 166–7; 'Diary of Alfred Lewis Castleman, April, 1862, in The Army of the Potomac, Behind the Scenes: A Diary of Unwritten History: from the Organization of the Army … to the Close of the Campaign in Virginia, About the First Day of January' (Milwaukee, Strickland & Co, 1863) 116; 'Letter from Richard Derby, December 15, 1861' in LM Post, *Soldiers' Letters, from Camp, Battle-field and Prison* (New York, Bunce & Huntington, 1865) 50.

[8] See A Gillespie, *A History of the Laws of War, Volume 1: The Customs and Laws of War with Regards to Combatants and Captives* (Oxford, Hart Publishing, 2011) 157.

[9] ibid, 153–6 (discussing the period between 1815 and 1861).

of war would not have given them any sort of special status as compared to other soldiers. Moreover, governments did not advocate providing protection or immunities to reconnaissance balloons comparable to those that would later be accorded to medical personnel and vehicles under the laws of war. Nonetheless, in the context of the time (and indeed even today), for a soldier not to be subject to punishment as a spy while engaging in a type of reconnaissance had significant legal consequences.

It is important to briefly situate the seemingly tangential legal issues raised by balloon reconnaissance in the broader context of the laws of war that were being debated and developed at the time. Despite several important precursors, many historians trace the modern origins of the laws of war to initiatives at rule-setting and codification within the Union Army that resulted in the so-called Lieber Code (or the General Orders No. 100, the 'Instructions for the Government of Armies of the United States in the Field').[10] This first major national military manual affected lawmaking efforts worldwide; at the same time, it was itself the product of a sort of international migration in the shape of Francis Lieber, who had spent the first part of his life in Europe and whose drafting of the manual relied on a range of foreign precedents. Numerous factors contributed to the spread and solidification of the laws of war, or in other words, helped sustain the relevant norms. To begin with, the Union Army's efforts were a codification of earlier practices and therefore already embedded in existing normative expectations, at least among the relevant circles of military commanders and soldiers. Moreover, they directly guided the military conduct of the victorious Union Army and its leadership. As one of the first national codifications of this sort, the Lieber Code's prescriptions spread by being disseminated and replicated globally, which affected contemporaneous efforts at developing so-called international humanitarian law. These efforts were drawn upon by others who sought to codify and develop the laws of war, such as the officials meeting at the 1874 Brussels Conference and later during the Hague Peace Conferences.

At the time of the American Civil War – and the operation of the Union Army's Balloon Corps – effective laws of war were in their infancy, but rules on the humane treatment of soldiers were slowly emerging and solidifying. Generally applicable rules for the conduct of warfare, such as the principles of distinction, military necessity, and proportionality, were considered to apply to balloons as well. By the first half of the twentieth century, a legal scholar noted that while reconnaissance balloons were fair targets of attack under the laws of

[10] See eg SC Neff, *War and the Law of Nations: A General History* (Cambridge, Cambridge University Press) 186–7; see also JF Witt, *Lincoln's Code: The Laws of War in American History* (New York, Free Press, 2012); W Sandholtz, *Prohibiting Plunder: How Norms Change* (Oxford, Oxford University Press, 2007). On earlier developments, also with a focus on customary international law, see R Lesaffer, 'Siege Warfare in the Early Modern Age: A Study on the Customary Laws of War' in A Perreau-Saussine and JB Murphy (eds), *The Nature of Customary Law* (Cambridge, Cambridge University Press, 2007) 176, 195–202.

war, limits of a 'legitimate' attack needed to be observed, arguing that attacking a balloonist parachuting to safety would be impermissible.[11] This approach was in line with the then-existing laws of war – transposed to the particular case of balloon reconnaissance operators. However, no specific rules relating to balloons or their operators were included in the Lieber Code.

As noted, the introduction of balloon reconnaissance into the military domain prompted additional legal questions – domestic and international – concerning especially the legal status of captured balloonists.[12] Most relevant in this context was the fear that as a 'civilian', a captured aeronaut might be treated as a spy, rather than a prisoner of war.[13] A prisoner of war was entitled to protection and was not subject to ordinary criminal prosecution in the capturing state. In contrast, a spy was subject to often draconian and unspecified punishment under the criminal law of the other state, as Articles 56 and 88 of the Lieber Code illustrate. However, the Lieber Code did not specifically address the qualification of captured balloonists. Although unresolved in practice, the question of how 'aeronauts' captured by the enemy forces should be treated – as spies or as prisoners of war – remained a live one in the decades after the American Civil War and flared up again just a few years later during the Franco-Prussian War of 1870–1, a conflict that itself had a profound effect on the development of international law as a profession.[14] How this question was resolved by military officials and lawyers on the other side of the Atlantic offers an insight into relevant international lawmaking processes of the era.

During the Franco-Prussian War, Paris was separated from the rest of the country by siege. The Parisian population and besieged authorities relied on ballooning for a number of reasons, most importantly for the transmission of messages, reconnaissance, and transport.[15] As in the context of the American Civil War, reconnaissance balloons and their operators were considered to be legitimate objects of attack. Yet, the question of how captured aeronauts

[11] J Kroell, *Traité de droit international public aérien: L'aéronautique en temps de guerre. La guerre aérienne (Volume II)* (Issoudun, Éditions internationales, 1936) 89–119. JM Spaight, in the 1933 edition of his book *Air Power and War Rights*, also discusses the same issue by reference to the earlier practice. See JM Spaight, *Air Power and War Rights*, 2nd edn (London, Longmans Green & co, 1933) 137–44.

[12] See eg FS Haydon, *Military Ballooning During the Early Civil War* (Baltimore, John Hopkins University Press, 2000) 270.

[13] ibid, 270–1.

[14] On the relationship between nineteenth-century international lawyers and the Franco-Prussian War, see eg G De Baere and A Mills, 'T.M.C. Asser and Public and Private International Law: The Life and Legacy of "a Practical Legal Statesman"' (2011) 42 *Netherlands Yearbook of International Law* 3, 18–9; see also V Genin, 'The Institute of International Law's Crisis in the Wake of the Franco-Prussian War (1873–1899)' in I Van Hulle and RCH Lesaffer, *International Law in the Long Nineteenth Century (1776–1914) From the Public Law of Europe to Global International Law?* (Leiden, Brill Nijhoff, 2019) 214.

[15] AK Kuhn, 'The Beginnings of an Aerial Law' (1910) 4(1) *American Journal of International Law* 109, 116; Holmes, *Falling Upwards* (n 6) 251–301; see also T Baycroft and B Wilkin, 'The Balloon Post during the Siege of Paris, 1870–71' (2023) 42(3) *War & Society* 215.

should be treated was a controversial one,[16] as Bismarck's failed efforts to shape the law on the question suggests.[17] Bismarck was at the time the leading driver of the unification of the German states, later the first chancellor of the German Empire, and more generally the continental leader credited with the unravelling of the balance of power struck at the Congress of Vienna after the defeat of Napoleon I. At the time, Bismarck attempted to push for a norm that would have allowed armed forces to treat all enemy balloonists as spies – by definition. This claimed norm went against the nuanced definition of spies that was developing among specialists debating this legal question around that time. Many commentators, both contemporaneous and those writing from the vantage point of the late nineteenth or early twentieth century, seemed to think that Bismarck's approach was misguided or lacked foundation as a matter of international law.[18] But Bismarck unleashed a series of steps by other governments, legal experts, and others that eventually clarified (at least in the relevant context) the prevailing law on the question.

The actual effect of Bismarck's uncompromising stance is difficult to determine. At any rate, the treatment meted out by Prussia to several captured aeronauts – it appears that several were captured, but only one was condemned with a commuted sentence – was immediately tied by legal commentators of the time to the discussion over the definition of espionage under the laws of war. Using this analogy provided a way to contest Bismarck's view and propose a more nuanced treatment of captured balloonists than Bismarck's proposal would imply. Since the spy was traditionally defined as one acting secretly, in disguise, or under false pretences, the legal debate centred on whether a balloon and its operator should be seen as acting in secret when, at least in daylight, they were visible from the ground. Several legal scholars of that era went on the record to advance a range of doctrinal solutions. Many rejected Bismarck's absolutist position, which would have assimilated all aeronauts engaged in balloon reconnaissance to spies. Some went as far as absolving balloonists from any possible responsibility for acts of espionage, arguing that the 'covert' criterion could never be applied to them and they, therefore, could never be deemed and punished as spies.[19] Others argued that an activity's dangerousness was the most relevant criterion and that balloon reconnaissance certainly met

[16] Holmes, *Falling Upwards* (n 6) 281 (discussing Bismarck's threat to treat balloonists as spies).

[17] A Mattelart, *The Invention of Communication* (Minneapolis, University of Minnesota Press, 1996) 217–8.

[18] F Dahn, 'Der Deutsch-Französische Krieg und das Völkerrecht' (1871) 1 *Jahrbücher für die Deutsche Armee und Marine* 79, 90; EF Glenn, *Hand-Book of International Law* (St. Paul, West Publishing, 1895) 231; JF Lycklama à Nijeholt, *Air Sovereignty* (The Hague, Martius Nijhoff, 1910) 1; J Kohler, *Luftfahrtrecht* (Berlin, Springer, 1912) 26; L Oppenheim, *International Law: A Treatise, Volume II (War and Neutrality)* (London, Longmans, Green, and Co, 1906) 161.

[19] See H Pohl, *Luftkriegsrecht: ein Vortrag* (Stuttgart, W Kohlhammer, 1924). For a brief biographical commentary, see M Stolleis, *A History of Public Law in Germany, 1914–1945* (Thomas Dunlap trans. 2004) 267–8.

that threshold.[20] Contemporaneous studies of the laws of war – for instance, Bluntschli's treatise on international law of 1878 emphasises that already by then, the rule for the treatment of spies formally postulated under the codified laws of war had ceased to apply in practice. Instead, questions of 'dangerousness' (*Gefährlichkeit*) and proportionality (*Verhältnismäßigkeit*) had become valid considerations that needed to be taken into account when deciding on the treatment of a captured spy.[21] The same nuanced discussion also seems to have bled into the field of international aviation law in the first decades of the twentieth century where the question of the treatment of captured aviators was treated very differently than in the immediate context of the American Civil and the Franco-Prussian wars.[22]

The legal debate over the question of the treatment of aeronauts, as spies or as prisoners of war of some kind, offers a number of insights into lawmaking processes during this period.[23] First, the use of analogies was an important means of proposing and justifying new norms. Precedents and existing definitions allowed lawyers to thwart attempts by one party to dictate a new rule under novel factual circumstances merely on the basis of power in the shape of military capacity. In other words, analogical reasoning provided an important basis for effectively regulating new types of activities like balloon reconnaissance and for modulating the effect of sheer power on lawmaking. This was not necessarily because the analogies were appropriate, but because analogical reasoning effectively transferred the lawmaking process onto a more deliberative plane. Second, there is no doubt that the relevant lawmaking process was strongly shaped by powerful actors, but that did not necessarily determine its outcome. For instance, since Prussia adopted a position not widely shared by other powers at the time, Bismarck's attempts at norm change foundered. Bismarck's efforts could have been successful but, in fact, rallied opposition and were ultimately buried. Third, given that the law was applied by individual armies, a powerful government may have attempted to change norms through practice or by implementing and enforcing norms internally. The case of the Lieber Code offers a good example of the latter process. In contrast, when Bismarck tried to establish a norm concerning balloon operators, little effort was made by Prussia to enforce or

[20] See eg F Dahn, 'Der Deutsch-Französische Krieg und das Völkerrecht' (1871) 1 *Jahrbücher für die deutsche Armee und Marine* 79, 90–2.

[21] JC Bluntschli, *Das moderne Völkerrecht der civilisirten Staten als Rechtsbuch dargestellt*, 3rd edn (Nördlingen, Verlag der Beck'schen Buchhandlung, 1878) 353–4 (para 628).

[22] For example, the legal commentator Erwin Riesch highlights the nuanced treatment of aviator-spies in armed conflict, mentioning the unusual case of a hastily dispatched pilot who is captured wearing his pajamas and thereby formally in disguise. See E Riesch, 'L'aéronautique militaire au service de l'espionnage en temps de guerre' (1932) 1 *Revue générale de droit aérien* 813, 818–20.

[23] See also F Meili, *Das Luftschiff im internen Recht und Völkerrecht* (Zurich, Füssli, 1908) 51–2; WD Geisberg, *Bismarck und das Kreigsvölkerrecht* (Bonn, Rheinische Friedrich-Wilhlelms-Universität, 1913) 166–7; RF Williams, 'Developments in Aerial Law' (1926) 75 *University of Pennsylvania Law Review* 139 (with further references).

internally embed the suggested norm, presumably because the normative position was adopted opportunistically rather than on the basis of broader strategic considerations.

The rules concerning the treatment of spies as first articulated in the Lieber Code and as discussed in the wake of the capture by Prussia of aeronauts flying out of Paris during the Franco-Prussian War would also appear in the Brussels Declaration of 1874, the result of a conference during which '[l]e règlement du président Lincoln' was explicitly invoked and whose outcome in large part reflects its substance, even if it went beyond it in many ways.[24] Notably, the Brussels Declaration would go further by explicitly excluding balloonists from the definition of spies and thus aiming to formally codify existing law on the question. The Brussels Declaration was the outcome of a meeting in 1874 of the representatives of 15 European states (including Russia) in Brussels on the initial suggestion of the Russian Tsar.[25] The delegates were meant to discuss the emerging idea of the laws of war and, in fact, to codify 'universally accepted rules' which in the Tsar's expressed view had shown excessive vagueness, were characterised merely by general principles, were often ignored, and left much room for interpretation. The Tsar had sent instructions for the conference – designed to be mainly an affair between European states' representatives in line with the prevailing biases of nineteenth century international law – accompanied by a set of draft articles proposed as a starting point for the discussion. Comparing the initial proposal and the final result of the conference[26] on the question of spies reveals a considerable overlap. For the men meeting in Brussels in 1874, the treatment of balloonists during the recent American Civil War and the Franco-Prussian war were recent events. Their meeting, to be sure, attempted to address various issues of the laws of war rather than a particular one.[27] Nonetheless, sitting in a mode of expert-like deliberation, they also sought to discuss how the laws of war should deal with captured balloonists. Their conclusion was a repudiation of Bismarck's attempt at introducing new law that would have automatically assimilated balloonists engaging in reconnaissance to spies, with all the ensuing consequences under various domestic laws. Instead, the finally agreed articles even generally excluded certain types of balloonists from the very definition of a spy under the laws of war. Subsequently, the Institut de Droit

[24] 'Actes de la Conférence de Bruxelles de 1974 sur le projet d'une Convention Internationale Concernant la Guerre (Protocoles des séances plénières, Protocoles de la Commission déléguée par la conference, Annexes)' (Paris, Librarie des Publications Législatives, 1874) (Lincoln is referred to at page 7).

[25] ibid.

[26] Compare the provisions originally recommended by the Tsar (§18 to 22) to those finally agreed (Articles 19 to 22).

[27] TL Dowdeswell, 'The Brussels Peace Conference of 1874 and the Modern Laws of Belligerent Qualification' (2017) 54(3) *Osgoode Hall Law Journal* 805, 842 ('The *Draft Declaration* and the final *Brussels Declaration* that followed are the first formal articulations of the modern rules of belligerent qualification and the principle of distinction between civilian and military targets …').

International (IDI) presented a resolution analysing the Brussels Declaration. Without making any specific remarks about the rules governing spies, the IDI (Gustave Rolin-Jaequemyns serving as Rapporteur) noted that the initiative of the Tsar reflected numerous 'analogies' with the 'instructions américaines du président Lincoln'. The IDI referred to the Declaration as a project of 'science', but also pointed to the necessity of obtaining the 'entente entre les divers États, et d'assurer cette entente par des concessions mutuelles'. The Resolution of the IDI ended on a realist note, emphasising that the Declaration had avoided succumbing to 'utopian wishes', thus taking into account governments' demands relating to 'security' and the conduct of military operations.[28]

In later years, balloon reconnaissance became less practically relevant, but new norms concerning the treatment of spies and the distinction between captured spies and regular soldiers solidified, even if, in practice, the norms postulated in Brussels left a lot to be desired. Subsequently, these norms were also adopted at the 1899 and 1907 Hague Peace Conferences, lending them even broader support. The rules emerging from these early codification endeavours were later included in multilateral treaties that continue to be in force, such as the Hague Regulations (of 1899 and 1907), Article 24 of which (in the 1907 version) provides that 'the employment of measures necessary for obtaining information about the enemy and the country are considered permissible'.[29] As such, they have survived and been applied regularly, for instance, by domestic courts.[30]

In conclusion, as the new aerial reconnaissance technology spread, there was initial uncertainty about how reconnaissance balloonists should be treated. Over time, the confusion gave way to a norm prescribing that those who engaged in the novel activity enjoyed the same protections as other soldiers. Interest in this type of norm was driven by the recognition that aerial reconnaissance was key to successful military operations. The norm was developed through a complex process involving analogical reasoning by experts, domestic initiatives aimed at codifying the laws of war, contestation over norms prompted by military incidents, and deliberations among international legal experts and officials. Although balloon reconnaissance was a short-lived activity, lawmaking in the field sheds light on the various factors that supported the respective norm's stability. The norm was not simply the product of a normative equilibrium among powerful actors, nor was it the product of a simple agreement among experts or governments. Instead, reliance on precedents and analogies played a key role in shaping expectations of how captured balloonists should be treated.

[28] See Institut de Droit International, 'Examen de la Déclaration de Bruxelles de 1874 (Session de La Haye)' (1875).

[29] See Articles 24, and 29 to 31 of the Hague Regulations concerning the Laws and Customs of War on Land of 18 October 1907.

[30] See eg Y Dinstein, *The Conduct of Hostilities under the Law of International Armed Conflict* (Cambridge, Cambridge University Press, 2004) 208–13.

Moreover, lawmaking was driven by the normative objectives held by a wide range of lawmaking participants at the time who had an interest in supporting the emerging and increasingly promising technology of aviation. They coordinated to reject overly unilateral or particularistic attempts at normative change and instead sought ways of supporting the use of the emergent technology of aerial reconnaissance.

II. FROM BALLOONOMANIA TO THE CHICAGO CONVENTION

As noted, starting in the nineteenth century, human uses of airspace – including for aviation – began to pose a number of legal problems. One fundamental question concerned the legal concept of airspace and the related notion of aerial sovereignty. It was significant because it shaped the legal powers, rights, and duties of states in respect of foreign aircraft operating above their land territories and any maritime zones, as well as the corresponding rights and duties of other affected states. It was also linked to innumerable more specific questions, including about the rules applicable to conduct onboard an aircraft, restrictions on the kind of equipment that could be carried on board, and other questions of liability and jurisdiction. How these and related questions were addressed offers insights into the varieties of customary international law processes and resulting norms during a formative period of contemporary international law.[31] These examples illustrate the effects of contingent social, economic, and geographic circumstances on lawmaking processes. They exemplify the role of structural, participatory, procedural, and substantive factors on international lawmaking processes and their outcomes. In addition, they shed light on the close relationship between technology and international lawmaking.

The rise of the discipline of international law in nineteenth century Europe and the Americas – including its definition of sources, fields of regulation, its focus on the law of inter-state relations, and other intellectual and sociological features of the field – roughly coincided with the growing uses of airspace. In other words, technological innovations in the field of aviation, but also wireless communication, happened to coincide with the early development of international legal doctrines, as well as late imperialism and the rise of liberal

[31] On the role of customary international law in aviation, see eg S Michaelides-Mateou, 'Customary International Law in Aviation' in B Lepard (ed), *Reexamining Customary International Law* (Cambridge, Cambridge University Press, 2017) 309; but see BF Havel and GS Sanchez, *The Principles and Practice of International Aviation Law* (Cambridge, Cambridge University Press, 2014) 18; see also generally A Dobson, *A History of International Civil Aviation: From its Origins through Transformative Evolution* (New York, Routledge, 2017); PS Dempsey, 'Introduction: Multilateral Conventions and Customary International Law' in PS Dempsey and RS Jakhu (eds), *Routledge Handbook of Public Aviation Law* (New York, Routledge, 2016) 1; CJ Cheng (ed), *Studies in International Air Law: Selected Works of Bin Cheng* (Leiden, Brill Nijhoff, 2017).

internationalism.[32] All this placed aviation and the development of international law in a close and continuing relationship. This early connection between aviation and international law was also shaped by the fragmented political landscape of the European subcontinent, which made sovereign boundaries relatively pervasive just as the rise of aviation made such boundaries more easily traversable. In addition, the European imperial powers – including France, Germany, Britain, and Italy – quickly exported certain inventions of the aerial age to their colonies, in part as a demonstration of their imperial domination. For example, already in 1784, France launched 'the first colonial aerostat' (indeed, the first one in the Americas) in Sainte-Domingue, which would soon thereafter achieve independence as Haiti.[33] This confluence of factors explains – to some extent – why the late nineteenth century is a useful and meaningful, indeed necessary, starting point for this story. Yet as the surveyed events approach the present, new actors and regions gained in relative importance and would have a comparable bearing on processes and outcomes of customary international lawmaking.

Although international legal norms concerning a state's aerial sovereignty consolidated only in the course of the first decades of the twentieth century, the preceding century illuminates central aspects of customary international lawmaking in the field. This is true especially if we consider international lawmaking from a comprehensive perspective and pay attention to the varieties of customary international lawmaking. Developments relating to aviation since the nineteenth century laid the ground for several norms relating to aerospace that stabilised in the twentieth century, and some only after World War II. They included public debates and the forming of public opinion concerning the novelty, promise, risks, effects, and regulation of new technologies of aviation across local, domestic, and transnational arenas. They encompassed formal and informal, private and official, as well as successful and failed attempts at codifying, developing, and reforming international legal norms. Importantly, these were all supported by a dense and growing transnational network of individuals, groups, and organisations collecting and disseminating information about legal developments and practices.

Two global military conflicts coincided with key moments in the history of aviation as well as other technologies emerging in that era, such as wireless communication. The military and technological aspects of these conflicts, as well as related developments – including the emergence of fighter planes, cross-border propaganda, or the use of aerial reconnaissance and wireless communication in war – all gave aviation and its associated technologies significant policy relevance.

[32] On the concept of liberal internationalism, see JG Ikenberry, *A World Safe for Democracy: Liberal Internationalism and the Crises of Global Order* (New Haven, Yale University Press, 2020) xiii.

[33] JE McClellan III, *Colonialism and Science: Saint Domingue and the Old Regime* (Chicago, Chicago University Press, 1992 [2010]) 168–70.

Due to the violence and risk they involve, armed conflicts usually set the stage for frenzied decision-making – observers of such events report the impression of time moving more quickly than usual. Indeed, armed conflict can be understood as a form of lawmaking, such as when war is waged to vindicate a particular norm. More concretely, armed conflicts are usually followed by comprehensive discussions and agreements about post-war legal arrangements, as in the case of the peace treaties prepared and concluded during and following the two World Wars. They also tend to implicate a large share of the populations of affected countries and members of various social strata. In short, while military conflicts have destroyed and disrupted the lives of millions (even as they were sometimes fought to punish or prevent atrocities), they also tended to accelerate international lawmaking processes in various ways.

The domestic legal questions raised by the use of balloons in the nineteenth century were another important backdrop to the international law questions of aerial sovereignty, access, and jurisdiction. A century of ballooning – including a variety of uses, ranging from spectacle and propaganda, science, geography, war, to travel,[34] and the strong presence of the new technology in the public eye – spurred various expectations about a future regime for aviation. On both sides of the Atlantic, the chief legal concerns that arose in the field during the nineteenth century involved domestic law questions of aviator liability and aerial trespass, but these matters were not clarified until the (in some cases, mid-) 1900s.[35] For example, domestic court cases in the United States (US) and France throughout the nineteenth century addressed issues arising as a result of the growth of aviation.[36] Similar questions faced courts in other parts of the world as lighter-than-air aircraft spread and came into use in different countries as early as the nineteenth century. How the domestic legal questions raised by the use of balloons in the nineteenth century were dealt with laid the ground for the settlement of key international law questions, including aerial sovereignty, access, and jurisdiction. At the same time, as Stuart Banner has noted, the question of aerial sovereignty was 'simultaneously analogous to and more fundamental than the issue of aerial property rights'.[37] That one question is more 'fundamental' than the other does not mean that domestic regulation necessarily post-dated international agreement on issues such as aerial sovereignty, as one might assume. It can also mean that the content of the relevant domestic norm precluded some solutions

[34] Holmes, *Falling Upwards* (n 6) 90–1.

[35] S Banner, *Who Owns the Sky? The Struggle to Control Airspace from the Wright Brothers On* (Cambridge, Harvard University Press, 2008) 23–30.

[36] Domestic legal cases involving overflight appeared soon in the wake of the balloon's invention, for instance in a case before the New York Supreme Court in 1822 or the French Cour de Cassation in 1852. See eg PH Sand, JT Lyon, and GN Pratt, 'An Historical Survey of International Air Law before the Second World War' (1960) 7 *McGill Law Journal* 24, 26–7.

[37] Banner, *Who Owns the Sky?* (n 35) 43.

on the international level while making others more plausible. Paradoxically, national sovereignty over airspace was the one solution most compatible, in retrospect, with a solution under domestic law that was aviator-friendly rather than supportive of claims by landowners to superjacent airspace. At first, this might seem surprising. However, the argumentative framework in which claims between aviators and landowners initially occurred was a domestic one. Claims of outsiders to freely access and use national airspace could not be easily weighed against competing claims by local landowners. The idea of a 'public airspace' required the benefits to accrue to the 'public', rather than to the amorphous international community. Initially, Paul Fauchille, the first and perhaps most ambitious prominent lawyer writing about the international legal aspects of aviation at the turn of the century, called for a qualified 'freedom of navigation'.[38] It did not take hold, presumably since it failed to accord with processes of lawmaking that operated on a bottom-up path from the domestic to the international. In the long term, an international freedom of aviation of sorts was indeed forged by international treaties and regulation, but only after states had themselves asserted aerial sovereignty. World War I, as noted above, also played a key role in this regard because it reinforced claims for national sovereignty over airspace. Retrospectively, it turned out that a recognition of aerial sovereignty left states the freedom to decide whether to recognise landowner's claims for aerial trespass or to rather opt for the more common approach of a public but regulated airspace in the air column above a state's territory. That question could be resolved most effectively on the domestic level where the beneficiaries of one approach stood side by side with the beneficiaries of the other.

A noticeable normative shift in lawyers' understandings of state territory occurred in the first decades of the twentieth century. It is reflected, for example, in the 1898 edition of the jurist and statesman Franz von Liszt's textbook on international law, which notes that state territory includes the airspace above a state's land surface to the extent that it can actually be controlled by arms or balloons.[39] Several decades later, the 12th edition of the same textbook, by then under the editorship of the legal scholar Max Fleischmann, unequivocally declared that all airspace above both a state's land and the relevant maritime surface was part of its territory,[40] something said to have become decisive only

[38] On Fauchille see eg Banner, *Who Owns the Sky?* (n 35) 48–9. Jenny Lycklama a Niejholt adopted a contrasting position, arguing that there was no need to view sovereignty as an 'obstacle' to the 'normal development of international [air] circulation', a view that turned out to be considerably more prescient. See JF Lycklama à Nijeholt, 'La souveraineté aérienne' (1910) 1 *Revue juridique internationale de la locomotion aérienne* 229, 251.

[39] F von Liszt, *Das Völkerrecht: Systematisch Dargestellt* (Berlin, Haering, 1898) 48.

[40] F von Liszt and M Fleischmann, *Das Völkerrecht: Systematisch Dargestellt von Franz von Liszt*, 12th edn (Berlin, Springer, 1925) 140.

following World War I.[41] The textbook also extended the notion of aerial sovereignty to wireless telegraphy.[42] In contrast to the edition of decades earlier, which made do with no references, the 1923 edition furnished a huge number of authorities for these various claims.[43] As this example suggests, this period witnessed the rapid consolidation of the aerial sovereignty norm.

The failed Paris Aviation Conference of 1910[44] was a pivotal element of the lawmaking process that would establish the norm of aerial sovereignty under customary international law, would become codified and treaty-based within a decade, and later 'universalized' in the 1944 Chicago Convention. Despite the conference's role in the consolidation of the aerial sovereignty norm, scholars and commentators often alternatively exaggerate or minimise its role. One view contends that the diplomatic event was a failure and that it made no difference to the developing norms in the field of aviation. The other view suggests that the convention was the site of a decisive agreement on the question of aerial sovereignty and related questions of 'air law'. While the former view gives too little credit to the 1910 conference in its contemporaneous context, the latter view exaggerates its relevance in a more complex and protracted process of lawmaking that ultimately stabilised the aerial sovereignty norm and its entailments. One of the most influential legal scholars in the field of aerospace of the twentieth century, John Cooper, tried to counter the neglect that scholars have paid to the 1910 conference by noting that '[it was the 1910 conference rather than] the 1919 conference as usually supposed, [which] first evidenced general international agreement that usable space above the lands and waters of a State is part of the territory of that State'.[45] While Cooper's assessment is useful in suggesting the existence of an international (customary) norm on that particular question already before 1919, Cooper also places too much emphasis on the earlier conference, somewhat implausibly suggesting that the position of the conference participants already indicated an 'agreement' only achieved years later. It is important to keep in mind that the 1910 Paris Aviation Conference was both a diplomatic effort and part of a broader lawmaking process. That it was a diplomatic failure is not necessarily to say that it was a failure in other respects;[46] the question of its impact as an instance of lawmaking is a separate matter, requires a different type of analysis, and may have a fundamentally

[41] ibid, 141.
[42] ibid.
[43] ibid.
[44] *Conférence Internationale de Navigation Aérienne, Paris (18 mai-29 juin 1910): Procès-Verbaux des Séances et Annexes* (Paris, Imprimerie nationale, 1910).
[45] JC Cooper, 'The International Air Navigation Conference, Paris 1910' (1952) 19 *Journal of Air Law and Commerce* 127.
[46] See P Fauchille, *Louis Renault (1843–1918): Sa vie-son œuvre* (Paris, Pedone, 1918) 80–1; on the context, see also the review of two books by Paul Loubeyre and André Blachère (under 'Bulletin Bibliographique') in XVIII (1911) *Revue générale de droit international public* 587.

different answer. Many of the damning assessments of the 1910 conference, especially from the perspective of France's diplomacy or those who favoured a treaty-based agreement in 1910, are not without basis. However, to classify the 1910 conference as insignificant in comparison to the later efforts in Paris in 1919 and Chicago in 1944 would unduly inflate the importance of such meetings as discrete instances of conventional lawmaking, when in fact they are parts of a broader lawmaking process. In fact, subsequent events suggest that lawmaking activities in the field, in the absence of any codification resulting from the 1910 conference, essentially continued to develop at the domestic, bilateral, and transnational levels, as in previous decades.[47] Yet it would take another decade for the norm that several governments were trying to establish to become unequivocally accepted. To be sure, it can be argued that already after 1910, as Banner finds, a 'background norm' of aerial sovereignty seemed to exist, even if exceptions can be identified.[48] In any case, this emerging norm would become formally ratified, among others, in the 1919 Paris Convention, and thus after World War I had taken its course.[49]

The 1910 conference also illustrates the role of multiple stages, experimentation, and failed attempts as significant factors in processes of international lawmaking. The 1910 conference was presumably many things: The culmination of a scholarly debate,[50] the site of a political disagreement, the focal point of an expert debate that was going on independently given the practical relevance of the problem, and the confluence of various commercial and other interests in addressing legal questions surrounding aviation.[51] Its precise outcome is less important than its role as part of a broader lawmaking process. Given the relevance of the customary international law category in particular, debate, contestation, and experimentation are always potentially lawmaking. In that context, launching a quasi-public debate guarantees that lawmaking of some sort will take place, even if the progenitor of the debate loses control over a process that has left the confines of a smaller scholarly or expert debate or a political negotiation. Publicity, which in this case was facilitated by scholars and the media, further expanded the range of actors that would be informed of and potentially involved in this process. At the time when the 1910 conference was unceremoniously 'suspended', this group included scientists and

[47] See Sand, Lyon, and Pratt, 'An Historical Survey of International Air Law before the Second World War' (n 36) 29–31; see also Hallion, *Taking Flight* (n 6) 271; M Schladebach, *Lufthoheit: Kontinuität und Wandel* (Tübingen, Mohr Siebeck, 2014) 56–61.

[48] Banner, *Who Owns the Sky?* (n 35) 62 (Banner argues that the various steps (including legislation and bilateral agreements) taken by various countries after the failed 1910 conference suggest that states 'assumed a background norm of complete state sovereignty over the atmosphere'); see also TD Crouch, *Wings: A History of Aviation from Kites to the Space Age* (Washington, DC, Smithsonian National Air and Space Museum, 2003) 599.

[49] LH Slotemaker, *Freedom of Passage for International Air Services* (Leiden, Sijthoff, 1932) 14–6.

[50] Banner, *Who Owns the Sky?* (n 35) 44.

[51] ibid 38–41.

engineers, governmental officials, military experts, the media, scholars, and members of the public interested in the future of aviation for a myriad reasons. In the following years, an ever broader and more representative group of participants would join this process, directly and indirectly. Ultimately, even more relevant than the exact participants taking part in this lawmaking process are the various factors that contributed to sustaining the customary international law norm that eventually developed and stabilised.

World War I, which prompted numerous disputes over aerial overflight and led to the development of the fighter jet, with powerful capabilities to police airspace and destroy intruding aircraft, further strengthened support for the aerial sovereignty norm. The end of World War I led to a flurry of international lawmaking activities, of which the 1919 Convention Relating to the Regulation of Aerial Navigation was a particularly significant one.[52] Provisions concerning aviation were also included in the respective peace treaties, such as the Versailles Peace Treaty in respect of overflight over German territory.[53] Countries with important interests in the field of aviation, in particular the US, did not become a party to the 1919 Convention, however.[54] Nonetheless, the 1919 Convention was the first multilateral treaty concerning airspace and the range of states becoming parties to it reflected the expansion of the geographic scope of international air law since the pre-war years.[55] Its first Article 'recognized' every state's 'complete and exclusive sovereignty over the airspace above its territory', which was clarified in the same article to include both the territory 'of the mother country and of the colonies, and the territorial waters adjacent thereto'.[56] The Convention also included provisions pertaining to aerial reconnaissance. Thus, Article 27 provided for the right of each state to 'prohibit or regulate the carriage or use of photographic apparatus'. It added that 'such regulations shall be at once notified to the International Commission for Air Navigation'.[57] The latter is considered the predecessor of the ICAO, which was to play a significant role in the coming decades in developing international air law.[58]

'[S]ince its inception, air transportation has been subject to more restrictions than any other mode of communication'.[59] This observation, made by

[52] ibid, 65–7.
[53] See eg M Schladebach, *Lufthoheit: Kontinuität und Wandel* (n 47) 66.
[54] ibid, 67; see also Banner, *Who Owns the Sky?* (n 35) 66–7.
[55] See International Commission for Air Navigation, 'International Convention Relating to the Regulation of Aerial Navigation Dated October 13, 1919, With the Annexes to the Convention and Protocols of Proposed Amendments' (1944) iv.
[56] ibid, 1.
[57] State aircraft were defined in Chapter VII of the Convention and subjected to special rules.
[58] D Mackenzie, *ICAO: A History of the International Civil Aviation Organization* (Toronto, University of Toronto Press, 2010) 15–6.
[59] MS McDougal, HD Lasswell, and IA Vlasic, *Law and Public Order in Space* (New Haven, Yale University Press, 1963) 277.

McDougal, Lasswell, and Vlasic in their path-breaking 1963 work 'Law and Public Order in Space', can be applied to the entire post-World War II period, which saw an increasing consolidation of the basic norm of aerial sovereignty, sometimes at the expense of the attainment of global values that could have been achieved by a more integrated global aviation regime.[60] Indeed, air transportation remains heavily restricted globally, with states frequently making use of their powers within the air columns above their territories for reasons unrelated to public safety. In contrast, outer space has recently become the extreme opposite, a frontier for risk-prone entrepreneurs attracted by the relative freedom allowed in that domain by states and groups of states attempting to support their local aerospace industry, or else unable or unwilling to develop and enforce an effective regime that would adequately consider the various risks raised by such activities. The background to this divergent development can be traced to the immediate post-World War II period, when outer space become a relatively distinct field of international legal regulation negotiated chiefly among the two Cold War adversaries. Since that time, the law governing activities in outer space and those in airspace would be made through different, if related, processes.

To better illuminate this 'bifurcation', it is worth recalling that in late 1944, two seemingly unrelated events prepared the ground for the two principal paths on which the legal frameworks governing airspace and outer space would move in the post-World War II era. In Chicago, representatives of more than a dozen states met to sign the Convention on International Civil Aviation (the 'Chicago Convention'). The Soviet Union chose not to send a delegation, and, as in the case of other wartime peace conferences such as those at Bretton Woods and Dumbarton Oaks, only allied and neutral countries were invited. The Chicago Convention had been convened by the US government during wartime and would elaborate, solidify, and put under a stronger institutional footing the existing pre-World War II legal consensus among governments about a state's sovereignty in the air column above its territory (and territorial sea). More importantly, it would constitute the basis for a gradual harmonization of the law governing civil aviation, an industry that was expected to have a bright future in the post-World War II period. Indeed, the part of the Chicago Convention that legal experts and aviation administrators later found had triggered the most innovative aspect of that legal regime was Article 37.[61] The article prescribed the harmonization of standards and a corresponding procedure in the shadow of the Convention's key substantive provisions.[62] It facilitated the harmonization and indeed the development of

[60] ibid, 276–81.

[61] The point is made very persuasively in JC Cooper, 'The Chicago Convention – After Twenty Years' (1965) 19(3) *University of Miami Law Review* 333, 337–8. See for a more recent and detailed account in MacKenzie, *ICAO* (n 58).

[62] Cooper, 'The Chicago Convention – After Twenty Years' (n 61).

international aviation law and an international aviation industry by nudging states towards 'the highest practicable degree of uniformity in regulations, standards, procedures, and organization', all with the aim of improving air navigation, without requiring the onerous process of formal treaty amendment.

While this mechanism can be described as leading to 'soft law', it effectively led to a large degree of authoritative and controlling expectations about the legal regulation of aviation globally through a process of decentralised coordination – traditionally a characteristic *modus operandi* of customary international law – grafted onto and given life through the institutions created by the Chicago Convention and related agreements. At the same time, this regime did not upend the basic norm providing for aerial sovereignty in the air column above a state's territory (and territorial sea). On the contrary, it strengthened it. The Chicago Convention thus became the legal framework under which the development and commercialization of civil aviation would occur and the framework under which state aircraft would be prohibited from entering the airspace of other states (see Article 3 (c) of the Chicago Convention). Soon after the entry into force of the Chicago Convention in 1947, lawyers began discussing how international law would regulate the nascent industry of high-altitude flight – this issue would, however, be relegated to a different forum and sow the seeds of a specialised area of international lawmaking: international space law.[63]

As the signing of the Chicago Convention was underway, World War II still raged on the other side of the Atlantic and in the Eastern Pacific. Under Nazi rule, Germany had attempted to develop a space capability, but its efforts failed, with the technological baton later passing on to the US and the USSR. In a last-ditch effort to shore up its offensive capabilities, Nazi Germany's military officials had since early 1944 accelerated the development, testing, and production of the V-2, a technologically innovative rocket, the first to reach outer space in mid-1944. The V-2 was in some ways symbolic of the Nazi regime: It was developed as a way to defy the limitations imposed on Germany under the Versailles Peace Treaty. Its construction reportedly cost the lives of even more people, many working as slave labourers, than it killed as a weapon. Thousands of V-2 rockets were launched upon London in 1944 and until as late as early 1945, just a few months before Germany's formal surrender on 4 May 1945. Although the V-2 rocket failed to affect the outcome of the war, the technological innovation achieved by the rocket's principal developer and his associates caught the attention of the incoming American and Soviet forces, which continued efforts in the direction of rocket technology and, eventually, space flight. Indeed, in the immediate post-War period, versions of the V-2 were launched both in the US and in the USSR.[64]

[63] JC Cooper, 'High Altitude Flight and National Sovereignty' (1951) 4 *The International Law Quarterly* 411; Banner, *Who Owns the Sky?* (n 35).

[64] FI Ordway III et al, 'A Memoir: From Peenemünde to USA: A Classic Case of Technology Transfer' (2007) 60(1) *Acta Astronautica* 24.

Somewhat surprisingly, given the context, it was the Nazi regime-developed V-2 rocket that initially seemed to have symbolised the spatial reconnaissance capabilities of the incipient space age, even in the US public sphere. For example, in 1950, an article published in the widely read *National Geographic* magazine included a mosaic-panorama of a part of the globe shot from outer space entitled 'V-2 Rocket-Eye View from 60 Miles Up', without providing context as to its progenitors.[65] The subsequent Cold War would be defined by a competition between the USSR and the US for dominance in outer space as well as a stabilization of the normative expectations about permissible conduct in outer space. Although space technologies would continue to be put to military use during the post-World War II period, the focus of that use would be on reconnaissance and surveillance rather than the offensive uses the Nazi regime had pursued.

As these two trajectories suggest, a bifurcation defined the legal regimes governing airspace and outer space in the years following World War II.[66] Much has been written about the period immediately following World War II until the collapse of the Soviet Union and its regime of satellite-states. For reasons rooted in technological, economic, and political contingencies, the post-World War II period was characterised both by the emergence of commercial or civil aviation and by the entailments of the Cold War, in which the US and the USSR deployed military aviation technologies and engaged in what can be called the first space race. In this process, the basic rules of aerial sovereignty and outer space law were laid down, as were the rules concerning national jurisdiction over aircraft. In considering this era, the extent to which customary international law came to govern these two strands of international affairs and technology offers important insights into international lawmaking processes and resulting norms more generally. Substantively, in line with the preceding 1928 Havana Convention, the 1944 Chicago Convention would be limited to civil aviation – thus excluding '[a]ircraft used in military, customs and police services' as per the definition of 'state aircraft', a category of aircraft not permitted to 'fly over the territory of another State … without authorization by special agreement or otherwise, and in accordance with the terms thereof' (Article 3(c) 1944 Chicago Convention). The 1919 Convention still had a different, broader ambit, referring to all forms of aviation, state or civil. By implication, this exclusion of state aircraft from the Convention would henceforth relegate most questions concerning state aircraft more directly to customary international law. The two regimes of airspace and outer space, although having points of connection, came to be governed by different substantive areas of international (and other) law. Whereas space activities

[65] R Edgington, 'An "All-Seeing Flying Eye": V-2 Rockets and the Promises of Earth Photography' (2012) 28(3) *History and Technology* 363.

[66] At the same time, questions of international communication whose regulation often spanned the atmosphere, the near-Earth orbit, and state territory (as well as areas beyond national sovereignty or jurisdiction) developed in a distinctive direction.

would be guided by the norms and institutions developed to govern states' activities in outer space, aviation would be subject to the overlapping regulations and institutions established primarily under air law and the law of the sea. To be sure, both fields were integrated into cross-cutting areas of international law. For instance, the law relating to the use of force would apply to both; moreover, both would later come under the ambit also of newly developing substantive areas of international law, including international atomic law, environmental law, the law of sustainable development, and international human rights law, to mention but a few. But in order to understand the relevant customary international lawmaking processes during this period and their effects on substantive outcomes, the bifurcation is relevant and revealing.

Humanity's 'conquest' of air and outer space provides important insights into customary international lawmaking during a formative period of the international legal order. It highlights the link between domestic and international lawmaking processes, the role of public opinion on lawmaking, the varied effects of technological developments on lawmaking, the influence of decentralization and other structural features of international lawmaking processes on their outcomes, and the importance of a range of contingent circumstances. One lesson from this history is that local and domestic legal action is a key part of relatively decentralised and multi-stage international lawmaking processes and one that is particularly relevant for customary international lawmaking. The decentralisation that characterised international lawmaking in the field shifted in important ways over time and across different groups of actors and such shifts have informed key questions about the relationship between lawmaking processes and outcomes.[67] Until the end of World War I, lawmaking processes in the field were extremely decentralised and featured a large number of activists, scholars, and other experts. Both the aviation industry and lawmaking processes in the field seem to have transformed in the course of the early 1900s, leading up to World War I and culminating in the 1919 Paris Convention. Aviation eventually became more government-driven – growing resources were invested by governments into military aviation, the training of pilots, and related technologies. The rise of governmental supervision and ever-larger enterprises in the aviation sector were paralleled by the key role of states in the lawmaking process.[68] While the emergence of private-led diplomatic and expert efforts directed at international lawmaking or codification competed or even merged with official lawmaking efforts at times, these never managed to displace the key role of government officials. Decision-makers were at times well-aware of public opinion and the opinions of outside experts, but these were rarely able to affect the lawmaking process directly.

[67] Banner, *Who Owns the Sky?* (n 35) 101.
[68] ibid 169–85.

However, already during this period, change was afoot and visible in the ways in which public concerns increasingly entered the lawmaking agenda. This change is visible, for example, in the different lawmaking processes involved in setting the basic rules or principles concerning airspace and more specific regulations of the technical and military aspects of aviation. The absence of third-party dispute settlement also had an important effect on international lawmaking processes by creating room for decentralised processes of customary international lawmaking. The history of aviation also shows that international law is made just as much on the conference table (or the courtroom) as on the battlefield. Here, the mentioned monopoly of governments over action was even more significant than elsewhere. Private organisations or individuals who thought they could shape lawmaking on the level of formal international law or various non-binding declarations had to contend with the fact that the lawmaking process continued in the application phase. There, governments were mostly dominant. However, organisations such as the International Committee of the Red Cross (ICRC), created in the second half of the nineteenth century, tried to insert a third voice into less public but no less significant fora of customary international lawmaking.

Finally, the seemingly administrative task of compiling, translating, comparing, and disseminating information about decentralised lawmaking efforts itself played an important role in furthering international lawmaking by imposing a unified framework on local legal developments. The simultaneity of international lawmaking efforts and domestic legal action made the collection and dissemination of local information, often by international organisations, especially important. At the same time, the very technologies that were being regulated – such as aerial transportation or wireless communication – facilitated information collection and dissemination and made transportation and cooperation among a rising class of transnationally active lawyers easier, thereby indirectly transforming international lawmaking. At a time when barriers to and costs of long-distance communication and transportation were falling, the lawmaking process could become more decentralised while also embedding itself more strongly in domestic legal systems, something that further buttressed the stability of any substantive international legal norms that happened to stabilise as a result of this process. In that sense, because a range of technological innovations directly impacted on the quality, speed, and dissemination of communication, these technologies affected the relevant lawmaking processes by making them more responsive to actual developments, progressively more global and inclusive, and improving our capacity to track developments in customary international lawmaking.

III. SHAPING RESTRAINTS ON AERIAL BOMBARDMENT

Improvements in military and aviation technologies paved the way for the use of aerial bombardment in the course of World War I. This raised the question of the legality of this military tactic and any constraints on aerial bombardment under the laws of war, which remains a regular subject of debate up to the present. In 1899, several governments decided to ban aircraft-delivered weapons. Importantly, this ban occurred in an era of technological transition – following the invention and deployment of balloons and airships but preceding the rise of the airplane. As a result, the episode offers valuable insights into customary international lawmaking at the intersection of technological innovation, military competition, and changing social norms.

When governmental representatives gathered in The Hague in 1899 to discuss the various proposals made by Tsar Nicholas II, military ballooning had still been of limited interest to the armies of the participating governments, but the broader development of military aviation was becoming ever-more promising. Despite considerable efforts, nineteenth-century attempts at launching weapons of some sort from aerial vehicles,[69] particularly balloons, were widely perceived as unsuccessful. The one frequently cited case of balloon-launched weapons,[70] the attempted bombing of Venice by Austrian troops in 1849,[71] was in retrospect often judged a 'failure' by commentators.[72] Though a military failure, one should keep in mind that its effects went beyond the sphere of the military commanders involved. After all, this experiment with aircraft-delivered weaponry created apprehension both in the public sphere and among experts, as would become apparent later.[73] Even some of the governmental representatives at the Second Hague Peace Conference would later relay, but dismiss, fears about aerial bombardment in the course of their deliberations.[74]

To be sure, while the issue of bombardment was related to the question of aviation (that is, as aerial bombardment), it was not limited to it. After all, already by the nineteenth century, the legal definition of bombardment included various types of attack at long-distance. For example, the earlier Brussels Conference of 1874 had already introduced explicit provisions on bombardment into its outcome document, the 'Project of an International Declaration Concerning the Laws and Customs of War'. The Brussels Declaration of 1874 was followed by a study by the IDI, which tabled its own attempt at codifying the laws of war in 1880 in the form of the 'Oxford Manual of the Laws and

[69] See more generally AW Crosby, *Throwing Fire: Projectile Technology through History* (Cambridge, Cambridge University Press, 2002).

[70] But see Banner, *Who Owns the Sky?* (n 35) 45, citing GB Davis, 'The Launching of Projectiles from Balloons' (1908) 2 *The American Journal of International Law* 528.

[71] G Pepe, *Narrative of Scenes and Events in Italy: From 1847 to 1849 Including the Siege of Venice* (London, Henry Colburn, 1850) 116 (mentioning the use of 'balloons and other aerostatic devices').

[72] Haydon, *Military Ballooning During the Early Civil War* (n 12) 17–8.

[73] Banner, *Who Owns the Sky?* (n 35) 45.

[74] See eg Thomas, *The Ethics of Destruction* (n 1) 87 (quoting Marius de Robilant's statement from 'The Proceedings of the Hague Peace Conferences of 1907'). See 'Statement by de Robilant' in JB Scott (ed), *The Proceedings of the Hague Peace Conferences: Translation of the Official Texts, The Conference of 1907, Volume III* (New York, Oxford University Press, 1921) 150.

Customs of War'. All of these codifications had something to say about the question of bombardment in general, rather than merely aerial bombardment, which was at the time largely hypothetical.

As noted, like the Brussels Conference of 1874, the 1899 Hague Peace Conference also originated in a Russian proposal that was met by a diplomatically coded mix of enthusiasm and suspicion on the part of other governments,[75] the press, and members of the interested public. Eventually, the delegates meeting at the First Hague Peace Conference agreed to a five-year moratorium on the 'launching of projectiles and explosives from balloons, and other methods of similar nature'.[76] The temporal limitation had been inserted following a last-minute intervention by the US delegate, Captain Crozier[77] – the ban was easily approved and swiftly implemented by the various participating governments.[78] After the five-year term ended on 4 September 1905, the delegates meeting at the Second Hague Peace Conference in 1907 agreed to a further extension of the prohibition of 'the discharge of projectiles and explosives from balloons or by other new methods of a similar nature' for an unspecified period until the end of an anticipated Third Peace Conference, which never came to pass.[79]

Both conferences took place in an 'intermediate' phase – after balloons had failed to prove any significant military worth, but before widely anticipated improvements in aviation technology arrived.[80] At the same time, the delegates at both conferences were clearly well-informed about the various relevant national initiatives in the field. For example, one of the American delegates to the Second Hague Peace Conference, Joseph H. Choate, reported that even very recent news about the development of aviation technology had directly affected the participants' views.[81] The 1907 Declaration[82] remains formally in force[83] – however, the limited formal adherence to the Declaration and the carve-out in respect

[75] See eg CD Davis, *The United States and the Second Hague Peace Conference: American Diplomacy and International organization, 1899–1914* (Durham, Duke University Press, 1975) 6.

[76] Declaration (IV,1), to Prohibit, for the Term of Five Years, the Launching of Projectiles and Explosives from Balloons, and Other Methods of Similar Nature. The Hague, 29 July 1899.

[77] JH Choate, *The Two Hague Conferences* (Princeton, Princeton University Press, 1913) 96; see also WI Hull, *The Two Hague Conferences and Their Contributions to International Law* (Boston, Ginn & Company, 1908) 76–82; Davis, *The United States and the Second Hague Peace Conference* (n 75) 26.

[78] Davis, *The United States and the Second Hague Peace Conference* (n 75) 34.

[79] See Hull, *The Two Hague Conferences and Their Contributions to International Law* (n 77) 82. See also Choate, *The Two Hague Conferences* (n 77) 14–5; AD White, *The First Hague Conference* (Boston, World Peace Foundation, 1905 (1912 reprint)).

[80] Choate, *The Two Hague Conferences* (n 77) 13–4.

[81] ibid, 14.

[82] Declaration (XIV) Prohibiting the Discharge of Projectiles and Explosives from Balloons. The Hague, 18 October 1907.

[83] See the ICRC's IHL database, which cites J Toman and D Schindler, *The Laws of Armed Conflicts: A Collection of Conventions, Resolutions, and Other Documents*, 3rd edn (Leiden, A.W. Sijthoff, 1973) 202–4.

of non-parties means that it has hardly been relevant.[84] At the same time, the Hague Regulations on Land Warfare of 1907 included a catch-all prohibition on the bombardment of 'undefended' settlements,[85] a norm later understood as declaratory of customary international law by the International Military Tribunal at Nuremberg.

In sum, it does not seem that the underlying norm – a ban of aerial bombardment – had much traction in diplomatic circles after the adoption of the 1907 Declaration and Regulations.[86] Of course, the temporal limitation of the declaration makes it difficult to infer any sort of agreement on a complete ban of aerial bombing to begin with. Statements by peace activists largely confirm that already before World War I, any agreement on the prohibition of aerial bombardment had been ineffective. For example, introducing a 1912 'Memorial against the Use of Armed Airships',[87] which is said to have been signed by three hundred persons in Britain, Evans W. Darby, an English peace activist, seems exasperated by the fruitlessness of the 1899 and 1907 Hague Peace Conferences.[88] For Darby, the only realistic option to address the 'peril' of aerial warfare in light of states' failure to address the problem was 'the creation of opinion and sentiment, which shall result in action when the time comes'.[89] Nonetheless, while there was apparently some support for an indefinite ban on aerial bombardment, it failed to gain traction in the relevant circles and any emerging norm completely disintegrated in the course of the subsequent global conflicts.

Law continued to apply to the conduct of war, but it would concern itself with the conditions under which aerial bombardment was to be deemed lawful, rather than its legality as such. However, this process was drawn out and did not lead to any effective norms during this period, but would only consolidate during the post-World War II era.[90] Why did governments attempt to regulate the discharge of weapons from balloons and other aerial platforms but fail to establish an effective norm against aerial bombardment in the early twentieth century? More importantly for our purposes, what does this tell us about

[84] Hull, *The Two Hague Conferences and Their Contributions to International Law* (n 77) 76–82.

[85] See on its interpretation eg Davis, *The United States and the Second Hague Peace Conference* (n 75) 206–7.

[86] E Barak (ed), *Deadly Metal Rain: The Legality of Flechette Weapons in International Law. A Reappraisal Following Israel's Use of Flechettes in the Gaza Strip* (2001–2009) (Leiden, Martinus Nijhoff, 2011) 89–91.

[87] 'A Memorial against the Use of Armed Airships', publ. International Arbitration League, London (UNOG Registry, Records and Archives, Ref. code BvS/6/29/1) (1912).

[88] WE Darby, 'The Peril of the Air' (1912) 74(10) *The Advocate of Peace* 244–5; WE Darby, 'The Peril of the Air (concluded from the November issue)' (1912) 74(11) *The Advocate of Peace* 263–5.

[89] ibid.

[90] See eg JM Henckaerts and E Debuf, 'The ICRC and the Clarification of Customary International Humanitarian Law' in BD Lepard (ed), *Reexamining Customary International Law* (Cambridge, Cambridge University Press, 2017) 161; see also J-M Henckaerts and L Doswald-Beck (eds) *Customary International Humanitarian Law* (Cambridge, Cambridge University Press, 2005).

customary international lawmaking during this period and in this context? One factor was the timing of the 1899 Hague Peace Conference, which helps explain why there was sufficient diplomatic momentum for government representatives to only temporarily ban the launching of projectiles from balloons. The Hague Peace Conferences were called at a time when the effects of the military deployment of balloons had been limited. At the same time, as contemporaneous reports suggest, the 1899 and 1907 Hague Peace Conferences took place during an era in which informed observers expected significant improvements in military aviation technology, implying that time was on the side of those governments who perceived themselves or hoped to be in the comparative technological lead.

From that perspective, the five-year moratorium on the discharge of projectiles from aerial vehicles declared in 1899 was not a major achievement; to the contrary, it may have motivated governments to pursue further investments and innovation in military aviation given the foreseeable expiry of the ban. A number of scholars have offered analyses of the two Hague Peace Conferences and their impact. Maartje Abbenhuis has argued that the Hague Peace Conferences of 1899 and 1907 formed a focal point for popular views about states' external conduct and helped shape public perceptions about possible restraints on warfare during subsequent periods.[91] At the same time, governments were interested in gaining a competitive military advantage over their perceived rivals, which meant that any decisions on arms control, including those about balloon-launched projectiles, occurred in the context of domestic interests and endowments and the projected benefits of an international moratorium. Eyal Benvenisti and Doreen Lustig have offered a broader historical account of why the nineteenth-century efforts to codify the laws of war were not the result of humanitarian efforts or civil society pressures[92] but instead the product of closed-door diplomacy seeking to counter-act the democratising tendencies that affected the European governments both internally and externally after the failed revolutions of 1848.[93] While Benvenisti and Lustig make a general point about the laws of war, it applies as well to the failure to develop stable norms restraining aerial bombardment during this period.

The case of aerial bombardment is an illustrative example of the difficulty of sustaining legal norms in this field, as also confirmed by Ward Thomas' study of the relationship between norms and the use of force. Thomas had earlier offered a detailed legal history of the rise, fall, and eventual rise in the post-World War II period of norms seeking to restrain aerial

[91] MM Abbenhuis, *The Hague Conferences and International Politics, 1898–1915* (London, Bloomsbury Academic, 2018) 3.

[92] See also Whitman, *The Verdict of Battle* (n 4) 12.

[93] E Benvenisti and D Lustig, 'Monopolizing War: Codifying the Laws of War to Reassert Governmental Authority, 1856–1874' (2020) 31(1) *European Journal of International Law* 127. See also, by reference to Schmitt, Whitman, *The Verdict of Battle* (n 4) 15.

bombardment.[94] Thomas argues against what he terms the 'conventional view of the bombing norm',[95] proposing first that 'something in the nature of the norm itself made it particularly brittle' and further that it is necessary to examine the 'gradual revitalization' of the norm after 1945, something ignored by the conventional view.[96] Thomas attributes the weakness of the norm to the fact that it 'was not internalised by the military and political institutions of the major states, [giving rise] to only a very tenuous understanding that such actions were inappropriate'.[97] Telling a nuanced story about the various factors affecting the regulation of aerial bombing in the early twentieth century, Thomas emphasises how the difficulty of embedding a new technology of warfare into existing legal categories made for a particularly weak norm.[98]

In addition, the lawmaking process in the field was almost completely decentralised, with virtually no third-party adjudication in place, with the limited exception of the immediate post-World War II period, only to be followed by the limited development of international criminal law since the 1990s. All this made the customary international lawmaking process in this field especially susceptible to patterns of retribution that unravelled any initial restraint military commanders might have shown in the course of the World Wars. Moreover, the limited representativeness of the lawmaking process, as reflected in the absence of civil society participation despite the existence of several pacifist movements, likewise ensured that little heed was given to popular fears about the looming threat of 'total' war. At the same time, various actors and groups, including civil society organisations, tried but failed to influence international lawmaking at the time. There was widespread popular apprehension about the destructiveness of an imagined aerial weapon.[99] And indeed, public awareness of such risks was growing precisely during this period thanks to the spread of the press.[100] And yet, all this did not help turn the normative dial.

The public apprehension about aerial bombardment, which was largely ignored by governments and which failed to lead to an effective ban, turned out to be prescient: Already during World War I, aerial bombardment was used both by the Central Powers and the Entente despite the defects of an infant technology, with significant civilian casualties on all sides. Various peace and similar movements of that era played a role in supporting some diplomatic initiatives,

[94] Thomas, *The Ethics of Destruction* (n 1) 87–146 (discussing aerial bombing until 1945).
[95] ibid, 89.
[96] ibid, 90–1.
[97] ibid, 91.
[98] ibid, 97–9.
[99] See eg G de Syon, *Zeppelin!: Germany and the Airship, 1900–1939* (Baltimore, John Hopkins University Press, 2002) 11–3; B Holman, *The Next War in the Air: Britain's Fear of the Bomber, 1908–1941* (Farnham, Ashgate Publishing, 2016).
[100] See eg A Pettegree, *The Invention of News: How the World Came to Know About Itself* (New Haven, Yale University Press, 2014) 364.

even though the actual impact of such movements on disarmament conferences such as the one convened on behest of the Russian Tsar in 1899 seems to have been minimal.[101] This particular case of normative failure[102] – the declaration of a norm, followed shortly thereafter by its unravelling in the course of World Wars I and II – offers a revealing insight into the features and defects of international lawmaking processes of this period.[103] If nothing more, recent scholarship and contemporaneous sources suggest that lawmaking processes in this field explain a good part of the substantive outcomes achieved, with strong echoes into the present.

IV. THE SECOND SPACE RACE: FROM REMOTE SENSING TO SPACE COLONIZATION

In the third decade of the twenty-first century, the prospect of humans travelling to, exploring, exploiting the resources of, and potentially 'colonising' proximate and more distant space objects is becoming an increasingly likely scenario. Many scholars have critically examined both popular ideas about humanity's future in outer space and the corresponding debates in the field of international law. For example, Matthew Craven has argued that the outer space regime envisaged during the Cold War reflects deeply problematic aspects of extraction-based economics and forms of neocolonialism.[104] Moreover, despite high hopes and some commercial success, the economic landscape of the so-called 'New Space' sector remains beset by a number of failures that cast doubt on its prospects, leaving aside issues of regulation on matters ranging from safety to competition.[105] Nonetheless, many space entrepreneurs and scientists see outer space as a frontier humans need to explore if they want to develop, test, and realise technologies that will improve life prospects for humanity.[106] Moreover, the same technologies used for the exploration and exploitation of space objects could help deflect possible 'extinction events', such as an asteroid collision with the Earth. At any rate, while the intellectual

[101] On parallel and more effective efforts to prohibit offensive war, see OA Hathaway and SJ Shapiro, *The Internationalists: How a Radical Plan to Outlaw War Remade the World* (New York, Simon & Schuster, 2017).

[102] See also Thomas, *The Ethics of Destruction* (n 1) 87–146.

[103] See more generally Benvenisti and Lustig, 'Monopolizing War: Codifying the Laws of War to Reassert Governmental Authority, 1856–1874 (n 93).

[104] M Craven, '"Other Spaces": Constructing the Legal Architecture of a Cold War Commons and the Scientific-Technical Imaginary of Outer Space' (2019) 30(2) *European Journal of International Law* 547, 567–9; see also HA Durrani, 'Interpreting "Space Resources Obtained": Historical and Postcolonial Interventions in the Law of Commercial Space Mining' (2019) 57 *Columbia Journal of Transnational Law* 403.

[105] See eg MC Weinzierl, 'Space, the Final Economic Frontier' (2018) 32(2) *Journal of Economic Perspectives* 173.

[106] See eg M Kaku, *The Future of Humanity: Terraforming Mars, Interstellar Travel, Immortality, and Our Destiny Beyond Earth* (New York, Doubleday, 2018).

history of contemporary outer space law points to an instrumental perspective, and while such a perspective is front and centre in recent regulatory drives by the US, Luxembourg, the United Arab Emirates, and others, there is arguably no inherent connection between outer space-related technologies (for exploration, transportation, and resource management) and any particular economic or political model. At any rate, increasing travel in and out of the Earth's atmosphere and the expansion of small satellite constellations in low Earth orbit (LEO) already feature prominently in the recent wave of so-called 'New Space' activities. Entrepreneurs and investors, such as SpaceX's Elon Musk or Blue Origin's Jeff Bezos, have combined their entrepreneurial ambition and significant resources with a heavy reliance on public funding to promote goals like space travel and even the longer-term aim of 'space colonisation'. These figures – similar in style to certain pioneers of the aerial age – have popularised and made more accessible what increasingly seems likely from a scientific, engineering, and economic perspective. But the range of legal issues arising in the context of the 'New Space' sector is vast, including questions about environmental regulation and the ownership of outer space resources.[107]

This section will briefly highlight the chief legal issues that have recently attracted attention in this field and then focus on the associated customary international lawmaking processes. They relate to two main kinds of current or envisaged space uses, namely the use of near-Earth satellite technologies, on the one hand, and the planned exploitation of space-based resources, such as resources located on the Moon, Mars, or on asteroids, on the other. When it comes to the use of near-Earth satellite technologies, some of the relevant issues include the coordination and allocation of orbits and frequencies, the prevention and management of space debris, other aspects of the regulation of the space sector's activities, including from a human rights angle, as well as the relationship between civilian and military uses of outer space. In recent decades, these issues were driven by the combined trends of more economical launch technologies, new constellations of smaller and ever-cheaper satellites with powerful communications and remote sensing capabilities, and the threats that military technologies (including Anti-satellite weapons (ASATs) and potential new space weapons) can pose to the sustainability of the near-Earth environment.

One important application of near-Earth satellite technologies, in addition to the provision of communication services, has been remote sensing and geolocation. Indeed, a huge variety and number of civilian and military applications rely on satellite-based remote sensing. Since the 1980s, the significant community interests served by remote sensing have prompted a notable, if limited, degree of cooperation, both bi- and multilateral, in the field. During the Cold War, cooperation in this field was chiefly bilateral, as with the Anti-Ballistic Missile

[107] See eg M Byers and A Boley, *Who Owns Outer Space? International Law, Astrophysics, and the Sustainable Development of Space* (Cambridge, Cambridge University Press, 2023).

Treaty (ABM Treaty) of 1972, whose article XII required the US and the USSR to refrain from interfering with the other party's 'national technical means of verification' conducted 'in a manner consistent with generally recognised principles of international law'. Since the 1980s, cooperation in the field has expanded significantly, even if a select group of space-faring powers continue to play a leading role in the field and resist binding international law commitments. As in other areas closely related to military and intelligence objectives, remote sensing has seen only a limited degree of multilateral cooperation. However, some cooperative efforts did support the development of more community-oriented norms with respect to remote sensing. A significant diplomatic episode illustrating the movement towards more community-oriented lawmaking in the field was the negotiation of the 'Principles Relating to Remote Sensing of the Earth' of 1986, adopted as UN General Assembly (UNGA) resolution 41/53 ('Remote Sensing Principles').[108]

The negotiations leading up to the Remote Sensing Principles were 'organized' based on a draft text tabled by the Austrian government, whose representatives managed to insert themselves as credible mediators.[109] A number of governments with strong interests in the field actively participated in the discussions, including the US, France, the Soviet Union, as well as members of the G77 group. Although the US did not initiate the debate over remote sensing at the UN level, it participated in the debates and finally did not object to the outcome reached. The negotiations' outcome reflected intense deliberations by many governments, was strongly promoted by France, and acquiesced to by the Eastern European and Soviet bloc. The Remote Sensing Principles themselves and their successor initiatives did not, on their own, usher in any paradigm shift in relation to the norms applicable to remote sensing. Over the subsequent decades, remote sensing by the growing number of states and other organisations with the requisite capabilities became widely accepted. The Remote Sensing Principles and their reception cemented broad international support for the right of states to engage in remote sensing of the Earth from outer space. However, it is more doubtful whether they spurred new legal norms concerning the distribution of benefits from remote sensing activities. Nonetheless, the Remote Sensing Principles suggested that there was demand for cooperative arrangements placing obligations of information and technology transfer on technologically advanced space-faring nations, while highlighting difficulties of achieving that goal through UN fora. Although the Remote Sensing Principles – like other UNGA resolutions – are not a legally binding instrument, their elaboration provides important

[108] UNGA Res 41/53 'Principles Relating to Remote Sensing of the Earth from Space' (3 December 1986) GAOR 41st Session Supp 53, 115.

[109] JI Gabrynowicz, *The United Nations Principles Relating to Remote Sensing of the Earth from Space: A Legislative History – Interviews of Members of the United States Delegation* (National Center for Remote Sensing and Space Law 2002) 56–161.

insights into customary international lawmaking in the field. The institutional framework in which the Remote Sensing Principles were elaborated and the procedural factors shaping their elaboration had profound downstream effects on the respective lawmaking process and its outcome. Moreover, given the important distributional questions at issue during the negotiations, their elaboration puts into focus the role of normative factors, be they procedural, formal, or substantive, in processes of international lawmaking. In parallel, we can discern the limited presence of participatory or democratic factors during this period, characterised both by the Cold War and growing interest from a broad range of countries and organisations in remote sensing for various purposes. Finally, the legally non-binding nature of the outcome of the discussions raises questions about the relationship between informal forms of lawmaking and customary international law.

Since the end of the Cold War, many other international initiatives have focused on better information exchange, which often implicates access to remote sensing technologies and data. For example, the Sendai Framework (2015), a legally non-binding document endorsed by the UNGA, emphasised the importance of various forms of cooperation and defines the 'reduction of disaster risk [as] a common concern for all States'.[110] The Sendai Framework identifies priorities of action, one of which connects the principle of cooperation to spatial reconnaissance and surveillance by pointing to the 'importance' of the 'promotion' and 'enhancement' of 'access to and the sharing and use of non-sensitive data and information, as appropriate, communications and geo-spatial and space-based technologies and related services'.[111] From the Remote Sensing Principles to the Sendai Framework, the issue of international cooperation to improve access to reliable information in response to (or in advance of) disasters has thus remained on the agenda of many governments and UN bodies, becoming even more pressing with the aggravation of climate change and its impacts especially on low-lying and low per capita income countries.

When it comes to plans for the exploitation of various space objects, questions of ownership, sharing, and regulation from the environmental and health perspectives feature prominently. To some extent, these issues have been discussed since the Cold War and form the backdrop to the current outer space law regime. For example, the question of pollution, be it of outer-space environments or of the Earth itself, through space activities has been discussed as early as 1963.[112] David Tan has suggested that sufficient customary norms relating to the protection of the outer space environment are lacking, even if they are sorely

[110] United Nations, 'Sendai Framework for Disaster Risk Reduction 2015–2030' (UN 2015) para 19(a).
[111] ibid, para 25(c).
[112] MS McDougal, 'Emerging Customary Law of Space' (1963) 58 *Northwestern University Law Review* 618, 636.

needed.[113] Many other scholars have likewise investigated the role of customary international law and 'soft law' in relation to harms and risks to near-earth and outer space environments.[114]

The relevance of these issues is illustrated by the fact that on 6 April 2020, the President of the US issued an Executive Order on a topic that could not be further from the minds of many at the time: space resources recovery and use. The Executive Order, entitled 'Encouraging International Support for the Recovery and Use of Space Resources', acknowledged the uncertainty surrounding the legal regulation of space resource recovery and use but rejected the notion that space was a 'global commons'.[115] It reiterated the US government's position on the topic of the 'recovery' and use of space resources, simultaneously directing the US Secretary of State to gather support for it with other governments. The document also rejected the idea that the Moon Agreement, in which states had adopted a 'common heritage of mankind' approach to the Moon, reflected customary international law. As such, the order was the first instrument of its kind to explicitly direct the Secretary of State to object to any claims that the Moon Agreement reflected customary international law.

This Executive Order was remarkable from at least two perspectives. On one level, it is the rare instance of a country's leader invoking customary international law so explicitly. As such, the Executive Order reflected both a recognition of the relevance of customary international law in this field and a degree of transparency about the US government's view about the relationship between customary international law and its policy position on this question. On another level, the Executive Order embodied a unilateral approach to international lawmaking. Although the issue of space resources 'recovery' and use is one ideally suited for an international agreement, the Executive Order avoids any reference to a multilateral solution. Instead, it adopts a particular legal position and directs the Secretary of State to gather 'international support' for it. To be sure, the order itself leaves its implementation open; implicitly, it does seem to recognise the need for an international normative regime, since the Secretary of State is directed to 'take all appropriate actions to encourage international support for the public and private recovery and use of resources in outer space

[113] D Tan, 'Towards a New Regime for the Protection of Outer Space as the Province of All Mankind' (2000) 25 *Yale Journal of International Law* 145, 175.

[114] See V Gupta, 'Critique of the International Law on Protection of the Outer Space Environment' (2016) 14(1) *Astropolitics* 20; JM Beard, 'Soft Law's Failure on the Horizon: The International Code of Conduct for Outer Space Activities' (2016) *University of Pennsylvania Journal of International Law* 38; P Chatterjee, 'Legality of Anti-Satellites Under the Space Law Regime' (2014) 12 *Astropolitics* 27; R Kocse, 'Final Detonation: How Customary International Law Can Trigger the End of Landmines' (2014) 103 *Georgetown Law Review* 749; DA Koplow, 'ASAT-isfaction: Customary International Law and the Regulation of Anti-Satellite Weapons' (2008) 30 *Michigan Journal of International Law* 1187; ND Welly, 'Enlightened State-Interest – A Legal Framework for Protecting the 'Common Interest of All Mankind' from Hardinian Tragedy' (2010) 36(1) *Journal of Space Law* 273.

[115] See eg Byers and Boley, *Who Owns Outer Space?* (n 108) 157–61.

[by seeking] to negotiate joint statements and bilateral and multilateral arrangements with foreign states regarding safe and sustainable operations for the public and private recovery and use of space resources'. In other words, the Executive Order directs the Secretary of State to try to block adverse developments in customary international lawmaking and to seek support for the US position on the international stage. As such, it does recognise that international legal norms concerning outer space resources exploitation cannot be made unilaterally, even if it reflects a confident position that the US government's approach would garner sufficient international support. The US government's initiative was of course only a step in an ongoing process and includes the 'Artemis Accords' initiative, which seeks to reshape the applicable law governing the use of outer space resources.

Several actors quickly expressed opposition to the White House's approach, instead favouring the negotiation of an international agreement. At the same time, in many ways, the lawmaking arena in the outer space field has already become significantly more multilateral and decentralised over the last few decades, not least through the involvement of the private sector, more governments, regional organisations, and still limited but growing public awareness and interest in outer space as a global public good. As to the Artemis Accords and the former White House's Executive Order, rather than reflecting a clear national consensus among a wide range of governmental and civil society actors in the US, such initiatives seem to rest on a rather brittle footing. Efforts by some countries – including the US – to alter the basic building blocks of the international legal regime governing outer space resources, which emerged in the 1960s and solidified over the coming decades,[116] are due to uncertainty over the legal basis for exploitative commercial activities in outer space.[117] For several years, the US government has argued that the commercial exploitation of outer space resources is compatible with current rules.[118] However, various groups have expressed doubts about this approach. Some of this opposition has also come from non-US civil society organisations, members of the scientific and academic community, and other governments.

These isolated lawmaking initiatives in the outer space field are embedded in a changed lawmaking landscape. The change can be traced to a number developments, but it can best be described as the transformation of the largely inter-governmental and bilateral lawmaking processes during the Cold War's first 'space race'. In contrast to Cold War-era international lawmaking in this field, which can be described as a form of dynamic and bilateral lawmaking between the US and the Soviet Union, the current state of outer space lawmaking is considerably more democratised. Even in the context of the above-mentioned

[116] BJ Egan (Legal Adviser USDoS), 'Remarks at the Galloway Symposium on Critical Issues in Space Law' (7 December 2016); see generally Byers and Boley, Who Owns Outer Space? (n 108) 130–85.

[117] ibid.

[118] ibid.

2020 Executive Order, the US was not seeking an arrangement with its chief economic or geopolitical adversary, but rather 'international support' for an already determined position. At the same time, the US government's initiative largely reflected the concerns of a powerful US-based but by now transnationally operating private and commercial space industry. Current developments in the outer space field have been labelled by some as part of the so-called 'second space race', accompanied by growing interest in various new uses of outer space by military, civilian, and commercial actors since roughly the 2000s, in the shadow of increasing trends towards multipolarity and military tension among the great powers and others.[119] These economic, social, and geopolitical trends have prompted renewed discussions about the law applicable to the regulation of both civilian and military uses of outer space.[120] Lawmaking activities in the field continue to occur through a range of national and regional initiatives, through scholarly and other expert projects, and through coordination within international and regional organisations. For example, in 2022, NATO announced an 'overarching Space Policy', while the EU has been developing its own strategic posture in the outer space domain[121] and is currently in the process of developing an 'EU Space Law'. In early 2022, China issued a paper outlining its space policy, entitled 'China's Space Program: A 2021 Perspective'.[122] As noted, since 2020, the US has promoted accession to the so-called Artemis Accords, which have been joined by a significant number of states.[123] Trends towards multipolarity fed by the pursuit of national or regional economic or other forms of security are also becoming apparent and could have important effects on lawmaking in the field. Meanwhile, the Russian government recently announced a plan to withdraw from the International Space Station after 2024,[124] while China has been developing its own LEO satellite constellation as part of a broader effort under its most recent five-year plan.[125] Regional efforts

[119] See also JC Moltz, *The Politics of Space Security: Strategic Restraint and the Pursuit of National Interests* (Stanford, Stanford University Press, 2019) 305–35.

[120] RS Jakhu and S Freeland (eds), *McGill Manual on International Law Applicable to Military Uses of Outer Space (MILAMOS), Volume I – Rules* (Montreal, Centre for Research in Air and Space Law, 2022).

[121] Joint Communication of the European Commission and the High Representative of the Union for Foreign Affairs and Security Policy to the European Parliament and the Council, 'European Union Space Strategy for Security and Defence' (10 March 2023) JOIN(2023) 9 final.

[122] State Council Information Office of the People's Republic of China, 'China's Space Program: A 2021 Perspective' (28 January 2022).

[123] See also R Deplano, 'The Artemis Accords: Evolution or Revolution in International Space Law' (2021) 70 *International & Comparative Law Quarterly* 799; Byers and A Boley, *Who Owns Outer Space?* (n 108) 157–61.

[124] M Byers and A Boley, 'Russia often threatens to leave the International Space Station. This time could be different' *The Globe and Mail* (29 July 2022).

[125] Central Commission for Cybersecurity and Informatization (PRC), '14th Five-Year Plan for National Informatization (28 December 2021)' (edited and translated by the DigiChina Project, based at Stanford University) (24 January 2022).

at integrating space-oriented projects are underway among countries in Africa, notably with the aim to strengthen the role of the African Space Agency.[126] In the Latin American and Caribbean region, the creation of the Latin American and Caribbean Space Agency also points in the direction of a greater regional emphasis on the development of space-oriented capabilities.

The contemporary international law regime in the outer space field can best be described as a set of written and unwritten legal norms stabilised by a broad-based Cold War consensus that is coming under increasing strain through the dual trends of outer space industry commercialization and the growth in the number of space powers and space actors. To be sure, the various uses of outer space and corresponding legal issues have not all come to be regulated in the same way. For example, the allocation of orbits and frequencies in the geostationary orbit is largely regulated in the context of the International Telecommunication Union and its associated legal instruments, as well as under domestic law. Because the outer space field is one of advanced technological innovation and because key technologies in the field require extraordinary precision and skill, scientific insights and knowledge, including advances in engineering, themselves exert an independent normative pull. This is especially clear in the satellite sector, where operators have an interest in reducing damage to their space assets and limiting liability. To achieve both aims, scientific or technical solutions are usually the most immediate and effective ones. As such, engineers and scientists are, in fact, driving actors of the international lawmaking process in some areas. To be sure, that does not obviate the need for other kinds of regulation but simply factors into the broader international lawmaking landscape.

In parallel, various domestic, regional, and international bodies or groups have developed instruments meant to steer the conduct of outer space actors. Notable examples include the recently adopted COPUOS Guidelines on the 'Long-term Sustainability of Outer Space Activities' and similar documents.[127] Like the Remote Sensing Principles, these Guidelines were developed in a multilateral setting, with all attendant implications for the respective process and outcome. Others were developed in smaller fora, such as inter-state groupings of military experts seeking to develop ways of preventing or mitigating space debris. At the intersection of such high-level instruments and engineering solutions lie concrete technical standards.[128] In theory, these are meant to connect

[126] Statute of the African Space Agency, adopted by the 30th Ordinary Session of the Assembly of the African Union, held in Addis Ababa, Ethiopia on 29 January 2018.

[127] See also UNOOSA, 'Awareness-raising and capacity-building related to the implementation of the Guidelines for the Long-term Sustainability of Outer Space Activities' (LTS Guidelines) (May 2022).

[128] See eg H Stokes et al, 'Evolution of ISO's Space Debris Mitigation Standards' (2020) 7(3) *Journal of Space Safety Engineering* 325. For an analogous discussion in respect of the ICT field, see O Kanevskaia, *The Law and Practice of Global ICT Standardization* (Cambridge, Cambridge University Press, 2022).

and translate high-level principles to the level of standards that can be applied to particular problems, but that path is not always straightforward since technical standards can themselves pre-empt certain higher-level principles.

Finally, popular awareness can be an important, if under-appreciated, factor affecting the stability of the relevant norms, including those of customary international law. Take the SpaceX Tesla stunt (in which the company launched an electric car into space as a marketing campaign), which may have had a negative impact on normative expectations about the proper conduct of space operators in the sensitive outer space environment and the regulation of the New Space sector more broadly, or the movie 'Gravity' and other kinds of cultural production that advance or propagate particular views about the permissible or desirable uses of outer space. At the same time, as a bigger share of the world's population becomes aware of the fact that space technologies are key elements for navigation, information gathering about the state of the global ecosystem, Internet connectivity, and associated social functions, issues like the risks deriving from space debris will rise on the global lawmaking agenda. This also illustrates the link between technological change and customary international lawmaking, suggests why norms that are general and community-oriented tend to be more effective, and points to lawmaking factors that support the democratisation of customary international lawmaking.

4

The Treatment of the 'Other' at the Heart of Global Law

THE TREATMENT OF the 'other' (or 'others') traditionally lies at the conceptual and practical heart of international law. How customary international law developed (or did not develop) around questions like the treatment of various types of minorities or aliens (non-citizens), including merchants, refugees, stateless persons, and others offers revealing insights into processes of customary international lawmaking and their transformation over time. Indeed, international law's focus on intergroup relations runs like a red thread through the field's past and present. It remains visible in a world of increasing interconnectedness, consolidating states, and continuing global inequalities, as well as the persistence of genocidal violence, rising nationalism, and armed conflict. Beyond international law's concern with the treatment of the 'other', the very *telos* of international law can be linked to a slowly and fitfully developing 'idea of humanity', allowing human societies to transcend narrow conceptions about the extent of the in-group and its relationship to various foreigners.[1] From that angle, the encounter between members of different groups also prompted the development of inter-group law and laid the ground for the formation of new ideas about a universal humanity. Other links between international law and the treatment of the 'other' are visible in the international legal profession's 'outsider' ethos, reflected in its traditionally liminal status in the legal profession, the central role of the 'independent' judge or arbitrator in the development of international law, and the 'wandering' background of some of its principal figures (from Grotius, Kelsen, Lauterpacht, Friedman, Alexandrowicz, to many more).[2]

The treatment of the 'other' – of persons or groups considered as the 'other' by members of another group – is not a modern phenomenon. Therefore, to start this story in the nineteenth century means passing over other periods in which the treatment of aliens was associated with slavery, genocide, and

[1] See generally S Stuurman, *The Invention of Humanity* (Cambridge, Harvard University Press, 2017); SC Neff, *Justice among Nations: A History of International Law* (Cambridge, Harvard University Press, 2014) 13.

[2] See G Simmel, *The Sociology of Georg Simmel* (translated, edited, and with an introduction by KH Wolff) (Glencoe, The Free Press, 1950) 404.

exploitation, including genocides of native populations in the Americas, the enslavement of more than 15 million persons of African origin, the extraction of resources and other property from native populations in most parts of the non-European world, and the brutal rule by colonial metropolises over their subjects, a history that only the post-World War II era has begun to address. As this chapter concerns customary international lawmaking in the context of the treatment of the 'other', it concentrates on the period when customary international law was an available intellectual category in the contemporary sense. Nevertheless, the early history of inter-group relations is linked to and should be considered also in the context of contemporary discussions of public international law dealing with the treatment of the 'other'.[3]

In multiple world regions, early forms of interpolity law have addressed the treatment of traders or merchants, in addition to other privileged groups of aliens. Today, international economic law has expanded far beyond those embryonic stages. Cross-border economic relations have become – imperfectly, but still – democratised and universalised to an unprecedented degree due to growing global interconnectedness, digitalisation, and migration flows. Many of the international legal norms governing cross-border economic relations are institutionally, intellectually, and academically specialised fields of legal practice, doctrine, scholarship, and education – with all these dimensions relating to each other in a feedback loop that progressively increases the density of the respective sub-fields. While this chapter also refers to what is conventionally called international economic law, which has traditionally been linked to the 'treatment of aliens', its focus is broader. Indeed, while international law has a close connection to the regulation of cross-border economic relations, it is difficult to demarcate the latter from the regulation of migration, global public health, or transboundary environmental harm.

I. BREAKING DOWN DISCRIMINATORY RESTRICTIONS ON MIGRATION

The key to understanding migration as a phenomenon also governed by international law is the rise and consolidation of the modern state as a basic unit of international society during the nineteenth and twentieth centuries.[4] As governments consolidated their rule internally and as the idea of the state slowly spread worldwide – commonly only as a result of violent opposition to colonisation – the need to manage the movement of an ever-growing number of persons across borders became acute. However, rather than adopting a unified approach, countries largely went their own ways, opening the way to the decentralised regulation of restrictive immigration practices. The example of the

[3] See eg ET Achiume, 'Migration as Decolonization' (2019) 71 *Stanford Law Review* 1509, 1573.
[4] MH Fisher, *Migration: A World History* (Oxford, Oxford University Press, 2013) 79.

US is instructive: After more than a century of restrictive immigration practices, the US imposed 'comprehensive' origin-based immigration quotas in the 1920s.[5] While the US was a forerunner of such immigration policies, other countries adopted similar measures during this period. Practically immediately, widespread opposition emerged from the side of the origin countries affected, such as Japan. At the time, Japan had gained a relatively important stature in international affairs as a non-European colonial power during an age of imperialism.[6] The Japanese government, aware that the US government's immigration policies were shaped by popular sentiment, sought to direct its communication also towards public opinion in the US in order to shape international norms on the topic.[7] Rather than advocate complete freedom of movement, the foreign governmental officials who tried to influence US policies on immigration restrictions had more limited aims directed at non-discrimination. For instance, in a Memorandum from the Japanese Embassy in the US to the US Department of State, dated 15 January 1924, which discusses certain proposed legislative measures as well as a Supreme Court Opinion of 13 November 1922 (*Takao Ozawa vs. the United States*), Japanese diplomats clarified their country's position as aiming at a norm of non-discrimination, rather than seeking the complete liberalisation of immigration for its nationals to the US.[8] The government's Memorandum suggests that the question of discriminatory immigration policies was mostly related to Japan's desire to be treated equally as a state in international affairs. The argumentative structure adopted by Japan reflects the logic of diplomatic protection, rather than, for example, a claim based on the interests or rights of the individuals affected. Thus, Japan claimed that it did not seek to 'send [its] nationals' abroad and accepted that some of its nationals may not be 'desired' by the US. However, discriminatory treatment offended the 'proper consideration ordinarily given by one nation to the self-respect of another'. Indeed, Japan invoked the standard of 'civilisation' as an argument to contest the US government's policies. Japan's position was shaped by the relevant context, characterised by its ambiguous international status and imperial expansion. Analogous approaches are reflected in the policies of many other states, whose governments tended to push for non-discrimination abroad while introducing discriminatory immigration policies at home.

[5] See eg MM Ngai, *Impossible Subjects: Illegal Aliens and the Making of Modern America*, updated edn (Princeton, Princeton University Press, 2014) 3.

[6] See eg WG Beasley, *Japanese Imperialism, 1894–1945* (Oxford, Clarendon Press, 1987) 34; see also RH Myers and MR Peattie (eds), *The Japanese Colonial Empire, 1895–1945* (Princeton, Princeton University Press, 1984); see also SCM Paine, *The Japanese Empire: Grand Strategy from the Meiji Restoration to the Pacific War* (Cambridge, Cambridge University Press, 2017).

[7] A telegram from the US Ambassador in Japan, Bancroft, to the Secretary of State, dated 22 January 1925, reports on a speech by the Japanese Foreign Minister at the (Imperial) Diet. US Department of State, 'Papers Relating to the Foreign Relations of the United States: 1924, Volume II' (US Government Printing Office, 1939) 411 (Document 313).

[8] US Department of State, 'Papers Relating to the Foreign Relations of the United States: 1924, Volume II' (US Government Printing Office, 1939) 334–7 (Document 277).

The early twentieth century was thus a period of normative contestation regarding the imposition of discriminatory restrictions to migration. Many governments limited the perceived 'kinds' of persons that were allowed to enter, discriminating along the lines of gender, disability, ethnicity, race, origin, and class, among others. In a study of the 'rise and relative demise of ethnic selection' in the Americas, David Scott FitzGerald and David Cook-Martín note that '[t]he first independent country to restrict black immigration was the United States'.[9] Somewhat counterintuitively, although these sorts of restrictions were widespread, many governments still pushed and lobbied on behalf of migrants from their own regions.[10] As such, transnational and international efforts at repudiating and contesting discriminatory migration policies were an important factor shaping the content of national immigration laws. Like diplomatic protection, this process allowed governments to leverage their power in international affairs to prompt changes that would benefit their nationals, though indirectly also governments themselves, including their ruling elites. Of course, a government cannot leverage more power than it has or can assemble in coalition with others. This explains why smaller and less powerful governments tended to join forces to push for a norm of non-discrimination. Weaker states in the global system often, though often hypocritically, invoked anti-discrimination norms to successfully promote an end to policies of 'ethnic selection' – that is, restrictions to immigration based on race, ethnicity, origin, and similar attributes. The League of Nations was one important institutional avenue that allowed such smaller states to coordinate their efforts and disseminate their views. But efforts to address the discriminatory nature of US measures were not merely an intergovernmental affair; they were promoted by a number of private associations and activists, developed through transnational networks, and supported through domestic political, administrative, and judicial processes.[11] In short, many countries imposed discriminatory migration restrictions during this period based on factors such as race, ethnicity, origin, religion, gender, disability, illness, and other factors. While some of these policies enjoyed strong support domestically, they also faced growing internal and external opposition. It took until the post-World War II period for the last holdouts, that is, states who adopted explicitly discriminatory migration policies, to fall. However, the seeds for limiting such discriminatory restrictions, especially based on race and origin, emerged much earlier and relied on a number of mechanisms that offer key insights into customary international lawmaking.

[9] DS FitzGerald and D Cook-Martín, *Culling the Masses: The Democratic Origins of Racist Immigration Policy in the Americas* (Cambridge, Harvard University Press, 2014) 1 and 39–40.

[10] ibid, 8.

[11] See eg I Hirobe, *Japanese Pride, American Prejudice: Modifying the Exclusion Clause of the 1924 Immigration Act* (Stanford, Stanford University Press, 2001); see also I Hirobe, 'American Attitudes toward the Japanese Immigration Question, 1924–1931' (1993) 2(3) *The Journal of American-East Asian Relations* 275.

To be sure, it is hard to argue that anything resembling a non-discrimination norm concerning immigration restrictions emerged during this period, or that it was one of customary international law. Nonetheless, the normative developments of the era are instructive as they point to the drivers of normative developments that sought to limit discriminatory restrictions to migration. Several sets of factors tended to support a developing norm of non-discrimination in this context. For one, institutional factors were clearly essential in supporting a non-discrimination norm. This era saw the rise of an unprecedented experiment in international organisation through the creation of the League of Nations, whose work concerned a variety of topics in the fields of movement, migration, and social affairs. The institutional framework provided by the League of Nations and other regional and international organisations allowed less powerful actors to augment their voices and agitate for normative change. International organisations enabled especially groups of relatively less powerful states to translate their collective power into efforts at global normative change. Contingent factors, from processes of national democratisation and state-building, the intensification of communication and information dissemination, the upheavals of World War I and II, and geopolitical changes all also affected the relevant lawmaking processes.

Although the scholarly discussion on normative shifts in respect of discriminatory restrictions on migration is differentiated, many scholars in the field give pride of place to participatory aspects of domestic politics, albeit always occurring in a broader transnational domain and affected by external pressures. In many countries, popular opinion and pressure from powerful domestic constituencies long buttressed discriminatory immigration restrictions. At the same time, when popular opinion shifted, and this could occur for a variety of reasons, restrictions were lifted. While hardly inevitable, an established non-discrimination norm tended to be stickier than its opposite and could not simply be rescinded, even in the face of subsequent popular backlash. In that way, customary international law norms can be supported through domestic-level internalisation to such an extent that the very line between the domestic and international is blurred.

A non-discrimination norm is stickier than its opposite because perceptions of normative justice render it more legitimate and effective. This is especially true in the pluralistic context of international law. Countries collectively and indirectly benefit from non-discrimination norms that affect their citizens in the global arena. Moreover, the non-discrimination norm is inherently general and community-oriented. The power of 'community-oriented' norms is particularly clear in this case: As FitzGerald and Cook-Martin note, several governments advocating 'anti-racist' norms in relation to immigration restrictions did so hypocritically. Nonetheless, their efforts were effective; indeed, so effective that they would come to restrain these governments too.[12] This suggests that norms

[12] See FitzGerald and Cook-Martín, *Culling the Masses* (n 9) 30.

with a community-oriented *telos* have a reinforced normative pull, as they tend to become rooted widely and deeply in legal expectations.

Although only a trend towards a non-discrimination norm developed during this era, the stability of this emerging norm can be traced to a number of structural factors characterising the respective lawmaking processes. International lawmaking in this field was highly decentralised. There were no central legal institutions that could mediate between divergent approaches relating to the admission of foreign nationals. The only element of centralisation concerned the rise of international and regional organisations during this period. They allowed governments and various transnational actors to coordinate their efforts on the international level. They also facilitated the dissemination of information about various national immigration policies and their potential critiques, thereby supporting decentralised lawmaking processes and allowing transnational actors to become involved. This explains why lawmaking occurred relatively slowly. In terms of its temporal dimension, this field also saw a huge number of stages and interactions at all levels. More generally, domestic authorities had considerable discretion to apply the law. Incidents affected numerous individuals over long periods of time, resulting in a multi-stage lawmaking process. Finally, in terms of legalisation, the field was poorly legalised on the international level. States used diplomacy to develop international norms and standards, but there was limited appetite for formal legalisation of any sort. Interestingly, the resistance to legalisation in this field continues to this day, as visible in the context of debates over the two Global Compacts of 2018, on migration and refugees.[13]

II. ENTERING AND EXITING: THE STANDARDISATION OF CROSS-BORDER MOVEMENT

The rise of globalised capitalism, imperialism, and various forms of cross-border exchange since the nineteenth century created a dilemma for governments. On the one hand, governments tried to manage and limit migration, sometimes on the basis of explicitly or implicitly discriminatory criteria, as shown above. On the other hand, governments were faced with pressure from influential constituencies, be it businesses, workers, or consumers – increasingly operating across borders – to enable forms of migration deemed desirable. In response, rather than simply prohibiting or capping immigration, governments sought to develop ways to manage and regulate the movement of citizens and aliens across borders. Given the inherently global or at least bilateral nature of migration, international law almost inevitably entered the picture as well.

An important set of tools that governments used individually and collectively to manage cross-border movement were entry and exit formalities for

[13] See eg V Chetail, *International Migration Law* (Oxford, Oxford University Press, 2019) 293–339.

aliens and citizens, including through the standardisation of travel documents like passports and associated procedures. Today, these two phenomena are only a small part of a vast and complex normative infrastructure sustaining significant cross-border movements of goods, people, capital, and services amidst economic globalisation, but they were historically important shapers of the international law affecting the treatment of the 'other'. The law of consular relations also played a key role in undergirding the standardisation of movement. Today, consular law is codified in the Vienna Convention on Consular Relations (VCCR), which is largely seen as reflective of but also supplemented by customary international law. But the harmonisation of practices and norms in this field has a far longer history. Even rudimentary forms of consular relations meant that governments were reciprocally 'exchanging' dedicated administrative representatives that could provide some of the various consular 'functions' now listed in Article 5 of the VCCR, from issuing passports and visas, to assisting and protecting nationals, while 'furthering' various dimensions of cross-border exchange.[14] While this type of regulation may appear as just an administrative solution to the practical problems faced by nationals abroad, the infrastructure of consular relations thus established had wide-ranging normative effects.

The harmonisation of travel documentation – covering everything from visas and passports to biometric technology standards – has been closely related to the explosion of cross-border travel that occurred since the nineteenth century as well as the consolidation of the 'nation'-state. A major role in this process was played by the railroad, the most significant and widely used transportation technology that transformed societies worldwide in the nineteenth and early twentieth centuries. For instance, the period from 1870–1910 saw an explosion in railway passenger traffic in Western Europe;[15] similar developments are recorded for other world regions. Growing cross-border movement put pressure on governments to harmonise cross-border travel documentation and procedures, a seemingly mundane effort shaping a central feature of the individual experience of crossing national borders. The entrenchment of norms surrounding the crossing of borders continues to be surprisingly deep, as recent debates around the UK's withdrawal from the EU suggest, which were accompanied by the symbolic reintroduction of the former's 'blue' passport.[16]

The development of such 'border-crossing' norms was not limited to the field of consular affairs or travel documentation. In the field of railroad transport, as early as the nineteenth century, coordination between governments and railway operators ensured a certain degree of technical standardisation. At the same time, failures of coordination ensured that early decisions about gouges would haunt cross-border movement to this day. As Douglas Puffert has shown, while

[14] Vienna Convention on Consular Relations (signed 24 April 1963, entered into force 19 March 1967) 596 UNTS 261.

[15] See eg P Bagwell, *The Transport Revolution 1770–1985* (New York, Routledge, 1988) 97–8.

[16] UK Home Office, 'Iconic Blue Passports Return Next Month' (Press Release, 22 February 2020).

contingency and path-dependent divergences characterised the development of rail gauges across regions, there were also considerable cross-border standardisation efforts among the governments of various European polities.[17] Of course, there is little 'customary law' amid such practices, and they were hardly examples of international lawmaking, but the impetus towards standardisation was the result of the desire by governments and allied actors to enable and manage cross-border movement. Efforts to standardise aspects of cross-border movement can thus be seen as part of a broader set of normative practices that undergirded the management of cross-border movement, keeping in mind the various restrictions examined in the preceding section.

To understand how ever-more harmonised infrastructures and procedures of border-crossing, including travel documents, developed, it is important to look back at nineteenth-century developments. Even within Europe, cross-border travel up to the nineteenth century was a complicated affair, despite claims of a 'liberal' pre-twentieth century migration regime. Governments frequently restricted movement within their territories, empires restricted movement from colonies to the respective metropolitan territories, and a plethora of distinct procedures faced those venturing abroad. Moreover, cross-border travel was often limited to certain classes of persons. At the same time, incentives to standardise both transportation infrastructures and procedures for managing cross-border travel grew. Contemporaneous observers were aware of the links between new transportation technologies and issues of border control. For example, there are reports of thoughtful balloonists in the 1830s who made sure to pack several 'passports' that would allow them to enter whatever polity they would happen to land in.[18] Moreover, during aviation's infancy, legal scholars often had trouble even imagining how 'airspace' could be effectively patrolled, which led to suggestions for flexible entry-and-exit procedures.[19]

Although the passport and its analogues have a long history,[20] it is today perhaps the most widely known and the most universal, albeit mundane,

[17] See DJ Puffert, 'Path Dependence in Spatial Networks: The Standardization of Railway Track Gauge' (2002) 39(3) *Explorations in Economic History* 282, 288. See also DJ Puffert, *Tracks Across Continents, Paths through History: The Economic Dynamics of Standardization in Railway Gauge* (Chicago, University of Chicago Press, 2009).

[18] See E Lausanne, *The Romance of Ballooning: The Story of the Early Aeronauts* (New York, Viking Press, 1971). The episode is also recounted in JE Hodgson, *The History of Aeronautics in Great Britain: From the Earliest Times to the Latter Half of the Nineteenth Century* (Oxford, Oxford University Press, 1924) 249–55. For a brief and popular account of early travel documents, see T Topol, 'A History of Passports and their Design: Passport Function and Feature Changes through the Centuries' (June 2018) *Keesing Journal of Documents & Identity* 12.

[19] J Kohler, *Luftfahrtrecht* (Berlin, Springer, 1912) 23–4.

[20] See also DF Trask, 'A Short History of the U.S. Department of State, 1781–1981' (reprinted from the *Department of State Bulletin* of January 1981) 11 (noting that the 'Department of State did not receive exclusive authority to issue passports until 1856 … [and that they] would not be required of all travelers until 1914'); T Topol, 'A History of Passports and their Design' (n 18) 12–5.

embodiment of the 'international'.[21] A number of scholars have devoted attention to the passport, and associated policies of entry and exit control, surveillance, and efforts towards international harmonisation. They have shown the intimate connection between the passport as a means of surveillance and the constitution of the state,[22] questioned the universality of the passport by identifying disparities in the ways members of different groups benefit from the freedom of movement,[23] and studied the role of the passport from the perspective of international law.[24] At the same time, even well into the twentieth century, the passport was not a mass phenomenon in most countries. As an instrument facilitating movement and migration, the passport also instantiated status distinctions, often characterised by widely different sets of rights and opportunities for citizens as compared to aliens, in addition to other distinctions shaped by nationality, race, gender, class, disability, and other attributes. While preceded by a long process of experimentation, in its modern form the passport was a product of international standardisation, with country-specific design elements hardly masking near-global uniformity. The passport became increasingly necessary for a combination of reasons, including the very rise of the interstate system, the acceleration of cross-border movement, which lowered transportation costs, the fitful process of domestic democratisation, which both increased the demand for travel and made elites more concerned about controlling and policing their compatriots, and broader trends of bureaucratisation and the development of associated technologies. These factors also encouraged international cooperation of various sorts, which itself required cross-border travel, though mainly among legal, political, and business elites.

The second half of the nineteenth century saw a significant relaxation or abandonment of passport requirements in Europe, particularly in the period from around 1860s until the First World War – though amidst a plethora of class, gender, and race-based movement restrictions.[25] Yet World War I and its various entailments spurred both the regulation and surveillance of

[21] MB Salter, *Rights of Passage: The Passport in International Relations* (Boulder, Lynne Rienner Publishers, 2003).

[22] JC Torpey, *The Invention of the Passport: Surveillance, Citizenship and the State* (Cambridge, Cambridge University Press, 2018); see also J Caplan and J Torpey (eds), *Documenting Individual Identity: The Development of State Practices in the Modern World* (Princeton, Princeton University Press, 2001); C Robertson, *The Passport in America: The History of a Document* (Oxford, Oxford University Press, 2010); DC Turack, *The Passport in International Law* (Toronto, Lexington Books, 1972); DC Turack, 'Freedom of Movement and the International Regime of Passports' (1968) 6 *Osgoode Hall Law Journal* 230; E Higgs, *Identifying the English: A History of Personal Identification 1500 to the Present* (London, Continuum, 2011); J Doulman and D Lee, *Every Assistance & Protection: A History of the Australian Passport* (Sydney, Federation Press, 2008).

[23] Salter, *Rights of Passage* (n 21).

[24] DC Turack, *The Passport in International Law* (n 22) 259.

[25] M Lloyd, *The Passport: The History of Man's Most Travelled Document* (Gloucestershire, Sutton Publishing, 2003) 115–20.

international travel and international agreements on the issue. The Interwar period saw initiatives aimed at standardising procedures of emigration and immigration. The League of Nations played a key role in this respect, convening the influential 'International Conference on Passports, Customs Formalities and Through Tickets' in 1920 in Paris.[26] The French government had initiated it through what the League of Nations later described as a 'semi-official' body 'for the study of the freedom of Communications and Transit' in 1919.[27] That body, which provisionally met in October 1919, was then integrated into the League of Nations, and composed of 'experts' from mostly European countries, as well as China, Japan, and Uruguay.[28] Originally, the 'Provisional Committee of Communications and Transit' had been directed, among others, to find a way for the world to return to pre-World War I conditions. Thus, the official account of the origins of the International Conference notes that the League of Nations had requested it 'to lay before it urgent propositions in order to remedy, as soon as possible, a state of affairs hampering personal relations between the nationals of different States and seriously delaying a return to normal and commercial conditions necessary for the economic restoration of the world'.[29] These remedies were motivated by 'the difficulties existing at present for the transport of travelers, due chiefly to passport and customs formalities, and to the impossibility which too often exists of obtaining through tickets'.[30] However, the conference's Final Resolution, adopted on 21 October 1920, already displayed a marked change in direction, emphasising that 'the legitimate concern of every Government for the safeguarding of its security and right, prohibits, for the time being, the total abolition of restrictions and that complete return to pre-war conditions which the Conference hopes, nevertheless, to see gradually re-established in the near future'.[31] In addition to influencing non-parties, subsequent treaties dealing with the matter of the passport referred explicitly to the conference's outcomes (for example, the 'Agreement concerning Passports and Visas' of 1922). Moreover, the process of standardisation of travel documents did not end with the League of Nations but was carried forward by a variety of other international organisations in subsequent decades.

Sara Kalm, who has examined the link between consolidating territorial states and the standardisation of passport controls,[32] suggests that standardisation, in fact, democratised movement while also making it more bureaucratised since earlier 'freedoms' of movement had been restricted to

[26] ibid, 130.

[27] 'Provisional Committee of Communications and Transit' (Nov./Dec. 1920) 1(8) *League of Nations O.J.* 52.

[28] ibid, 52.

[29] ibid, 53.

[30] ibid.

[31] ibid, 58.

[32] S Kalm, 'Standardizing Movements: The International Passport Conferences of the 1920s' (2017) 8 *STANCE Working Papers Series* 1.

particular socio-economic and ethnic groups.[33] Examining the International Passport Conferences that formed a central part of the League of Nations' early efforts at international regulation, as well as related diplomatic exchanges during the 1920s, Kalm focuses on the normative effect of standardisation itself. According to Kalm, the standardisation of passports was at once a technical project and a means of 'normaliz[ing] the state system' that was consolidating during the post-World War I period.[34] Kalm illustrates the radical shift in governments' official positions to the control of international travellers: While many countries publicly called for an alleged 'return' to pre-World War I 'liberalism', the political mood quickly shifted so that by the mid-1920s only a few governments called for the abolition of passports.[35] The international deliberations on the regulation of entry and exit formalities also revealed the general point noted above: The relevant lawmaking processes and the substantive outcomes were strongly affected by the geographical, social, and geopolitical context affecting the issue.[36]

In short, notwithstanding the slow emergence of a norm proscribing discriminatory restrictions to immigration during this period, governments were standardising entry and exit procedures in various ways, using international organisations and conferences as fora in which to develop standards and templates. Technical forms of standardisation and coordination were part of this larger process of both enabling and managing movement and migration during an age of growing interconnectedness. The passport was just one invention that was standardised, internationalised, and normalised through a process of international lawmaking. But to say that the passport was an 'invention' does not mean it appeared on a normative blank slate. Passport-like documents had been connected to identity and movement in the inter-state system since at least the late eighteenth century. In the subsequent century, many countries adopted forms of identification documentation and control to surveil the movement of persons across borders. These precedents partly explain why international lawmaking efforts were so effective – they grew in the soil of existing expectations about movement, allegiance, and governmental power that had been forming in a decentralised fashion for generations.

For all intents and purposes, it became a customary international law norm that a state shall establish a procedure of entry and exit in subsequent decades.

[33] ibid, 25–6. In this context, Kalm also refers to League of Nations, Passport Conference held at Geneva from May 12th to 18th, 1926, League of Nations Doc. C.423.M.156.1926.VIII (6 July 1926) 44.

[34] Kalm, 'Standardizing Movements' (n 32) 32; see also P Becker, 'Remaking Mobility: International Conferences and the Emergence of the Modern Passport System' in P Becker and N Wheatley, *Remaking Central Europe the League of Nations and the Former Habsburg Lands* (Oxford, Oxford University Press, 2020) 193.

[35] ibid.

[36] See eg the exchange between the Hungarian and the Japanese delegates at the 1926 Conference in League of Nations, 'Passport Conference held at Geneva from May 12th to 18th, 1926', League of Nations Doc. C.423.M.156.1926.VIII (6 July 1926) 14.

This type of norm was essentially midway between a deeply entrenched background custom and one replicated by analogy from the basic norm of state sovereignty and supported by millions of everyday interactions by citizens of various classes and origins over a long period of time. As in the case of limits to restrictions on migration based on discriminatory criteria, the lawmaking processes were essentially pluralistic, decentralised, and not legalised at all, at least on the international level. International organisations played a key role as information conduits and as fora allowing states to coordinate their efforts. Although the standardisation of travel documentation and entry and exit procedures may appear unglamorous and mundane, important distributional issues were at play. After all, while all states benefited from the standardisation of passports and entry and exit procedures, states that sought to control immigration were most interested in consolidating control over their borders. As a result, it is not surprising that this system of cross-border control emerged just as the European interstate system was universalising, with leading European governments still in firm control of their colonial empires. Despite this distributional aspect, the generality and basic community orientation of the relevant set of norms, in addition to important network effects caused by the standardisation of travel documents, helped entrench the relevant norms.

III. INTERNATIONAL MINORITIES' RIGHTS: A FAILED PRECURSOR OF THE HUMAN RIGHTS MOVEMENT?

During the crystallisation of the European interstate system following the Reformation, the protection of some religious minorities was a central element of emerging international legal arrangements.[37] The Congress of Vienna saw the inclusion of specific minority-related provisions into the Congress' Final Act.[38] During the nineteenth century, as European states consolidated and slowly morphed into modern states, minorities felt increasing pressure to assimilate. As new 'nations' were carved onto heterogeneous populations in Europe, the protection of minorities became an issue of concern, notably for minorities themselves and their advocates. However, despite the efforts of transnationally operating activists before and after 1900 and some backing by the era's dominant powers, the persecution of minorities by imperial powers continued. As the genocide of the Herero and Nama at the hands of German colonial forces showed, the mistreatment of the 'other' was also closely related to colonialism. Moreover, as the Armenian genocide proved, transnational efforts at changing

[37] See eg J Jackson-Preece, *National Minorities and the European Nation-States System* (Oxford, Oxford University Press, 1999) 54–66; see also H Weber, 'Der Minderheitenschutz des Völkerbundes' in M Mohr (ed), *Friedenssichernde Aspekte des Minderheitenschutzes in der Ära des Völkerbundes und der Vereinten Nationen in Europa* (Berlin, Springer, 1996).

[38] See eg S Bartsch, *Minderheitenschutz in der Internationalen Politik* (Opladen, Westdeutscher Verlag, 1995) 63–5.

international norms were insufficient to affect the conduct of states towards their most vulnerable populations.[39] This process accelerated through World War I and its aftermath, which saw the creation of many new nation-states and minorities in Europe and further promoted the universalisation of the state.[40]

The post-World War I minorities regime was enabled by the confluence of massively increasing risks to minorities in the wake of imperial disintegration and the window of opportunity created for the victors to impose a legal regime on the vanquished.[41] One important characteristic of the League of Nations minorities regime was a network of treaties and unilateral commitments that included a series of generic provisions about standards for the treatment of minorities that were essentially copied across treaties in respect of the various, mostly Central and Eastern European, states that were bound by them.[42] In contrast to other examples of networks of similarly worded treaty provisions (for example, in the bilateral investment treaty context), these minority treaties or instruments were applied selectively. Nonetheless, the standardisation of minority protection provisions expressed a growing expectation about what customary international law required of states in respect of 'their' minorities. Moreover, while these minority provisions were applied selectively, the victorious powers made efforts to present their demands as expressions of established practices reflecting centuries of European diplomatic precedent.[43] As Tarcisio Gazzini has shown, the protection obligations under the Interwar minorities regime were the first example of an *erga omnes* type of legal obligation, a legal construction developed chiefly by the international judiciary.[44] But the experience of Jewish and other victims of Nazi rule show that claims about the customary international law nature of the relevant legal norms remained aspirational.[45]

[39] See eg ED Weitz, *A World Divided: The Global Struggle for Human Rights in the Age of Nation-States* (Princeton, Princeton University Press, 2019).

[40] CS Maier, 'Leviathan 2.0' in ES Rosenberg (ed), *A World Connecting*, Volume 5 of A Iriye and J Osterhammel (general editors), *A History of the World* (Cambridge, Belknap Press, 2013) 29, 34.

[41] See Bartsch, *Minderheitenschutz in der Internationalen Politik* (n 38) 65.

[42] See eg P Kovács, 'The Protection of Minorities under the Auspices of the League of Nations' in D Shelton (ed), *The Oxford Handbook of International Human Rights Law* (Oxford, Oxford University Press, 2013) 327 (citing Clémenceau's letter to Paderewski). See, for a compilation, League of Nations, 'Protection of Linguistic, Racial and Religious Minorities by the League of Nations: Provisions Contained in the Various International Instruments at Present in Force', LoN Doc I.B.2. (1927).

[43] See Kovács, 'The Protection of Minorities under the Auspices of the League of Nations' (n 42) 327.

[44] T Gazzini, 'The Protection of Minorities at the Origins of the Notion of Erga Omnes Obligations' in A Ziegler and J Küffer (eds), *Les minorités et le Droit / Minorities and the Law: Mélanges en l'honneur du Professeur Barbara Wilson* (Zurich, Schulthess Verlag, 2016) 13, 18.

[45] One notable example concerns unpublished parts of the Annex to James G. McDonald's 1935 letter of resignation as High Commissioner for Refugees (Jewish and Other) Coming from Germany. These parts were later published in OI Janowsky and MM Fagen, *International Aspects of German Racial Policies* (New York, Oxford University Press, 1937) 30–2. On the history of the drafting of McDonald's letter, see MN Penkower, 'Honorable Failures Against Nazi Germany: McDonald's Letter of Resignation and the Petition in its Support' (2010) 30(3) *Modern Judaism* 247.

The second – and of course related – key characteristic of the post-World War I minorities regime was its institutional and procedural infrastructure, built around the League of Nations, its Assembly, Council, and Secretariat,[46] which together and in different ways exemplified the twentieth-century rise of international organisations and an international civil service.[47] Although the League of Nations Covenant did not refer to minorities, the various post-World War I minorities treaties established that their protection was an obligation of 'international concern' and placed them under its 'guarantee', as an influential report on this topic noted.[48] The institutional compromise reached after World War I was relatively modest, but marked an important shift from how minority issues had been managed by European powers since the preceding century.[49] The fact that the League of Nations was itself not a party or otherwise formally bound to most of the relevant instruments[50] and the 'general' nature of their substantive content suggests that the relevant obligations were viewed as more than simply treaty-based, or bilateral, ones. Moreover, the procedural and institutional involvement of the League of Nations in this area developed over several years.[51] Nonetheless, by placing its institutional support at the disposal of the minorities regime, the League of Nations' work in the field both reinforced and further developed the relevant norms.

Although the legal regime that developed in this field was highly state-driven, it represented an important innovation by internationalising minority issues through the option of a direct complaints procedure not requiring the exhaustion

[46] See also R Veatch, 'Minorities and the League of Nations' in United Nations Library (ed), *The League of Nations in Retrospect / La Société des Nations: rétrospective* (Berlin, Walter de Gruyter, 1983) 369, 375.

[47] S Pedersen, *The Guardians: The League of Nations and the Crisis of Empire* (Oxford, Oxford University Press, 2015) 5–7; see also D Gorman, *The Emergence of International Society in the 1920s* (Cambridge, Cambridge University Press, 2012) 52–81; D Hammarskjöld, *The International Civil Servant in Law and in Fact: Lecture delivered to Congregation at Oxford University 30 May 1961* (Oxford, Clarendon Press, 1961) 329–30; for a contemporary legal analysis of the international civil service, see G Ullrich, *The Law of the International Civil Service: Institutional Law and Practice in International Organisations* (Berlin, Duncker & Humblot, 2018).

[48] The so-called Tittoni report, authored by the Italian diplomat and later Mussolini-supporter Tommaso Tittoni. See League of Nations, 'Procès-verbal of the Tenth Session of the Council Held in Burssels, 20th to 28th October, 1920' (Nov./Dec. 1920) 1(8) *League of Nations O. J.* 8.

[49] On the drafting history, see L Castellanos-Jankiewicz, 'Negotiating Equality: Minority Protection in the Versailles Settlement' in M Erpelding, B Hess, and H Ruiz Fabri (eds), *Peace Through Law: The Versailles Peace Treaty and Dispute Settlement After World War I* (Baden Baden, Nomos, 2019) 123, 149–53.

[50] P de Azcarate, *League of Nations and National Minorities: An Experiment* (translated by EE Brooke) (Washington, D.C., Carnegie Endowment for International Peace, 1945) 94.

[51] For a detailed account of the development of this system, see C Raitz von Frentz, *Lesson Forgotten: Minority Protection Under the League of Nations: The Case of the German Minority in Poland, 1920–1934* (Münster, Lit-Verlag, 1999); see also D Macfadyen et al, *Eric Drummond and his Legacies: The League of Nations and the Beginnings of Global Governance* (Cham, Palgrave Macmillan, 2019) 242; B Heyking, 'The International Protection of Minorities. The Achilles' Heel of the League of Nations' (1927) 13 *Transactions of the Grotius Society* 31; JS Roucek, 'Procedure in Minorities Complaints' (1929) 23 (3) *The American Journal of International Law* 538.

of local remedies and managed through the filter of a committee composed of three members of the League's Council and supported by the Minorities Section of the Secretariat of the League of Nations.[52] A total of 473 petitions were dealt with by the League of Nations between 1928 and 1938.[53] This function was supplemented by the role of the Permanent Court of International Justice (PCIJ), an institution formally separate from the League but granted contentious, advisory, and even appellate jurisdiction under Article 14 of the League of Nations Covenant and other agreements.[54] During its tenure, the Court rendered a series of judgments and advisory opinions dealing with the treatment of minorities.[55]

The case concerning minority schools in Albania offers an illustration of both dimensions of the novelty introduced by the Interwar minorities regime. In 1921, Albania had been admitted to the League of Nations on the condition of its adherence to the substantive 'principles of the Minorities Treaties', with some variations that made Albania's commitment appear more stringent.[56] When Albania attempted to restrict minority schooling by banning private schools,[57] it faced the League of Nations' complaints procedure and ultimately a request by the Council for an advisory opinion from the PCIJ.[58] The advisory opinion concerned the extent to which an Albanian constitutional amendment was compatible with its obligations under the 'Albanian Declaration' of 1921. The Court emphasised that despite some differences, the Albanian Declaration essentially reflected 'the analogous régime of the protection of minorities'.[59] It went on to essentially develop – also by reference to its earlier jurisprudence – basic principles of minority law.[60] Specifically, the Court emphasised the implications of equality to be guaranteed both 'in law and in fact'.[61] The Court's findings influenced the field of human rights far into the post-World War II period.[62] It essentially developed a norm judicially that would become deeply entrenched following many decades of application. Furthermore, the Court also

[52] Macfadyen et al, *Eric Drummond and his Legacies* (n 51) 135–6.

[53] Bartsch, *Minderheitenschutz in der Internationalen Politik* (n 38) 103.

[54] See Article 14 of the League of Nations Covenant. On the PCIJ's appellate jurisdiction, see 'International Agreements Regarding the Financial Obligations of Hungary Resulting from the Treaty of Trianon' (1931) 25(1) *The American Journal of International Law* 19, 28 (see Article 10 of the Agreement No II). See eg *The Pajzs, Csáky, Esterházy Case (Hungary v Yugoslavia)* (Judgment) PCIJ Series A/B No 68; *Peter Pázmány University v State of Czechoslovakia* (Merits) PCIJ Series A/B No 61; see also J Crawford, 'Continuity and Discontinuity in International Dispute Settlement: An Inaugural Lecture' (2010) 1(1) *Journal of International Dispute Settlement* 3, 15.

[55] For a list, see Kovács, 'The Protection of Minorities under the Auspices of the League of Nations' (n 42) 330 (footnotes 22 to 25).

[56] *Minority Schools in Albania* (Advisory Opinion) [6 April 1935] PCIJ, Series A/B No. 64, 3, 9.

[57] ibid, 13–4.

[58] ibid, 14.

[59] ibid, 17.

[60] ibid.

[61] ibid, 19.

[62] For a domestic-level parallel see eg RM Cover, 'The Origins of Judicial Activism in the Protection of Minorities' (1982) 91(7) *The Yale Law Journal* 1287.

made an important contribution to international legal doctrine by developing the basis of the idea of *erga omnes* obligations.[63] It is, of course, problematic to speak of anything like customary international law norms in the conventional sense in this context. After all, the Court was interpreting a particular national declaration in light of a broader regional regime established by a network of treaties with identical provisions (though constituting a 'régime', in the words of the Court).

Not only was the League of Nations minorities regime an explicitly treaty-based one, but it was also hardly general since it applied mainly in Europe and in a differentiated way even there.[64] However, the introduction of a norm whose ambit is initially limited can still be significant, especially if it is replicated or becomes grafted onto a new legal regime subsequently. This is because normative expectations are shaped both by experiences and concrete needs. This was the case for the minorities regime of the League of Nations in two respects. First, basic norms about the treatment of 'aliens' (more generally, including minorities) had long taken root in international law, to some extent as customary law norms, even if they may initially have been entirely of judicial origin. Second, while the Interwar minorities regime as such collapsed, the concerns that motivated it and the lessons learned did not disappear but were incorporated into the post-World War II human rights regime.[65] This process was mediated through individuals, groups, and organisations that tended to operate cross-substantively and helped carry ideas and practices across different contexts, both in space and in time.

In the course of the nineteenth and twentieth centuries, elites and powerful international institutions became persuaded that minorities themselves (rather than their treatment) were a 'problem' to be solved, leading to massive efforts at forced population transfers that would affect over ten million people just on the European continent.[66] The practice of so-called population 'transfers' or 'exchanges' offers another revealing insight into an important type of customary international lawmaking. Such population transfers became a widely used policy during the twentieth century meant to further homogenise populations and thus address the minority 'problem'. Although such practices also tried to address some concerns of minority populations, they were in direct tension with several norms developing at the time, including those proscribing the expulsion of aliens and denials of justice, norms prescribing respect for minority rights, as well as the basic tenets of refugee protection. And yet, population exchanges were not only tolerated but generally seen as an accepted practice throughout the

[63] See Gazzini, 'The Protection of Minorities at the Origins of the Notion of Erga Omnes Obligations' (n 44) 18.

[64] See eg LB Sohn, 'The New International Law: Protection of the Rights of Individuals Rather Than States' (1982) 32 *American University Law Review* 1, 6 (see footnote 16).

[65] Minorities issues continued to raise separate issues of international law also after World War II. See eg MG Frank, *Making Minorities History: Population Transfer in Twentieth-Century Europe* (Oxford, Oxford University Press, 2017) 311–55.

[66] ibid, 2.

pre-World War II period and to some extent beyond.[67] While the idea and policy of population transfers would influence decision-makers up to the present, the approach was traditionally the product either of bilateral negotiation or so-called great power decision-making. This is understandable since population exchanges constituted large-scale attempts at social engineering, requiring significant political support.[68] As Howard Adelman and Elazar Barkan note, decision-making about minority or refugee 'problems' were, especially in the first half of the twentieth century, consistently marked by a disregard or lack of consideration for those affected.[69] That context greatly influenced the ways in which the applicable norms concerning the desirability and indeed acceptability of population exchanges were formed, sustained, and could change.

While norms about population 'exchanges' were part of a larger normative universe concerning the situation of minorities and refugees, it is notable that shared assumptions about the acceptability of population exchanges shifted rapidly depending on the context since they were based on a temporary consensus among the relevant powers. As the historical record suggests, while the practice of population transfers was accepted by key actors during this period, this permissive norm was weakly embedded and, as a result, highly unstable. This is illustrated persuasively by Frank in a study of notable episodes of population transfers concerning minorities in the period from 1913 to 1948.[70] Adelman and Barkan also point to a radical shift in the relevant norms since the 1950s.[71] In short, normative expectations surrounding population transfers were highly unstable. Moreover, being poorly legalised and institutionalised while having little support from actors on the ground, population exchanges were governed by a highly dynamic lawmaking process.

The Interwar minorities regime also illustrates how different international lawmaking processes can affect each other. As noted, key features of the contemporary international human rights regime, as a set of ideas and practices, can be traced to the League of Nations minorities regime. The Interwar experience introduced a set of legal norms and institutional practices that became deeply entrenched through a range of decentralised practices and other factors that supported their continuity in the post-World War II period. Generally, the Interwar minorities regime was innovative by imposing duties on states for the treatment of their nationals and created an international system of supervision that was unprecedented. The protection of minorities was somewhat legalised, in contrast to some of the other fields examined here. The presence of a relatively active set of third-party dispute settlement mechanisms, including

[67] H Adelman and E Barkan, *No Return, No Refuge: Rites and Rights in Minority Repatriation* (New York, Columbia University Press, 2011) 24.
[68] ibid, 50.
[69] ibid, 24–46 (focusing on the period before 1945).
[70] See Frank, *Making Minorities History* (n 65) 8–10 (see generally Chapters 4 to 9).
[71] Adelman and Barkan, *No Return, No Refuge* (n 67) 52.

the role of the PCIJ, helped develop norms that would later permeate many aspects of international human rights law. Moreover, analogously to the case of the international human rights movement that blossomed since the 1960s, the rights of minorities were promoted by groups of transnational activists since at least the nineteenth century, albeit often with little success.

To be sure, the protection of minorities themselves during the first half of the twentieth century and beyond was largely a failure. Moreover, while innovative and relatively legalised, the Interwar minorities regime was not detached from the logic of diplomatic protection. Particular states often advocated most vocally for the protection of those minorities they claimed an affiliation with. Minorities without a protecting state had a far harder time shaping international lawmaking. Indeed, in situations where minorities made up a significant portion of a state's population, dissolution, the creation of a new state, or population transfers were seen as viable avenues to protect minorities. As noted, even the application of practices like population transfers was, to some extent, law-governed. There are multiple reasons why no strong norms of minority protection emerged during this period. A major one is that the regime was too particularistic. In contrast to the human rights regime of the post-World War II period, the minorities regime was selectively applied mainly to Central and Eastern European countries. This made it difficult to entrench norms domestically and to sustain norms in an environment of heightened nationalism and in the face of shifts in the balance of power. The selective application of minority protection therefore undermined the stability of the regime and stymied the development of corresponding customary international law norms.

All in all, despite these weaknesses, and despite being unable to withstand the shock of Nazi violence and World War II, the Interwar minorities regime offers revealing insights into customary international lawmaking processes and resulting norms, displaying examples of dynamic forms of custom, emerging forms of entrenched background custom, analogical custom, and pure judicial custom. In short, the whole international lawmaking palette is revealed, with enduring lessons for twenty-first-century international lawmaking given the important continuities connecting the League of Nations and the PCIJ to their successors.

IV. THE RIGHTS OF STATELESS PERSONS AND REFUGEES

Refugee law represents the most striking anomaly in the state-based international legal order and has been the subject of extensive study by political scientists, economists, sociologists, legal scholars, and others.[72] I rely on some of this work but try to link it to broader questions about customary international lawmaking.

[72] See eg CM Skran, *Refugees in Inter-War Europe: The Emergence of a Regime* (Oxford, Clarendon Press, 1995); P Orchard, *A Right to Flee: Refugees, States, and the Construction of International*

Before coming to the construction of the post-World War I refugee regime itself, it is worth emphasising that despite its innovativeness, it drew on prior normative expectations concerning the treatment of aliens and minorities that had been formulated and reflected in a range of social practices. These precedents were created and reinforced at the domestic and bilateral levels as well as on the international plane,[73] where types of alien-related and humanitarian norms had developed for decades, and in some cases, centuries. They were promulgated in treaties and other international instruments, expert reports, codifications, domestic court decisions, and featured in public debates. In many cases, these normative expectations were also reflected in popular culture, literature, and popular opinion.

Two factors contributed to bringing the refugee issue to the forefront of the international agenda in the 1920s and prompting specific forms of transnational action and international lawmaking. The first was the consolidation and progressively increasing capacities of territorial nation-states, at least in Europe but also in the Americas.[74] This development accelerated as new states were created in Eastern Europe and Western Asia in the wake of World War I and continued throughout the wave of post-World War II decolonisation. The corollary of this process of 'national' consolidation was practical and activist pressure calling for a humanitarian exception to this very same statism. This call enjoyed significant support among civil society organisations and was amplified through a network of transnational activists. But it also had the ear of governments, whose leaders and officials understood that accepting a limited degree of refugee protection would stabilise and even legitimise their own governments and the consolidating interstate system built around the idea and practice of state sovereignty.[75] As a result, several scholars have argued that the very concept of the refugee cannot be divorced from this period's rise of the state in international affairs.[76] Indeed, Phil Orchard has pointed to the

Cooperation (Cambridge, Cambridge University Press, 2014) 14; R Bubb, M Kremer, and D Levine, 'The Economics of International Refugee Law' (2011) 40 *Journal of Legal Studies* 367; TJ Hatton, 'Asylum Migration to the Developed World: Persecution, Incentives, and Policy' (2020) 34(1) *The Journal of Economic Perspectives* 75; see also A Hammerstad, *The Rise and Decline of a Global Security Actor: UNHCR, Refugee Protection, and Security* (Oxford, Oxford University Press, 2014); A Betts, G Loescher, and J Milner (eds), *The United Nations High Commissioner for Refugees (UNHCR): The Politics and Practice of Refugee Protection*, 2nd edn (New York, Routledge, 2013); G Loescher, *The UNHCR and World Politics: A Perilious Path* (Oxford, Oxford University Press, 2001); A Betts, 'International Relations and Forced Migration' in E Fiddian-Qasmiyeh et al (eds), *The Oxford Handbook of Refugee and Forced Migration Studies* (Oxford, Oxford University Press, 2014) 60; A Betts and G Loescher (eds), *Refugees in International Relations* (Oxford, Oxford University Press, 2010).

[73] Orchard, *A Right to Flee* (n 72) 5.

[74] See MN Barnett, 'Refugees and Humanitarianism' in E Fiddian-Qasmiyeh et al (eds), *The Oxford Handbook of Refugee and Forced Migration Studies* (Oxford, Oxford University Press, 2014) 241, 245.

[75] ibid, 245–6.

[76] S Behrman, *Law and Asylum: Space, Subject, Resistance* (Abingdon, Routledge, 2018) 72. See also Barnett, 'Refugees and Humanitarianism' (n 74) 245.

functional role of the refugee category, serving the international system as a 'release valve'.[77]

The second triggering factor for the development of the refugee regime at this time was practical. The plight of millions of Russians and Armenians during and in the aftermath of World War I led millions of refugees to try and spill across, often shifting, borders.[78] The enormous and sudden rise of the refugee population in Europe put pressure on the era's dominant powers to accept or at least manage the flow of refugees.[79] Earlier forms of displacement, because of their lesser scope and more porous borders, could have been ignored or addressed in other ways – for example, locally or bilaterally. However, the unprecedented displacements that occurred during the first decades of the twentieth century prompted concerted international action to protect refugees. The resulting solutions turned out to be highly innovative and created institutions and norms that would be carried forward well into the post-World War II period.[80]

As noted, while the chief governmental decision-makers of the era may have been motivated by political and security considerations, the developing refugee regime drew on deeper and wider legal and moral concerns that were voiced and disseminated by a coterie of transnationally operating activists at the time.[81] Notably, the treatment of aliens was already a recognised field of international law that had solidified and shaped the expectations of officials, merchants, scholars, and others groups for generations. At the same time, transnational social movements had long invoked humanitarian arguments for the protection of various minorities. Nationalism and processes of democratisation across many domestic societies during this era further created pressure on governments to restrict migration and take responsibility for managing cross-border movement. When all these strands coalesced in the particular context of the 1920s just described, the resulting regime would go considerably beyond the simple security concerns of the chief actors among the era's dominant powers. It became legally entrenched on the global level and difficult to unsettle even when the interests of particular governments changed.[82]

In response to the massive swell of Russian refugees following the Russian Revolution and World War I and its aftermath, an international regime was improvised very rapidly in the early 1920s. While unprecedented as such, it drew on layers of existing normative expectations concerning the protection of aliens and minorities which were brought together by individuals who took action and, in effect, created the relevant regime. Without several key

[77] Orchard, *A Right to Flee* (n 72) 4–5.

[78] M Foster and H Lambert, *International Refugee Law and the Protection of Stateless Persons* (Oxford, Oxford University Press, 2019) 19–20.

[79] See eg K Knox and T Kushner, *Refugees in an Age of Genocide: Global, National and Local Perspectives during the Twentieth Century* (New York, Routledge, 1999) 43.

[80] ibid, 9. See also Barnett, 'Refugees and Humanitarianism' (n 74) 245–6.

[81] ibid, 245.

[82] See generally Orchard, *A Right to Flee* (n 72) 4–5.

individuals, the result would likely have turned out very differently. Initially managed by the enterprising explorer and activist Fritjof Nansen, the regime was built in several stages amid a close relationship between the ICRC, the League of Nations system, a number of governments, and the International Labor Organization.[83] As Atle Grahl-Madsen observed more than half a century ago, the very development of the regime suggests that the normative framework supporting refugee protection during this period had already been based also on customary international law.[84]

One notable feature of the Interwar refugee regime was its reliance on a relatively small number of people who operated a global network on what has been described as a 'shoestring budget'.[85] More generally, the quick creation of an institutional infrastructure applying a rapidly developing international refugee law, the relatively small number of persons involved in its creation, and its lasting normative impact raise many questions about processes of international lawmaking. Of the several individuals who played leading roles as both advocates and shapers of the refugee regime that developed in the League of Nations context, Gustave Ador and Fritjof Nansen stand out. Gustave Ador, a Swiss lawyer and prominent politician with a formidable international network, served as president of the ICRC between 1910 and 1928 and played a key role in the early history of international refugee law and policy. In 1921, Ador publicly called on the Council of the League of Nations to take action, specifically asking the League to appoint a special 'Commissioner for the Russian refugees'.[86] Ador's letter, as well as an attached memorandum, were published in the League of Nations Official Journal in full in 1921, as annexes to a Memorandum by the League's Secretary-General of 16 March 1921, which explicitly called on the League's Council to act.[87] Ador's letter of 20 February 1921, as well as the attached memorandum, were a carefully

[83] See A Grahl-Madsen, 'The League of Nations and the Refugees' in United Nations Library (ed), *The League of Nations in Retrospect* (n 46) 358. See also LW Holborn, 'The League of Nations and the Refugee Problem' (1939) 203 *The Annals of the American Academy of Political and Social Science* 124–35; G Jaeger, 'On the History of the International Protection of Refugees' (2001) 83 (843) *RICR/IRRC* 727, 729; United Nations Office at Geneva (Library Archives), 'Refugees Mixed Archival Group (Nansen Fonds)' (information on the 'Administration History'); H Sallinen, *Intergovernmental Advocates of Refugees: The Refugee Policy of the League of Nations and the International Labour Organization in the 1920s and 1930s* (Dissertation, University of Helsinki, 2013) 107.

[84] See eg A Grahl-Madsen, 'The European Tradition of Asylum and the Development of Refugee Law' (1966) 3(3) *Journal of Peace Research* 278, 281.

[85] A Grahl-Madsen, 'The League of Nations and the Refugees' (n 83) 363.

[86] G Loescher, *Refugees and the Asylum Dilemma in the West* (University Park, Pennsylvania State University Press, 1992) 24; see also A Grahl-Madsen, *The Land Beyond: Collected Essays on Refugee Law and Policy* (edited by P Macalister-Smith and G Alfredsson) (Leiden, Brill Nijhoff, 2001) 125–37; GA Goodwin-Gill, 'International Refugee Law: Where it Comes From, and Where It's Going …' (2017) 45 *International Journal of Legal Information* 24; Orchard, *A Right to Flee* (n 72) 104–39.

[87] 'The Question of the Russian Refugees' (March/April 1921) 2(2) *League of Nations O.J.* 225, 227.

planned exercise in agenda-setting – as the letter itself and other contemporaneous sources indicate.

At the time, indeed, since April 1920, Fritjof Nansen had already served as the League's 'High Commissioner for the Repatriation of Prisoners-of-War'.[88] A range of factors played into the quick agreement within the League of Nations that Nansen was the right person for the job.[89] Nansen's effectiveness seems in large part to have derived from his demonstrated specialisation and independence, eschewing any statements or actions that may have suggested political bias, while also rejecting accusations of political bias when he adopted unpopular views that, in his view, served the humanitarian cause.[90] Notably, Nansen refused to be drawn into related political disputes between the emerging Soviet Union and other countries.[91] Many of Nansen's initiatives appear in retrospect as precursors of later institutions, even if many of them were launched in an informal fashion, such as the 'Nansen passport', based on what was called an 'arrangement' and adopted at an international conference on 5 July 1922.[92] Further initiatives and extensions of the arrangement followed in subsequent years, including the 'Plan for the Issue of a Certificate of Identity to Armenian Refugees'.[93] Was the 'arrangement' a treaty, and does it matter?[94]

[88] See M Housden, *The League of Nations and the Organisation of Peace* (New York, Routledge, 2012) 59–72; see also Grahl-Madsen, *The Land Beyond* (n 86) 127.

[89] M Fosse and J Fox, *Nansen: Explorer and Humanitarian* (Lanham, Rowman & Littlefield, 2016) 35–7.

[90] B Cabanes, *The Great War and the Origins of Humanitarianism, 1918–1924* (Cambridge, Cambridge University Press, 2014) 153–6; Grahl-Madsen, *The Land Beyond* (n 86) 127–8; see also V Chetail, 'Fridtjof Nansen and the International Protection of Refugees: An Introduction' (2003) 22 *Refugee Survey Quarterly* 1; FP Walters, *A History of the League of Nations* (2 Volumes) (New York, Oxford University Press, 1952); B Blukacz-Louisfert, 'The Nansen Archival Collection at the Library of the United Nations Office at Geneva' (2003) 22(1) *Refugee Survey Quarterly* 52; IC Jackson, 'Dr. Fridtjof Nansen: A Pioneer in the International Protection of Refugees' (2003) 22(1) *Refugee Survey Quarterly* 7.

[91] MR Marrus, *The Unwanted: European Refugees in the Twentieth Century*, 2nd edn (Philadelphia, Temple University Press, 2002) 90–1.

[92] See MR Alborzi, *Evaluating the Effectiveness of International Refugee Law: The Protection of Iraqi Refugees* (Leiden, Martinus Nijhoff, 2006) 160–1; see also League of Nations, 'Arrangement with respect to the issue of certificates of identity to Russian Refugees, 5 July 1922' LNTS Vol XIII, No 355 (1922) 237; League of Nations, 'Arrangement Relating to the Legal Status of Russian and Armenian Refugees, 30 June 1928' LNTS Vol LXXXIX, No 2005 (1929) 53; O Hieronymi, 'The Nansen Passport: A Tool of Freedom of Movement and of Protection' (2003) 22(1) *Refugee Survey Quarterly* 36; 'Conference on the Question of the Russian Refugees' (2003) 22(1) *Refugee Survey Quarterly* 74.

[93] CM Skran and E Easton-Calabria, 'Historical Development of Refugee Law' in A Zimmermann et al (eds), *The 1951 Convention Relating to the Status of Refugees and its 1967 Protocol: A Commentary*, 2nd edn (Oxford, Oxford University Press, 2024) 8; see also E Fripp, *Nationality and Statelessness in the International Law of Refugee Status* (Oxford, Hart Publishing, 2016) 105; C Lewis, *UNHCR and International Refugee Law: From Treaties to Innovation* (New York, Routledge, 2012) 16–8.

[94] Some argue that the arrangement was not a treaty, see eg P Fitzmaurice, 'Between the Wars – The Refugee Convention of 1933: A Contemporary Analysis' in D Keane and Y McDermott (eds), *The Challenge of Human Rights Past, Present and Future* (Cheltenham, Edward Elgar, 2012) 244; Skran and Easton-Calabria, 'Historical Development of Refugee Law' (n 93) 6–15.

The documentary records of the League of Nations certainly give the impression that it was treated as such, despite its designation and a certain degree of ambiguity over its nature. Thus, the arrangement was 'amended' in subsequent acts, which were promulgated in the League of Nations Treaty Series.[95] Moreover, 'accessions' to the 'arrangement' were likewise dutifully recorded.[96] At the same time, the very wording of the 'arrangement' suggests that it formally imposed no strict obligations, even if it were to be classified as a treaty.[97]

The regime created during the 1920s went through a rapid succession of stages and ultimately led to a set of customary and treaty-based norms[98] as well as an institutional infrastructure that served as a focal point for developing, applying, and disseminating the relevant norms. I do not attempt here to provide a detailed legal analysis of refugee law during this period. Moreover, as noted, it can hardly be claimed that anything like a solid set of customary international law norms developed in the field. Nonetheless, the rise of the refugee as a legal category in international law emerged and took root quickly during this time. It implied, in particular, a general duty on the part of states to aid refugees and a more specific duty not to expel or refuse them entry at the border.[99] To be sure, neither the 'arrangements' of the 1920s nor the 1933 Refugee Convention as such established a customary international law norm concerning the *non-refoulement* rule or principle. Nonetheless, the norm was first formulated during this period and later became the cornerstone of the refugee law regime. Although the application of these general norms remains defective to this day, they have been broadly accepted. In particular, in respect of the general duty to aid refugees, states have continuously supported collective measures and the international institutions that have helped implement this duty. As much as many governments have neglected the plight of refugees, most states have never repudiated the principal legal norms of refugee law. As to the duty of *non-refoulement*, it was recognised as a customary international law norm early on and never placed in doubt as such, even if its interpretation and application in particular contexts remain contested.

Early efforts to protect refugees and the stateless also exemplify the role of norm-entrepreneurs in the development of deeply entrenched background custom. Indeed, Ador's actions, as well as those of other activists at the time,

[95] League of Nations, 'Arrangement Relating to the Issue of Identify Certificates to Russian and Armenian Refugees' (12 May 1926) LNTS Vol LXXXIX, No 2004 (1929) 47.

[96] For instance, the LNTS records that on 1 April 1926 the Saar Territory 'adhered' to the 5 July 1922 arrangement. See LNTS Vol XLV, No 355 (1926) 103.

[97] League of Nations, 'Arrangement with Respect to the Issue of Certificates of Identity to Russian Refugees' (5 July 1922) LNTS Vol XIII, No 355 (1922) 237.

[98] JC Hathaway, 'The Evolution of Refugee Status in International Law: 1920–1950' (1984) 33(2) *The International and Comparative Law Quarterly* 348, 379–80.

[99] See eg JC Hathaway, *The Rights of Refugees under International Law*, 2nd edn (Cambridge, Cambridge University Press 2021) 313–464; see also GS Goodwin-Gill and J McAdam, *The Refugee in International Law*, 4th edn (Oxford, Oxford University Press, 2021). See also Article 3 of the 1933 Convention Relating to the International Status of Refugees.

have been understood by scholars as notable instances of 'norm entrepreneurs' at work.[100] These particular actors were successful in part for very specific reasons that suggest that without a constellation of supportive factors, efforts by norm entrepreneurs can founder. Such supportive factors included political incentives for governments to tolerate and cooperate with an international administration, well-connected individuals who could act rapidly as intermediaries and drivers of the regime, and external pressure on key decision-makers to respond quickly. In addition, the generality and community orientation of the relevant norms, which were embedded in prior normative practices and expectations, helped give the refugee regime solid support.

As much as both the pre-World War II refugee and minorities regimes foundered despite significant support from civil society groups, many of the basic norms that emerged in those contexts did not go away, but informed developments that contributed to the rise of an international human rights movement and the UN-based refugee regime. Norm entrepreneurs are therefore important also because they allow legal regimes to survive major setbacks, notably by socialising those who can continue their work, effectively becoming repeat players in a changing political environment. Organisations like the ICRC regularly invoke the storied past of their and their members' involvement in the shaping of the international refugee regime.[101] While such invocations may be partly rhetorical, and while it is important to emphasise the contingencies of any social movement, they also point to the mechanisms that help stabilise international norms across long periods of time, against significant odds.

By necessity, rather than deliberate design, Nansen adopted an approach to law and policymaking in the field that was gradual and 'soft' in terms of its legal ambitions. In many ways, this approach set a precedent for similar processes of international regime formation. Nansen's approach – proceeding through action and non-binding instruments, relying on early forms of crowd-funding and support (the sale of postcards), and a certain pluralism of world-views reflected in the wide-ranging networks Nansen managed to maintain – seems strikingly contemporary, in the sense that it reflects the realist and bottom-up approach to lawmaking that would become popular in international law only much later. This does not mean that informal forms of ordering are normatively desirable in all circumstances. After all, the refugee regime faced considerable strain in the face of the rise of Nazism, Germany's pull-out from the League, the general weaknesses of the League of Nations, and the unwillingness of many countries to open their borders to refugees. Whether a different lawmaking arrangement would have changed this path is impossible to tell, but we can draw lessons about the factors that can, under certain conditions, sustain effective customary international law norms.

[100] See Orchard, *A Right to Flee* (n 72) 109–10.

[101] See eg *Submissions of the Intervener: The Queen (on the Application of B) v The Director of the Legal Aid Casework* (2015) 26(4) *International Journal of Refugee Law* 700, 701.

From a broader perspective, the refugee regime experiment points to some advantages of informal lawmaking regimes. They tend to be more malleable, adaptable, and accommodating to shifting understandings or definitions of a problem. At the same time, they also tend to be more reflective of inequalities in power relations. In contrast, more formal lawmaking processes, such as codifications, have their own drawbacks. In particular, they show a tendency towards specialisation, which can lead to siloed regimes for refugees, migrant workers, or prisoners of war, not to mention various regimes relating to international economic relations, sustainable development, or the environment. This siloisation can make policy-makers blind to links that tie these fields together. Although the absence of formalisation and institutionalisation can be defects of relatively more informal regime structures, their upside is reactivity to the concerns of those affected by them. Such concerns are commonly not siloed. For example, while refugees usually face the primary challenge of finding refuge, they have additional social and economic needs as well. And indeed, one remarkable feature of the refugee regime up until today is the degree to which it concerned itself with the social and economic rights of refugees in their host countries. This substantive normative outcome can be traced to the relatively informal processes in which norms were developed in this field early on. Both substantive and institutional questions could be adapted rapidly to changing circumstances, as the role of the International Labor Organization in the early history of the regime suggests.[102] And the basic norms and design of the international refugee regime were then carried forward into the post-World War II period.

One important contrast between the refugee and minorities regimes of the Interwar period was the lack of any significant third-party dispute settlement bodies in the former case, at least on the international level. Part of the explanation for this difference is surely practical, in that the non-deliberative emergence of the refugee regime made it already a priori difficult to establish international institutions with appropriate jurisdiction. Moreover, unlike the minorities regime, whose judicial infrastructure was essentially imposed on some states selectively, the refugee regime was structurally not amenable to this sort of solution since obligations towards refugees could affect decisions that states came to believe were key aspects of their sovereignty. Creating binding third-party dispute settlement in this field would have represented a major shift in the balance of power between powerful states and international organisations. As a result, judicial decision-making in the field shifted to domestic and transnational actors. This would be carried forward to the post-World War II period, as domestic courts and agencies, the UNHCR, and regional courts became the main actors in the development of refugee law.

The rise of Nazism meant a wholesale repudiation of several emerging norms of international law at the time and ended up destroying anything resembling an effective refugee regime until the end of World War II. After Adolf Hitler

[102] Grahl-Madsen, 'The League of Nations and the Refugees' (n 83) 362.

was appointed Chancellor of Weimar Germany on 30 January 1930, the country quickly slid into authoritarianism. Following the formal grant of emergency powers on 28 February 1933, the new German leadership systematically went about purging first the bureaucracy and then its entire population of persons it considered 'alien' or non-Aryan, most significantly the Jews. In the course of the period of Nazi rule, and particularly in Eastern Europe, this led to the extermination on a massive scale of European Jews.[103] By the time the Soviet and Allied troops entered the former Reich, more than 6 million Jews had been murdered, in addition to numerous other victims. Before Hitler's rise to power in Germany and the Holocaust, a small but increasing number of members of Jewish and other groups persecuted by the Nazi regime attempted to leave Germany (and other European countries). The rising numbers of refugees led to the reactivation of the office of the High Commissioner for Refugees,[104] an organisation originally created in the League of Nations framework, whose operation continued but largely fell into desuetude after the death of its first and until then only High Commissioner, Nansen.[105]

The inability of the rudimentary international framework concerning minorities and refugees to deal with Nazi Germany meant that any normative developments had to move away from the institutions that were premised on a degree of mutual cooperation between governments. In other words, Nansen's approach was no longer an option. The recreated High Commissioner for Refugees was in 1933 made into a considerably weaker institution than the earlier one led by Nansen.[106] James G. McDonald, who became its head in the fall of 1933 and whose work remained largely ineffective, eventually resigned in 1935. McDonald was aware of the deteriorating situation in Germany as early as August 1933.[107] On 27 December 1935, McDonald famously resigned from his post as 'High Commissioner of the League of Nations for Refugees (Jewish and Other) Coming from Germany'.[108] McDonald's letter of resignation (with Annexes, only a part of which was published), which he carefully prepared in consultation with several advisers, was reprinted and reported on widely across the world.[109] Interestingly, in his letter, McDonald explicitly referred both to the

[103] See eg M Mazower, *Hitler's Empire: How the Nazis Ruled Europe* (New York, Penguin Press, 2008) 11; see also T Snyder, *Bloodlands: Europe between Hitler and Stalin* (New York, Basic Books, 2010).

[104] S Milton and H Friedlander (eds), *Archives of the Holocaust: An International Collection of Selected Documents*, Volume VII (New York, Garland, 1989) x–xi.

[105] UN General Assembly, Refugees and Stateless Persons: Report of the Secretary-General, 26 October 1949, UN Doc A/C.3/527.

[106] Milton and Friedlander (eds), *Archives of the Holocaust* (n 104) xii–iv.

[107] ibid, 2 (see the letter of 22 August 1933 to Mildred Wetheimer, a fellow member of the Foreign Policy Association, of which McDonald had served as the chairman until 1933).

[108] Penkower (n 45).

[109] Including Hersch Lauterpacht, who would later serve on the World Court. See ibid, 286. Penkower (n 45) notes (at 286) that 'Fagen and Janowsky turned to publishing their exised chapters … in book form'. Those chapters appeared in Janowsky and Fagen, *International Aspects of German Racial Policies* (n 45). The issue is also discussed in P Sands, 'Of Refugees and Resignation' (2017) 6(2) *UCL Journal of Law and Jurisprudence* 1, 2–3.

notion of 'practice' and 'customary international law'. After discussing the extent to which Germany was bound by basic international norms concerning the treatment of religious minorities,[110] McDonald concludes rather modestly by noting as follows:

> It is not within my province to state to what extent the practice in this matter of the community of nations in the last hundred years and of the League of Nations has become a rule of customary international law; neither am I called upon to judge how far the declarations and the conduct of Germany prior to 1933 are in themselves sufficient to establish legal presumptions. But both, I believe, are sufficient to establish an appeal to those broad considerations of humanity and of international peace which are the basis of the public law of Europe in the matter of racial and religious minorities.[111]

Interestingly, the 'erased' parts of the Annex to McDonald's letter are less equivocal about the customary nature of the relevant minority rights under international law. At any rate, McDonald's letter is the rare instance of this rather technical notion being communicated widely and deliberately to a large audience worldwide. Thus, one compilation of reactions to the letter – included in a documentary history of the Holocaust – refers to a variety of newspapers, pamphlets, books, and specialised journals, among others.[112] Reports of the letter percolated to other specialised outlets, suggesting that the letter must have been disseminated widely and that the public must have had a fairly good impression of the ethical and legal implications of Nazi Germany's actions.[113] The refugee regime that was constructed in the 1920s faced a number of challenges in the ensuing decades. However, the basic norms and institutions of the regime survived. In the immediate post-World War II period, those who met to codify the law concerning refugees and stateless persons relied heavily on the precedents of the post-World War I period. For example, norms such as the duty of *non-refoulement* were uncontroversially recognised as ones of customary international law during the relevant international conferences following World War II.

Given the tragic failure of the Interwar refugee regime, it is challenging to utter anything positive about its design. At the same time, the broader international lawmaking process shaping the status and treatment of refugees in this era offers important insights into the factors shaping customary international lawmaking processes and resulting norms.[114] Thus, legal norms can emerge for reasons that are motivated chiefly by the political and security concerns of an era's dominant powers, as was the case here. As a result, emerging legal norms

[110] 'Letter of Resignation of James G. McDonald, High Commissioner for Refugees (Jewish and Other) Coming from Germany, addressed to the Secretary General of the League of Nations' (with an Annex) (27 December 1935) LoN Doc C.13.M.12.1936.XII, viii-ix, para 12.

[111] ibid, para 14.

[112] Milton and Friedlander (eds), *Archives of the Holocaust* (n 104) 239–86.

[113] See eg FK Wentz, 'Book Review: So It Was True: The American Proestant Press and the Nazi Persecution of the Jews. By Robert W. Ross (1980)' (2009) 51 *Church History* 364.

[114] See in particular Orchard, *A Right to Flee* (n 72) 5.

in the field can initially apply selectively to particular groups of refugees, as was the case here. However, when states create a legal regime they often lose control over its development. This explains why other pre-existing normative currents begin to affect the regime and shape it in new ways. By creating a legal regime that can be affected by new actors and institutions, a legal norm that may originally have been treaty-based, or a dynamic norm of customary international law that could change if the interests of the era's dominant powers altered, can become deeply entrenched. This is what slowly began to occur here for several reasons. First, the new regime was supported by a long-standing series of precedents relating to the protection of aliens and minorities that could be extended by analogy to refugees. Second, the consolidation of statehood itself supported the relevant norms and vice versa. In that sense, basic norms concerning the status and rights of refugees drew on the same sources of stability as the norm of state sovereignty. In turn, they suffered from the same limitations inherent in a state-centred lawmaking process (or, in other words, they had to be compatible with the norm of state sovereignty). Third, the rise of an institutional framework on the international level to protect refugees created a kind of third-party lawmaker that could amplify and support a set of emerging, but highly fragile, legal norms. This was a particularly weak, informal, and non-legalised international institutional framework, even as compared to the above-discussed minorities regime. Indeed, that system was practically destroyed with the rise of Nazism and the failure of states to effectively protect persons fleeing from Nazi persecution. But it was resuscitated in new garb following World War II when it would become recast amid new waves of refugee movements both during the immediate post-World War II period and the Cold War.[115] Moreover, even during the final stages of the League of Nation's operation, there was an awareness that certain of its institutional innovations could and should be carried forward.[116] Indeed, a leading scholar and practitioner in the field has emphasised the close connection between the institutional framework and the broader lawmaking process shaping contemporary refugee law.[117]

V. THE INTERNATIONAL LAW OF SOVEREIGN DEBT: INVISIBLE CUSTOM

In recent years, international tribunals and domestic courts have increasingly dealt with issues of sovereign default, notably as a result of the Argentine

[115] See C Lewis, *UNHCR and International Refugee Law* (n 93) 89; see also Orchard, *A Right to Flee* (n 72) 173–202.

[116] See League of Nations, 'The Committees of the League of Nations: Classified List and Essential Facts', LoN Doc C.99.M.99.1945.V. (20 September 1945). On the 'Bruce Report', see eg MD Dubin, 'Toward the Bruce Report: The Economic and Social Programs of the League of Nations in the Avenol Era' in United Nations Library (ed), *The League of Nations in Retrospect* (n 46) 42.

[117] GS Goodwin-Gill, 'The Office of the United Nations High Commissioner for Refugees and the Sources of International Refugee Law' (2020) 69 *International and Comparative Law Quarterly* 1, 40.

economic and financial crisis, stretching from the country's default in 2001 to fairly recent settlements with certain remaining holdout creditors. This and similar episodes – involving Greece, Ireland, and Venezuela, for example – have brought a recurrent phenomenon of international economic history to the attention of legal scholars: sovereign debt and sovereign defaults. In general terms, debt has served an important function in both socio-economic life and politics for millennia. Economists view debt as an instrument that allows savings to be put to productive use, supports economic specialisation, allows for improved resource allocation, and permits enterprises and governments to realise large-scale and long-term endeavours. Credit has also played a key role in the global expansion of capitalism and has tended to entrench social hierarchies and class relationships.[118] As a result, issues of debt and default draw on a deep socio-political context on both the domestic and international levels.[119]

While debt comes in various forms, I will concentrate here on external sovereign debt, which is usually issued by governments in the form of bonds.[120] Incidentally, since a major share of external sovereign debt has traditionally been held by private foreign creditors, the issue of external sovereign debt also concerns the broader theme of the law governing the treatment of aliens.[121] External sovereign debt is an important tool for governments to manage their finances, with countries at practically all levels of per capita income tied together in a dense network of debt obligations to investors from around the world. The significant role of sovereign debt throughout history has prompted a vibrant literature on the topic.[122] Although the domestic legal orders of key financial centres, notably London and New York, are at the heart of global finance, various legal orders, including international law, affect how debt is created and managed in cross-border settings.[123] For example, domestic property and contract laws

[118] A considerable literature exists on the history of money and credit. See eg A Turner, *Between Debt and the Devil: Money, Credit, and Fixing Global Finance* (Princeton, Princeton University Press, 2017); J Beckert, *Imagined Futures: Fictional Expectations and Capitalist Dynamics* (Cambridge, Harvard University Press, 2016) 102–4; N Dodd, *The Social Life of Money* (Princeton, Princeton University Press, 2016) 89–134; D Graeber, *Debt: The First 5,000 Years* (New York, Melville, 2011); F Martin, *Money: The Unauthorized Biography from Coinage to Cryptocurrencies* (New York, Knopf, 2015); S Eich, *The Currency of Politics: The Political Theory of Money from Aristotle to Keynes* (Princeton, Princeton University Press, 2022).

[119] See also CM Reinhart and KS Rogoff, *This Time Is Different: Eight Centuries of Financial Folly* (Princeton, Princeton University Press, 2009) 66.

[120] On definitions, see eg M Megliani, *Sovereign Debt: Genesis – Restructuring – Litigation* (Cham, Springer, 2014); see also H Kupelyants, *Sovereign Defaults Before Domestic Courts* (Oxford, Oxford University Press, 2018); P Bolton, M Gulati, and U Panizza, 'Sovereign Debt Puzzles' (2023) 15 *Annual Review of Financial Economics* 239.

[121] An important early work on sovereign debt is NE Politis, *Les emprunts d'état en droit international* (Paris, Durand, 1894). See also O Lienau, *Rethinking Sovereign Debt: Politics, Reputation, and Legitimacy in Modern Finance* (Cambridge, Harvard University Press, 2014); P Pénet and JF Zendejas, *Sovereign Debt Diplomacies: Rethinking Sovereign Debt from Colonial Empires to Hegemony* (Oxford, Oxford University Press, 2021).

[122] See eg RW Kolb, 'The Economics of Sovereign Debt' in *Elgar Research Reviews in Economics* (9 December 2016).

[123] K Pistor, *The Code of Capital: How the Law Creates Wealth and Inequality* (Princeton, Princeton University Press, 2019) 132.

are often the main determinants for how debt instruments are organised and managed both domestically and globally, and this can shape the allocation of resources and the stability of economies worldwide.[124] At the same time, aspects of private international law and public international law are central to the interaction among sovereign legal orders.

When it comes to external sovereign debt – that is, debt borrowed by a sovereign entity from foreign persons – there is ultimately no centralised system of debt enforcement on the global level.[125] Whereas until the early twentieth century, powerful governments occasionally employed so-called gunboat diplomacy to enforce debts owed by sovereigns, the norm against the use of force save in the case of self-defence or collective (UN Security Council) authorisation shifted the relevant legal landscape.[126] Moreover, states have traditionally been reluctant to engage in international dispute settlement concerning their external sovereign debt obligations.[127] In addition, doctrines of state immunity generally bar domestic enforcement action against a state, though not necessarily other disputes relating to sovereign debt instruments that may arise in domestic courts.[128] Given these inauspicious background conditions, scholars have puzzled over the presence of a global market for sovereign debt and a relatively robust repayment norm. While the sovereign debt market is not entirely without a means of enforcement (such as through domestic judicial proceedings), the absence of any international bankruptcy law together with state immunity rules, which in many cases restrict the territorial state's enforcement jurisdiction, raise the question of what holds the sovereign debt regime together at all. Prompted by such questions and considering the expansion of sovereign borrowing and the emergence of significant cases of sovereign default or near-default in recent years, scholars have developed a range of explanations for the relative stability of sovereign debt markets. The answers provided to this basic question – how can a sovereign debt market exist – have come from a variety of angles, usually reflecting the disciplinary perspectives of their respective authors. Economists, in particular, have devoted considerable attention to investigating the mechanisms that explain sovereign debt markets in the absence of formal enforcement possibilities against sovereigns.[129] The most

[124] Reinhart and Rogoff, *This Time Is Different* (n 119) xxv.

[125] ibid 53.

[126] RW Kolb, 'Sovereign Debt: Theory, Defaults, and Sanctions' in RW Kolb (ed), *Sovereign Debt: From Safety to Default* (Hoboken, Wiley, 2011) 3, 3–4.

[127] M Waibel, *Sovereign Defaults before International Courts and Tribunals* (Cambridge, Cambridge University Press, 2011) 7.

[128] H Fox and P Webb, *The Law of State Immunity*, 3rd edn (Oxford, Oxford University Press, 2013) 480.

[129] See eg Reinhart and Rogoff, *This Time Is Different* (n 119) 55–8; see also E Borensztein and U Panizza, 'The Costs of Sovereign Default' (2008) 238 *International Monetary Fund Working Paper* 5; see also B Hébert and J Schreger, 'The Costs of Sovereign Default: Evidence from Argentina' (2017) 107 (10) *American Economic Review* 3119.

illuminating scholarship in this area combines economic, social, and political explanations for what might be called the sovereign debt regime.[130]

This section concentrates on two basic normative questions relating to sovereign debt and default. The first asks what the entire sovereign debt regime can tell us about customary international lawmaking – does that modality of international lawmaking play a role in this field at all, and if so, which one? The second question concerns the frequently invoked debt repayment norm. In particular, that norm can be divided into both the general principle of a repayment obligation and some special cases, such as alleged repayment exceptions in cases of so-called odious debt. These aspects are both important because even though the overwhelming majority of external sovereign debt is governed by domestic laws, some scholars have suggested that a general global norm concerning debt repayment exists as well. Some have also suggested a nascent doctrine of odious debt. Even if neither is recognised as a norm of customary international law today, the relevant discussion offers valuable insights into customary international lawmaking more generally.

Does customary international law play a role in respect of key legal questions concerning external sovereign debt? In particular, does it apply to the obligation of a state to repay its private bondholders or in relation to the so-called odious debt doctrine? The answer, I will try to show, is largely negative but also more complex and illuminating as to the nature of customary international law than may at first appear. Legal scholars in the field tend to suggest that customary international law plays a limited role in respect of sovereign debt in particular.[131] To be sure, the law of treaties and the law of state responsibility, widely understood as forming part of customary international law, have been relevant also in relation to some sovereign debt disputes.[132] Moreover, basic norms of state sovereignty and jurisdiction naturally affect the field indirectly. Nonetheless, it is widely thought that a general norm of debt repayment under customary international law is not recognised. Indeed, numerous scholars who have specifically examined the existence of any customary norm in the field tend to deny its presence. For instance, Florentino Feliciano, as part of a detailed collective study of external sovereign debt conducted under the auspices of the Hague Academy of International Law in 1995, noted that 'there appears as yet very little evidence of the subjective element of *opinio juris*' in relation to certain legal principles governing debt repayment.[133]

[130] See Lienau, *Rethinking Sovereign Debt* (n 121); J Roos, *Why Not Default? The Political Economy of Sovereign Debt* (Princeton, Princeton University Press, 2019) 4; see also M Tomz, *Reputation and International Cooperation: Sovereign Debt Across Three Centuries* (Princeton, Princeton University Press, 2012); P Pénet and JF Zendejas, 'Introduction' in Pénet and Zendejas, *Sovereign Debt Diplomacies* (n 121) 5.

[131] Waibel, *Sovereign Defaults before International Courts and Tribunals* (n 127) 13.

[132] ibid 169–206.

[133] FP Feliciano, 'Report of the Director of Studies of the English-speaking Section of the Centre' in D Carreau and MN Shaw (eds), *La dette extérieure/The External Debt* (Dordrecht, Martinus Nijhoff, 1995) 25, 50.

A subsequent work by Tai-Heng Cheng, in which the author sought to explain succession to commercial debt obligations comprehensively using a policy-oriented approach, also rejected the existence of relevant customary international law rules concerning debt succession.[134] While Cheng focused on a slightly different topic than merely sovereign debt (namely the fate of any commercial obligation in cases of both state succession and regime change), the absence of an agreed general rule certainly appears widely shared among lawyers. In a comprehensive study of the public international law aspects of sovereign debt disputes before a variety of international tribunals, Michael Waibel similarly pointed to the irrelevance of customary international law in the field, observing that '[c]urrent international law plays a remarkably limited role in the resolution of sovereign debt crises' and that both '[t]reaty and customary law on sovereign debt is sparse'.[135]

And yet, scholars who explicitly focus on something like a general norm of debt repayment in the field (namely the debt repayment norm discussed in works by Odette Lienau and Jerome Roos, for example) do identify such a norm. However, in both authors' frameworks, customary international law does not figure. Thus, according to Lienau, the so-called 'norm of sovereign debt continuity' applies in contemporary international law and is tied to a 'strictly *statist* concept of sovereignty'.[136] According to Lienau, the 'basic expectations [of market participants] resolve into one background rule: sovereign borrowers must repay, regardless of the circumstances of the initial debt contract, the actual use of loan proceeds, or the exigencies of any potential default'.[137] Lienau's account (which also equates cases of state succession with those of regime change)[138] provides a valuable and persuasive framework for understanding the history of sovereign debt restructuring in the twentieth century. Lienau also offers a normative critique of the background rule, which she suggests is essentially a dominant myth serving 'to immunize the debt regime from serious challenge and to stabilize the massive sums at stake'.[139] According to Lienau, the nature of the relevant background rule remains relatively unspecified; at any rate, it is not a recognised rule of customary international law, but simply one that the relevant participants follow.

Like Lienau, Jerome Roos has highlighted the persistence of a seeming repayment norm for sovereign debt. Indeed, such a norm appears to have been gaining strength since the 1980s.[140] As Eduardo Borensztein and Ugo Panizza

[134] See TH Cheng, *State Succession and Commercial Obligations* (Ardsley, Transnational Publishers, 2006) 379.

[135] See Waibel, *Sovereign Defaults before International Courts and Tribunals* (n 127) 20.

[136] O Lienau, 'Sovereignty, Legitimacy, and Creditworthiness' in Kolb (ed), *Sovereign Debt: From Safety to Default* (n 126) 245, 246.

[137] Lienau, *Rethinking Sovereign Debt* (n 121) 1.

[138] ibid.

[139] ibid, 243 (note 15, referring to Cheng).

[140] Roos, *Why Not Default?* (n 130) 7–8.

note, that period coincided with the rise of a new wave of sovereign borrowing involving developing countries.[141] Roos has found that this norm's surprising existence or persistence reflects the power of the global financial infrastructure on which states depend.[142] However, Roos has contended that even at times when so-called gunboat diplomacy was a permissible enforcement route, compliance was usually secured through 'the more subtle and indirect influence of *haute finance* itself'.[143] Roos' argument, which develops the idea of a 'peculiar … structural' form of power at some length,[144] is consistent with the existence of a complex sort of normative equilibrium relying on deeply entrenched expectations within the relevant legal community.

The situation is slightly different in the case of various purported exceptions to the debt repayment norm. Some of these exceptions are part of the law of state responsibility. Thus, the so-called necessity defence is understood as being anchored in customary international law. Another possibly relevant norm in the sovereign debt context is the so-called odious debt doctrine. The idea that a legal duty can be affected by its genesis, as noted, is hardly new – it is a feature of both the law of treaties and many domestic or transnational contract law systems. However, the notion of odious debt is not widely acknowledged in international finance[145] despite strong popular backing.[146] To a large extent, the odious debt doctrine thus remains untested and not accepted as a customary international law norm. However, some scholars have argued that the norm is or should be one of customary international law. For instance, Jeff King has argued that an odious debt doctrine under specific circumstances should apply under both domestic and international law.[147] Similarly, Ilias Banektas has argued that while 'lawfully incurred' debt must be repaid, under certain circumstances international law recognises the right of a debtor state to repudiate 'debt that is odious, illegal, illegitimate, or unsustainable'.[148] Even if a specific version of the odious debt doctrine is not vindicated in the future, efforts have been underway to address some of the underlying policy concerns that prompted this debate.[149]

[141] Borensztein and Panizza, 'The Costs of Sovereign Default' (n 129) 7.
[142] Roos, *Why Not Default?* (n 130) 4.
[143] ibid, 6–7.
[144] ibid, 10.
[145] See eg S Ludington and M Gulati, 'A Convenient Untruth: Fact and Fantasy in the Doctrine of Odious Debts' (2008) 48 *Virginia Journal of International Law* 595.
[146] Roos, *Why Not Default?* (n 130) 309.
[147] J King, *The Doctrine of Odious Debt in International Law: A Restatement* (Cambridge, Cambridge University Press, 2016) 28.
[148] I Bantekas, 'The Right to Unilateral Repudiation of Odious, Illegal, and Illegitimate Sovereign Debt as a Human Rights Defence' in I Bantekas and C Lumina (eds), *Sovereign Debt and Human Rights* (Oxford, Oxford University Press, 2018) 536, 554.
[149] ibid, see also AM Dickerson, 'Insolvency Principles: The Missing Link in the Odious Debt Debate' in Kolb (ed), *Sovereign Debt: From Safety to Default* (n 126) 261; P Bolton and DA Skeel Jr, 'Odious Debts or Odious Regimes?' in Kolb (ed), *Sovereign Debt: From Safety to Default* (n 126) 253.

One meaningful way to understand these efforts is as a slow accretion of informal guidelines and instruments aimed at solidifying globally applicable expectations to address the need for the law of sovereign debt to strike a better balance among the interests of creditors and debtor governments and their populations. In that regard, instruments such as the UNCTAD's 'Principles on Promoting Responsible Sovereign Lending and Borrowing' (2012)[150] or the UNGA's 'Basic Principles on Sovereign Debt Restructuring Processes' (2015) represent but the tips of a longstanding intellectual and political effort involving a wide variety of participants.[151] Here too, international organisations serve as sites of information exchange, negotiation fora, codification platforms, and norm dissemination mechanisms.

In sum, customary international law structures important aspects of the law governing external sovereign debt. For example, a range of norms of customary international law have played a role in the context of negotiations concerning state succession to debt. Customary international law is also relevant in relation to the law of treaties and the law of state succession to treaties when treaties or any institutions created by them affect sovereign debt. Where private debt contracts are internationalised in some way, customary international law plays a role in regulating that process. Moreover, customary international law may affect the substantive outcomes reached on the basis of general concepts such as 'equitable proportion' as well other norms of customary international law. Customary international law may further concern the permissible forms of enforcing international legal obligations. At the same time, while it is widely acknowledged that there is a fairly effective repayment norm on the international level, it is hardly ever seen or discussed as one of customary international law. However, we can easily imagine a scenario where an international court would be called upon to adjudicate a dispute implicating this norm, and it might declare it as a norm of customary international law. Judging from its wide acceptance, an international court might even feel comfortable seeing such a norm enforced, given that it is already acceptable to states and the relevant professional communities. Similarly, the so-called 'odious debt' doctrine – widely not accepted as forming part of customary international law – could also be discussed from that angle if we consider the multifaceted nature of customary international lawmaking and view the global lawmaking process from a more dynamic and comprehensive angle.

[150] UNCTAD, 'Principles on Promoting Responsible Sovereign Lending and Borrowing' (amended and restated as of 10 January 2012).

[151] See eg S Blankenburg and R Kozul-Wright, 'Preface: Sovereign Debt Restructurings in the Contemporary Global Economy: The UNCTAD Approach' (2016) 41(2) *The Yale Journal of International Law Online* 1, 6–7; L Buchheit et al, 'The Restructuring Process' in SA Abbas et al (eds), *Sovereign Debt: A Guide for Economists and Practitioners* (2019) 328.

VI. INTERNATIONAL ORGANISATIONS: POWER AND ACCOUNTABILITY

Traditionally, diplomatic protection only involved states and their respective nationals. In the twentieth century, with the rise of international organisations and the multiplication of their activities, diplomatic protection came to be extended to these new 'subjects' of international law. Despite a rich debate about their legal nature and powers, international organisations are generally understood as legal entities established under international law by at least two states, including a host state with which they maintain a special legal relationship. International lawyers see them as having the capacity to exercise a form of diplomatic protection, meaning the entitlement to bring claims on their own behalf and on behalf of their officials against states or other entities, be it the host state or another state or entity. Intriguingly, their capacity to exercise diplomatic protection has been understood in the judicial practice of the ICJ as deriving in part from customary international law.

Notably, the advisory proceedings concerning *Reparation for Injuries Suffered in the Service of the United Nations* raised the question of the UN's capacity to espouse claims on behalf of Folke Bernadotte, the slain UN envoy to Palestine against various entities. Abraham Feller, a senior UN lawyer pleading for the organisation before the Court,[152] emphasised both the treaty-based and customary basis of the UN's right to exercise diplomatic protection.[153] He noted that the UN's legal personality and the rights entailed by it derived 'both from general international law' and treaty (or 'conventional') law. The Court's majority gave an affirmative answer to the questions concerning the UN's legal capacity, not only in respect of bringing a claim to obtain reparation owed 'in respect of the damage caused to the United Nations' but also 'to the victim or to persons entitled through him'. Moreover, the majority agreed that such a power existed even with respect to non-UN member states.[154] On the first two questions, the Court's findings were based on a theory of 'implied powers'. In respect of the latter point, which most obviously should raise an issue of general or customary international law, the Court's decision was based on the theory of 'objective personality'. Several judges criticised the Court's reasoning as an impermissible application of analogy that only pretended to be based on accepted notions of international law. For instance, Judge Badawi Pasha of Egypt, in a Dissenting Opinion, complained that 'the use of analogy has never been a customary technique in international law'.[155] The Court was wrong, in Badawi Pasha's view, for there was 'in fact no common law for

[152] On Feller, see T Lie, *In the Cause of Peace: Seven Years with the United Nations* (New York, Macmillan, 1954) 399.

[153] ICJ, Memorials, Pleadings and Documents: *Reparation for Injuries Suffered in the Service of the United Nations*, Public Sitting Held on 7 March 1949, Statement by Mr. Feller, 76.

[154] See *Reparation for injuries suffered in the service of the United Nations* (Advisory Opinion) [1949] ICJ Rep 174.

[155] ibid (Dissenting Opinion by Judge Badawi Pasha) 211.

international persons'.[156] Judge Hackworth of the US also admonished the majority for its 'liberality' in the construction of the UN Charter, its ignorance of 'practice', and the freewheeling use of analogy to come to the desired result.[157] Judge Krylov of the Soviet Union criticised the Court for a decision he felt was 'outside the limits of the international law in force' when it came to the idea that the UN was even entitled to bring a claim against an agent's state of nationality.[158] Furthermore, the idea that non-member states of the UN should be under a legal obligation with respect to the UN was unimaginable to Krylov in the absence of 'a special agreement with these States'.[159]

This brief excursus into the *Reparation for Injuries* case illustrates two basic points. First, international organisations (and their officials) progressively began to play a role in the context of what in an earlier context would have been understood as the 'treatment of aliens'. Even with respect to their own respective state(s) of nationality, we can thus conceive of an international organisation's official as a relative 'other', suggesting a significant transformation of the international legal landscape during the contemporary period. Second, the digression also illustrates how the power of international organisations (here the UN) to espouse claims on behalf of its officials was established in international legal practice. We see the beginning of an argument in Feller's pleading before the Court, where he notes that an international organisation's rights derive both from general, or customary, and treaty-based international law.[160] While the Court never adopts this position explicitly, it develops a theory of implied powers and 'objective personality' that essentially amounts to the development of law that is not treaty-based but also not based on 'practice'. As the dissenting judges' criticisms illustrate, and the opinion itself suggests, the Court's finding on this point was an application of analogy and entailed the development, to borrow Judge Badawi Pasha's words, of a 'common law for international persons'. The advisory opinion thereby opened the way for a broadening of legal personality under international law.[161]

The other side of this development, which is linked to the growing power of international organisations, lies in the long-standing but increasingly relevant issue of international organisations' accountability or responsibility under international law for the treatment of their respective 'others', including persons affected by their activities. In this context, the discussion concerning the legal consequences of the 2010 cholera epidemic in Haiti is illustrative. In 2010, one of the most deadly and destructive cholera epidemics in recent

[156] ibid, 205.
[157] ibid (Dissenting Opinion by Judge Hackworth) 197–203.
[158] ibid (Dissenting Opinion by Krylov) 218.
[159] ibid, 218–9.
[160] See quoted text at footnote 153.
[161] See eg M Karavias, 'Corporations and Responsibility under International Law' in P Pazartzis and P Merkouris (eds), *Permutations of Responsibility in International Law* (Leiden, Brill Nijhoff, 2019) 43, 44.

history struck Haitians, leading to nearly 10,000 deaths in Haiti alone. At the time, the Haitian population was affected by high rates of poverty and was still recovering from the consequences of a major earthquake.[162] As was later determined by various experts, the disease had been inadvertently imported to Haiti through UN peacekeepers previously based in Nepal. Insufficient sanitary precautions by the UN peacekeeping mission, in combination with other environmental factors, led to its further spread.[163] After the full extent of the catastrophe became clear, the first task was to manage and eradicate the disease, a momentous task that took nearly a decade – only in 2019 was Haiti declared free of cholera. In parallel, various civil society groups and lawyers began to identify legal remedies, document evidence, establish the responsibility of the UN bodies and officials who had handled the matter and seek reparations, a process that remains ongoing.[164]

The case of the UN's involvement in the 2010 cholera outbreak in Haiti points to a number of issues at the intersection between public health, environmental law, the law of armed conflict, the law of international organisations, and customary international law. First, it suggests a close connection between situations of armed conflict and both environmental and health risks.[165] Second, it points to new but predictable types of disease transmission, the role of new types of actors in this context, and the operational and legal deficiencies in the work of the UN. Third, it illustrates the legal challenges that persons affected by such risks and harms face when they seek legal remedies on the domestic or international levels.[166] Fourth, it demonstrates the important but limited role of transnational and international actors in supporting the interests and rights of the affected populations. As Adam Houston notes, 'if any longstanding principle relating to any disease can be thought to have attained the status of customary international law, it is [the obligation to prevent the transnational spread of cholera]',[167] even though Houston admits that the case of the UN's role in Haiti's cholera epidemic stands as an exception to this finding.[168] Still, the case of the cholera epidemic in Haiti offers an opportunity to examine both the relevant lawmaking processes and the place of the UN in this context.

[162] See A Cravioto et al, 'Final Report of the Independent Panel of Experts on the Cholera Outbreak in Haiti' (Independent Panel of Experts on the Cholera Outbreak in Haiti, 2011).

[163] See RR Frerichs, *Deadly River Cholera and Cover-Up in Post-Earthquake Haiti* (Ithaca, Cornell University Press, 2016).

[164] Transnational Development Clinic (Yale Law School) et al, 'Peacekeeping without Accountability: The United Nations' Responsibility for the Haitian Cholera Epidemic' (2013) 3.

[165] M Tignino and Ö Irmakkesen, 'Water in Peace Operations: The Case of Haiti' (2020) 29(1) *Review of European, Comparative and International Environmental Law* 33.

[166] I Kurzban, B Lindstrom, and S Jonsson, 'UN Accountability for Haiti's Cholera Epidemic' (2014–15) 108 *AJIL Unbound* 17.

[167] AR Houston, 'Applying Lessons from the Past in Haiti: Cholera, Scientific Knowledge, and the Longest-Standing Principle of International Health Law' in M Eccleston-Turner and I Brassington (eds), *Infectious Diseases in the New Millennium Legal and Ethical Challenges* (Cham, Springer, 2020) 13, 30.

[168] ibid.

As noted, one major question raised by this incident concerned the legal framework that would govern the UN peacekeepers' behaviour and any issues of liability or responsibility. Various lawyers, public health experts, NGOs, and student volunteers attempted to aid victims and their descendants by helping establish the relevant facts and calling for the legal responsibility of the UN for the events of 2010 and their consequences. In this context, they relied on a range of legal obligations,[169] many of which were claimed to derive from customary international law. While these arguments were highly persuasive, the reaction of the UN's leadership suggested considerable uncertainty about the applicable law. On the one hand, the UN did try to support efforts to remedy the consequences of the incident. However, although UN Secretary-General Ban Ki-moon publicly apologised for the UN's handling of the cholera outbreak, there has been no formal acknowledgment of the UN's legal responsibility by its political leadership or legal advisers. In 2016, Philip Alston, who served as the UN's 'Special Rapporteur on extreme poverty and human rights', summed up his evaluation of silence from the UN on this legal question as 'morally unconscionable, legally indefensible … politically self-defeating [and] entirely unnecessary'.[170]

States have historically claimed to possess a considerable degree of discretion in taking measures to prevent the spread of epidemics. As became clear during the COVID-19 pandemic, states took the liberty to suddenly and severely restrict the entry of non-citizens or otherwise restrict forms of movement that could introduce epidemics. While there was some push-back against discriminatory or abrupt border closures, notably on the part of scientists, medical professionals, lawyers, and the World Health Organization's leadership, that criticism had limited effect. However, in the case of Haiti, UN peacekeepers created a new situation, in part because of the exceptional powers, privileges, and immunities granted to the UN, and in part because of the dire security situation in the countries in which UN peacekeepers operate. In such a scenario, with the territorial state having limited control over the movement of various persons into its territory, it might seem logical for the UN to bear some legal responsibility for the consequences of incidents like the 2010 epidemic. However, this did not occur because basic legal norms to ensure the UN's legal responsibility were not in place or were not applied.

The legal assessment of the UN's role in the cholera epidemic in Haiti and its consequences was largely shaped by the fora in which it could occur. The route of domestic litigation was foreclosed due to the broad jurisdictional immunities afforded to international organisations, and notably the UN, before domestic courts. While those immunities usually derive from treaties, they

[169] Transnational Development Clinic (Yale Law School) et al, 'Peacekeeping without Accountability' (n 164) 35.

[170] Statement by Professor Philip Alston, 'UN Responsibility for the Introduction of Cholera into Haiti', 71st session of the UNGA, Third Committee, Item 68 (b&c), New York (25 October 2016).

are also understood as mandated by customary international law. Attempts to challenge the UN's immunity in this scenario did not succeed and no alternative international fora were available. Instead, those affected had to rely on voluntary support from foreign donors, the UN's varied human rights mechanisms and relevant mandate holders, various expert bodies, civil society organisations, and the public.

The UN-Haiti cholera situation thus highlights the link between lawmaking processes and substantive outcomes. On the one hand, numerous substantive rules were invoked and undoubtedly can be established in this field, including both treaty-based and customary international law rules or principles. At the same time, there are important outstanding legal questions concerning the international legal personality of the UN and the extent to which the UN, as such, is bound by customary international law, including the secondary rules concerning the responsibility of the UN. However, given the absence of a domestic judicial forum – with immunity on the domestic level shielding international organisations from litigation – there was little opportunity to identify, let alone apply, the legal standards that were invoked by activists and advocates.[171] Furthermore, no alternative international judicial forum – such as an administrative tribunal – was made available either. This situation stands in contrast to the one applying to UN staff or in the context of other international organisations, such as the EU or the World Bank, both of which allow individuals to bring direct actions before independent bodies (though even there, significant limitations exist). For example, a series of cases against the Council of the EU heard by the Court of Justice of the EU have challenged the conclusion of agreements by the EU and its member states with Morocco that were alleged to be contrary to the right to self-determination of the Sahrawi people and other norms of customary international law applicable also to the EU. More broadly, however, there is a dearth of legal avenues to ensure responsibility for events implicating international organisations. This lack of third-party dispute settlement shapes norms in this area to a significant extent. Notably, it reduces the effectiveness of the relevant rules and principles and makes it less likely for customary international law to develop in this area. In short, access to legal fora that could interpret and apply the relevant rules and principles is foreclosed, and legal development is therefore stifled. No international or domestic tribunal can adjudicate the UN's responsibility, leading to

[171] See eg R Freedman and N Lemay-Hebert, 'Towards an Alternative Interpretation of UN Immunity: A Human Rights-Based Approach to the Haiti Cholera Case' (2015) *Questions of International Law* 5; R Freedman, 'UN Immunity or Impunity? A Human Rights Based Challenge' (2014) 25 *European Journal of International Law* 239; S Hollenberg, 'Immunity of the UN in the Case of Haitian Cholera Victims' (2015) 19 *Journal of International Peacekeeping* 118; RG Bode, 'Cholera in Haiti: United Nations Immunity and Accountability' (2016) 47 *Georgtown Journal of International Law* 759; RB Larson, 'Law in the Time of Cholera' (2017) 92 *Notre Dame Law Review* 1271; see also RB Larson, *Just Add Water: Solving the World's Problems Using its Most Precious Resource* (Oxford, Oxford University Press, 2020).

the handling of the whole question being left to activists, victims, and academics – all groups with relatively limited clout and legitimacy in legal and policy debates. In the few diplomatic fora that remain, however, the cards are stacked in favour of the UN and its member states, whose leaders and legal representatives are careful to avoid creating precedents that may indirectly implicate the legal responsibility of its member states – at least this is the interpretation that Alston's critique allows.

As such, the case of the UN's lack of legal accountability in this context is but a reflection of states' broader refusal to acknowledge legal responsibility for collective action. The absence of adjudicative mechanisms in relation to important crises in the international arena is striking and can hardly be explained merely by inertia. The important role of third-party adjudication in lawmaking, which can be identified across many areas of law, points to at least one important reason for the reluctance of governments and international organisations to consent to it – namely that such third-party adjudicators could become effective legal institutions and thus challenge existing bases of power, which also explains why powerful states are usually reluctant to submit to international adjudication. The practical challenge for those seeking to improve legal outcomes on the global level is thus to find ways of incentivising governments and international organisations to submit to expanding forms of international adjudication, which would have significant implications for customary international lawmaking.

5

Habitat and Health: Constructing Global Environmental and Health Law

HUMANS HAVE ALWAYS been affected by 'natural' phenomena of diverse kinds, including seismic events, currents and tides, and zoonoses. At the same time, humans have shaped the planet's biological sub-systems in profound ways, especially starting with the extensive use of fossil fuels since the late eighteenth century, less than 300 years ago.[1] The last three centuries also saw the rise of imperialism, the advent and spread of industrialisation and forms of globalised capitalism, explosive population growth, and the development of an unprecedented degree of interconnection through the regional and global movement of persons, goods, information, and capital.[2] The long struggle for decolonisation eventually led to a reshuffling of the world's map and geopolitical arrangements, but not a diminution of the world's ever-expanding need for resources, many of them exhaustible. Amid huge disparities in resource use across and within countries, and despite efforts at the diversification of energy sources, humanity today relies on fossil fuels for an overwhelming proportion of its energy use.[3] During the last several decades, climate change has become the most widely discussed and intensively studied global environmental challenge. As the Paris Agreement illustrates, it has also triggered important international lawmaking processes, with implications also for customary international law. Transboundary risks posed by nuclear technologies, both military and civil, as well as the varied uses of biological and chemical innovations, have prompted calls for limits on their use and stricter regulation on the national, regional, and global levels. Major environmental risks have tended to be a consistently important focus of concern across societies and a prominent cause for civil society engagement. Global issues of public health have similarly shot up on the agenda of governments, businesses, civil society organisations, and citizens over the last several decades. A major part of the explanation is that people,

[1] V Smil, 'A New World of Energy' in JR McNeill and K Pomeranz (eds), *The Cambridge World History*, Volume VII (Cambridge, Cambridge University Press, 2015) 164.

[2] See JR McNeill and ES Mauldin (eds), *A Companion to Global Environmental History* (Chichester, John Wiley & Sons, 2012) 7–8; see also J Osterhammel, *Die Verwandlung der Welt: eine Geschichte des 19. Jahrhunderts*, 3rd edn (Munich, C.H. Beck Verlag, 2009).

[3] See V Smil, *Energy and Civilization: A History* (Cambridge, MIT Press, 2017) 295–6.

animals, pathogens, and information can move around more rapidly today than in previous eras, also thanks to increasing urbanisation. Health-related knowledge and information are much more widely disseminated today than ever before. Differences in health outcomes across societies can be monitored, tracked, and evaluated in nearly real-time – to the chagrin of some governments. More importantly, these innovations are supported by a wide array of groups and individuals, including research organisations, philanthropists, businesses, governments, international organisations, and individuals.

This chapter surveys episodes of customary international lawmaking relating to the environment and public health. International environmental law is one of the most vibrant, innovative, and arguably consequential fields of contemporary international law. Customary international law in what is today seen as the 'environmental' area first developed around the use, management, and protection of cross-border resources, including waterways and aquifers, marine mammals, fisheries, and a healthy environment, linked to challenges like air pollution. Although the notion of the environment and something like contemporary international environmental law were unknown before the mid-twentieth century, the post-World War II environmentalist movement and contemporary international environmental law owe much to preceding developments. Indeed, in the hands of savvy activists and lawyers, even decidedly questionable legal precedents of the pre-World War II period were turned into important pillars of the evolving field of international environmental law in the second half of the twentieth century. Contemporary environmentalism truly took off only starting in the 1960s. Post-World War II economic growth and the US–USSR rivalry put significant strain on natural resources, leading to debates about access to and the distribution of resources, sustainable development, and the management of cross-border resources and risks. Since the 1960s, the world witnessed the consolidation of the contemporary law of the sea regime, which recast the staid but centuries-old body of law governing some aspects of maritime affairs into a more modern package of legal norms codified in the United Nations Convention on the Law of the Sea (UNCLOS) and its various related agreements, most recently the Agreement on the Conservation and Sustainable Use of Marine Biological Diversity of Areas beyond National Jurisdiction (BBNJ).[4] The evolution of modern environmentalism continues in an age when the dramatic scope and complexity of environmental challenges are becoming apparent, just as the legal and policy responses to address them remain deficient in spite of their innovativeness, as with the design of the Paris Agreement. In parallel, efforts to constrain the devastating human and environmental effects of warfare and militarisation continue unabated in the twenty-first century.

[4] See also G Novak, 'Reading the Waves: Continuity and Change in Ocean Lawmaking' (2022) 47(2) *Columbia Journal of Environmental Law* 359.

Similarly, global public health law is another central concern of contemporary international law, just as forms of public health have been long-standing preoccupations across the world. From quarantines to projects of sanitation, there are countless examples of inter-polity coordination on issues of public health in all world regions. Nonetheless, the notion of public health or 'sanitation' as an issue of 'international concern' coincided with the nineteenth century rise of contemporary international law – as limited as its ambit was at the time, focusing on the management of infectious diseases by European powers in an age of globalisation, colonialism, and imperial competition. This set of concerns later morphed into what is now called global public health, a field that covers nearly every aspect of human, animal, and plant health.[5] Across the last century, we have seen the expansion of what is best described as a global public health consciousness extending beyond issues of contagious disease control and increasingly intersecting with adjacent issue areas, including human rights, sustainable development, trade, and warfare (where health-related aspects emerged early on). In particular, the growth of global interconnection – physical and virtual – since the 1990s has made global public health into one of the most important fields of transnational, if not global, regulation. Global public health law thus illustrates, probably more directly than most other areas, the radical transformation of the international legal order over time.[6] Customary international law is generally thought to play a limited role in the field, given the preponderance of non-binding guidelines, treaties, expert reports, and domestic regulatory instruments. Nonetheless, if we consider customary international lawmaking from a more comprehensive perspective, we see that unwritten norms are constantly being developed in this field through complex and decentralised interactions between a range of actors.[7] Lawmaking in the field – involving scientists, medical professionals, international organisations, governments, civil society organisations, businesses, and research institutions – therefore offers a unique perspective on the role of customary international law.

[5] See eg BM Meier and LO Gostin (eds), *Global Health Law and Policy: Ensuring Justice for a Healthier World* (Oxford, Oxford University Press, 2023); A Gross, 'The Past, Present, and Future of Global Health Law Beyond Crisis' (2021) 115 (4) *American Journal of International Law* 754; GL Burci and B Toebes (eds), *Research Handbook on Global Health Law* (Cheltenham, Edward Elgar, 2018); LO Gostin, *Global Health Law* (Cambridge, Harvard University Press, 2014); LO Gostin, *Global Health Security: A Blueprint for the Future* (Cambridge, Harvard University Press 2021); JP Ruger, *Global Health Justice and Governance* (Oxford, Oxford University Press, 2018); S Sekalala, *Soft Law and Global Health: Problems Lessons from Responses to HIV/AIDS, Malaria and Tuberculosis* (Cambridge, Cambridge University Press, 2017).

[6] See eg M Cueto, 'The History of International Health: Medicine, Politics, and Two Socio-Medical Perspectives, 1851 to 2000' in C McInnes, K Lee, and J Youde (eds), *The Oxford Handbook of Global Health Politics* (Oxford, Oxford University Press, 2020) 18; M Cueto, TM Brown, and E Fee, *The World Health Organization: A History* (Cambridge, Cambridge University Press, 2019).

[7] See eg A Kamradt-Scott, *Managing Global Health Security: The World Health Organization and Disease Outbreak Control* (Basingstoke, Macmillan, 2015).

I. AN UNEXPECTED TRAIL: TOWARDS THE DUTY TO PREVENT TRANSBOUNDARY HARM

The town of Trail in British Columbia hosts one of the largest zinc-lead smelters in the world.[8] The smelter's environmental impacts continue to be scrutinised on both sides of the US-Canada border and beyond, but it is chiefly remembered by international lawyers as the origin of a prominent diplomatic dispute and arbitration that catalysed, shaped, and came to symbolise the development of twentieth-century international environmental law. The Trail Smelter dispute and its context and legacy have been studied extensively by historians, political scientists, and legal scholars.[9] At heart, the underlying dispute concerned the emissions of the smelter at Trail and its impact on surrounding populations and properties in the neighbouring US state of Washington. Decades of diplomatic negotiation and expert scrutiny preceded the creation of two arbitral tribunals based on a bilateral treaty concluded in 1935.[10] Notably, before arbitration commenced, the International Joint Commission, a bilateral mechanism created by the US-Canadian Boundary Waters Treaty of 1909,[11] had already examined certain factual issues concerning the Trail Smelter dispute[12] on the basis of Article IV of the 1909 Treaty, which included the obligation to prevent pollution carried across shared watercourses.[13] Much later, the *Trail Smelter* arbitration would come to be recognised as the first international 'judicial' decision dealing with transboundary environmental harm, and specifically air pollution.[14] The impact of the *Trail Smelter* arbitral tribunal's decision of 11 March 1941 can be measured by the impact of its most cited passage, which reads as follows:

> ... [U]nder the principles of international law ... no State has the right to use or permit the use of its territory in such a manner as to cause injury by fumes in or to the

[8] Teck Resources Limited, *Annual Report* (2023) 19.

[9] See eg RM Bratspies and RA Miller (eds), *Transboundary Harm in International Law: Lessons from the Trail Smelter Arbitration* (Cambridge, Cambridge University Press, 2006).

[10] 'Convention for the Final Settlement of the Difficulties arising through Complaints of Damage done in the State of Washington by Fumes discharged from the Smelter of the Consolidated Mining and Smelting Company, Trail, British Columbia (United States – Canada)' (signed 15 April 1935, entered into force 3 August 1935) 162 LNTS 73.

[11] Treaty between Great Britain and the United States relating to Boundary Waters and Questions (signed 11 January 1909, entered into force 5 May 1910) 208 CTS 213.

[12] As summarised in the 'Trail Smelter Arbitral Tribunal Decision, April 16, 1938', reprinted as Annex B in Bratspies and Miller (eds), *Transboundary Harm in International Law* (n 9) 314, 317; see on the treaty also AO Gibbons, 'Sir George Gibbons and the Boundary Waters Treaty of 1909' (1953) 34 *Canadian Historical Review* 124; see also JH Knox, 'The Boundary Waters Treaty: Ahead of Its Time, and Ours' (2008) 54 *Wayne Law Review* 1591.

[13] See Article IV of the Boundary Waters Treaty of 1909.

[14] See, also by reference to the abundant literature about the case, AL Springer, *Cases of Conflict: Transboundary Disputes and the Development of International Environmental* Law (Toronto, University of Toronto Press, 2016) 22–53; see also JE Read, 'The Trail Smelter Dispute' (1963) 1 *Canadian Yearbook of international Law/Annuaire canadien de droit international* 213; JD Wirth, 'The Trail Smelter Dispute: Canadians and Americans Confront Transboundary Pollution, 1927–41' (1996) 1(2) *Environmental History* 34.

> territory of another or the properties or persons therein, when the case is of serious consequence and the injury is established by clear and convincing evidence.[15]

At the time of the arbitration, international lawyers were increasingly concerned with what would later be called 'environmental' issues,[16] even if there was no established notion of environmental (let alone international environmental) law until well into the twentieth century. By the early 1900s, practices and norms had nonetheless developed around issues ranging from localised air and water pollution, wildlife conservation and management, and various uses of international waterways. However, it took decades before major cross-border incidents prompted the development of something resembling a coherent set of legal norms aimed at regulating cross-boundary environmental problems.

The qualification of the *Trail Smelter* case as 'mythical' and a 'precedent' in the international environmental law field has naturally attracted scepticism. As David Caron pointed out with respect to the *Trail Smelter* arbitration, it achieved the status of a landmark case of 'environmental law' only decades after it was handed down.[17] Patrick Kelly faulted legal scholars and judges for relying on the *Trail Smelter* case as a precedent or as indicative of customary international law, arguing that the tribunal did not, in fact, examine or apply any kind of 'state practice' and thus could not have identified customary international law.[18] However, others have interpreted the role of the decision in a more contextual way. For example, Günther Handl has argued that to doubt the relevance of the arbitral decision is to misunderstand the nature of the customary international law norms at issue and the reasons why important judicial institutions still indirectly invoke the norm expressed in the *Trail Smelter* case.[19] Duncan French has proposed another framework for understanding the influence or effect of the *Trail Smelter* case, noting that the pithy formulation of a general principle by the tribunal and the time and place of its making contributed to its dissemination and influence.[20] It is true that the tribunal did not in fact identify a general practice in the case. But this suggests that we may need to adopt a different perspective to 'customary international law' in the judicial versus in other contexts.

[15] *Trail Smelter* case, 'Decision reported on March 11, 1941, to the Government of the United States of America and to the Government of the Dominion of Canada, under the Convention signed April 15, 1935', RIAA, Volume III, 1938–82, at 1965.

[16] EB Weiss, 'The Evolution of International Environmental Law' (2011) 54 *Japanese Yearbook of International Law* 1, 2–3.

[17] See DD Caron, 'Foreword' in Bratspies and Miller (eds), *Transboundary Harm in International Law* (n 9) xix, xx.

[18] JP Kelly, 'The Twilight of Customary International Law' (2000) 40 *Virginia Journal of Intenrational Law* 449, 471–2.

[19] G Handl, 'Trail Smelter in Contemporary International Environmental Law: Its Relevance in the Nuclear Energy Context' in Bratspies and Miller (eds), *Transboundary Harm in International Law* (n 9) 125, 127–8.

[20] See D French, 'Trail Smelter (United States of America/Canada) (1938 and 1941)' in E Bjorge and C Miles (eds), *Landmark Cases in Public International Law* (Oxford, Hart Publishing, 2017) 159, 160.

The history of what would today be called environmental concerns began in local settings and involved what were essentially disputes over the use of and damage to property or shared resources. In the *Trail Smelter* case, that chiefly meant air pollution affecting farmers' properties; in the case of boundary-crossing rivers, that could mean concerns over access to waterways for purposes of irrigation or electricity production. Even at the time of the *Trail Smelter* dispute, the questions at issue were focused on physical and chemical processes affecting orchards, water, and the air; for example, the expert documentation collected for purposes of the arbitration included specific measurements of sulphur dioxide in the air, as well as photographs of individual trees recording the alleged damage inflicted by the smelter's emissions. However, the *Trail Smelter* tribunal did not refer to the 'environment' and to the extent that its decision was understood as concerning the 'environment',[21] the latter had a different connotation than it would later achieve.

In revisiting the case, however, it is worth recalling that it was local Washington farmers and politicians who initially drew attention to the smelter's emissions and advocated for a settlement. Washington newspapers started to report on the smelter at Trail early on and frequently, presumably given popular interest. The 25 December 1927 edition of the Seattle Daily Times, for example, noted that 'at the request of Senator Wesley L Jones' the '[d]amage caused to orchards in Eastern Washington by fumes from a smelter at Trail, British Columbia has ... become a subject of diplomatic negotiation with Canada'.[22] However, it took a long time for the diplomatic process, mediated through the nation's capital, to produce results.[23] Indeed, Secretary of State Kellogg (of the Kellogg-Briand Pact) had already in 1928 formulated the key questions that would in 1935 (when Kellogg was no longer Secretary of State) be directed at the arbitral tribunal pursuant to the 1935 Convention (Article III).[24]

The assessments undertaken both by the International Joint Commission and the arbitral tribunal involved extensive recourse to scientific, including statistical, evidence. For example, two experts appointed to investigate the matter by the International Joint Commission, Deans Howes and Miller,[25]

[21] But see the comments on the smelter's effect on 'nature' rendered in JR Allum, '"An Outcrop of Hell"': History, Environment, and the Politics of the Trail Smelter Dispute' in Bratspies and Miller (eds), *Transboundary Harm in International Law* (n 9) 13, 14.

[22] Seattle Daily Times (Seattle, Washington), 'Smelter Fumes are Discussed by Diplomats' (25 December 1927) 46; Seattle Daily Times (Seattle, Washington), 'U.S. Will Survey Smoke Damage in Stevens Country' (4 July 1928) 2; Seattle Daily Times (Seattle, Washington), 'Board to Judge Smelter Damage' (16 April 1935) 9. Incidentally, in 1928, readers of local Washington newspapers could read reports about the diplomatic efforts to resolve the US-Canadian dispute side by side with reports about the recently concluded Kellogg-Briand Pact.

[23] See KA Murray, 'The Trail Smelter Case: International Air Pollution in the Columbia Valley' (1972) *BC Studies: The British Columbian Quarterly* 68.

[24] ibid, 75–6.

[25] See eg Read, 'The Trail Smelter Dispute' (n 14) 213, 214; Murray, 'The Trail Smelter Case (n 23) 76.

proceeded to evaluate claims of physical damage to the properties of the complaining Washington farmers. In their assessments, which later also informed the arbitral tribunal's findings, they devoted considerable space to justifying their conclusion that more than physical damage should be relevant for the tribunal's evaluation of the matter. They wrote: 'We do not think that any remedy, based upon actual physical damage appraisal, fully meets the situation'.[26] Such a claim must have seemed far-reaching to them, for they littered their findings with qualifiers and descriptions supporting this apparently alternative view. The farmers they interviewed in elaborating their reports, Howes and Miller noted, were 'kindly and courteous'.[27] True, some were 'either auto-intoxicated or else plainly bluffing', but many seemed 'absolutely sincere'.[28] Yet these poor folks did not, for the most part, seek to 'squeeze' that 'great enterprise embodied by the Trail smelter'.[29] The farms at issue were the 'very modest holdings' and 'the homes of a people' who 'mistakenly' but sincerely thought that 'smelter fumes furnish the prime cause of the decadence of their profession of farming' in the valley.[30] And yet, Professor Howes and Miller suggested that something more was at stake – yet they did not seem to be able to find their own words to express what seems in retrospect like the commonsense insight supplied by a farmer ('landholder'). Thus, they noted:

> All we have said, and we could have said much more, as a tribute to the great enterprise embodied by the Trail smelter, does not give this great organization any right to 'park their smelter fumes upon other peoples' property without paying rent', an expression used by one of the landholders.[31]

Beyond this remarkable passage, it is notable that the tribunal in the *Trail Smelter* case needed to rely on a domestic precedent for its basic finding on the duty of prevention. In contrast, on the incidental question concerning the status of the principle of *res judicata*, the *Trail Smelter* tribunal in its 1941 decision had referred to international precedents.[32] Eighty years later, in The Hague, the need for an international tribunal to look to domestic courts for precedents on environmental law matters gave way to the International Court of Justice's confident proclamation – by reference to its own precedents, albeit echoing the *Trail Smelter* case – that 'the principle of prevention'

[26] Trail Smelter Question, Documents. Series A, 'The Deans' Report: Appendix A1' (Ottawa 1936) 28.
[27] ibid.
[28] ibid, 20 and 28.
[29] ibid, 28.
[30] ibid.
[31] ibid.
[32] *Trail Smelter* case, 'Decision reported on March 11, 1941' (n 15) at 1951.

was 'a customary rule', and had 'its origins in the due diligence that is required of a State in its territory'.[33]

If the degree of attention accorded to the affected individuals is an indication of progress, the practice of international environmental law has come a long way since the first decades of the twentieth century. As compared to the Deans' Report, no condescension towards, for example, farmers or other affected groups was suggested in the context of that case. The relevant discussion by the ICJ in the *Pulp Mills* case focused on whether there had been an obligation to consult affected populations (including farmers, incidentally) before the pulp mills' construction (there was none, in the Court's view)[34] and whether such consultations (mandated or not) had taken place (they had). Interestingly, the Court, despite finding no such obligation, devoted considerable attention to the matter, referring to a host of examples indicating forms of consultation by Uruguay of affected groups and populations.[35]

In the *Pulp Mills* case, the 14 present judges of the ICJ had to decide whether Uruguay had breached certain obligations under the 1975 River Statute between Argentina and Uruguay and related obligations arising under general international law whose relevance was contested among the parties.[36] The Court made a notable – if confusing – finding on the existence of a requirement to conduct an Environmental Impact Assessment (EIA) under customary international law,[37] which it confirmed in several subsequent cases.[38] However, despite the fact that both parties agreed that 'consultations of the affected populations should form part' of an EIA, the Court explained that there was no 'legal obligation' of consultation with individuals affected.[39] While the Court suggested that an EIA was required under general international law in some circumstances, its substance was left notably vague.[40] Part of the reason could have to do with the fact that customary international law (or general international law) was invoked here incidentally.[41] Moreover, the Court did not find that this duty had been breached. Indeed, the population seemed to have been consulted anyhow and a discussion of the law could therefore be sidestepped by the Court. Despite this rather hesitant approach, the judgment reflects a fairly dramatic shift in the role of public participation since the era of the *Trail Smelter*

[33] *Pulp Mills on the River Uruguay (Argentina v Uruguay)* (Judgment) [2010] ICJ Rep 14, para 101.

[34] ibid, para 216.

[35] ibid, paras 218–9.

[36] On issues of terminology when it comes to the unwritten parts of international law, see eg *Iron Rhine Arbitration (Belgium/Netherlands)* (Final Award (24 May 2005) para 58; *Pulp Mills on the River Uruguay (Argentina v Uruguay)* (Separate Opinion of Judge Cançado Trindade) [2010] ICJ Rep 135, 143, para 19.

[37] See *Pulp Mills* (n 33) para 204.

[38] *Dispute over the Status and Use of the Waters of the Silala (Chile v. Bolivia)* (Merits) [2022] ICJ Rep 614, para 114.

[39] *Pulp Mills* (n 33) para 215.

[40] ibid, para 205.

[41] ibid, paras 55–66.

arbitration. In this case, the respondent gave evidence of consultation with affected populations, and both parties explicitly agreed on the desirability of that practice. That the Court would not suggest that a 'legal obligation' attached to this practice is another matter.

The *Trail Smelter* case is today seen as a seminal episode in the history of international environmental law. It was also the only international judicial case dealing squarely with a case of transboundary air pollution. This is unsurprising because domestic courts were then at the forefront of developing standards for the management of cross-border resources. The translation of domestic legal innovations occurred largely through scholarly endeavours, diplomatic exchanges, and activities of various river commissions, some of them emerging in the early 1800s. For contingent reasons, the *Trail Smelter* case became an important site for just such a translation of a domestic precedent into a purported rule of customary international law concerning cross-boundary emissions. In that sense, the second *Trail Smelter* decision is a prime example of the close connection between domestic or local precedents or analogies and international lawmaking.[42] While it may seem puzzling why a decision relying largely on domestic US case law would become a precedent of international law, it is much less surprising when we consider the mutually reinforcing relationship between entrenched background custom, analogical custom, and pure judicial custom.

II. CONSTRUCTING INTERNATIONAL WATER LAW

Whereas international environmental law is a relatively recent concept, international lawyers have tried to actively construct a so-called 'international water law' for more than a century. Drawing on earlier jurists' often hypothetical discussions, legal scholars of the late nineteenth and early twentieth century attempted to compile and synthesise the sparse and often inconsistent precedents concerning the management of rivers, usually among neighbours.[43] Many of these early works of international fluvial law explicitly referred to customary international law.[44] By the first decades of the twentieth century, there were already numerous examples for the legal regulation of water resources, some on the local level, some on the level of empires, and some on various inter-polity levels, often as part of some kind of pluralistic order. Notably, following the Napoleonic wars, the Paris Peace Treaty of 1814 and the Vienna Congress of 1815 formalised an agreement by the major European

[42] This is not to say that the Court was 'correct' or even technically skilful in articulating the rule it identified. Indeed, the ambiguity of its legal finding has rightly been critiqued. See eg French, 'Trail Smelter (United States of America/Canada) (1938 and 1941)' (n 20) 174.

[43] See eg K Schulthess, *Das internationale Wasserrecht* (Zurich, Rascher, 1915) 5.

[44] ibid.

powers of the time concerning certain principles governing navigation on international rivers. The nineteenth century saw the conclusion of a wide array of river-related treaties meticulously documented by a range of early scholars of 'international water law'. Later on, the gist of the relevant principles in the Final Act of the Congress of Vienna of 1815 found its way into a series of other treaties, including the Versailles Treaty of 1918 and other post-World War I agreements.

The regulation of the Rhine provides an exemplary insight into the history of cross-border lawmaking concerning the use of so-called 'international rivers' for navigation.[45] During the late eighteenth century, users of this important Western European economic artery increasingly called for a more commerce-friendly regime.[46] This push was buoyed by the liberal intellectual climate of the era and prompted by the river users' perception that the fragmented regulatory regime in place at the time stymied the growth of commercial activity across the region.[47] However, reforms only came to fruition for contingent reasons. Post-Revolutionary France had already pushed for free navigation on international rivers,[48] notably in relation to the river Scheldt.[49] This policy of liberalising navigation on international rivers was also extended to the Rhine and supplemented by a relatively complex institutional infrastructure, including a form of third-party dispute settlement.[50] The 'small bureaucracy' established pursuant to an 1804 agreement (the 'Octroi') created a template for riverine cooperation that was maintained, modified, and expanded elsewhere even after Napoleon's defeat.[51] While the Rhine was under French patronage for several years, Napoleon's defeat risked calling into question the institutional innovations supporting Rhine commerce. However, a unified legal regime was largely maintained, though with some regressive features.[52] More importantly, it would become an influential precedent for the management of international rivers for two centuries.

[45] On the post-World War II era, see eg C Henrich-Franke and I Tölle, 'Competition for European Competence: The Central Commission for Navigation on the Rhine and the European Economic Community in the 1960s' (2011) 27(3) *History and Technology* 331; see also generally H Kümper and A Maurer (eds), *150 Jahre Mannheimer Akte: Festschrift zum 150jährigen Bestehen der Revidierten Rheinschifffahrtsakte vom 17. Oktober 1868* (Baden Baden, Nomos, 2018).

[46] See RM Spaulding, 'Revolutionary France and the Transformation of the Rhine' (2011) 44(2) *Central European History* 203; see also J Schenk, *The Rhine and European Security in the Long Nineteenth Century: Making Lifelines from Frontlines* (Abingdon, Routledge, 2021).

[47] J Schenk, 'The Central Commission for the Navigation of the Rhine: A First Step towards European Economic Security?' in B de Graaf, I de Haan, and B Vick (eds), *Securing Europe after Napoleon: 1815 and the New European Security Culture* (Cambridge, Cambridge University Press, 2019) 75, 78–82.

[48] See Spaulding, 'Revolutionary France and the Transformation of the Rhine' (n 46) 204; see also Schenk, 'The Central Commission for the Navigation of the Rhine' (n 47) 75.

[49] ibid, 78.

[50] ibid, 82.

[51] Spaulding, 'Revolutionary France and the Transformation of the Rhine' (n 46) 216.

[52] See Schenk, 'The Central Commission for the Navigation of the Rhine' (n 47) 85.

Attempts to improve river management during this era were not limited to the Rhine,[53] but due to its location and commercial importance in Europe it was the site of the most significant early efforts at 'international organisation'. Moreover, while similar debates about the freedom of navigation occurred in other parts of the world, the early creation of river commissions during this period was for a significant period limited to Europe.[54] This was due to the inherently unequal relations between European powers and their colonies, which meant that the translation of important European precedents was incompatible with the reality of colonial exploitation, as the case of the Congo River suggests.[55] In short, during this period, the lawmaking that took place did not result in a generally applicable regime addressing navigational uses of international rivers around the world. Nonetheless, the regime that was built for Rhine commerce turned out to be an influential precedent for 'international organisation', even though comparable forms of institutionalisation in other parts of the world were only realised in the post-World War II period. At the same time, it is increasingly understood that the construction of international river law over the last two centuries is far more than simply the story of evolutionary progress in the technical management of riverine commons. As a result, the design, purposes, and effects of the Central Commission for the Navigation on the Rhine and similar institutions, also in their imperial context, have been subjected to critical scrutiny, just like other forms of inter-polity cooperation.[56]

This early experience offers another important insight into customary international lawmaking. As Joep Schenk notes, the Treaty of Paris of 1814 and its context still reflected a strong dose of 'natural law'-style reasoning about the freedom of navigation on international rivers, including the Rhine.[57] Many of the legal claims about free navigation and commerce on international rivers were formulated – if not necessarily meant – in general terms,

[53] See generally B de Graaf, I de Haan, and B Vick (eds), *Securing Europe after Napoleon: 1815 and the New European Security Culture* (Cambridge, Cambridge University Press, 2019); C Ardeleanu, *The European Commission of the Danube, 1856–1948: An Experiment in International Administration* (Leiden, Brill, 2020); E Krehbiel, 'The European Commission of the Danube: An Experiment in International Administration' (1918) 33(1) *Political Science Quarterly* 38; YJ Yao, *Constructing the Ideal River: the 19th Century Origins of the First International Organizations*, LSE Dissertation (September 2016); J Yao, *The Ideal River: How Control of Nature Shaped the International Order* (Manchester, Manchester University Press, 2022).

[54] In relation to the Amazon, see eg B Garcia, *The Amazon from an International Law Perspective* (Cambridge, Cambridge University Press, 2011) 66. In relation to waterways in Africa during the colonial period, see J Lautze and M Giordano, 'Transboundary Water Law in Africa: Development, Nature, and Geography' (2005) 45(4) *Natural Resources Journal* 1053.

[55] See Yao, *Constructing the Ideal River* (n 53) 170; see also Yao, *The Ideal River* (n 53).

[56] See generally de Graaf, de Haan, and Vick (eds), *Securing Europe after Napoleon* (n 53); Yao, *Constructing the Ideal River* (n 53) 12; see also Schenk, 'The Central Commission for the Navigation of the Rhine' (n 47) 88–94.

[57] See Schenk, *The Rhine and European Security in the Long Nineteenth Century* (n 46) 22.

deemed to be applicable to all states, including non-riparians, and in principle to all rivers. Such arguments for a quasi-absolute freedom of navigation had a strong natural law flavour as well as an unmistakable imperial dimension. They were the same sort of principles that the US advocated in Latin America[58] and that European powers would later impose in respect of the Congo and Niger rivers at the Congress of Berlin.[59] As such, they were comparable in their generality to customary international law claims. However, during the negotiation of the relevant provisions of the Final Act of the Congress of Vienna, a more positivistic approach prevailed. As Schenk notes, it reflected the idea that the '[f]reedom of navigation was not considered a natural right, but an act of goodwill by each individual riparian state', even if the institutional innovations that had begun to shape the field were maintained.[60] This turn to positivism initially barred any expansive move towards a general international river law.[61] However, the repudiation of 'natural law' thinking meant that efforts to develop general rules would need another outlet, a more 'dynamic' source of international law. Indeed, that is what occurred over the next century as 'international water law' came to be frequently discussed in terms of customary international law, a development that continued well into the twentieth century.

The basic outcome of the Congress of Vienna held sway for more than a century. The Covenant of the League of Nations foresaw the development of rules concerning a number of issues, including the 'freedom of communications and of transit and [the] equitable treatment for the commerce of all Members of the League', as stipulated in Article 23(e) of the Covenant. In 1921, a Committee of Enquiry of the League of Nations produced a report to accompany the 'Draft Convention on the International Regime of Navigable Waterways' (the Barcelona Convention), which evaluated legal developments in the field. Notably, the Report referred to the governing law as quasi-customary, though without using the phrase,[62] and identified important changes to the uses of waterways in the previous decades that were seen as having implications for their legal governance.[63] In the first decades of the twentieth century, that idea was also endorsed by the newly created PCIJ.

[58] B Garcia, *The Amazon from an International Law Perspective* (Cambridge, Cambridge University Press, 2011) 62–3.

[59] DA Caponera and M Nanni (revised and updated by), *Principles of Water Law and Administration: National and International*, 3rd edn (London, Routledge, 2019) 273.

[60] See Schenk, 'The Central Commission for the Navigation of the Rhine' (n 47) 92.

[61] Caponera and Nanni, *Principles of Water Law and Administration* (n 59) 271.

[62] League of Nations (Barcelona Conference), 'Verbatim Records and Texts Relating to the Convention on the Regime of Navigable Waterways of International Concern and to the Declaration Recognising the Right to a Flag of States Having No Sea-Coast' (1921) 414–5 (see the 'Report on the Draft Convention on the International Regime of Navigable Waterways' in the Annex to Section IV (at 414)).

[63] ibid, 415.

In 1928, the PCIJ had to address an issue of navigational rights concerning the jurisdiction of the Oder River Commission in relation to sections of a tributary of the Oder located on Polish territory. In that case, the Court was faced with a question of interpretation relating to Article 331 of the Treaty of Versailles, which concerned so-called international rivers. In its Judgment of 10 September 1929 in the case concerning the *Jurisdiction of the International Commission of the River Oder* (*Oder* case), the Court found the so-called 'Barcelona Statute' (annexed to the Convention, the above-mentioned treaty indirectly and prospectively referred to in the Treaty of Versailles, which Poland was not a party to) inapplicable. However, it went on to identify what it called the 'principles governing international fluvial law in general',[64] drawing on the Final Act of the Congress of Vienna, the Versailles Treaty, and other unspecified treaties.[65] The Court here was applying legal principles that it thought were generally applicable as a matter of quasi-unwritten law, even if it did not refer to customary international law. For example, in response to the Polish argument that the freedom of navigation was meant to protect the rights of the 'upstream States' to access the sea, the Court developed the fairly general 'conception' on which it found 'international river law' to be based, namely that of a 'community of interest in a navigable river'.[66] The teleological and community-oriented form of interpretation adopted by the Court and the considerable ambiguity reflected in the Court's definition of legal sources make the case appear as a precursor to similar innovations in international environmental law of later decades, be it in the form of 'codifications' or far-reaching judicial pronouncements.[67]

But can we really speak of an 'international fluvial law' at the time of the PCIJ's *Oder* judgment, or – to stretch the question even further – during the more than century before it was invoked by the Court in support of the respective principles? From today's perspective, clearly not. On the one hand, this was hardly international law in the global sense in which it may be understood today. It was thoroughly European intellectually and practically: The principles were agreed upon by an exclusive group of European powers. Even when they were applied to colonised peoples and polities, their application remained an essentially inter-imperial law, in law and fact regulating the relationships between the European colonial powers. On the other hand, the parochial character of this legal order raises questions about the nature and effect of the type of judicial custom on display in the *Oder* judgment. After all, if this was not international law properly speaking, why were such principles carried forward in the post-World War II period in a thoroughly altered international context?

[64] *Territorial Jurisdiction of the International Commission of the River Oder (Six Governments v Poland)* (Judgment) (10 September 1929) [1929] PCIJ Series A, No. 23, 26.

[65] ibid, 29.

[66] ibid, 27.

[67] See eg, referring to McCaffrey, E Louka, *International Environmental Law: Fairness, Effectiveness, and World Order* (Cambridge, Cambridge University Press, 2006) 44.

One answer, of course, is that the context has *not* fundamentally changed and that the inheritance of an imperial past still permeates contemporary international law. The more plausible answer is that the existing norms were sufficiently acceptable even to a changing international society and sufficiently general to be applied to new contexts. In particular, the PCIJ's strong emphasis on communitarian values (the 'community of interest' idea) reflects a legal principle with deep roots in a multitude of legal contexts. In that sense, this initially pure judicial custom became generally effective because it reflected socially acceptable norms. To be sure, social acceptance is not always a requirement for effective law. However, in situations lacking any system of compulsory adjudication and where enforcement occurs piecemeal, if at all, as is still the case in many parts of the international legal order, social acceptance can be very important, if not necessary, for effective lawmaking. Judicial pronouncements purporting to state the law thus play a part in an elaborate and protracted process in which legal ideas and expectations are reiterated, discussed, disseminated, and made effective in a range of contexts. One such context is the work of professional associations of lawyers, which had tried to address the relevant questions well before the *Oder* judgment.[68]

Following a focus on the navigational uses of international waterways, non-navigational uses gained prominence in tandem with the growth of agricultural production and the exploitation of new energy sources. Because non-navigational uses of international waterways raised significant distributional questions, cooperation was slower to emerge. The field also saw tense disputes over resource control by riparians, as exemplified in the debate over the Harmon doctrine. That doctrine's emphasis on territorial sovereignty created considerable international controversy. From today's perspective, it offers an example of an attempt at establishing 'dynamic custom' by a powerful actor. As would be expected in such a lawmaking scenario, norms of this sort were fickle and liable to change quickly under the pressure of changing political currents or more solidly established norms. In parallel, legal scholars did attempt to draw on local precedents to propose legal norms relating to the non-navigational uses of rivers. Max Huber was one such scholar whose work had significant influence in the field. Huber's 1907 article concerning 'sovereignty in respect of boundary rivers' was based on the author's work as an expert on behalf of the Swiss canton of Zurich in a dispute with the canton of Schaffhausen. The article was later often invoked by scholars as an important precedent for the development of 'international fluvial law' since one of its sections devotes considerable

[68] SC McCaffrey, 'Introduction: The Path to the UN Watercourses Convention and Beyond' in L Boisson de Chazournes et al (eds), *The UN Convention on the Law of the Non-Navigational Uses of International Watercourses: A Commentary* (Oxford, Oxford University Press, 2018) 1, 2; LA Teclaff, *The River Basin in History and Law* (The Hague, Martinus Nijhoff, 1967) 153.

attention to the international law applicable to international watercourses.[69] According to Huber, the international law concerning non-navigational uses of watercourses was at the time limited to 'some few, general, and mostly natural law-derived principles'.[70] Nonetheless, Huber went on to list a number of principles[71] 'generally recognised both by theory and presumably also state practice'.[72] Huber found these principles to be relatively general and presumably drawn by analogy from Roman law, despite noting that 'Roman private law is neither by theory nor by states – by treaty or by custom – recognised as a subsidiary norm of international law'.[73] To be sure, these efforts, like others at the time, had a strong European flavour and likely had a limited effect on positive law, as much as they may have been acknowledged by a small group of practitioners and scholars. Nonetheless, they showcase efforts to construct 'international water law' as a field, which included attempts to distil relevant legal norms by analogy from various precedents.

The history of international lawmaking concerning international rivers affirms the significance of the relevant socio-political context, marked by deep-seated inequalities on the global and local levels, for lawmaking. As such, it demonstrates the role of power in the creation of legal norms. However, it also highlights the multifaceted nature of customary international lawmaking processes and resulting norms. As in other examples surveyed in this book, it points to the role of unintended consequences. Policies and norms like freedom of navigation and commerce, although proposed and often imposed in particular political contexts, tended to gain a life of their own and shaped international water law for more than a century. This was no doubt due in part to the generality of the respective norms and their congruence with the needs of managing inherently connected water basins. The example of international water law also highlights the role of domestic practices, precedents, and analogies for the development of customary international law. It further illustrates how the demise of natural law reasoning among legal scholars by the nineteenth century meant that there was an increased need for customary international law to fill the emerging gaps. Another running theme characterising lawmaking processes in this field concerns the role of expertise, popular pressures, and commercial interests. In addition, the early creation of international bodies in this field with supervisory, regulatory, or adjudicatory functions demonstrates the role of international organisations, including international courts and tribunals, both for developing and entrenching norms of customary international law.

[69] M Huber, 'Ein Beitrag zur Lehre von der Gebietshoheit an Grenzflüssen' (1907) 1 *Zeitschrift für Völkerrecht und Bundesstaatsrecht* 29, 159.

[70] ibid.

[71] See, including a translation, SC McCaffrey, *The Law of International Watercourses* (Oxford, Oxford University Press, 2019) 136.

[72] Huber, 'Ein Beitrag zur Lehre von der Gebietshoheit an Grenzflüssen' (n 69) 160–3 (translation by the author).

[73] ibid, 160 (translation by the author; Huber refers to Triepel and Phillimore as authorities on this point).

III. TREATY DESIGN AND CUSTOMARY INTERNATIONAL LAWMAKING

Environmental law instruments on the global level share – or are burdened by – many of the basic structural features, and defects, of the state-centric international legal order. However, those who helped design international treaties in the environmental sphere since the 1970s have dynamically responded to a changing international environment and tried to rope into their operation a wide array of actors on all levels – no small feat given the novelty of such arrangements in diplomatic circles.[74] As a result, many key treaties in the environmental sphere, from the Framework Convention on Climate Change to the Convention on Environmental Impact Assessment in a Transboundary Context, form cooperative frameworks of general principles rather than fully effective or self-enforcing legal regimes.

Take, for example, the Convention on the Law of the Non-navigational Uses of International Watercourses of 1997. Its provisions are the product of many decades of practice and expert deliberation in a variety of contexts. Its key provisions reflect a compromise on the relative importance of the principles of 'no harm' and 'equitable and reasonable utilisation and participation' and restate a range of prescriptions that are largely procedural, even if they serve substantive aims.[75] But few would argue that the Convention itself establishes an effective or comprehensive legal regime; it is rather the top-level anchor to a rich array of watercourses-related lawmaking activities (understood broadly) on all levels.

How are this and similar treaty arrangements connected to customary international law? There are two basic approaches to an answer: The usual one considers whether and to what extent the provisions of a treaty reflect customary international law. That, of course, is significant especially in scenarios where universal treaty adherence is lacking. It can be decisive in both diplomatic negotiations and international or domestic litigation. However, the more vital question from the broader perspective of customary international lawmaking concerns the particular design of such treaties as frameworks for longer-term

[74] See EB Weiss, 'The Five International Treaties: A Living History' in EB Weiss and HK Jacobson (eds), *Engaging Countries: Strengthening Compliance with International Environmental Accords* (Cambridge, MIT Press, 1998) 89.

[75] The history of the 'no harm' rule, its relationship to the principle of 'equitable and reasonable utilisation', and its permeation, as a matter of customary international law, into 'global water law' is particularly instructive. For a pre-Convention perspective, see L Caflisch, 'Emerging Rules on International Waterways: The Contribution of the United Nations' (1996) 15 *Political Geography* 273, 278–80; see also SMA Salman, 'Misconceptions Regarding the Interpretation of the UN Watercourses Convention' in FR Loures and A Rieu-Clarke (eds), *The UN Watercourses Convention in Force: Strengthening International Law for Transboundary Water Management* (London, Earthscan, 2013) 28; K Wegerich and O Olsson, 'Late Developers and the Inequity of "Equitable Utilization" and the Harm of "Do no Harm"' (2010) 35 *Water International* 707; T Tvedt, O McIntyre, and TK Woldetsadik (eds), *A History of Water, Series III, Volume 2: Sovereignty and International Water Law* (London, IB Tauris, 2015).

action to address cross-border environmental issues. This raises the question of how their design and the mix of substantive and procedural obligations they embody, their broader institutional infrastructure, and the availability of third-party dispute settlement contributes to customary international lawmaking in the field and beyond.

Many contemporary legal instruments relating to the management and protection of natural resources or the environment have been designed in the shape of a so-called 'framework convention-protocol' model,[76] even if it is also used in other areas, from public health to minority rights. That basic setup masks a wide variety of arrangements but essentially refers to a procedural, iterative, dynamic, and decentralised arrangement meant to be jurisgenerative. The adoption of this model was driven by a combination of functionalist and bureaucratic ambitions that sought effective tools to manage fields that were inherently complex and dynamic, coupled with public and expert pressure that catalysed the political and economic resources needed to implement such arrangements on the international level. In addition, such regimes were supported by reference to domestic administrative law models developed in relation to environmental problems. In short, the model accorded well with the public participatory and science-based approach that has characterised the field in fits and starts since as early as the twentieth century, but only gained sufficient public and political traction by the late 1980s.

On the one hand, the procedural character of much of contemporary international environmental law is an indictment of its effectiveness and power. On the other, the relevant procedural norms (like the duty to act in due diligence to prevent transboundary harm or the more specific procedural rules codified in treaties) serve substantive ends and influence both how 'substantive' norms of international environmental law develop and the role of customary international law in the field. Procedural norms often relate to access to information, cooperation, mutual regard, information exchange, prior notification, and similar issues. Because the activities required or encouraged by such norms tend to expand participation in the broader lawmaking process and encourage repeated interactions among different actors across various levels and across time, they can become motors of customary international lawmaking. Even if such lawmaking initially occurs in the shadow of formal treaty law, the existence of a framework provides the reasonable expectation that it will eventually shape the respective legal regime. This process tends to encourage or incentivise additional participation, resulting in a potentially virtuous feed-back loop in which law is continuously generated in the face of changing socio-economic and technological circumstances.

[76] D Bodansky, 'The United Nations Framework Convention on Climate Change: A Commentary' (1993) 18 *Yale Journal of International Law* 451, 493–4; see also MP Carazo and D Klein, 'Implications for Public International Law: Initial Considerations' in D Klein et al (eds), *The Paris Agreement on Climate Change Analysis and Commentary* (Oxford, Oxford University Press, 2017) 389.

Most recently, the Paris Agreement offers probably the most vivid example of how international treaties interact with quasi-customary international lawmaking processes. Several features of the agreement seem particularly notable in that they reduce the relevance of inter-state bargaining or competition, give sub-state actors a role in the implementation of the agreement, and generally allow for more transparency.[77] All of these aspects also mirror the factors that help sustain deeply entrenched background custom. Climate change is rarely, but sometimes, discussed in the context of customary international law.[78] Indeed, it seems plausible to tie the ongoing normative developments in the climate change field – as complex, treaty-based, and technical as it may be – to customary international lawmaking processes and resulting norms. On the most basic level, customary international law plays a significant role in framing the relevant debate and creating a legal and political basis for a more elaborate and detailed treaty-based structure.[79] In turn, a legally binding agreement can affect subsequent customary international law more powerfully than a (potentially more easily achievable) non-binding instrument or UNGA resolution. Even the negotiation of the Framework Convention on Climate Change, and more recently, the Paris Agreement, have had significant impacts on the dissemination of key customary international law norms, as reflected both in debates about the design of such agreements and in the context of attempts by powerful actors to withdraw from them.[80]

In parallel, in recent years, international, regional, and domestic courts have increasingly been called on to pronounce themselves on issues of international environmental law, including climate change law – from a range of domestic courts, to the IACtHR, the ECtHR, the ITLOS, and the ICJ.[81] I will have more to say on the role of courts in the next section. For now, it is important to recall that where courts become involved in lawmaking processes, their impact can be significant: the design of judicial institutions affords them a powerful role in shaping and steering the legal regimes over which they have jurisdiction. At the same time, if judicial decision-makers fail to properly perform their particular role in this process, an otherwise virtuous – participatory and problem-oriented – lawmaking process can be stymied.

[77] See eg D Bodansky, 'The Paris Climate Change Agreement: A New Hope?' (2016) 110 *American Journal of International Law* 388, 290–1; D Bodansky, 'The United Nations Climate Change Regime Thirty Years on – A Retrospective and Assessment' (2022) 62 *Washburn Law Journal* 1.

[78] C Bakker, 'The Paris Agreement on Climate Change: Balancing "Legal Force" and "Geographical Scope"' (2016) 25(1) *The Italian Yearbook of International Law* 299; C Bakker and F Francioni (ed), *The EU, the US and Global Climate Governance* (New York, Routledge, 2014); see also C Voigt and F Ferreira, 'Differentiation in the Paris Agreement' (2016) 6 *Climate Law* 58.

[79] See eg, by reference to Principle 21 of the Stockholm Declaration and Principle 2 of the Rio Declaration, F Yamin and J Depledge, *The International Climate Change Regime: A Guide to Rules, Institutions and Procedures* (Cambridge, Cambridge University Press, 2004) 68–9.

[80] See eg RO Keohane, 'The International Climate Regime Without American Leadership' (2017) 15(3) *Chinese Journal of Population Resources and Environment* 184.

[81] See UNEP, 'Global Climate Litigation Report: 2023 Status Review' (Nairobi, UNEP, 2023).

For that reason, international courts and tribunals face the challenge of needing to consider the broader lawmaking process in which they are intervening and query whether, in addition to resolving a dispute at hand, the relevant judicial decision is likely to block, encourage, or leave unaffected a regime's jurisgenerative potential.

In short, the rise of the framework convention-protocol model and the spread of procedural norms in the international environmental law field have significantly affected customary international lawmaking. The practical effects of adopting, implementing, and operating such setups are far-reaching, also for customary international lawmaking. By creating quasi-permanent frameworks for cooperation, by enabling dynamic changes to lawmaking processes and legal norms under the umbrella of a global concern about, for example, climate change, by being more inclusive in terms of the range of relevant actors, and by allowing for a significant participation of the scientific community, such regimes operate in ways that are inherently dynamic and have the potential to produce distinct types of customary international law norms. On the level of the climate change regime itself, the framework convention-protocol model leads to an institutionalisation of action around a particular issue, with dynamism built into the treaty setup, which supports its continuation and evolution. Legal regimes such as those to tackle climate change, including the Paris Agreement, have a series of features that ensure their stickiness. Additionally, by serving as continuous public fora for the airing, collection, and indeed stimulation of what could no doubt be drawn on later as 'state practice' or 'opinio juris', such mechanisms can serve as motors of customary international lawmaking – this not only makes formal withdrawal from such agreements less likely or useful for any potential defector, but also creates incentives for participation. To be sure, disadvantages of such regimes include their usually slow pace of lawmaking, weak enforcement mechanisms, the risk of entrenching silos, and possible inconsistencies with other legal regimes. However, in that context, customary international law can serve as an additional integrative element.[82]

IV. THIRD PARTY DISPUTE SETTLEMENT AND CUSTOMARY INTERNATIONAL LAW

As noted, the availability of custom as a formal modality of lawmaking serves as a powerful signal to a host of civil society organisations and experts who may seek ways to achieve legal and social change. It both legitimates the work of such actors and renders it at least potentially meaningful. Inversely, independent courts and arbitral tribunals benefit (from the perspective of their

[82] See eg Carazo and Klein, 'Implications for Public International Law' (n 76).

typical ends, which is to render enforceable and effective decisions or steer future behaviour in socially beneficial ways) when their decisions enjoy legitimacy and become socially effective. Therefore, they have incentives to anticipate and steer normative changes even when they are not yet reflected in positive law. Therefore, in the context of customary international lawmaking, third-party dispute settlers, civil society organisations, experts, and international organisations are engaged in relationships of co-dependency or complementarity, with potentially strong jurisgenerative effects.

Like in other areas of law, landmark cases of international environmental law are significant less on account of their specific holdings, or even their direct impact, as for how they allowed subsequent generations to organise and plan their conduct and served as a source of analogical reasoning in the broader international lawmaking arena. For example, during the Cold War, the duty of states to act in due diligence to prevent transboundary harm and risk was buttressed in a number of diplomatic, judicial, and other fora. Already the seminal *Corfu Channel* case – the first case decided by the Court in a highly eventful year 1949 – turned out to be particularly influential, even if it did not explicitly deal with an issue of transboundary environmental harm. For example, international lawyers have emphasised the lasting influence of the *Corfu Channel* case, including in international environmental law, on issues of the burden of proof, and on the law of state responsibility.[83] In later decades, and together with other canonical decisions in the field, the Court's holdings have been relied on, among others, in a number of cases and in the work of the ILC on issues of transboundary harm and risk management.[84] Another post-World War II case that influenced international environmental law, the *Lake Lanoux* arbitration, become a widely invoked precedent in the field of international water law, and environmental law more generally. Scholars were quick to seize upon and publicise the intellectual merits of the award, decided by some of the leading international lawyers of the era. Its status in the legal community has added to its general authority, while its reasoning proved useful beyond the specific matter in dispute.[85]

[83] *Corfu Channel Case* (Judgment of April 9th, 1949) [1949] ICJ 4. See also MA Fitzmaurice, 'The Corfu Channel Case and the Development of International Law' in N Ando et al (eds) *Liber Amicorum Judge Shigeru Oda*, Volume I (The Hague, Kluwer, 2002) 119.

[84] K Bannelier, 'Foundational Judgment or Constructive Myth? The Court's Decision as a Precursor to International Environmental Law' in K Bannelier, T Christakis, and S Heathcote (eds), *The ICJ and the Evolution of International Law: The Enduring Impact of the Corfu Channel Case* (Abingdon, Routledge, 2012) 242.

[85] See eg A Gervais, 'L'affaire du lac Lanoux, étude critique de la sentence arbitrale du Tribunal arbitral' (1960) 6 *Annuaire Français de Droit International* 372; L Boisson de Chazournes, 'The Notion of Environmental Flows and the Law Applicable to International Watercourses' (2014) 108 *Proceedings of the Annual Meeting (American Society of International Law)* 295; B MacChesney, 'Lake Lanoux Case (France-Spain)' (1959) 53 *The American Journal of International Law* 156; JG Laylin and RL Bianchi, 'The Role of Adjudication in International River Disputes: The Lake Lanoux Case' (1959) 53 *The American Journal of International Law* 30.

The balanced, careful, and general nature of the Tribunal's reasoning makes it eminently transferable to new situations – similarly to the ICJ's judgment in the *Gabčíkovo–Nagymaros* case, and perhaps in contrast to cases like *Pulp Mills*. Moreover, upper riparians have found it useful in litigation – as the *Indus Waters Kishenganga Arbitration* illustrates.[86] Incidentally, during the *Lake Lanoux* arbitration, Spain relied not only on local custom (of the Pyrenees region), but also on customary international law, proffering a large number of treaties as purported evidence for the existence of a rule of general international law,[87] even if the Tribunal rejected these arguments.[88]

As noted, the last three decades have seen an increasing involvement of international and regional courts in problems relating to international environmental law. Aspects of the design of a third-party dispute settlement body that shape customary international lawmaking include its composition, the appointment and tenure of its members, its jurisdictional scope, formal and informal aspects of its procedure, and the degree of publicity and deliberativeness characteristic of its working methods. But how third-party dispute settlement affects a field depends not only on its design but also the broader context in which it takes place. This includes the central role of scientific knowledge for decision-making in this area and the involvement of a wide array of civil society groups with broad-based public support.

Rather than actually 'identifying' customary international law, or simply being in a position to 'create' law, as domestic courts might be in a position to do under certain circumstances, international courts and tribunals tend to play a role in the international legal systems that is at once more complex and potentially more consequential. On the one hand, when international courts are called to apply customary international law, awareness of this fact can incentivise social actors to engage in (potentially) norm-generating behaviour of various sorts. In other words, the recognition that legal decision-making is an inexact science, coupled with the openness of the legal doctrine of customary international law, signals to a myriad social actors that their participation in lawmaking is at least potentially relevant. This makes what might appear to be a rather old-fashioned type of law – custom – a potentially potent source of legal and social change. At the same time, in the decisional phase, when courts – judges – are faced with handing down a final judgment or advisory opinion, they remain keenly aware of their limited powers. This is especially true of courts like the ICJ, compared to courts of a specialised jurisdictional ambit (like the ECtHR)

[86] See the restatement by the tribunal of India's argument on this point, *Case in the Matter of the Indus Water Kishenganga Arbitration (Pakistan v. India)*, PCA (Partial Award of 18 February 2013), paras 187–8.

[87] See Gervais, 'L'affaire du lac Lanoux' (n 85) 406. The Court refers (in French) to 'droit international commun', rather than custom, a term that is essentially equivalent to the English 'general international law'.

[88] ibid.

or the courts of close-knit regional organisations (like the EU's Court of Justice), whose jurisdictional powers may appear more solidly entrenched. While courts can always declare particular norms as ones of customary international law, even if they are truly new, support for any legal norm identified by an international court always remains tenuous. Continuously updating their expectations about potentially effective legal norms, judges are thus engaged in a task that at best involves accurately anticipating which legal norms will be widely accepted or have the potential to become effective. Although legal norms can become effective in various ways, the position of powerful actors and their expectations and preferences seem to be a central factor. To be sure, all this occurs in the context of a particular court or tribunal, which includes not only relevant past decisions, legal arguments proffered to it by the parties or other actors, but also the legal doctrine of customary international law.

The *Gabčíkovo–Nagymaros* case was undoubtedly the first major case dealing with international environmental law that came before the ICJ in the late twentieth century. It offers insights into a broader – and ongoing, but nonetheless contingent – transformation of the international law relating to the environment and the uses of shared resources on the local, regional, and international levels. The end of the Cold War left an opening for states to address the often-disastrous legacy of communist-era governance on the environment.[89] From today's perspective, the discontinuance of most aspects of this Slovak-Hungarian dispute before the ICJ and the integration of 'Green' concerns into mainstream European politics mark the end of an era in which civil society movements in Europe managed to achieve important social transformations – not only, but particularly in the field of environmental protection – on the local, regional, and global levels. In this context, environmentalisms, with different national connotations, found expression across the world.

Many scholars have examined the historical, including the political, social, and economic context of the *Gabčíkovo–Nagymaros* case.[90] Here, I simply wish to point to the broader context of the dispute to show the landscape in which landmark cases like *Gabčíkovo–Nagymaros* are embedded. The range of factors that shaped the dispute are myriad. Somewhat analogously to the background

[89] For a comparison of the tension between communist hydroelectricity projects in two eastern European countries, Romania and Czechoslovakia, and environmentalism in the period from 1948–1989, see A Štanzel, *Wasserträume und Wasserräume im Staatssozialismus: Ein umwelthistorischer Vergleich anhand der tschechoslowakischen und rumänischen Wasserwirtschaft, 1948–1989* (Göttingen, Vandenhoeck & Ruprecht, 2017) 166.

[90] *Gabčíkovo-Nagymaros Project (Hungary/Slovakia)* (Judgment) [1997] ICJ Rep 7; see eg T Fleischer, 'Jaws on the Danube: Water Management, Regime Change and the Movement Against the Middle Danube Hydroelectric Dam' (1993) 17 *International Journal of Urban and Regional Research* 429; See also Štanzel, *Wasserträume und Wasserräume im Staatssozialismus* (n 89); J Fitzmaurice, *Damming the Danube: Gabčíkovo and Post-Communist Politics in Europe* (Boulder, Westview Press, 1996). See also E Benvenisti, *Sharing Transboundary Resources: International Law and Optimal Resource Use*

situation preceding the *Trail Smelter* case, the underlying conflict(s) pitted different groups and interests that were not tied to any particular locale, but rather understood themselves as operating transnationally. As several studies dealing with the history and background of the *Gabčíkovo–Nagymaros* case have shown, already before the collapse of the communist regimes in the two countries, alliances transcending not only states and governments, but even ostensibly radically opposed regimes existed. Those supporting the project's continuation as it stood were initially the Slovaks, parts of the Hungarian government,[91] and those representing Austrian industrial, economic, and financial interests.[92] As the conspicuous role of corporate and economic interests in the context of the dispute suggest, these transnational entanglements were not limited to pressure groups lobbying for and against a project for ideational reasons, as many environmentalists were. Rather, transnational entanglements were often tied to economic and legal interests.[93] On the other side of the fence was a relatively diffuse and decentralised movement of environmentalists. This movement was visible to the public in a variety of forms, such as in public debates about the underlying dispute in various countries, including the US, through the voices of prominent political leaders in Austria, through the opinions of scientists and other figures who enjoyed public authority while being untarred by overly close links to the collapsed communist regimes, through public actions that regularly made the news, through mass protests on the streets of Austrian and Hungarian towns, including a major protest in Budapest in 1994, through the physical obstruction of construction sites, petitions, and in other ways. Importantly, those involved – activists and business representatives – were aware of these transnational linkages and their legal implications.[94] In short, when we consider the role of customary international lawmaking in the judicial context, the seemingly unrelated transnational aspects of political, environmental, and legal agitation form an essential part of the story. When courts identify or develop customary international law, in cases like *Pulp Mills*, *Indus Waters Kishenganga*, or *Gabčíkovo–Nagymaros*, it is these aspects of the

(Cambridge, Cambridge University Press, 2002) 199 (arguing that the 'decision raises serious doctrinal questions concerning the legitimacy of the court's innovative moves').

[91] Reuters, 'Papers Show Government Divisions over Danube Dam' (29 September 1988).

[92] See Štanzel, *Wasserträume und Wasserräume im Staatssozialismus* (n 89) 166 (citing Walter Fremuth in particular as exemplifying a quasi-transnationally operating actor in this context); see also New Scientist (Micha Glenny), 'Political Walz on the Danube Takes an Ugly Turn' (30 April 1987) 32–3; Fitzmaurice, *Damming the Danube* (n 90) 81–3 (referring to the Austrian link to the project); Fleischer, 'Jaws on the Danube' (n 90) 435.

[93] Thus, when Hungary backed off from the construction of the Nagymaros dam, the consortium of Austrian companies that had concluded a series of contracts with the respective Hungarian contractor, Oviber, engaged in a protracted, but relatively short, legal battle that led to a substantial settlement in November of 1991. See WIFO (A Keil), 'Wirtschaftschronik, IV. Quartal 1990' (1991) 1/91 *WIFO Monatsberichte* (1991) 18.

[94] See eg AP, '2,000 Protest Danube Power Project' (27 May 1988); see eg Die Presse, 'Firms Involved in Nagymaros Project Consider Legal Action against Politicians' (30 September 1988).

broader international lawmaking landscape that they have the power to shape, support, or stifle.

Another notable case in the international environmental law sphere that explicitly invoked customary international law, the *Indus Waters Kishenganga* arbitration, marked the first occasion for the judicial settlement of a dispute based on the Indus Waters Treaty. The Indus Waters Treaty – concluded by Pakistan, India, as well as the World Bank in 1960 – found its origin in the proposal of a leading US political figure, David E. Lilienthal.[95] In 1951 Lilienthal had essentially tried to draw the world's attention to the security risks inherent in the dispute over water in the Indus valley.[96] According to Lilienthal, solutions based on purported 'legal' claims to territory (adjudicated or arbitrated), politics, or religion would not be helpful – instead, cooperation for the mutual benefit of the riparians was needed and should be achieved through negotiation.[97] While Lilienthal may have seemed overly idealistic in the face of formidable obstacles, his approach is best understood as a strategy for transcending existing political antagonisms creatively by using legal means selectively and strategically. It is comparable to the strategy of producing 'concrete achievements which first create a de facto solidarity' among European nations, as outlined in the so-called Schuman Plan of 9 May 1950. That neo-functionalist approach was in high favour with technocratic internationalists in the Post-World War II period. While Lilienthal's preferred solution did not in fact translate into the agreement the parties actually reached with the Indus Waters Treaty, his comprehensive, holistic, and engineering-based approach was nonetheless influential. In addition, the challenges associated with the implementation of the treaty offer a good illustration of the force of background norms at work in the design of an agreement to regulate riparian rights.[98]

In 2013, an arbitral tribunal administered by the PCA issued its partial and final awards in a case concerning a dispute under the Indus Waters Treaty between Pakistan and India concerning the Kishenganga Hydro-Electric Project.[99]

[95] See on the role of David E. Lilienthal in the context preceding the conclusion of the Indus Water Treaty, especially, D Haines, '(Inter)Nationalist Rivers? Cooperative Development in David Lilienthal's Plan for the Indus Basin, 1951' (2014) 6 *Water History* 133; see also SM Neuse, *David E. Lilienthal: The Journey of an American Liberal* (Knoxville, University of Tennessee Press, 1996).

[96] See JG Laylin and RL Bianchi, 'The Role of Adjudication in International River Disputes' (n 85) 32 (footnote 7).

[97] DE Lilenthal, 'Another 'Korea' in the Making?' (4 August 1951) *Collier's* 58.

[98] See eg AA Arthur Michel, *The Indus Rivers: A Study of the Effects of Partition* (New Haven, Yale University Press, 1967) 518. A contextual analysis of the factors that may have affected the conclusion of the Indus Waters Treaty is offered in M Akhter, 'The Hydropolitical Cold War: The Indus Waters Treaty and State Formation in Pakistan' (2015) 46 *Political Geography* 65; see also, from the perspective of an engineer, IH Siddiqui, *Hydro Politics & Water Wars in South Asia* (Lahore, Vanguard Books, 2010) 51–92; very critical also BA Malik, *Indus Waters Treaty in Retrospect* (Lahore, Brite Books, 2005) 128–200.

[99] *Case in the Matter of the Indus Waters Kishenganga Arbitration (Pakistan v. India)* PCA (Partial Award of 18 February 2013 and Final Award of 20 December 2013); J Ahmad, 'The Indus Waters

The tribunal hearing the case was composed of an eminent panel of judges – many of them having already been involved in several landmark cases in the field of international environmental law.[100] The *Pulp Mills* case and the *Indus Waters Kishenganga* case shared the presence of two key decision-makers: Peter Tomka, who replaced the President in *Pulp Mills* given his then role as Vice-President (the *Pulp Mills* case was decided on the merits during a temporary absence of the then-President of the Court) as well as Bruno Simma, a notable dissenter in the *Pulp Mills* case, who might have had the opportunity to put some of his (and Judge Al-Khasawneh's) critical comments relating to evidentiary matters in the *Pulp Mills* case into practice in a case that similarly raised the problem of a tribunal's handling and evaluation of scientific and technical evidence. Beyond this, the two cases differ in some important respects, notably in the size and nature of the respective decision-making organ: in one case, the ICJ, in the other a five-member arbitral tribunal also composed of leading international law experts. The arbitrators faced the task of addressing two key substantive questions concerning India's proposed hydroelectric plant on the Kishenganga/Jelum River, which also raised many complex technical, hydrological, and environmental questions. While the dispute mainly came down to an exercise in the interpretation of detailed provisions of the 1960 Treaty and its Annexures, customary international law played a notable role. This was due partly to the fact that the Court of Arbitration was competent to settle certain disputes between the parties also by reference to customary international law as well as because under the applicable rules of treaty interpretation as codified in Article 31(3)(c) of the Vienna Convention on the Law of Treaties, 'relevant rules of international law applicable in the relations between the parties' were anyhow pertinent for the interpretation of the treaty.[101]

Finally, the mentioned *Pulp Mills* case was also the product of a complex set of domestic and transnational circumstances.[102] The underlying industrial project represented one of the largest instances of foreign investment in the country's history. At the height of the dispute, tensions between the two countries were extremely high, even if the reported deployment by Uruguay of its army to protect mills from protesters can be characterised as posturing.[103]

Kishenganga Arbitration and State-to-State Disputes' (2013) 29(3) *Arbitration International* 507; J Moussa, 'Implications of the Indus Water Kishenganga Arbitration for the International Law of Watercourses and the Environment' 64 *International and Comparative Law Quarterly* 697.

[100] Thus, the tribunal's Chair, Stephen M. Schwebel, had served as ICJ President during the *Gabčíkovo-Nagymaros* Project case. Judge Tomka, who acted as an advocate for Slovakia in that case, was the ICJ's acting President when the *Pulp Mills* case was decided. Bruno Simma further also sat on the Court when *Pulp Mills* was decided, offering a joint dissenting opinion which criticised the majority for its handling and consideration of evidence in that case.

[101] *Indus Waters Kishenganga Arbitration (Pakistan v. India)* (Partial Award of 18 February 2013), paras 447–52.

[102] Springer, *Cases of Conflict* (n 14) 197–221.

[103] ibid, 197.

At the same time, following the Court's decision, countries of the Latin American and Caribbean region accelerated domestic and regional-level diplomatic efforts at implementing Principle 10 of the Rio Declaration, on 'access to information, access to public participation and access to justice'.[104] At any rate, the *Pulp Mills* case explicitly dealt with matters of customary international law but was also marred by confusing drafting: Many readers, including ICJ judges writing in their official capacity, expressed difficulty making sense of the Court's findings on general international law and the requirement to undertake an environmental impact assessment (EIA) contained in para 204. Nonetheless, in subsequent cases brought under similar legal bases and concerning environmental disputes, parties began to focus on the EIA as an obligation explicitly arising under customary international law. This was visible in a set of cases between Costa Rica and Nicaragua as well as in a case between Chile and Bolivia.[105] In contrast, the *Indus Waters Kishenganga* awards were more cogent in their treatment of customary international law. This is not to say that the Awards were 'models' in applying an abstract legal doctrine of customary international law. Rather, when it came to the key relevant categories, the Awards avoided unnecessary ambiguity as to categories like 'requirements', 'practices', customary international law, or general international law, let alone custom, principles, rules, etc. With minor exceptions, the Awards were instead clear and transparent when labelling key concepts relating to customary international law. As such, the two decisions offer contrasting models of how courts and tribunals can use the legal doctrine of customary international law not only as a tool of decision-making but also to steer and encourage bottom-up international lawmaking.

V. FROM THE SILENCES OF INTERNATIONAL LAW TO GLOBAL PUBLIC HEALTH LAW

Following the European colonisation of the Americas starting in the late fifteenth century, many of the native populations in the 'New World' faced both genocide and the less visible death and disease caused by pathogens against which they often had no immunities.[106] Somewhat remarkably, much of the earlier experience of inter-polity cooperation in the management of epidemics

[104] See eg ECLAC, 'Regional Agreement on Access to Information, Public Participation and Justice in Environmental Matters in Latin America and the Caribbean: Implementation Guide' (Santiago, United Nations, 2023) 206.

[105] *Dispute over the Status and Use of the Waters of the Silala (Chile v. Bolivia)* (Merits) [2022] ICJ Rep 614, para 114.

[106] See eg JR McNeill and ES Mauldin (eds), *A Companion to Global Environmental History* (Chichester, John Wiley & Sons, 2012) 326; W McNeill, *Plagues and Peoples* (New York, Anchor Books, 1976) 176–207; see also JN Hays, *The Burdens of Disease: Epidemics and Human Response in Western History*, revised edn (New Brunswick, Rutgers University Press, 2009) 72.

seems to have been ignored. After all, city-states in the Mediterranean had successfully deployed merchant quarantines just as transoceanic conquest, slavery, and commerce had begun in the fifteenth century. This is explained only in part by lagging advances in science and medicine. It was also due to the geopolitical and economic context of a lawmaking process that structurally favoured the 'centre' over the 'periphery'. At the same time, it was only in the nineteenth century that public health would become associated with the ever-more institutionalised field of international law.

What is today called global public health law and policy was – in its embryonic state – the site of several early and instructive examples of international lawmaking.[107] Since at least the nineteenth century, public health was closely connected to competition among empires, the consolidation of statehood, and the professionalisation of health-related fields.[108] The proximity of the dominant European powers of that era and their global imperial expansion resulted in growing cross-border exchanges motivating governments to coordinate their health policies, if only to avoid contagion in Europe. At the same time, the close connection between public health policies and statehood also explains why governments were often reluctant to agree on legally binding norms that could constrain their action in times of crisis. We can distinguish two broad varieties of health-related public policies adopted by governments and other collectivities to this day.[109] One aspect of public health consists of general measures aimed at addressing a wide variety of health concerns in the long term. These include the development of a health care infrastructure, measures of sanitation and environmental protection, as well as education, training, and licensing. Over time, the meaning of health expanded continuously, beginning to encompass issues like occupational disabilities, mental health, and preventative medicine. The other aspect of public health consists of emergency measures aimed at managing usually temporally limited events like natural or human-made disasters, epidemics, as well as the health effects of armed conflicts or terrorist attacks. These two aspects of public health law and policy have never been truly separate but have multiple connecting points and overlaps. Nonetheless, they are understood

[107] On 'global public health', see eg AE Birn, Y Pillay, and TH Holtz, *Textbook of Global Health*, 4th edn (Oxford, Oxford University Press, 2017). The literature on global public health, including its legal history, is immense and gaining increasing attention. See eg G Rosen, *A History of Public Health*, revised and expanded edn (Baltimore, John Hopkins University Press, 2015); RM Packard, *A History of Global Health: Interventions into the Lives of Other Peoples* (Baltimore, John Hopkins University Press, 2016); D Porter, *Health, Civilization and the State: A History of Public Health from Ancient to Modern Times* (London, Routledge 1999); SA Wempe, *Chronic Disparities: Public Health in Historical Perspective* (Oxford, Oxford University Press, 2020).

[108] See eg AE Birn, 'The Stages of International (Global) Health: Histories of Success or Successes of History?' (2009) 4(1) *Global Public Health* 50; see also CO Pannenborg, *New International Health Order: An Inquiry into the International Relation of World Health and Medical Care* (Alphen aan den Rijn, Sijthoff & Noordhoff, 1979) 15–27.

[109] On the former, see eg P Baldwin, *Contagion and the State in Europe, 1830–1930* (Cambridge, Cambridge University Press, 1999) 2–10.

as distinct aspects of the field across the world, notwithstanding significant differences in access to public health across countries.

Most contemporary legal scholarship covering international cooperation in the public health field begins with the nineteenth century.[110] Yet, the individuals and groups developing international 'sanitary' law in the nineteenth and twentieth centuries were not working from a blank slate. Historians of public health have identified and documented numerous precursors going back several centuries, including instances of organised public health policies and bodies on the municipal level, as well as cases of inter-polity cooperation on public health matters. To be sure, important scientific breakthroughs, as well as developments in technology, transportation, and communication played important roles in expanding the field since the nineteenth century. However, some of the ideas that undergird both contemporary and earlier international public health law are age-old. For example, quarantines have long been used to minimise the virological risks of cross-border exchanges and were also subject to various forms of legal or quasi-legal constraints. Well before the International Health Regulations, the first documented cases of quarantines in modern times were introduced by comparatively wealthy coastal city-states that relied on maritime commerce.[111] Another early example of proto-customary forms of cooperation in the public health field is visible in inter-polity cooperation between Italian city-states in the context of the so-called 'concerto', a decentralised format conducive to forms of customary lawmaking.[112] Although systems of inter-polity cooperation on public health existed in various regions, the extent to which they have been studied varies widely.[113] Moreover, as Paul Weindling notes, decades prior to the major international sanitary conferences and almost a century before the creation of international bodies in the public health field, there were already regional and quasi-international quarantine authorities in place, notably in Egypt and Constantinople (Istanbul).[114]

[110] See eg N Howard-Jones, *The Scientific Background of the International Sanitary Conferences, 1851–1938* (Geneva, World Health Organization, 1975); Pannenborg, *New International Health Order* (n 108) 27.

[111] MD Grmek, 'Les débuts de la quarantaine maritime' in C Buchet (ed), *L'Homme, La Santé et La Mer* (Paris, H. Champion, 1997) 39, 51–6 (contesting the claim that Marseille introduced the first maritime quarantine of forty days, and instead arguing that Dubrovnik invented the practice in 1377, while 'Venice perfected it after 1403'); see also PS Sehdev, 'Arcanum: The Origin of Quarantine' (1 November 2002) 35 *Clinical Infectious Diseases* 1071, 1072; E Tognotti, 'Lessons from the History of Quarantine, From Plague to Influenza A' (2013) 19(2) *Emerging Infectious Diseases* 254.

[112] CM Cipolla, *Fighting the Plague in Seventeenth-century Italy* (Madison, University of Wisconsin Press, 1981) 3 and 49–50 (linking this type of 'international health cooperation' to its nineteenth-century successors).

[113] See eg KW Bowers, *Plague and Public Health in Early Modern Seville* (Rochester, University of Rochester Press, 2013); see also NM Goodman, *International Health Organizations and their Work* (Philadelphia, Blakiston, 1952) 32.

[114] P Weindling, 'Introduction: Constructing International Health Between the Wars' in P Weindling (ed), *International Health Organisations and Movements, 1918–1939* (Cambridge, Cambridge University Press, 2009) 1, 5–6.

This early period saw the development of common standards for addressing issues of public health, prompted by a variety of contingent geopolitical, commercial, and ethical motives. In parallel, public health 'experts' and 'scientists' collaborated across borders through scholarship, debate, and training. However, governments have traditionally been reluctant to accept far-reaching intrusions into their freedom of manoeuvre in this area. The simultaneous rejection of legally binding international instruments combined with a good deal of decentralised coordination and the role of scientific expertise made forms of bottom-up lawmaking, including forms of customary international lawmaking, particularly relevant. To be sure, most legal scholars writing about the field of international public health law today put limited emphasis on customary international law. For example, David Fidler, whose work ranges from in-depth studies of the international law of infectious diseases[115] to customary international law more generally,[116] has argued that customary international law played a very limited role in global public health.[117] Nonetheless, even the field's early history illustrates the presence of various lawmaking factors,[118] with important parallels to contemporary processes of customary international lawmaking in several areas.

To be sure, the beginnings of what we might today call 'global public health' law and policy were seen more as European 'sanitary' control than international law. Largely in response to the perceived threat from repeated waves of cholera outbreaks that had begun to affect European populations since the early nineteenth century, the dominant European powers of the era engaged in forms of cross-border cooperation and coordination that would later be seen as the origin of global public health law. Indeed, the initially European but increasingly more representative International Sanitary Conferences that began in the mid-nineteenth century are routinely referred to as the backdrop of contemporary international health cooperation. Both the official publications of leading contemporary international organisations in the health field, such as the World Health Organization (WHO) and

[115] See DP Fidler, *International Law and Infectious Diseases* (Oxford, Oxford University Press, 1999); DP Fidler, 'Bioterrorism, Public Health, and International Law' (2002) 3(1) *Chicago Journal of International Law* 7; DP Fidler, 'From International Sanitary Conventions to Global Health Security: The New International Health Regulations' (2005) 4(2) *Chinese Journal of International Law* 325 (describing the process leading from the International Sanitary Conventions to the 2005 revision of the International Health Regulations); DP Fidler, '"Geographical Morality" Revisited: International Relations, International Law, and the Controversy over Placebo-Controlled HIV Clinical Trials in Developing Countries' (2001) 42(2) *Harvard International Law Journal* 299; DP Fidler, 'Microbialpolitik: Infectious Diseases and International Relations' (1998) 14(1) *American University International Law Review* 1 ('provid[ing] a framework with which to analyze the global politics of infectious disease control').

[116] DP Fidler, 'Challenging the Classical Concept of Custom: Perspectives on the Future of Customary International Law' (1996) 39 *German Yearbook of International Law* 198.

[117] See Fidler, *International Law and Infectious Diseases* (n 115) 98–9.

[118] See eg Baldwin, *Contagion and the State in Europe, 1830–1930* (n 109) 235–6.

many scholars writing in the field point to the important role of this series of international conferences. As one scholar puts it, this early conference diplomacy served to both 'legitimise' and 'organise' an incipient regulatory field.[119] The desire for legitimation by pedigree is also visible in the work of many contemporary organisations working in the public health field. For instance, the 10th-anniversary report of the WHO, published in 1958, opens by observing that '[i]nternational public health had its origin, just over a century ago, in the International Sanitary Conference which opened in Paris on 23 July 1851'.[120] However, many of these nineteenth-century meetings did not produce 'hard law'. As Fidler notes, until the late nineteenth century, none of the proposed International Sanitary Conventions entered into force.

The fact that it took so long for hard law to emerge in this field can obscure the development of a shared set of expectations with regard to public health-related duties and powers of states on the international plane. In addition, it can be argued that even before any of the nineteenth-century conferences of European powers, the idea that governments were under a kind of international duty concerning public health had gained currency, namely in the form of mutual expectations that governments in control of important ports in the Mediterranean region would implement policies to limit the spread of infectious diseases. Moreover, while earlier efforts at international health regulation seemed to have been hampered by various forms of national resistance,[121] the International Sanitary Conferences starting in the mid-nineteenth century appear to have had an impact on domestic legislative developments, which in turn shaped international legal norms in the field. Note, for example, a 25 August 1860 Report of the British House of Commons containing summaries of domestic quarantine regulations across several countries.[122] The brief report on France stands out in underlining that the 'existing laws and regulations in all French ports are based' on 'the recommendations and conclusions' discussed at the 1851–2 International Sanitary Conference.[123] Although a report by Gavin Milroy, which is appended to the 1860 report, concludes that only a handful of states adopted the outcomes of the conference, the conference record actually shows considerable alignment on some basic ideas and principles; notably the idea of proceeding from scientific considerations and the recognition that governments were limited in the extent to which they could impose restrictive measures in the face of actual or potential health risks.

[119] See eg Birn, 'The Stages of International (Global) Health: Histories of Success or Successes of History?' (n 108) 53.

[120] World Health Organization, *The First Ten Years of the World Health Organization* (Geneva, World Health Organization, 1958) 3.

[121] MJ Echenberg, *Plague Ports: The Global Urban Impact of Bubonic Plague, 1894–1901* (New York, NYU Press, 2007) 15.

[122] 'Quarantine. Abstract of regulations in force in Foreign Countries respecting Quarantine, communicated to the Board of Trade' (Her Majesty's Stationery Office, 25 August 1860).

[123] ibid, 9.

Although they were the most visible diplomatic events in the health field during the nineteenth century, the International Sanitary Conferences were hardly the only international fora at which coordinated policies or norms in the field of public health were discussed and developed. Other international meetings with similarly expert participation included the International Medical Congresses, the International Military Health Congresses, as well as various more specialised conferences dealing with diseases such as tuberculosis. Less widely discussed, presumably in part due to their links to imperialism and paternalism, were transnational efforts and projects to discuss and develop norms to address so-called venereal diseases.[124]

We can identify one example of a quasi-international lawmaking process, albeit not commonly labelled as such, in the context of a widely-studied outbreak of the plague between 1910–1 in various parts of Manchuria, parts of which were then ruled by China, Japan, and Russia, resulting in an estimated sixty thousand fatalities.[125] As the epidemic spread through the region, the various powers, alone and occasionally in cooperation with one another, tried to address it partly by reference to past practices. As noted, while some of these practices went back centuries, they had been articulated and brought on the international agenda in the context of the numerous International Sanitary Conferences at which selected governments had assembled in various European cities since the mid-nineteenth century. Drawing on informal norms and practices developed in Europe since the nineteenth century and applying them to the Manchurian context not only accelerated their internationalisation. It also transformed them. Following the plague's outbreak, the Chinese government convened an international conference of experts, the 1911 International Plague Conference, in Mukden (present-day Shenyang). By deliberately framing the conference as one of experts, the Chinese government both set and followed existing practices in the field. It drew on experts, scientists, and medical professionals, while leaving to one side possible political and territorial interests that would otherwise have determined such interactions. As William Summers observed, amid many changes to the fight against infectious diseases since the nineteenth century, the significance of 'networks of scientists' and other experts became a stable feature of international efforts to address infectious diseases globally. As Summers notes: '… [I]nternational networks of scientists, from Mukden in 1911 to Geneva in the twenty-first century, serve as a counterweight to the nationally focused work of diplomats and politicians'.[126]

[124] For a discussion of the 19th century background to the 'abolitionists' in France see eg E Camiscioli, *Reproducing the French Race: Immigration, Intimacy, and Embodiment in the Early Twentieth Century* (Durham, Duke University Press, 2009) 101–4.

[125] See WC Summers, *The Great Manchurian Plague of 1910-1911: The Geopolitics of an Epidemic Disease* (New Haven, Yale University Press, 2012).

[126] ibid, 159.

As noted, already before Mukden, a series of cholera epidemics had prompted the development of tentative forms of international cooperation on infectious diseases in Europe.[127] To be sure, in this context, international law has a particular meaning, ideas of 'global public health' were not current, and profound inequalities and the peak of European imperialism marked the limits of anything like global public health policy. More broadly, neither international law nor the field of international public health in particular were well-institutionalised. For example, according to Anne-Emmanuelle Birn, the chief achievement of international public health until 1902 was the 'holding of meetings',[128] an assessment still raising the question of their potential broader normative effects. Alongside a flurry of diplomatic initiatives, a set of incidents during the mid-nineteenth century concerning the spread of infectious diseases such as cholera and the plague thus led to recurrent intergovernmental efforts at cross-border lawmaking in the field. Even if the results of such efforts were not ratified, they eventually served as a basis for more expansive forms of public health regulation.

The outcomes of the 1911 International Plague Conference also feature in a major work by the medical doctor Wu Lien-Teh entitled 'Treatise on Pneumonic Plague', which was published and distributed by the League of Nations in 1926 and would remain authoritative even into the post-World War II period.[129] In this work, Wu drew on his experiences during and after the plague that hit Manchuria in 1910–1. Wu had played a key role as a scientist and policy-maker in the context of the 1910–1 plague and the 1911 conference in Mukden.[130] As Wu recalls in his 1926 Treatise, the 1911 International Plague Conference was meant to assemble 'experts from eleven countries … to recommend plans for preventing future outbreaks of a similar disastrous nature'.[131] As Summers observes, the Chinese government, which had initiated the conference, intentionally tried to ensure that it would be one of experts rather than governmental officials or diplomats. It was understandably feared by several governments at the time that a conference that did not have a purely scientific or consultative focus would have allowed various governments to use the occasion to try to advance particular strategic or geopolitical aims.[132] Such sentiments could apply with no less force to the twenty-first century's first major global pandemic. Wu's treatise is the work of a scientist and medical professional: In addition to detailed studies of the plague's aetiology and the ecological context of the 1910–1 outbreak, it

[127] See Fidler, *International Law and Infectious Diseases* (n 115) 26–35 (with further references).

[128] See eg Birn, 'The Stages of International (Global) Health: Histories of Success or Successes of History?' (n 108) 53.

[129] According to Summers, Wu's work was only 'superseded' by a work published by the WHO in 1954 and authored by a 'protégé' of Wu's. See Summers, *The Great Manchurian Plague of 1910–1911* (n 125) 105.

[130] See LT Wu, *A Treatise on Pneumonic Plague* (Geneva, League of Nations, 1926); see also Summers, *The Great Manchurian Plague of 1910–1911* (n 125) 63–4.

[131] Wu, *A Treatise on Pneumonic Plague* (n 130) vii.

[132] eg Summers, *The Great Manchurian Plague of 1910–1911* (n 125) 80–93.

contains recommendations concerning the prophylaxis and prevention of the plague both on the local and the international levels. The recommendations Wu makes in his 1926 treaties relate to a number of design features of the developing infrastructure of international health policy, including the structure and communication of cross-border efforts for the prevention and management of diseases such as the plague. The recommendations also concern a variety of other practical measures dealing with both infected and (presumably) non-infected areas.[133] Although the work of medical professionals like Wu rarely features in discussions of global public health law, it helped shape international law norms for the preparation for, management of, and response to infectious diseases. As this and other examples highlighted in this book show, scientific, medical, and technical knowledge play crucial roles in the context of customary international lawmaking. Wu's impact also highlights the central role that individuals, with their distinct mix of professional experiences, knowledge, and personal qualities play in shaping international lawmaking processes. Their role and selection are thus not ancillary but often central features of customary international lawmaking processes.

Up until the beginning of World War I, international cooperation in the health sphere thus progressed at speed: Following numerous proposed but unratified International Sanitary Conventions, a legally binding document was achieved with the International Sanitary Convention of 1892, the first to enter into force.[134] During this period, one of the deadliest modern pandemics, the 1918–20 flu (H1N1) pandemic, swept through the world[135] and also prompted, among others, momentous changes to public health systems in many countries, with broader normative effects.[136] The early decades of the twentieth century also saw a growing institutionalisation of international public health law, with the creation of regional[137] and international public and private organisations dealing with public health,[138] notably in the context of the League of Nations' activities in the social and economic sphere.[139] The period between 1902 and 1939 witnessed important institutional innovations, with both the 'Office Internationale d'Hygiène Publique' (OIHP) and later on the League of Nations

[133] Wu, *A Treatise on Pneumonic Plague* (n 130) 418–48.

[134] See Howard-Jones, *The Scientific Background of the International Sanitary Conferences, 1851–1938* (n 110) 64–5; Fidler, *International Law and Infectious Diseases* (n 115) 25.

[135] The popular misnomer for the 1918–1920 flu pandemic is the 'Spanish Flu', see eg A Trilla et al, 'The 1918 "Spanish Flu" in Spain' (2008) 47 *Clinical Infectious Diseases* 668; SK *Kent, The Influenza Pandemic of 1918-1919: A Brief History with Documents* (2013) 7–11.

[136] M Martini et al., *The Spanish Influenza Pandemic: a lesson from history 100 years after 1918*, 60(1) *Journal of Preventive Medicine and Hygiene* E64–E67 (29 March 2019).

[137] See eg M Cueto and S Palmer, *Medicine and Public Health in Latin America: A History* (Cambridge, Cambridge University Press, 2014) 126–8.

[138] See generally Weindling (ed), *International Health Organisations and Movements, 1918–1939* (n 114).

[139] MD Dubin, 'The League of Nations Health Organisation' in P Weindling (ed), *International Health Organisations and Movements, 1918–1939* (n 114) 56.

Health Organization playing important, if parallel, roles.[140] After World War I, the OIHP coexisted with the League of Nation's own Health Committee and Health Section (created in 1922), but the two bodies did not coordinate their activities;[141] only after World War II was a common global health organisation created with the WHO.

Customary international law has played a limited role in global public health law. However, we can trace contemporary global public health law to complex and decentralised international lawmaking processes that drew on numerous precursors. The emergence of legal norms in the field is best understood by reference to the efforts by various actors and institutions to advance public health outcomes at the domestic, regional, and global levels. Health is a characteristically universal concern, even if access to healthcare has traditionally been distributed in highly unequal ways. This basic context has affected not only the *telos* of global public health law but also how global health law has been made and the actors that have shaped it. Running like a red thread through the history of global public health law is the significant role of scientists and doctors, educational and research institutions, merchants and businesspeople, activists, the pharmaceutical and chemical industries, as well as philanthropic organisations. Keeping this context in mind allows us to better understand the lawmaking factors shaping global public health law, as dynamic as they remain.[142] At least so far, customary international lawmaking processes in this field have been characterised by a strong degree of decentralisation, multiple stages, and the involvement of a diverse cast of actors. At the same time, the legal norms emerging in this field have tended to collide with more deeply entrenched norms invoked by governments that seek to restrict interference with what are perceived as core sovereign functions. From that perspective, the rise of treaty-making in the field since the nineteenth century should not obscure the fact that lawmaking in this area has always included informal, decentralised, localised, and expert-driven efforts, something that continues to this day. This insight allows us to better understand the seemingly limited role of customary international law in the global public health field and can inform the design of treaty-based processes in ways that support existing customary international law norms and incentivise further jurisgenerative efforts.

[140] See eg Birn, 'The Stages of International (Global) Health: Histories of Success or Successes of History?' (n 108) 50, 53–5.

[141] Pannenborg, *New International Health Order* (n 108) 181–2; N Howard-Jones, *International Public Health between the Two World Wars: The Organizational Problems* (Geneva, World Health Organization, 1978).

[142] See eg WHO, 'Global Strategy on Digital Health 2020–2025' (Geneva, World Health Organization, 2020) 42 (defining 'multistakeholder groups').

6

Reconsidering the Legal Doctrine of Customary International Law

BECAUSE THIS BOOK'S framework centres around four types of customary international law, it is crucial to establish how it relates to the dominant legal doctrine of customary international law, which is likely to remain unitary but plays an important role in the international legal order, also as a kind of legal fiction. This chapter therefore focuses on the central yet often neglected relationship between customary international law as a set of ideas and legal doctrines, on the one hand, and as a broader social phenomenon, the 'law in action', on the other. It traces the intellectual history of the contemporary legal doctrine of customary international law, illuminating its role and the possibilities and limits of potential changes to it. It considers the various factors that stabilise the legal doctrine of customary international law, the ILC's contribution to it, and its role in global lawmaking. Finally, the chapter considers the role of customary international law in the context of aspirations for global democracy and an international lawmaking landscape populated by a variety of social movements and increasingly structured by the activities of international organisations.

I. FROM THE IDEA TO THE LEGAL DOCTRINE OF CUSTOMARY INTERNATIONAL LAW

As noted above, participants to nearly every legal order recognise unwritten forms of law as authoritative.[1] To be sure, legal systems are diverse and internally complex and there is a huge variety in the nature, extent, and role of such unwritten law. Furthermore, forms of unwritten law in various legal systems go by different names ('unwritten law', 'common law', 'custom', 'customary law', 'unwritten principles', etc, and their respective cognates in different languages). Despite the plethora of designations and unwritten law's patchy presence, hardly a legal order exists in which some form of unwritten law is not at least sometimes recognised. Nonetheless, legal scholars have a tendency

[1] On the *lex non scripta*, see also the discussion in Chapter 1, Section IV.

to underestimate, downplay, if not largely ignore the presence and relevance of unwritten law.[2]

This is significant because the idea and legal doctrine of customary international law did not develop in a vacuum. Although some express scepticism on that point,[3] there is ample evidence that customary international law has been shaped, indeed built upon, layers of prior thinking and experience related to unwritten law (the *lex non scripta*). That aspect of its intellectual genealogy explains why it is associated with 'unwritten' law and other relatively dynamic, malleable, and community-derived forms of law. To be sure, not everything that goes by the name of 'customary law' reflects such forms of law[4] and the same is true, to some extent, of 'customary international law'. However, insights into various forms of unwritten law can be leveraged for a better understanding of customary international law.[5]

When the legal doctrine of the 'sources' of international law was progressively defined in the early and still influential works that established international law as a discipline and, importantly, when the PCIJ Statute was drafted (see more on that in the subsequent section), its authors were familiar with prior thinking about unwritten and customary law. Even had they intended and gone about trying to create something entirely different, they inevitably drew on received ideas linked to earlier thinking about customary law, for instance, in the context of canon law or Roman Law. Even if they had succeeded in introducing into international law a truly novel idea, its meaning could not have remained fixed but would rather be continually negotiated in social practice, especially in the context of a relatively decentralised international legal order in which domestic courts, activists, scholars, and lawyers significantly shape the meaning of the legal doctrine of customary international law. In short, customary international law's central role in international law does not derive simply from having been posited in the ICJ (and earlier, the PCIJ) Statute but rather from its status as a multifaceted form of the international *lex non scripta*, which is shaped through the daily users of international law, including lawyers, judges, those using the legal system to vindicate their interests or rights, and ultimately all those who seek to invoke the global legal order. Those individual legal operators are the

[2] Lawyers and judges also tend to be reluctant to acknowledge the significance of unwritten forms of law in so-called 'modern' legal orders or those whose popular legitimation and authority is thought to depend on their perception as code or text-based. See also A Ross, *On Law and Justice* (Berkeley, University of California Press, 1959) 95; HLA Hart, *The Concept of Law*, 2nd edn (Oxford Clarendon Press, 1994) 233.

[3] See eg J d'Aspremont, *The Discourse on Customary International Law* (Oxford, Oxford University Press, 2021) 5–9.

[4] See eg MSH Kim, 'Customary Law and Colonial Jurisprudence in Korea' (2009) 57 *American Journal of Comparative Law* 205, 213.

[5] See eg LL Fuller, *The Principles of Social Order: Selected Essays of Lon L. Fuller* (Kenneth I. Winston ed., Durham, Duke University Press, 1981) 213; see also WM Reisman, *Law in Brief Encounters* (New Haven, Yale University Press, 1999) 3; M Barkun, *Law Without Sanctions: Order in Primitive Societies and the World Community* (New Haven, Yale University Press, 1968) 75.

portals through which ideas about unwritten law can shape customary international law.

There is an important normative implication of the finding that forms of unwritten law are omnipresent across legal systems, albeit in particular manifestations, such as customary international law. It relates to the fact that only relatively recently has 'international law' moved towards becoming a truly globalised or universal language.[6] The universality of unwritten forms of law makes them relatively more compatible with global legal orders than more particularistic modalities of lawmaking. At the same time, to the extent that customary international law is multifaceted, as I argue in this book, this conclusion may apply more to some types of customary international law norms than others. At any rate, while the idea of customary international law displays many idiosyncratic elements, its universal characteristics could allow it to serve as an anchor, or at least as an important integrative element, of a truly global international legal order.

Beyond the debate over contingency versus universality – or the extent to which customary international law is both an instance of a quasi-universal form of law and an idiosyncratic part of modern international law – the role of customary international law has been supported by at least four additional mutually reinforcing processes – path dependence,[7] lock-in, the structure of the international legal order, and network effects – which further stabilise the position of customary international law as an 'authoritative' source of law in the international domain. Without entering the debate over the precise type of path dependence at issue, the choice of the drafters of the PCIJ Statute, later incorporated into the ICJ Statute, was a fateful one and meant that customary international law became the default non-treaty source that judges could invoke to decide cases raising issues of international law. The continued role of customary international law was ensured through the lock-in created by the difficult process of treaty amendment, and the ICJ Statute in particular (notably, Article 69 of the ICJ Statute refers to the same amendment procedure envisaged for the Charter of the UN). In addition, over the years, the ICJ has developed a central, though not necessarily hierarchically superior or actually influential, position in the international legal order. Through its close relationship to the UN, including the ILC, and the broader community of

[6] See eg CW Jenks, *The Common Law of Mankind* (New York, Praeger, 1958) 62–172; E McWhinney, *The International Court of Justice and the Western Tradition of International Law: The Paul Martin Lectures in International Relations and Law* (Dordrecht, Martinus Nijhoff, 1987) 3–5; H Thirlway, 'Reflections on Multiculturalism and International Law' in S Yee and JY Morin (eds), *Multiculturalism and International Law: Essays in Honor of Edward McWhinney* (Leiden, Martinus Nijhoff, 2009) 95; O Yasuaki, *International Law in a Transcivilizational World* (Cambridge, Cambridge University Press, 2017); A Roberts, *Is International Law International?* (Oxford, Oxford University Press, 2017).

[7] On path dependency, see eg OA Hathaway, 'Path Dependence in the Law: The Course and Pattern of Legal Change in a Common Law System' (2001) 86 *Iowa Law Review* 104. See also M Prado and M Trebilcock, 'Path Dependence, Development, and the Dynamics of Institutional Reform' (2009) 59(3) *The University of Toronto Law Journal* 341, 350.

international lawyers that helps sustain international law, the ICJ's legal findings have enjoyed powerful reach, also feeding into the ILC's codification efforts. From that perspective, in a global society that is diverse and fragmented, the lawyers that operate in symbolic core nodes like the ICJ, ILC, and other parts of the UN – perhaps simply because of the symbolic or forum-creating character of such institutions – can serve as important points of connection. From this perspective, the structure of the social relationships undergirding international law serves to augment the role of customary international law. Network effects – meaning positive externalities resulting from the widespread adoption of customary international law as a recognised source of law – further support its role and significance. In that context, a factor that helps sustain and stabilise customary international law is the conceptual dichotomy between domestic and international law.[8] Notably, the idea of relatively distinct domestic legal systems reflecting particular political, social, or cultural ideas of law, which undergirds the state-centric system of international law, tends to stifle changes to received categories of lawmaking. Similarly, the division between distinct international legal sub-fields tends to reduce incentives for wholesale changes to the intellectual categories used across those fields (including customary international law).

In addition to these structural and intellectual factors supporting customary international law's role in the international legal arena, customary international law meets several functional and socio-political needs of contemporary (twentieth and twenty-first century) international lawmaking. This has allowed it to be drawn on repeatedly by legal practitioners, which further entrenched its role (indeed, the meta-norm positing customary international law as a relevant 'source of law' can itself be understood as an entrenched background custom). Notably, there is a functional need for a particularly flexible modality of lawmaking especially in the decentralised but strongly power-oriented international system. While most legal systems are characterised by a duality of written and unwritten forms of law, the need for adaptability is particularly acute in international law given the absence of an effective means of centralised law enforcement. Moreover, entry and exit into the society of states cannot be very effectively regulated by treaty (thus, the law of state succession). This makes it imperative for unwritten law to govern the gaps that inevitably arise in the application of basic international legal norms, including those concerning the prohibition of genocide, international humanitarian law, the law of the sea, or fundamental rules of the law of treaties and state responsibility.

[8] The rigid distinction between domestic and international law reached its zenith in the nineteenth century and in some ways remains with us today. See eg C Chinkin, 'Monism and Dualism: The Impact of Private Authority on the Dichotomy Between National and International Law' in JE Nijman and A Nollkaemper (eds), *New Perspectives on the Divide Between National and International Law* (Oxford, Oxford University Press, 2007) 134, 135; see also A Mills, 'The Private History of International Law' (2006) 55(1) *The International and Comparative Law Quarterly* 1.

Moreover, over the last more than 70 years, the international legal order has become more democratic. A host of new countries and their peoples formally gained access to the international diplomatic table, represented by their governments as states and thus recognised actors on the world stage. This has led to a proliferation of more diverse and inclusive diplomatic exchanges, incidents, and countless legal disputes, some before international courts and tribunals. In addition, and relatedly, international law has become a subject of everyday debate in and across countries. To be sure, treaties and other more formal modes of international lawmaking are the main tools used by an increasing number of governments, and their constituencies, to shape international law. However, customary international law is arguably a modality of lawmaking that is (at least potentially) especially attuned to this recent democratisation of international law due to its dynamism, unwritten nature, responsiveness to normative discourses of various sorts, and its important role in litigation and arbitration. This helps explain why customary international law remains attractive to the principal actors and constituencies of contemporary international law. It displays a unique fit at a moment when the democratisation of global society coincides with the persistence of a decentralised and strongly power-oriented international system.

II. THE ROLE OF THE LEGAL DOCTRINE OF CUSTOMARY INTERNATIONAL LAW

Within public international law narrowly understood, the inclusion of customary international law as a formal 'source' of law was given a consequential impetus through the drafting of Article 38 of the PCIJ Statute and its perpetuation in the almost identical Article 38 of the ICJ Statute.[9] In a widely cited phrase, Article 38 (2) of the PCIJ Statute provided that '[t]he Court shall apply: … [i]ternational custom, as evidence of a general practice accepted as law'.[10] Following World War II and the founding of the United Nations and its 'principal judicial organ', a nearly identical formulation found its way into the respective article of the ICJ Statute. Throughout the following century, the history of the idea and legal doctrine of customary international law was thus linked to this formulation. In its brevity, generality, and partly confusing and indeterminate nature, it is the axis around which subsequent discourse has turned. In that

[9] O Spierman, *International Legal Argument in the Permanent Court of International Justice: The Rise of the International Judiciary* (Cambridge, Cambridge University Press, 2005) 14–23; see generally CJ Tams and James Sloan (eds), *The Development of International Law by the International Court of Justice* (Oxford, Oxford University Press 2013); H Lauterpacht, *The Development of International Law by the International Court: Being a Revised Edition of The Development of International Law by the Permanent Court of International Justice* (1934) (London, Stevens, 1958).

[10] See generally P Haggenmacher, 'An Archaeological Look at "International Custom as Evidence of a General Practice Accepted as Law" and Article 38 of the World Court's Statute' (2021) 34(3) *Leiden Journal of International Law* 1.

sense, a big part of the intellectual history of customary international law is the history of the interpretation of that instrument, article, and formulation.

The drafting of Article 38(2) of the PCIJ (and ICJ) Statute goes back to the Advisory Committee of Jurists, established by the League of Nations Council in February 1920 based on Article 14 of the League of Nations Covenant.[11] The records of the Council's public meeting in London on 13 February 1920 already reveal a strong degree of political backing and intellectual foundation for the proposal.[12] After the original members of the Committee changed slightly, the Advisory Committee met for the first time in The Hague on 16 June 1920 and a report of this meeting was published in the League of Nations Official Journal.[13] Present at that meeting were a number of individuals representing the leading powers of the day: Mineichirō Adachi, Rafael Altamira, Raoul Fernandez (who replaced Clovis Bevilaqua), Édouard Descamps, Francis Hagerup, Albert de Lapradelle, Bernard Loder, Walter Phillimore, Arturo Ricci-Busati, and Elihu Root. By September 1920, a 'draft scheme' for the to be established PCIJ was circulated to the League's membership.[14] Legal scholars have devoted considerable attention to understanding the context and reasons for the particular phrasing the Committee of Jurists chose to describe the relevant 'sources' of law, which later found its way into the ICJ Statute. As Peter Haggenmacher points out, it is only with the benefit of hindsight that this event obtains a larger significance as a quasi-founding moment of the contemporary legal doctrine of sources of international law.[15] Indeed, the official records of the meetings of the Advisory Committee of Jurists, which drafted the PCIJ's Statute, are notably reticent as to a debate on the inclusion of custom. At any rate, the fateful drafting coincided with the rise of an international judiciary, something that ensured that the formulation would be replicated and attain remarkable longevity and relevance. At the same time, in the early years of the twentieth century, the idea that adjudication played a key role in the development of law was widely shared among legal experts. Notably, it was commonly understood that the creation of courts like the Central American Court of Justice and the PCIJ meant a decisive turning point for the international legal order, and both institutions attracted significant attention from the leading legal thinkers of that time.[16] It is therefore plausible to assume that those who drafted the PCIJ

[11] See Article 14 of the League of Nations Covenant.

[12] See League of Nations Council, 'Second Public Meeting, held in London at St. James's Palace, on Friday, 13th February, 1920, at 12 noon' (March 1920) 1(2) *League of Nations O.J.* 33–8.

[13] 'Meeting of the Advisory Committee of Jurists' (Jul./Aug. 1920) 1(5) *League of Nations O.J.* 226–41.

[14] See *League of Nations O.J.*, Special Supplement No 2 (September 1920) 3–14.

[15] Haggenmacher, 'An Archaeological Look' (n 10) 4–5.

[16] See Spierman, *International Legal Argument in the Permanent Court of International Justice* (n 9) 14–23.

Statute considered the potentially far-reaching consequences of including a catalogue of sources in its text, at least in principle.

However, there is more to the legal doctrine of customary international law than Article 38 of the ICJ Statute. In particular, many domestic constitutions explicitly or implicitly provide for the applicability of international law, including customary international law.[17] Consequently, the relevant provisions and doctrines of domestic law that deal with the status, nature, and applicability of that 'source of law' also belong to the legal doctrine of customary international law.[18] Similarly, legal doctrines developed or expressed by international courts, arbitral tribunals, domestic courts, and scholars or scholarly associations also shape the legal doctrine of customary international law.[19] In addition, the International Law Commission made an effort to codify the 'meta-law' of custom in 2019, when it finalised its work concerning the 'identification of customary international law'.[20] That recent development merits separate treatment because of the unique institutional context and composition of that body, the scope of its work, and because much has already been written about the ILC's role and output.

How custom is described in the PCIJ Statute has faced significant critique (notably, circular and imprecise), yet obscurity is neither an unusual nor necessarily dire feature of legal provisions, especially if third-party adjudicators are at hand to interpret them. Indeed, given that the definition refers to a 'source' as multifaceted as custom and authorises a court to apply it, its vagueness may be seen as the key merit of its institutional design as a legal doctrine. To go a step further, uncertainty about the reasons for its vagueness (accidental, intentional, the product of a compromise, etc) can also be seen not as a defect but as the merit of a provision meant to remain open-ended and subject to adaptation. We can only speculate about the future course of customary international law if another wording had been chosen – for example, the one drafted by Kelsen.[21]

[17] See eg PH Verdier and M Versteeg, 'International Law in National Legal Systems: An Empirical Investigation' in A Roberts et al (eds), *Comparative International Law* (Oxford, Oxford University Press, 2018) 209, 225; see also D Shelton, *International Law and Domestic Legal Systems: Incorporation, Transformation, and Persuasion* (Oxford, Oxford University Press, 2011).

[18] See among many others H Meijers, 'On International Customary Law in the Netherlands' in HHG Post (eds), *On the Foundations and Sources of International Law* (The Hague, T.M.C. Asser Press, 2003) 77; S Besson and O Ammann, 'La pratique suisse relative à la détermination du droit international coutumier' (2016) 21 *Cahiers fribourgeois de droit européen* 1. See also CA Bradley, *International Law in the US Legal System*, 3rd edn (Oxford, Oxford Unviersity Press, 2021); F Lusa Bordin, AT Müller, and F Pascual-Vives, *The European Union and Customary International Law* (Cambridge, Cambridge University Press, 2022); HP Aust and T Kleinlein (eds), *Encounters between Foreign Relations Law and International Law: Bridges and Boundaries* (Cambridge, Cambridge University Press, 2021).

[19] In particular, this includes aspects of the case law of the PCIJ, the ICJ, the ITLOS, the ICTY and the ICTR, the ICC, as well as the case law of various ad-hoc arbitral tribunals and regional courts.

[20] Originally, the ILC had designated this item as 'Formation and evidence of customary international law/Identification of customary international law'.

[21] Hans Kelsen, eg in his Oliver Wendell Holmes lectures in 1940–1, emphasised the central role of adjudication in the development of an international legal system. See H Kelsen, *Law and Peace*

But it is clear that these early steps allowed customary international law to – at least symbolically – assume the role it plays in contemporary international legal practice. Although it has been argued that the two-pronged definition of customary international law – which does not appear in the PCIJ Statute – was an invention of the twentieth century, similar ways of conceptualising customary law, by reference to a practical and an ideal element, the latter being acceptance, consensus, or another similar notion, were long widespread. To be sure, the idea of a strict separation of the legal doctrine of customary international law into two 'elements', which was subsequently read into the ICJ Statute, is largely the product of twentieth-century interpretations and scholarly work – arguably representing an aberration in the history of customary law doctrine.[22] However, the Statute's drafters did little more than apply a preexisting formula, albeit somewhat confusingly, to international law. What is crucial is that the article, as eventually adopted, included custom as an authoritative source of international law and happened to endow it with a description broad enough to encompass various approaches to the identification and interpretation of customary international law.

As I have argued above, the element of practice is a crucial one in allowing disparate and diverse forms of conduct to shape the lawmaking process. Though its definition might seem self-evident, even the broad contours of the mainstream understanding of practice in international law as tied to a mythical type of 'state practice' (be it verbal or non-verbal) is – on closer inspection – relatively recent and artificial.[23] As a term of art in international law, 'practice' has a particular meaning, although what precisely constitutes authoritative instances of practice varies widely both by area and forum.[24] A domestic court adjudicating a refugee

in International Relations: The Oliver Wendell Holmes Lectures, 1940–41 (Cambridge, Harvard University Press, 1942) (Lecture VI). In the subsequent H Kelsen, *Peace Through Law* (Chapel Hill, University of North Carolina Press, 1944), Kelsen provided an annexed draft of a 'Covenant of a Permanent League for the Maintainance of Peace'. Its article 33, which deals with the law to be applied by the League's court, does not refer to custom or customary law explicitly; instead, Kelsen refers simply to 'the rules of International Law' and '[t]he general principles of law recognised by civilised nations [which] are considered to be part of International Law'. But in earlier work purporting to provide a theory of customary international law, Kelsen made it clear that he attributed a central role to the judge in the development of customary international law.

[22] The point is made emphatically in J D'Aspremont, 'The Four Lives of Customary International Law' (2019) *International Community Law Review* 229. But see Haggenmacher, 'An Archaeological Look' (n 10).

[23] J Kammerhofer, 'Between Pragmatism and Disenchantment: The Theory of Customary International Law after the ILC Project' in P Merkouris, J Kammerhofer, and N Arajärvi (eds), *The Theory, Practice, and Interpretation of Customary International Law* (Cambridge, Cambridge University Press, 2022) 3, 11–7.

[24] An example of the extent to which the meaning and practical value of the kind of 'state practice' considered as relevant is contextual and contingent is offered by a debate held in the German Reichstag in 1869, involving Otto von Bismarck, then the Chancellor of the German Empire. See O von Bismarck, *Die Politischen Reden des Fürsten Bismarck, Vierter Band 1868–1870* (critical edition by H Kohl) (Stuttgart, Cotta, 1893) 196–202. Bismarck's speech and the practice of European countries in creating official collections of 'state practice' is referred to, eg, by Louis Renault in an introductory textbook on international law, notably in a section dealing with customary international law. See L Renault, *Introduction à l'étude du droit international* (Paris, Larose, 1879) 42–3.

claim will consider different materials than an international tribunal concerned with transboundary environmental risks. A civil society association submitting an *amicus curiae* brief before a domestic court will rely on different precedents than a diplomat who is negotiating an investment agreement. At some point in the nineteenth century, the emerging circle of international lawyers appeared to adopt a particular definition of relevant practice, which has largely been perpetuated in the twentieth and twenty-first centuries. So-called 'state practice' has become essentially synonymous with 'practice' in the field, thus narrowing and simplifying its meaning.

As part of both the legal doctrine and broader intellectual history of customary international law, the notion of *opinio juris* or *opinio juris sive necessitatis* is also highly significant. Crucially, *opinio juris* serves as a corrective to an otherwise purely empirical, and thereby strongly positivist, conception of customary law. To be sure, *opinio juris* may at first appear as empirical as the 'practice' element of custom. However, because of its open-ended nature and ability to justify community-oriented legal developments, a finding of *opinio juris* resembles in some respects an assertion of natural law. Indeed, after the nineteenth century saw the disappearance of natural law as a recognised 'source' of international law, customary law arguably stepped in to fill the gap left and supplement what was understood as strictly consent-based treaty law. This role made it imperative for a 'non-empirical' element, such as in practice *opinio juris*, to play an important role in the legal doctrine of customary international law.

Today, the most authoritative insights into the 'internal' perspective on what constitutes the 'elements' relevant for the identification or interpretation of customary international law are furnished by pronouncements of international courts such as the ICJ, relevant scholarly writings used by practitioners, as well as the work of the ILC. While conceptions of governmental authority have developed throughout the last centuries, and while legal realism has infiltrated and transformed the legal academy in many parts of the world, mainstream conceptions of international law – including when it comes to the decisive notions of 'state practice' and 'opinio juris' – seem to have maintained a remarkably static form as a matter of legal doctrine, which tends in the relevant fora to be almost exclusively focused on 'states'. Indeed, the recent work of the ILC maintains this view by noting, for example, in Conclusion 4 that 'general practice, as a constituent element of customary international law, refers primarily to the practice of States that contributes to the formation, or expression, of rules of customary international law'.[25]

[25] ILC, 'Draft Conclusions on Identification of Customary International Law, with Commentaries' (2018) UN Doc A/73/10 122, 130. The ILC also continued to sustain the so-called 'persistent objector' doctrine. On the latter, see eg T Meron, 'International Law in the Age of Human Rights: General Course on Public International Law' (2004) 301 *Collected Courses of The Hague Academy of International Law* 9, 394; JA Green, 'The Persistent Objector Rule in the Work of the International Law Commission: On the Identification of Customary International Law' (2017) 27(1) *Italian Yearbook of International Law* 175.

III. CODIFYING INTERNATIONAL LAWMAKING OR THE LIMITS OF FORMALISATION

The development and systematisation of legal rules or principles under the guise of expert codification has a long and storied history, even if in its modern form codification is chiefly associated with the Enlightenment.[26] Codification projects span nearly all fields of law, levels, and historical eras, even if their roles varied significantly depending on the context. Carried out by individuals on their own accord, by government officials, by learned societies, or various other groups, codification projects have long served as an important avenue of legal development in the shadow of formal lawmaking institutions, such as legislatures. Codification projects have also occurred in the field of international law, where they have often played a significant role in the elaboration of both treaties and similarly authoritative instruments, such as the ILC's Articles on the Responsibility of States for Internationally Wrongful Acts.

The ILC has a distinctive role in the context of the development of the legal doctrine of customary international law. Notably, it considered the topic of the 'identification of customary international law' between 2011 and 2018, even if the ILC and its individual members had already been vocal about this topic for a long time. Although the ILC should be seen in the context of a broader set of institutions and actors shaping the legal doctrine of customary international law, it merits separate treatment given its distinct role, institutional context, methods of work, and the fact that it has concluded its consideration of the topic of the 'identification of customary international law' only several years ago.[27]

The ILC is a recent institution drawing on nineteenth and early twentieth century precursors.[28] It was established in 1948 by the UNGA pursuant to a mandate explicitly enshrined in the UN Charter. Although the ILC was established by the UNGA, the idea of an expert body codifying international legal

[26] See eg HP Glenn, 'The Grounding of Codification' (1998) 31 *UC Davis Law Review* 765; M Reimann, 'Historical Jurisprudence' in MD Dubber and C Tomlins (eds), *The Oxford Handbook of Legal History* (Oxford, Oxford University Press, 2018) 397, 413–4; on the American Law Institute, see eg W Twining, *General Jurisprudence: Understanding Law from a Global Perspective* (Cambridge, Cambridge University Press, 2009) 306–9.

[27] See eg M Wood and O Sender, *Identification of Customary International Law* (Oxford, Oxford University Press, 2024). On the work of the ILC in the area of environmental law, see eg AE Boyle, 'State Responsibility and International Liability for Injurious Consequences of Acts not Prohibited by International Law: A Necessary Distinction?' (1990) 39 *International and Comparative Law Quarterly* 1. On the codification work of the ILC in the area of 'state responsibility' and its effects, see eg DD Caron, 'The ILC Articles on State Responsibility: The Paradoxical Relationship between Form and Authority' (2002) 96 *American Journal of International Law* 857. For a critique of the ILC's work on the topic of state responsibility, see eg P Allott, 'State Responsibility and the Unmaking of International Law' (1988) *Harvard International Law Journal* 1.

[28] See RP Dhokalia, *The Codification of Public International Law* (Manchester, Manchester University Press, 1970); see also M Wood, 'Statute of the International Law Commission' (2009) *Audiovisual Library of International Law*.

norms was not new but drew (at the very least) on nineteenth-century precedents. The question of the codification of international law had also been raised in the League of Nations context[29] on several occasions. Notably, on the basis of a Swedish proposal tabled before the Assembly of the League of Nations in 1924, the Assembly adopted a resolution requesting the Council to 'convene a committee of experts' with a relatively limited ambit but which came to be known as the 'Committee of Experts for the Progressive Codification of International Law'.[30] That committee had been explicitly tasked to – and indeed did – consult with a range of non-governmental organisations, such as the International Law Association and the International Law Institute.[31] However, the 1930 Hague Conference, which was meant to see the culmination of the League of Nations' codification efforts, is today largely regarded as a failure.[32] Other private initiatives aimed at what might be called the 'codification and progressive development of international law' were somewhat more successful, including the 'Harvard Research in International Law', whose influence would be felt well into the post-World War II period.[33]

Under Article 20 of its Statute, the ILC is called upon to prepare draft articles and corresponding commentaries and submit them to the UNGA. A 'commentary' is meant to contain an '[a]dequate presentation of precedents and other relevant data, including treaties, judicial decisions and doctrine' and '[c]onclusions defining … (i) [t]he extent of agreement on each point in the practice of States and in doctrine … [,] (ii) [d]ivergencies and disagreements which exist, as well as arguments invoked in favour of one or another solution'. As a subsidiary body of the UNGA, the ILC was conceived of and remains an essentially intergovernmental mechanism (see on the selection of Members of the ILC Articles 3 to 14 of the ILC Statute) with a traditionally glacial and fundamentally conservative working method. The UN Secretariat is entrusted with a great deal of the preparatory work that the ILC's members develop during the sessions of its Working Groups in the course of its relatively short annual meetings at the UN Office at Geneva. The ILC plays an important, though today perhaps diminished role, which can be explained by a number of factors. One part of its considerable influence is due to the involvement of highly experienced members of the international legal profession in the ILC's work.[34] Another explanation

[29] See eg Seventeenth Plenary Meeting, LoN Official Journal, Special Supplement 23 (Geneva, 1924).

[30] MO Hudson, 'The Progressive Codification of International Law' (1926) 20(4) *The American Journal of International Law* 655, 660–62.

[31] ibid, 665.

[32] See S Rosenne, 'Codification Revisited After 50 Years' (1998) 2(1) *Max Planck Yearbook of United Nations Law Online* 1, 22.

[33] See, in particular, JP Grant and JC Barker, 'The Harvard Research: Genesis to Exodus and Beyond' in JP Grant and JC Barker (eds), *The Harvard Research in International Law: Contemporary Analysis and Appraisal* (Buffalo, Hein, 2007) 1, 39–40.

[34] See on this point SC Neff, *Justice Among Nations* (Cambridge, Harvard University Press, 2014) 401 (referring to Scelle, Brierly, Lauterpacht, and Hudson).

for the ILC's influence lies in its institutional link to the UN and the fact that many of its members have concurrently or subsequently held influential positions in the legal profession, be it as judges, diplomats, officials, or scholars.[35]

Today, the ILC's work is frequently drawn upon by various international, regional, and domestic courts and tribunals as evidence of customary international law or its absence on a particular matter. Although the mandate of the ILC includes, according to Article 1(1) of its Statute, 'the promotion of the progressive development of international law and its codification', it is driven to a large extent in its agenda by the UNGA (and notably its Legal Committee) in addition to the members of the Commission itself.[36] As noted, the ILC's influence is less a feature of its own formal role than the group of international lawyers that tend to fill its ranks and those of various associated organisations. From that perspective, the ILC reflects a particular conception of legal expertise in the international legal field with strong continuities to the nineteenth century and to earlier forms of government-driven international law codification projects. At the same time, the ILC's changing composition also reflects an expansion of the UN's membership, changes in the composition of the international legal profession, and regional and national differences in legal practice and scholarship. As a subsidiary body of the UNGA, the ILC is also directly and indirectly connected to ongoing processes of formalisation, bureaucratisation, and legalisation that shape the UN and its various sub-organisations.

In addition, the practical utility of the ILC's output, which is due to its unhurried and deliberative working method and the authority many of its members enjoy in the international legal profession, offers another reason for the ILC's influence. For example, Fernando Lusa Bordin has argued that 'institutional features of the ILC, combined with certain properties of the texts that it produces, converge to convey the image that the resulting texts constitute the most authoritative restatements of the substance of customary international law'.[37] While it is difficult to gauge the precise impact of the ILC's work and that of its individual members as such, it is undeniable that the ILC has both given the impetus to important legal developments in the field of customary international law and directly affected several substantive areas of international law. Much has been written about the role of the ILC in the process of customary international law formation, identification, and interpretation, and each of its efforts at codification through the preparation of draft articles, guidelines, and reports is met with a (relatively) broad range of scholarly opinion and critique.[38]

[35] See eg G Gaja, 'Interpreting Articles Adopted by the International Law Commission' (2015) 85(1) *British Yearbook of International Law* 10.

[36] See the definition of the two concepts in Article 15 of the Statute of the International Law Commission.

[37] See FL Bordin, 'Reflections of Customary International Law: The Authority of Codification Conventions and ILC Draft Articles in International Law' (2014) 63 *International and Comparative Law Quarterly* 535, 536.

[38] United Nations, *The International Law Commission Fifty Years After: An Evaluation*, Proceedings of the Seminar Held to Commemorate the Fiftieth Anniversary of the International Law

Current or past members of the ILC have published numerous works connected to its work output or working methods[39] – with some having even called for the institution to be abolished.[40] What emerges from this set of assessments is that the ILC's work is widely seen as the most reliable and authoritative synthesis of the existence and scope of various customary international law norms by international courts and tribunals, and therefore many legal professionals.

It is important to keep in mind that the ILC's work product is directed to, and in fact mainly used by, international lawyers. Even the form of the ILC's work evokes a certain formal genre, reminiscent not only of legislation but of international treaties in particular. Its recommendations are phrased in the form of legislation that would be familiar in many countries (particularly civil law countries) and tend to be divided into 'Articles', 'Parts', but more recently also into 'Conclusions' (as in its recent customary international law-related project). To be sure, international lawyers are not a cohesive community – and the ILC's communications may be understood differently and enjoy different degrees of authority across this broader group. And indeed, the changing composition of the international legal profession shapes both the voice and impact of the ILC. For we might ask, who is the principal group of international lawyers to which the ILC speaks today? It is domestic lawyers litigating matters relating to international law, lawyers active in or before various international jurisdictions, such as the ICJ, the ITLOS, innumerable arbitral tribunals, WTO panels, the EU courts, regional human rights courts, private commercial litigators or transactional lawyers, or government lawyers in myriad specialised fields?

When it comes to calls for the 'clarification' or 'codification' of the 'law of customary international law', it is important to stress that these had been expressed as early as 1949[41] but were implicit in earlier discussions in the field. Moreover, although the ILC considered the topic of the 'identification' of customary international law only fairly recently, it had implicitly been engaged in it since its creation. This has placed the ILC in a somewhat awkward position in its most recent endeavour: If it simply affirmed its earlier approach (however coherent) to identifying customary international law, it could be deemed to have an institutional conflict of interest arising from a seeming attempt to retroactively validate or rationalise its earlier approach. In addition, a charge of futility could be raised against its effort since the consistent use of a method seems to obviate the need for its codification. However, if the ILC had instead departed from its earlier approach (if there indeed had been a consistent one that could be distilled

Commission, 21–22 April 1998 (United Nations, 2000); A Watts, *The International Law Commission 1949–1998, Volume I: The Treaties* (Oxford, Oxford Uniersity Press, 2000).

[39] See eg M Forteau, 'Comparative International Law Within, Not Against, International Law: Lessons from the International Law Commission' in A Roberts et al (eds), *Comparative International Law* (Oxford, Oxford University Press, 2018) 161.

[40] Lecture at the International Law Commission Seminar by Prof. A. Pellet (Geneva, July 2011).

[41] *See* GM Danilenko, *Law-Making in the International Community* (Dordrecht, Martinus Nijhoff, 1993) 128 (referring to H Lauterpacht, among others).

from its past practice at all), it would have run the risk of indirectly calling into question its own codification efforts. To be sure, this problem is largely hypothetical for several reasons. First, perhaps no one will attempt to juxtapose the ILC's past approach to the identification of customary international law with the outcome of its project on the identification of customary international law (the effort seems ridden with methodological challenges). In other words, the bases of the ILC's various codifications may be understood as irrelevant to the projects which have obtained a life of their own after leaving the ILC's hands. Second, perhaps the ILC has never had a truly consistent approach to the codification of customary international law, and consequently, the ILC's recent project marks a turning point that might streamline and perhaps alter future codification projects or at least make them more formally consistent. Third, perhaps the identification of customary international law is changing, and perhaps the ILC's approach simply represents the latest (soon to be dated) word on the question. Without entering into the debate over the substance of the ILC's conclusions relating to the 'identification of customary international law', this is just to emphasise a set of fundamental challenges that faced the ILC's attempt at codifying the legal doctrine of customary international law – ones that it did not face in other projects, be it concerning the law of treaties or the law of state responsibility, among others.

Finally, it should be noted that instruments such as the Vienna Convention on the Law of Treaties or the ILC's 'Conclusions on the Identification of Customary International Law' are usually seen as reflecting the prevailing international legal doctrine of sources. However, even such instruments need to be interpreted – textually, contextually, and teleologically. The proliferation of international legal instruments promoting the increased involvement in decision-making by particular communities (peasants, indigenous peoples, minorities, scientists, etc) or the public more generally, for example, raises important issues for the interpretation of such instruments.[42] It calls for balancing the relatively state-centric conception of the prevailing legal doctrine of sources with norms mandating more broad-based public participation in customary international lawmaking. After the conclusion of the ILC's project on the identification of customary international law, it remains to be seen what the impact of its Conclusions or approach will be – it will certainly depend in large part on whether its approach will be adopted by the relevant actors, including governments, scholars, and influential domestic and international courts. So far, there is little indication that the ILC's recent work has noticeably influenced the approach to the identification and interpretation of customary international law of even its most loyal disciples.

[42] Eg UNGA, 'United Nations Declaration on the Rights of Peasants and Other People Working in Rural Areas', UN Doc A/C.3/73/L.30, Annex (30 October 2018) Article 2(3).

IV. DEMOCRACY AND CUSTOMARY INTERNATIONAL LAW

As we consider the potential effects of ideas about customary international law, including its legal doctrine, on customary international law as a broader social phenomenon, it is worth recalling that generations of social scientists have tried to develop a better understanding of the mechanisms through which ideas affect social practices and conditions.[43] In the context of international law, the social and institutional contexts in which ideas and legal doctrines become actualised are especially significant.[44] This insight tends to be familiar to practising lawyers since an engagement with the law provides them with the awareness of the fact that ideas – be they legal doctrines or more general ideas concerning the *lex non scripta* – obtain concrete meaning only in particular social contexts and institutional settings. This also applies to the legal doctrine of customary international law and its sometimes-diffuse relationship to both consent and democracy.

In the absence of anything resembling global democracy, the role of international organisations as well as international courts and tribunals merits special attention, since they play an important role in the context of customary international lawmaking.[45] When it comes to international courts and tribunals, it is impossible to divorce the application and development of the legal doctrine of customary international law from their composition, jurisdiction, appointment, working methods, financing, and other elements affecting their operation and authority. When it comes to international organisations, they have directly or indirectly supported the very role of customary international law as a relevant modality of international lawmaking. This relates to international organisations' capacity and authority to collect and disseminate information about various actions and expectations and to bring disparate groups together. By developing mechanisms like periodic reports and reviews, rankings, ratings, fact-finding missions, and similar information-oriented tools, international organisations have had significant impacts on the role of customary international law. In addition, as important sites where lawyers

[43] See eg RJ Shiller, *Narrative Economics: How Stories Go Viral and Drive Major Economic Events* (Princeton, Princeton University Press, 2019); RJ Barro and R McCleary, *The Wealth of Religions: The Political Economy of Believing and Belonging* (Princeton, Princeton University Press, 2019).

[44] See eg R Cotterrell, *Law, Culture and Society: Legal Ideas in the Mirror of Social Theory* (Aldershot, Ashgate 2006).

[45] A separate, but related, discussion concerns international organisations' contribution to customary international lawmaking as such. See eg FL Bordin and J Odermatt, 'International Law of Regional Organizations: A Comparative Perspective' 19 (2024) *International Organizations Law Review* 19, 36–8; M Pacholska, 'New Kids on the Block International Organizations as Customary Rules Creators' (2019) 21(3–4) *International Community Law Review* 325; J Odermatt, 'The Development of Customary International Law by International Organziations' (2017) 66(2) *International & Comparative Law Quarterly* 491, 510–1; K Daugirdas, 'International Organizations and the Creation of Customary International Law' 31(1) *European Journal of International Law* 201; see also G Cahin, *La coutume internationale et les organisations internationales: L'incidence de la dimension institutionnelle sur le processus coutumier* (Paris, Pédone, 2001).

and public officials are socialised, international organisations facilitate a shared ethos among actors from a variety of national, regional, and disciplinary backgrounds. In this way, international organisations disseminate and stabilise implicit understandings of how norms are developed, identified, and interpreted, including norms of customary international law. This socialisation occurs not only in relation to legal experts but all individuals and groups participating in international organisations' activities, including various kinds of public officials, scientists or scholars, business representatives, civil society activists, and other individuals or groups.[46]

One way – and it is hardly the only one – in which customary international law relates to democracy is through the mediation of social movements and others who engage in forms of 'practice' that can be relied on by those entrusted to apply or adjudicate claims based on customary international law (often, but not only, courts). For that reason, the role of social movements and their relationship to law and legal change can help us assess the democratic quality of customary international lawmaking. Conversely, a narrow understanding of customary international law can obscure the potential, relevance, and versatility of customary international law, thereby limiting both its potential utility and the democratic quality of global lawmaking.[47]

Customary international law is commonly thought to suffer from a serious democratic deficit in a number of respects.[48] For example and despite significant differences across countries, it is often assumed that key decisions that shape customary international law can be made by executives at will, in contradistinction to treaties. In many countries, the negotiation, conclusion, and ratification of treaties are accompanied by legally enforceable forms of involvement from the side of national parliaments. In contrast, the 'practice' that contributes to customary international law can, in many cases, derive from less deliberative processes. This appears problematic in light of the rudimentary democratic tools available on the intergovernmental level and the often-limited supervision of domestic executive action by courts, civil society groups, or parliaments in the field of foreign affairs and defence. The alternative of the treaty (or even the non-binding instrument) is therefore often seen as the lesser evil, given that

[46] See eg RW Cox and HK Jacobson (eds), *The Anatomy of Influence: Decision Making in International Organization* (New Haven, Yale University Press, 1974).

[47] See the discussion on the relationship between international law and democracy in Chapter 2 (including further references). See also eg B Rajagopal, *International Law from Below: Development, Social Movements, and Third World Resistance* (Cambridge, Cambridge University Press, 2003); on the role of social movements, see eg JM Balkin and RB Siegel, 'Principles, Practices, and Social Movements' (2005) 154 *University of Pennsylvania Law Review* 927; WN Eskridge, 'Some Effects of Identity-Based Social Movements on Constitutional Law in the Twentieth Century' (2002) 100 *Michigan Law Review* 2062; T Brown-Nagin, 'Elites, Social Movements, and the Law: The Case of Affirmative Action' (2005) 105(5) *Columbia Law Review* 1436.

[48] See also Verdier and Versteeg, 'International Law in National Legal Systems: An Empirical Investigation' (n 17) 225–8.

treaties tend to be products of intergovernmental deliberation between (at least partially) democratic governments, many of which provide for at least indirect, though sometimes direct, democratic involvement on the national level both before treaties are signed and ratified.

While it is true that executive discretion in foreign affairs can undermine the quality if not the legality of governmental action,[49] this basic critique of customary international law's democratic features – alone or relative to treaties – is flawed in a few respects that derive from common misconceptions about both customary international lawmaking and treaty-making processes in a variety of countries. First, treaties are far more difficult to change than customary international law. To be sure, there are numerous kinds of treaties, some of which have developed elaborate structures that ensure quasi-parliamentary deliberation. However, for the most part, treaties tend to be relatively static, with onerous or non-existent possibilities of amendment. This creates low incentives for actors outside governmental circles to even try to agitate for legal change since hurdles for the invalidation of a treaty, treaty amendment, or treaty withdrawal by a significant number of parties can be very substantial. In contrast, customary international law is premised on the possibility of informal change. As noted, even the underlying processes by which various types of customary international law norms are created and sustained (its 'meta-law') are notoriously dynamic. Moreover, customary international law often serves as a signal to a widely dispersed set of actors that social pressure is potentially legally rewarding. It signals that various areas of international law are open for contestation, provided that an agitating group can leverage a sufficient degree of power. In contrast, even significant numbers of parties to many treaties are often unable to push through treaty amendments because of the usually onerous rules for treaty amendment under the law of treaties. In short, treaties have far greater sticking power than customary international law – for good or for ill – but purely from the perspective of democratic lawmaking (rather than a broader conception of the rule of law), that is not necessarily a strength. Moreover, treaties are rarely role models of democratic lawmaking. They are often negotiated far from any parliamentary or public scrutiny. Quite apart from the question of the extent to which domestic legislation in many countries conforms to a democratic ideal to begin with, treaties are therefore hardly paragons of democratic lawmaking. This point does not, of course, lessen any critique of customary international lawmaking as such. However, it puts the supposed second-best alternative of the treaty as a modality of lawmaking into perspective.

[49] For example, the results of an official inquiry into the role of the French government in the Rwandan genocide suggest that concentrated and unaccountable power of key decision-makers in the French external affairs field indirectly contributed to the Rwandan genocide. See eg Chapter 7 of Commission de recherche sur les archives françaises relatives au Rwanda et au génocide des Tutsi, 'La France, le Rwanda et le génocide des Tutsi (1990–1994)' (2021) 987.

Treaties – unlike customary international law – are rather rigid instruments under the law of treaties. This is not the case for custom whose processes of change are varied and relatively open-ended. Therefore, comparing customary international law and treaties along the democratic dimension is problematic unless we specify what types of treaties and, indeed, customary international law we are comparing.

Second, customary international lawmaking can be relatively fluid and dynamic – it can quickly respond to changing power relations. Power can, of course, derive from multiple sources, including popular opinion and democratic processes. In that sense, because customary international law is a dynamic and multifaceted modality of international lawmaking, it can be shaped to conform to changing practices of various sorts. In that sense, customary international law is potentially more responsive to public pressure and opinion than the hard and fast provisions of (most) treaty law. One could say the same about 'evaluation norms' in treaties since they give decision-makers discretion in considering a host of practices and expectations. But such evaluation norms are usually also understood by reference to prevailing norms of customary international law. To be sure, this also means that the presence and jurisdiction of third-party decision-makers is an important, though not a necessary, element for the development of customary international law, though one that usually cannot be established by customary international law itself.

In general, the availability of unwritten law as an authoritative 'source of law' at least potentially opens the door to a wider range of practices and expectations in the application, interpretation, and development of law. This appears to be true in many domestic legal orders but seems to be even more relevant in the international arena, whose range of participants is more varied and dispersed and whose institutional structure is more dynamic and less deeply entrenched than that of many domestic constitutional orders. In other words, because – at least compared to well-established domestic legal orders – international law's catalogue of sources is both vaguely defined and relatively dynamic, it seems to be comparatively inclusive and receptive to a diverse set of demands placed on the law. In practice, the existence of the customary international law category does indeed invite, provoke, and even give potential (prospective) legitimacy to practices and expectations of all kinds, notwithstanding the fact that customary international law itself is a multifaceted phenomenon. The legal doctrine of customary international law can thus serve as a signal, a magnet, an invitation, and an incentive for so-called 'norm-entrepreneurs'. Of course, the myriad practices and expectations that might vie for influence need to be accepted as authoritative by the relevant community before they can become determinative. As noted, in this process, third party decision-makers and international organisations, including bodies like the ILC, continue to play a key role – they can 'declare' some practices and expectations as relevant and signal their potential relevance to a wider audience. In this sense, the vagueness of the legal doctrine of customary international law and the lack of specificity when it comes to the kinds of practices and expectations that might be authoritative appears as both an inadvertently beneficial and far-reaching element of its institutional design. For example, by not artificially or prospectively limiting the range of 'acceptable' practices to 'state practice', customary international law can become more open and inviting as well as more amenable to changes in the kinds of practices deemed relevant in different contexts.

To be sure, all this only adds to the existing controversy about the elements that matter for customary international law identification and interpretation.[50] Moreover, uncertainty about the elements shaping customary international law could also be seen as a drawback from the perspective of legal predictability or stability, and therefore the rule of law. From that perspective, tension might exist between customary international law's dynamic and stabilising tendencies. This suggests that a normative evaluation of the appropriate degree of vagueness of the legal doctrine of customary international law should be the product of a balancing exercise. We might ask: What are the unavoidable but necessary costs in terms of legal predictability that should be incurred for world society to possess a source of law that is adaptable and open and can accommodate shifts in the kinds of practices and expectations relevant for lawmaking? Ultimately, this question can only be answered on the basis of some prescriptive criteria since trade-offs between legal predictability and change are not normatively neutral but reflect a preference for either change or the *status quo*. But as noted, even ambiguity about this sends a valuable signal to those who seek legal change by engaging in new practices or instigating others to do so. The presence of such a signal is compatible with democratic forms of lawmaking and with what Douglas North and associates have referred to as 'open-access orders'.[51] Such orders allow various decentralised actors to engage in economic, political, and other behaviour, a feature that both stabilises them and makes them more adaptable to changing circumstances than 'closed-access orders'.

However, it is important to keep in mind that ambiguity about the range of practices and expectations that are potentially relevant for customary international law does not need to lead to arbitrary or unpredictable decisions. This is the case, in particular, where courts or other third-party decision-makers are tasked to evaluate and sort through various practices and expectations (even if decentralised mechanisms for sifting and evaluating such inputs can be imagined as well). For example, to allow 'all practices to be relevant' is initially a convenient fiction that signals to individuals and groups: 'You may enter the conversation'. In scenarios where third-party adjudication is available and

[50] See eg Wood and Sender, *Identification of Customary International Law* (n 27) 299–300; KJ Heller, 'Specially-Affected States and the Formation of Custom' (2018) 112 *American Journal of International Law* 191.

[51] See generally DC North, JJ Wallis, and BR Weingast, *Violence and Social Orders: Conceptual Framework for Interpreting Recorded Human History* (Cambridge, Cambridge University Press, 2009) 111–5.

active, participation thus depends to a great extent on the persons making choices about inclusion and exclusion and on the extent to which their decisions are accepted in the relevant community and in society more generally. In that sense, as with various other forms of decision-making, the performance of international lawmaking can ultimately not be divorced from the effective personal qualities, including ethical values, of the individuals tasked with the exercise of power.

In conclusion, it appears that customary international law is in fact – contrary to widespread assumptions – at least potentially a versatile and significant part of international lawmaking, and the idea that it is 'primitive' or undemocratic is not particularly warranted, even if many specific criticisms could be directed against it in particular contexts. In practice, international lawyers and many scholars who adopt a narrow and limited understanding of customary international law and of legality have tended to obscure the potential, relevance, and versatility of customary international law. This has arguably limited both its potential utility and the democratic quality of international lawmaking.

Conclusion

BEFORE HIGHLIGHTING SOME of this book's descriptive and normative implications, it may be helpful to reiterate what it tried to accomplish. Most importantly, this book sought to reorient existing streams of scholarship towards a comprehensive view of customary international lawmaking and always with an eye to its relationship to social change. It tried to do this by reference to customary international law as a multifaceted social phenomenon, and without neglecting the role of the idea and legal doctrine of customary international law. The framework developed in this book is one tool that can help us understand and evaluate a complex reality shaped by and itself shaping customary international law. By offering a new descriptive account of customary international lawmaking, this book also tried to lay the ground for more solid normative critiques. Because the design of lawmaking processes affects substantive outcomes, it is important to ask how such processes can be made more equitable, inclusive, transparent, and sustainable. Answering and acting on this question can lead to improved social outcomes across a range of areas. Thus, from a normative perspective, a better understanding of customary international lawmaking offers a basic and necessary starting-point for reconsidering how the factors that affect customary international lawmaking processes, and their outcomes, can be improved. In that sense, by providing an analytical and explanatory framework, I sought to offer a roadmap to those interested in thinking about how global lawmaking could be shaped to better advance what Myres McDougal has referred to as a 'world public order of human dignity'.

As noted above, customary international law draws both on ideas about the *lex non scripta* in international society as well as on the legal doctrine of customary international law. International organisations as well as international, regional, and domestic courts and tribunals are key conduits for the socialisation of legal actors and for the application and shaping of the legal doctrine of customary international law. More importantly, without the various functions performed by international organisations (such as information collection, comparison, and dissemination), courts and tribunals, and social movements, customary international law would be a less relevant and less democratic modality of international lawmaking, *ceteris paribus*. This suggests that efforts to minimise the role of customary international law or to formalise its means of identification or interpretation in ways that do not take into account the broader customary international lawmaking process are at best misguided and at worst risk stifling a central jurisgenerative process within contemporary international law.

The reader will need to judge if Kurt Lewin's quip about there being 'nothing as practical as a good theory' can be applied to the framework developed in this book. However, it is hardly meant to be a final assessment of customary international law, which continues to transform, just as our ability to analyse it will improve. Tentatively, I hope that the framework developed in this book, other than spurring further thinking about the nature and role of customary international law, can provide useful insights to lawyers and legal scholars in several concrete ways.

I. MAPPING THE TERRITORY OF CUSTOMARY INTERNATIONAL LAWMAKING

Scholars, students, and practising lawyers are often faced with competing arguments about the existence, relevance, or precise scope (material, personal, territorial) of norms of customary international law. While the presence of competing arguments about what the law requires is hardly unusual in most legal orders, the complexity of the international legal system is distinctive due to a plethora of different fora and institutions, the coexistence of thoroughly legalised regimes with those barely distinguishable from warfare, as well as differences in legal cultures, languages, and education that have significant effects on international legal argument and practice. As a consequence, scholars are often exasperated by customary international law and propose solutions that include either its rejection in toto or a formalisation of its legal doctrine. Therefore, what is needed is a better map of the territory of customary international lawmaking. Once we realise that customary international law norms are sustained through particular factors and recognise certain patterns in customary international lawmaking and its resulting norms, it becomes easier to understand, interpret, and shape customary international law, including its legal doctrine. In other words, when faced with any scenario that raises (or could raise) questions of unwritten international law, the proposed framework helps us determine what type of customary international law norm is (or could be) at issue in a particular scenario. This offers not only descriptive insight but also suggests which legal strategies (argumentative or practical) are most likely to be persuasive in different contexts.

II. UNDERSTANDING THE LEGAL DOCTRINE OF CUSTOMARY INTERNATIONAL LAW

As suggested above, discussions about customary international law have traditionally focused either on the level of legal doctrine or on the level of norm-creation from a purely sociological (for example, economic or political science) perspective. While both are important, the framework I propose takes both perspectives seriously but tries to integrate so-called internal and external (or intermediate) perspectives on customary international law. The framework shows that the legal doctrine of customary international law has a particular and distinct role in different contexts (eg, in the judicial context). This insight helps inform normative proposals about the formalisation (or deformalisation) of the legal doctrine of customary international law. In particular, it points to the fact that a vague and open-ended definition of customary international law is a key merit of its institutional design, and is linked to its role as a signal to a widely dispersed set of actors to engage in jurisgenerative activities. To be sure, it is not as simple as that. As I have underlined above, when we evaluate the role and effect of the legal doctrine of customary international law, it is essential to consider the social and institutional contexts in which all ideas, including legal doctrines, become actualised.

III. IDENTIFYING THE LEVERS OF SOCIAL CHANGE THROUGH CUSTOM

This leads directly to perhaps the major implication of this book's proposed framework, which is that it highlights how the design of customary international lawmaking, and thus its outcomes, can be improved. It is widely recognised that lawmaking processes and legal norms should on the whole be flexible enough to allow social change to be realised without becoming indistinguishable from untrammelled power or crumbling in the face of challenges. The diversity of normative arrangements identified in this book's framework serves to organise and structure social change. The relationship between the design of lawmaking institutions and lawmaking outcomes is widely recognised. However, my framework tries to identify the specific factors that help explain the stability of different types of customary international law norms. Importantly, the book highlights that some of the factors that help sustain different types of customary international law norms are more amenable to change by conscious design or technological developments than others. This gives scholars, activists, and policymakers a practical roadmap for developing strategies to facilitate social change through the bottom-up (re)design of customary international lawmaking processes.

IV. EXPANDING THE SCOPE OF INTERNATIONAL LEGAL SCHOLARSHIP

Finally, and more generally, this book can help stimulate an expansion of conventional accounts of customary international lawmaking, which draw on highly influential but also overly limiting descriptive assumptions that reflect a state-centric conception of international lawmaking. The historical record contradicts the premise that international law is mainly explained by the actions of governments. This finding should have implications for any comprehensive approach to customary international law as well. Moreover, it is important to recall that the key legal doctrines and institutions underpinning customary international lawmaking as a multifaceted process are remarkably malleable and open-ended. This implies that a strictly formal approach to the legal doctrine of customary international law that centres state practice and the views of governments can inadvertently stifle especially those processes of international lawmaking that have historically contributed most significantly to legal and social change.

All this needs to be accompanied by the perhaps obvious proviso that customary international lawmaking is always in flux. To better understand and engage with customary international law, it is imperative to recognise that it is not a unitary phenomenon, but differs radically in operation depending on the context in which customary international law norms are created, applied, interpreted, and modified. One way of seeing customary international law anew is through the framework I propose in this book. But it is neither the only nor the final way to approach a phenomenon as complex and dynamic as customary international law. My aim in this book, more than anything else, was to prompt a reorientation in how lawyers and legal scholars think about customary international law and its relationship to social change. If my framework will be tested and developed further by others, the aims I set myself for this book will have been realised many times over.

Bibliography

BOOKS

Abbenhuis, MM, *The Hague Conferences and International Politics, 1898–1915* (London, Bloomsbury Academic, 2018).

Acemoglu, KD, and Johnson, S, *Power and Progress: Our Thousand-Year Struggle Over Technology and Prosperity* (London, Basic Books, 2023).

Ackerman, B, *We the People, Volume 2: Transformations* (Cambridge, Harvard University Press, 1991).

Adelman, H and Barkan, E, *No Return, No Refuge: Rites and Rights in Minority Repatriation* (New York, Columbia University Press, 2011).

Albert, R, Guruswamy, M, and Basnyat, N (eds), *Founding Moments in Constitutionalism* (Oxford, Hart Publishing, 2019).

Alborzi, MR, *Evaluating the Effectiveness of International Refugee Law: The Protection of Iraqi Refugees* (Leiden, Martinus Nijhoff, 2006).

Amar, AR, *America's Unwritten Constitution: The Precedents and Principles We Live By* (New York, Basic Books, 2012).

Anghie, A, *Imperialism, Sovereignty and the Making of International Law* (Cambridge, Cambridge University Press, 2004).

Arajärvi, N, *The Changing Nature of Customary International Law: Methods of Interpreting the Concept of Custom in International Criminal Tribunals* (Abingdon, Routledge, 2014).

Archibugi, D et al (eds), *Global Democracy: Normative and Empirical Perspectives* (Cambridge, Cambridge University Press, 2011).

Ardeleanu, C, *The European Commission of the Danube, 1856–1948: An Experiment in International Administration* (Leiden, Brill, 2020).

Arendt, H, *On Revolution* (New York, Penguin Press, 1963).

Arthur Michel, AA, *The Indus Rivers: A Study of the Effects of Partition* (New Haven, Yale University Press, 1967).

Aust, HP and Kleinlein, T (eds), *Encounters between Foreign Relations Law and International Law: Bridges and Boundaries* (Cambridge, Cambridge University Press, 2021).

Bagwell, P, *The Transport Revolution 1770–1985* (New York, Routledge, 1988).

Bakker, C and Francioni, F (ed), *The EU, the US and Global Climate Governance* (New York, Routledge, 2014).

Baldwin, P, *Contagion and the State in Europe, 1830–1930* (Cambridge, Cambridge University Press, 1999).

Banner, S, *Who Owns the Sky? The Struggle to Control Airspace from the Wright Brothers On* (Cambridge, Harvard University Press, 2008).

Barak, E (ed), *Deadly Metal Rain: The Legality of Flechette Weapons in International Law. A Reappraisal Following Israel's Use of Flechettes in the Gaza Strip (2001–2009)* (Leiden, Martinus Nijhoff, 2011).

Barkun, M, *Law Without Sanctions: Order in Primitive Societies and the World Community* (New Haven, Yale University Press, 1968).

Barro, RJ and McCleary, R, *The Wealth of Religions: The Political Economy of Believing and Belonging* (Princeton, Princeton University Press, 2019).
Bartsch, S, *Minderheitenschutz in der Internationalen Politik* (Opladen, Westdeutscher Verlag, 1995).
Beasley, WG, *Japanese Imperialism, 1894–1945* (Oxford, Clarendon Press, 1987).
Beckert, J, *Imagined Futures: Fictional Expectations and Capitalist Dynamics* (Cambridge, Harvard University Press, 2016).
Behrman, S, *Law and Asylum: Space, Subject, Resistance* (Abingdon, Routledge, 2018).
Benvenisti, E, *Sharing Transboundary Resources: International Law and Optimal Resource Use* (Cambridge, Cambridge University Press, 2009).
Bernholz, L, Landemore, H, and Reich, R (eds), *Digital Technology and Democratic Theory* (Chicago, University of Chicago Press, 2021).
Betts, A and Loescher, G (eds), *Refugees in International Relations* (Oxford, Oxford University Press, 2010).
Betts, A, Loescher, G, and Milner, J (eds), *The United Nations High Commissioner for Refugees (UNHCR): The Politics and Practice of Refugee Protection*, 2nd edn (New York, Routledge, 2013).
Bianchi, A, *International Law Theories: An Inquiry into Different Ways of Thinking* (Oxford, Oxford University Press, 2016).
Bicchieri, C, *Norms in the Wild: How to Diagnose, Measure, and Change Social Norms* (Oxford, Oxford University Press, 2017).
Birn, AE, Pillay, Y, and Holtz, T, *Textbook of Global Health*, 4th edn (Oxford, Oxford University Press, 2017).
Bix, B, *Jurisprudence: Theory and Context*, 9th edn (London, Sweet & Maxwell, 2023).
Blokker, P and Thornhill, C (eds), *Sociological Constitutionalism* (Cambridge, Cambridge University Press, 2017).
Bluntschli, JC, *Das moderne Völkerrecht der civilisirten Staten als Rechtsbuch dargestellt*, 3rd edn (Nördlingen, Verlag der Beck'schen Buchhandlung, 1878).
Bowers, KW, *Plague and Public Health in Early Modern Seville* (Rochester, University of Rochester Press, 2013).
Bradley, CA (ed), *Custom's Future: International Law in a Changing World* (Cambridge, Cambridge University Press, 2016).
Bradley, CA, *International Law in the US Legal System*, 3rd edn (Oxford, Oxford Unviersity Press, 2021).
Bratspies, RM and Miller, RA (eds), *Transboundary Harm in International Law: Lessons from the Trail Smelter Arbitration* (Cambridge, Cambridge University Press, 2006).
Brennan, G, Eriksson, L, Goodin, RE, and Southwood, N, *Explaining Norms* (Oxford, Oxford University Press, 2013).
Brölmann, C and Radi, Y (eds), *Research Handbook on the Theory and Practice of International Lawmaking* (Cheltenham, Edward Elgar, 2016).
Brownsword, R and Goodwin, M, *Law and the Technologies of the Twenty-First Century: Text and Materials* (Cambridge, Cambridge University Press, 2012).
Brunnée, J and Toope, SJ, *Legitimacy and Legality in International Law: An Interactional Account* (Oxford, Oxford University Press, 2010).
Burci, GL and Toebes, B (eds), *Research Handbook on Global Health Law* (Cheltenham, Edward Elgar, 2018).
Byers, M and Boley, A, *Who Owns Outer Space? International Law, Astrophysics, and the Sustainable Development of Space* (Cambridge, Cambridge University Press, 2023).
Byers, M, Custom, *Power and the Power of Rules: International Relations and Customary International Law* (Cambridge, Cambridge University Press, 1999).
Cabanes, B, *The Great War and the Origins of Humanitarianism, 1918–1924* (Cambridge, Cambridge University Press, 2014).

Cahin, G, *La coutume internationale et les organisations internationales: L'incidence de la dimension institutionnelle sur le processus coutumier* (Paris, Pédone, 2001).
Calabresi, G, *The Future of Law and Economics: Essays in Reform and Recollection* (New Haven, Yale University Press, 2016).
Camiscioli, E, *Reproducing the French Race: Immigration, Intimacy, and Embodiment in the Early Twentieth Century* (Durham, Duke University Press, 2009).
Caplan, J and Torpey, J (eds), *Documenting Individual Identity: The Development of State Practices in the Modern World* (Princeton, Princeton University Press, 2001).
Caponera, DA and Nanni, M (revised and updated by), *Principles of Water Law and Administration: National and International*, 3rd edn (London, Routledge, 2019).
Carlisle, C, *On Habit* (New York, Routledge, 2014).
Charlesworth, H and Chinkin, C, *The Boundaries of International Law: A Feminist Analysis* (Manchester, Manchester University Press, 2000).
Cheng, CJ (ed), *Studies in International Air Law: Selected Works of Bin Cheng* (Leiden, Brill Nijhoff, 2017).
Cheng, TH, *State Succession and Commercial Obligations* (Ardsley, Transnational Publishers, 2006).
Chetail, V, *International Migration Law* (Oxford, Oxford University Press, 2019).
Chimni, BS, *International Law and World Order: A Critique of Contemporary Approaches*, 2nd edn (Cambridge, Cambridge University Press, 2017).
Choate, JH, *The Two Hague Conferences* (Princeton, Princeton University Press, 1913).
Cipolla, CM, *Fighting the Plague in Seventeenth-Century Italy* (Madison, University of Wisconsin Press, 1981).
Coleman, J, *Foundations of Social Theory* (Cambridge, Harvard University Press, 1994).
Corten, O, *Le Discours du Droit International: Pour un Positivisme Critique* (Paris, Pedone, 2009).
Cotterrell, R, *Law, Culture and Society: Legal Ideas in the Mirror of Social Theory* (Aldershot, Ashgate 2006).
Cotterrell, R, *Law's Community: Legal Theory in Sociological Perspective* (Oxford, Oxford University Press 1997).
Cox, RW and Jacobson, HK (eds), *The Anatomy of Influence: Decision Making in International Organization* (New Haven, Yale University Press, 1974).
Craven, M, *The Decolonization of International Law: State Succession and the Law of Treaties* (Cambridge, Cambridge University Press, 2007).
Crawford, J, *Brownlie's Principles of Public International Law*, 9th edn (Oxford, Oxford University Press, 2019).
Crosby, AW, *Throwing Fire: Projectile Technology through History* (Cambridge, Cambridge University Press, 2002).
Crouch, TD, *Wings: A History of Aviation from Kites to the Space Age* (Washington, D.C., Smithsonian National Air and Space Museum, 2003).
Cueto, M, Brown, TM, and Fee, E, *The World Health Organization: A History* (Cambridge, Cambridge University Press, 2019).
Cueto, M and Palmer, S, *Medicine and Public Health in Latin America: A History* (Cambridge, Cambridge University Press, 2014).
D Ross, *The Origins of American Social Science* (Cambridge, Cambridge University Press, 1991).
D'Amato, AA, *The Concept of Custom in International Law* (Ithaca, Cornell University Press, 1971).
d'Aspremont, J, *The Discourse on Customary International Law* (Oxford, Oxford University Press, 2021).
Damaška, MR, *The Faces of Justice and State Authority: A Comparative Approach to the Legal Process* (New Haven, Yale University Press, 1986).
Danilenko, GM, *Law-Making in the International Community* (Dordrecht, Martinus Nijhoff, 1993).
Davis, CD, *The United States and the Second Hague Peace Conference: American Diplomacy and International organization, 1899–1914* (Durham, Duke University Press, 1975).

de Azcarate, P, *League of Nations and National Minorities: An Experiment* (translated by EE Brooke) (Washington, DC, Carnegie Endowment for International Peace, 1945).
de Graaf, B, de Haan, I, and Vick, B (eds), *Securing Europe after Napoleon: 1815 and the New European Security Culture* (Cambridge, Cambridge University Press, 2019).
de Syon, G, *Zeppelin! Germany and the Airship, 1900–1939* (Baltimore, John Hopkins University Press, 2002).
De, R, *A People's Constitution: The Everyday Life of Law in the Indian Republic* (Princeton, Princeton University Press, 2018).
Dhokalia, RP, *The Codification of Public International Law* (Manchester, Manchester University Press, 1970).
Dickson, B, *Writing the United Kingdom Constitution* (Manchester, Manchester University Press, 2019).
Dinstein, Y, *The Conduct of Hostilities under the Law of International Armed Conflict* (Cambridge, Cambridge University Press, 2004).
Dobson, A, *A History of International Civil Aviation: From Its Origins through Transformative Evolution* (New York, Routledge, 2017).
Dodd, N, *The Social Life of Money* (Princeton, Princeton University Press, 2016).
Donahue-Ochoa, TJ, *Unfreedom for All: How the World's Injustices Harm You* (Oxford, Oxford University Press, 2019).
Doulman, J and Lee, D, *Every Assistance & Protection: A History of the Australian Passport* (Sydney, Federation Press, 2008).
Droubi, S and d'Aspremont, J (eds), *International Organisations, Non-State Actors, and the Formation of Customary International Law* (Manchester, Manchester University Press, 2020).
Dumberry, P, *The Formation and Identification of Rules of Customary International Law in International Investment Law* (Cambridge, Cambridge University Press, 2018).
Dundes Renteln, A and Dundes, A (eds), *Folk Law: Essays in the Theory and Practice of Lex Non Scripta* (2 Volumes) (Madison, University of Wisconsin Press, 1994).
Dunoff, JL and Pollack, MA (eds), *International Legal Theory: Foundations and Frontiers* (Cambridge, Cambridge University Press, 2022).
Dupuy, PM (ed), *Customary International Law* (Cheltenham, Edward Elgar, 2021).
Durkheim, E, *The Rules of Sociological Method and Selected Texts on Sociology and its Method* (edited by S Lukes and translated by WD Halls) (New York, Free Press, 2013[1982]).
Echenberg, MJ, *Plague Ports: The Global Urban Impact of Bubonic Plague, 1894–1901* (New York, NYU Press, 2007).
Ehrlich, E, *Tatsachen des Gewohnheitsrechts, Inaugurationsrede, gehalten am 2. Dezember 1906* (Leipzig, Franz Deuticke, 1906).
Eich, S, *The Currency of Politics: The Political Theory of Money from Aristotle to Keynes* (Princeton, Princeton University Press, 2022).
Ellickson, RC, *Order Without Law: How Neighbors Settle Disputes* (Cambridge, Harvard University Press, 1991).
Ellis, TT, *Leaves from the Diary of an Army Surgeon: Or, Incidents of Field, Camp, and Hospital Life* (New York, John Bradburn, 1863).
Elon, M, *Jewish Law: History, Sources, Principles*, 1st English edn (Philadelphia, Jewish Publication Society, 1994).
Evans, CM, *The War of the Aeronauts: A History of Ballooning During the Civil War* (Harrisburg, Stackpole Books, 2002).
Fassbender, B. *The United Nations Charter as the Constitution of the International Community* (Leiden, Martinus Nijhoff, 2009).
Fauchille, P, *Louis Renault (1843–1918): Sa vie-son œuvre* (Paris, Pedone, 1918).
Fidler, DP, *International Law and Infectious Diseases* (Oxford, Oxford University Press, 1999).
Finnis, J, *Natural Law and Natural Rights*, 2nd edn (Oxford, Clarendon Press).
Fisher, MH, *Migration: A World History* (Oxford, Oxford University Press, 2013).

FitzGerald, DS and Cook-Martín, D, *Culling the Masses: The Democratic Origins of Racist Immigration Policy in the Americas* (Cambridge, Harvard University Press, 2014).
Fitzmaurice, J, *Damming the Danube: Gabčíkovo and Post-Communist Politics in Europe* (Boulder, Westview Press, 1996).
Fosse, M and Fox, J, *Nansen: Explorer and Humanitarian* (Lanham, Rowman & Littlefield, 2016).
Foster, M and Lambert, H, *International Refugee Law and the Protection of Stateless Persons* (Oxford, Oxford University Press, 2019).
Fox, H and Webb, P, *The Law of State Immunity*, 3rd edn (Oxford, Oxford University Press, 2013).
Franck, TM, *Fairness in International Law and Institutions* (Oxford, Oxford University Press, 1995).
Franck, TM, *The Power of Legitimacy among Nations* (Oxford, Oxford University Press, 1990).
Frank, MG, *Making Minorities History: Population Transfer in Twentieth-Century Europe* (Oxford, Oxford University Press, 2017).
Frerichs, RR, *Deadly River Cholera and Cover-Up in Post-Earthquake Haiti* (Ithaca, Cornell University Press, 2016).
Fripp, E, *Nationality and Statelessness in the International Law of Refugee Status* (Oxford, Hart Publishing, 2016).
Fuller, LL, *The Morality of Law* (New Haven, Yale University Press, 1964).
Fuller, LL, *The Principles of Social Order: Selected Essays of Lon L. Fuller* (edited by KI Winston) (Durham, Duke University Press, 1981).
Gabrynowicz, JI, *The United Nations Principles Relating to Remote Sensing of the Earth from Space: A Legislative History – Interviews of Members of the United States Delegation* (National Center for Remote Sensing and Space Law 2002).
Gagarin, M, *Writing Greek Law* (Cambridge, Cambridge University Press 2009).
Garcia, B, *The Amazon from an International Law Perspective* (Cambridge, Cambridge University Press, 2011).
Geisberg, WD, *Bismarck und das Kreigsvölkerrecht* (Bonn, Rheinische Friedrich-Wilhlelms-Universität, 1913).
Gerring, J, *Case Study Research Principles and Practices*, 2nd edn (Cambridge, Cambridge University Press, 2016).
Giacco, LL, *Judicial Decisions in International Law Argumentation: Between Entrapment and Creativity* (Oxford, Hart Publishing, 2022).
Gianni, G, *La coutume en droit international* (Paris, Pedone, 1931).
Gillespie, A, *A History of the Laws of War, Volume 1: The Customs and Laws of War with Regards to Combatants and Captives* (Oxford, Hart Publishing, 2011).
Glenn, EF, *Hand-Book of International Law* (St. Paul, West Publishing, 1895).
Goodman, NM, *International Health Organizations and their Work* (Philadelphia, Blakiston, 1952).
Goodwin-Gill, GS and McAdam, J, *The Refugee in International Law*, 4th edn (Oxford, Oxford University Press, 2021).
Gorman, D, *The Emergence of International Society in the 1920s* (Cambridge, Cambridge University Press, 2012).
Gostin, LO, *Global Health Law* (Cambridge, Harvard University Press, 2014).
Gostin, LO, *Global Health Security: A Blueprint for the Future* (Cambridge, Harvard University Press 2021).
Gould, WL and Barkun, M, *International Law and the Social Sciences* (Princeton, Princeton University Press, 1970).
Graeber, D, *Debt: The First 5,000 Years* (New York, Melville, 2011).
Grahl-Madsen, A, *The Land Beyond: Collected Essays on Refugee Law and Policy* (edited by P Macalister-Smith and G Alfredsson) (Leiden, Brill Nijhoff, 2001).
Green, JA, *The Persistent Objector Rule in International Law* (Oxford, Oxford University Press, 2016).
Grisel, F, *The Limits of Private Governance: Norms and Rules in a Mediterranean Fishery* (Oxford, Hart Publishing, 2021).
Günther, H, *Zur Entstehung von Völkergewohnheitsrecht* (Berlin, Duncker & Humblot, 1970).

Guzman, AT, *How International Law Works: A Rational Choice Theory* (Oxford, Oxford University Press, 2008).
Halliday, TC and Shaffer, G (eds), *Transnational Legal Orders* (Cambridge, Cambridge University Press, 2014).
Hallion, R, *Taking Flight: Inventing the Aerial Age from Antiquity Through the First World War* (Oxford, Oxford University Press, 2003).
Hammarskjöld, D, *The International Civil Servant in Law and in Fact: Lecture Delivered to Congregation at Oxford University 30 May 1961* (Oxford, Clarendon Press, 1961).
Hammerstad, A, *The Rise and Decline of a Global Security Actor: UNHCR, Refugee Protection, and Security* (Oxford, Oxford University Press, 2014).
Hanson, J, *Ideology, Psychology, and Law* (Oxford, Oxford University Press, 2012).
Hart, HLA, *The Concept of Law*, 2nd edn (Oxford, Clarendon Press, 1994).
Hathaway OA and Shapiro, SJ, *The Internationalists: How a Radical Plan to Outlaw War Remade the World* (New York, Simon & Schuster, 2017).
Hathaway, JC, *The Rights of Refugees under International Law*, 2nd edn (Cambridge, Cambridge University Press, 2021).
Havel, BF and Sanchez, GS *The Principles and Practice of International Aviation Law* (Cambridge, Cambridge University Press, 2014).
Haydon, FS, *Military Ballooning During the Early Civil War* (Baltimore, John Hopkins University Press, 2000).
Hayek, FA, Law, *Legislation and Liberty, Volume I: Rules and Order* (Chicago, University of Chicago Press, 1973).
Hays, JN, *The Burdens of Disease: Epidemics and Human Response in Western History*, revised edn (New Brunswick, Rutgers University Press, 2009).
Henckaerts, JM and Doswald-Beck, L (eds), *Customary International Humanitarian Law* (Cambridge, Cambridge University Press, 2005).
Hertogh, M (ed), *Living Law: Reconsidering Eugen Ehrlich* (Oxford, Hart Publishing, 2009).
Higgs, E, *Identifying the English: A History of Personal Identification 1500 to the Present* (London, Continuum, 2011).
Hirobe, I, *Japanese Pride, American Prejudice: Modifying the Exclusion Clause of the 1924 Immigration Act* (Stanford, Stanford University Press, 2001).
Hodgson, JE, *The History of Aeronautics in Great Britain: From the Earliest Times to the Latter Half of the Nineteenth Century* (Oxford, Oxford University Press, 1924).
Holman, B, *The Next War in the Air: Britain's Fear of the Bomber, 1908–1941* (Farnham, Ashgate Publishing, 2016).
Holmes, R, *Falling Upwards: How We Took to the Air* (London, William Collins, 2013).
Housden, M, *The League of Nations and the Organisation of Peace* (New York, Routledge, 2012).
Howard-Jones, N, *The Scientific Background of the International Sanitary Conferences, 1851–1938* (Geneva, World Health Organization, 1975).
Hull, WI, *The Two Hague Conferences and Their Contributions to International Law* (Boston, Ginn & Company, 1908).
Ikenberry, JG, *A World Safe for Democracy: Liberal Internationalism and the Crises of Global Order* (New Haven, Yale University Press, 2020).
Iurlaro, F, *The Invention of Custom: Natural Law and the Law of Nations, ca. 1550–1750* (Oxford, Oxford University Press, 2021).
Jackson-Preece, J, *National Minorities and the European Nation-States System* (Oxford, Oxford University Press, 1999).
Jakhu, RS and Freeland, S (eds), *McGill Manual on International Law Applicable to Military Uses of Outer Space (MILAMOS), Volume I – Rules* (Montreal, Centre for Research in Air and Space Law, 2022).
Janowsky, OI and Fagen, MM, *International Aspects of German Racial Policies* (New York, Oxford University Press, 1937).
JE Alvarez, *International Organizations as Law-makers* (Oxford, Oxford University Press, 2006).

Jenks, CW, *The Common Law of Mankind* (New York, Praeger, 1958).
Johnston, DM, *The Historical Foundations of World Order: The Tower and the Arena* (Leiden, Martinus Nijhoff, 2008).
Jouannet, E, *A Short Introduction to International Law* (Cambridge, Cambridge University Press, 2014).
Jouannet, E, *The Liberal-Welfarist Law of Nations: A History of International Law* (Cambridge, Cambridge University Press, 2012).
Juma, C, *Innovation and Its Enemies: Why People Resist New Technologies* (Oxford, Oxford University Press, 2016).
Kaku, M, *The Future of Humanity: Terraforming Mars, Interstellar Travel, Immortality, and Our Destiny Beyond Earth* (New York, Doubleday, 2018).
Kamradt-Scott, A, *Managing Global Health Security: The World Health Organization and Disease Outbreak Control* (Basingstoke, Macmillan, 2015).
Kanevskaia, O, *The Law and Practice of Global ICT Standardization* (Cambridge, Cambridge University Press, 2022).
Kelsen, H, *Écrits français de droit international* (edited by C Leben) (Paris, Presses universitaires de France, 2001).
Kelsen, H, *Law and Peace in International Relations: The Oliver Wendell Holmes Lectures, 1940–41* (Cambridge, Harvard University Press, 1942).
Kelsen, H, *Peace Through Law* (Chapel Hill, University of North Carolina Press, 1944).
Kennedy, D, *A World of Struggle: How Power, Law, and Expertise Shape Global Political Economy* (Princeton, Princeton University Press, 2016).
Kent, SK, *The Influenza Pandemic of 1918–1919: A Brief History with Documents* (Boston, Bedford/St. Martin's, 2013).
Keppeler, LM, *Oswald Spengler und die Jurisprudenz: Die Spenglerrezeption in der Rechtswissenschaft zwischen 1918 und 1945, insbesondere innerhalb der «dynamischen Rechtslehre», der Rechtshistoriographie und der Staatsrechtswissenschaft* (Tübingen, Mohr Siebeck, 2014).
King, J, *The Doctrine of Odious Debt in International Law: A Restatement* (Cambridge, Cambridge University Press, 2016).
Klötzer, CCW, *Versuch eines Beytrags zur Revision der Theorie vom Gewohnheitsrecht* (Jena, Mauke und Söhne, 1813).
Knox, K and Kushner, T, *Refugees in an Age of Genocide: Global, National and Local Perspectives during the Twentieth Century* (New York, Routledge, 1999).
Kohler, J, *Luftfahrtrecht* (Berlin, Springer, 1912).
Kolb, R, *Theory of International Law* (Oxford, Hart Publishing, 2016).
Korkunov, NM, *General Theory of Law* (translated by WG Hastings) (Boston, Boston Book Company, 1909).
Koskenniemi, M and Eisemann, PM (eds), *State Sucession: Codification Tested against the Facts* (The Hague, Martinus Nijhoff, 2000).
Koskenniemi, M, *From Apology to Utopia: The Structure of International Legal Argument* (reissue with a new Epilogue) (Cambridge, Cambridge University Press, 2006).
Koskenniemi, M, *The Gentle Civilizer of Nations: The Rise and Fall of International Law 1870–1960* (Cambridge, Cambridge University Press, 2001).
Krisch, N and Yildiz, E (eds), *The Many Paths of Change in International Law* (Oxford, Oxford University Press, 2023).
Kroell, J, *Traité de droit international public aérien: L'aéronautique en temps de guerre. La guerre aérienne (Volume II)* (Issoudun, Éditions internationales, 1936).
Kümper, H and Maurer, A (eds), *150 Jahre Mannheimer Akte: Festschrift zum 150jährigen Bestehen der Revidierten Rheinschifffahrtsakte vom 17. Oktober 1868* (Baden Baden, Nomos, 2018).
Kupelyants, H, *Sovereign Defaults Before Domestic Courts* (Oxford, Oxford University Press, 2018).
Landemore, H, *Open Democracy* (Princeton, Princeton University Press, 2020).
Latour, B, *Reassembling the Social: An Introduction to Actor-Network-Theory* (Oxford, Oxford University Press, 2005).

Lausanne, E, *The Romance of Ballooning: The Story of the Early Aeronauts* (New York, Viking Press, 1971).
Lauterpacht, H, *The Development of International Law by the International Court: Being a Revised Edition of The Development of International Law by the Permanent Court of International Justice (1934)* (London, Stevens, 1958).
Lepard, BD (ed), *Reexamining Customary International Law* (Cambridge, Cambridge University Press, 2017).
Lepard, BD, *Customary International Law: A New Theory with Practical Applications* (Cambridge, Cambridge University Press, 2010).
Lewis, C, *UNHCR and International Refugee Law: From Treaties to Innovation* (New York, Routledge, 2012).
Lie, T, *In the Cause of Peace: Seven Years with the United Nations* (New York, Macmillan, 1954).
Lienau, O, *Rethinking Sovereign Debt: Politics, Reputation, and Legitimacy in Modern Finance* (Cambridge, Harvard University Press, 2014).
Lin, J, *Governing Climate Change: Global Cities and Transnational Lawmaking* (Cambridge, Cambridge University Press, 2018).
Lloyd, M, *The Passport: The History of Man's Most Travelled Document* (Gloucestershire, Sutton Publishing, 2003).
Loescher, G, *Refugees and the Asylum Dilemma in the West* (University Park, Pennsylavania State University Press, 1992).
Loescher, G, *The UNHCR and World Politics: A Perilious Path* (Oxford, Oxford University Press, 2001).
Louka, E, *International Environmental Law: Fairness, Effectiveness, and World Order* (Cambridge, Cambridge University Press, 2006).
Lusa Bordin, F, Müller, AT, and Pascual-Vives, F, *The European Union and Customary International Law* (Cambridge, Cambridge University Press, 2022).
Lycklama à Nijeholt, JF, *Air Sovereignty* (The Hague, Martius Nijhoff, 1910).
Lynn, MR, *Popular Science and Public Opinion in Eighteenth-Century France* (Manchester, Manchester University Press, 2006).
MacCormick, N, *Institutions of Law: An Essay in Legal Theory* (Oxford, Oxford University Press, 2007).
Macfadyen, D et al, *Eric Drummond and his Legacies: The League of Nations and the Beginnings of Global Governance* (Cham, Palgrave Macmillan, 2019).
MacKenzie, D, *ICAO: A History of the International Civil Aviation Organization* (Toronto, University of Toronto Press, 2010).
Malik, BA, *Indus Waters Treaty in Retrospect* (Lahore, Brite Books, 2005).
Marks, S, *The Riddle of All Constitutions: International Law, Democracy, and the Critique of Ideology* (Oxford, Oxford University Press, 2003).
Marrus, MR, *The Unwanted: European Refugees in the Twentieth Century*, 2nd edn (Philadelphia, Temple University Press, 2002).
Martin, F, *Money: The Unauthorized Biography from Coinage to Cryptocurrencies* (New York, Knopf, 2015).
Martin, M and McIntyre, LC (eds), *Readings in the Philosophy of Social Science* (Cambridge, MIT Press, 1994).
Matte, NM, *La coutume dans les cycles juridiques internationaux* (Paris, Pedone, 1947).
Mattelart, A, *The Invention of Communication* (Minneapolis, University of Minnesota Press, 1996).
Maxeiner, JR, *Failures of American Methods of Lawmaking in Historical and Comparative Perspectives* (Cambridge, Cambridge University Press, 2018).
Mazower, M, *Hitler's Empire: How the Nazis Ruled Europe* (New York, Penguin Press, 2008).
McCaffrey, SC, *The Law of International Watercourses* (Oxford, Oxford University Press, 2019).

McClellan III, JE, *Colonialism and Science: Saint Domingue and the Old Regime* (Chicago, Chicago University Press, 1992 [2010]).
McDougal, MS, Lasswell, HD, and Vlasic, IA, *Law and Public Order in Space* (New Haven, Yale University Press, 1963).
McNeill, JR and Mauldin, ES (eds), *A Companion to Global Environmental History* (Chichester, John Wiley & Sons, 2012).
McNeill, W, *Plagues and Peoples* (New York, Anchor Books, 1976).
McWhinney, E, *The International Court of Justice and the Western Tradition of International Law: The Paul Martin Lectures in International Relations and Law* (Dordrecht, Martinus Nijhoff, 1987).
Meder, S, *Ius non scriptum – Traditionen privater Rechtsetzung*, 2nd edn (Tübingen, Mohr Siebeck, 2009).
Megliani, M, *Sovereign Debt: Genesis – Restructuring – Litigation* (Cham, Springer, 2014).
Meier, BM and Gostin, LO (eds), *Global Health Law and Policy: Ensuring Justice for a Healthier World* (Oxford, Oxford University Press, 2023).
Meili, F, *Das Luftschiff im internen Recht und Völkerrecht* (Zurich, Füssli, 1908).
Merkouris, P et al (eds), *Custom and Its Interpretation in International Investment Law* (Cambridge, Cambridge University Press, 2024).
Merkouris, P, Kammerhofer, J and Arajärvi, N (eds), *The Theory, Practice, and Interpretation of Customary International Law* (Cambridge, Cambridge University Press, 2022).
Milton, S and Friedlander, H (eds), *Archives of the Holocaust: An International Collection of Selected Documents, Volume VII* (New York, Garland, 1989).
Moltz, JC, *The Politics of Space Security: Strategic Restraint and the Pursuit of National Interests* (Stanford, Stanford University Press, 2019).
Moyn, S, *Not Enough: Human Rights in an Unequal World* (Cambridge, Harvard University Press, 2018).
Murphy, JB, *The Philosophy of Customary Law* (Oxford, Oxford University Press, 2014).
Myers, RH and Peattie, MR (eds), *The Japanese Colonial Empire, 1895–1945* (Princeton, Princeton University Press, 1984).
N Howard-Jones, *International Public Health between the Two World Wars: The Organizational Problems* (Geneva, World Health Organization, 1978).
Neff, SC, *Justice among Nations: A History of International Law* (Cambridge, Harvard University Press, 2014).
Neff, SC, *War and the Law of Nations: A General History* (Cambridge, Cambridge University Press, 2005).
Neuse, SM, *David E. Lilienthal: The Journey of an American Liberal* (Knoxville, University of Tennessee Press, 1996).
Ngai, MM, *Impossible Subjects: Illegal Aliens and the Making of Modern America*, updated edn (Princeton, Princeton University Press, 2014).
Nissel, A, and Weiler, J (eds), *International Law* (6 Volumes) (New York, Routledge, 2011).
North, DC, *Institutions, Institutional Change and Economic Performance* (Cambridge, Cambridge University Press, 1990).
North, DC, Wallis, JJ, and Weingast, BR, *Violence and Social Orders: Conceptual Framework for Interpreting Recorded Human History* (Cambridge, Cambridge University Press, 2009).
Noyes, JE, Dickinson, LA, and Janis, MW (eds), *International Law Stories* (New York, Foundation Press, 2007).
Onuf, NG (ed), *Law-Making in the Global Community* (Durham, Carolina Academic Press, 1982).
Oppenheim, L, *International Law: A Treatise, Volume II (War and Neutrality)* (London, Longmans, Green, and Co, 1906).
Orchard, P, *A Right to Flee: Refugees, States, and the Construction of International Cooperation* (Cambridge, Cambridge University Press, 2014).

Osterhammel, J, *Die Verwandlung der Welt: eine Geschichte des 19. Jahrhunderts*, 3rd edn (Munich, CH Beck Verlag, 2009).

Packard, RM, *A History of Global Health: Interventions into the Lives of Other Peoples* (Baltimore, John Hopkins University Press, 2016).

Pahuja, S, *Decolonising International Law: Development, Economic Growth and the Politics of Universality* (Cambridge, Cambridge University Press, 2011).

Paine, SCM, *The Japanese Empire: Grand Strategy from the Meiji Restoration to the Pacific War* (Cambridge, Cambridge University Press, 2017).

Pannenborg, CO, *New International Health Order: An Inquiry into the International Relation of World Health and Medical Care* (Alphen aan den Rijn, Sijthoff & Noordhoff, 1979).

Pauwelyn, J, Wessel R, and Wouters, J (eds), *Informal International Lawmaking* (Oxford, Oxford University Press, 2012).

Pedersen, S, *The Guardians: The League of Nations and the Crisis of Empire* (Oxford, Oxford University Press, 2015).

Penet, P and Zendejas, JF, *Sovereign Debt Diplomacies: Rethinking Sovereign Debt from Colonial Empires to Hegemony* (Oxford, Oxford University Press, 2021).

Pepe, G, *Narrative of Scenes and Events in Italy: From 1847 to 1849 Including the Siege of Venice* (London, Henry Colburn, 1850).

Peters, A, Boyle, A, and Alston, P, and Cassese, A (ed), *Realizing Utopia: The Future of International Law* (Oxford, Oxford University Press, 2012).

Petrazycki, L, *Law and Morality* (translated by HW Babb) (Cambridge, Cambridge University Press, 1955).

Pettegree, A, *The Invention of News: How the World Came to Know About Itself* (New Haven, Yale University Press, 2014).

Pirie, F, *The Anthropology of Law* (Oxford, Oxford University Press, 2013).

Pistor, K, *The Code of Capital: How the Law Creates Wealth and Inequality* (Princeton, Princeton University Press, 2019).

Pohl, H, *Luftkriegsrecht: ein Vortrag* (Stuttgart, W Kohlhammer, 1924).

Politis, NE, *Les emprunts d'état en droit international* (Paris, Durand, 1894).

Porter, D, *Health, Civilization and the State: A History of Public Health from Ancient to Modern Times* (London, Routledge 1999).

Porter, TM and Ross, D (eds), *The Cambridge History of Science, Volume 7, The Modern Social Sciences* (Cambridge, Cambridge University Press, 2003).

Posner, R, *Frontiers of Legal Theory*, 4th edn (Cambridge, Harvard University Press, 2001).

Post, LM, *Soldiers' Letters, from Camp, Battle-field and Prison* (New York, Bunce & Huntington, 1865).

Postema, GJ, *Bentham and the Common Law Tradition* (Oxford, Clarendon Press, 1986).

Puffert, DJ, *Tracks Across Continents, Paths through History: The Economic Dynamics of Standardization in Railway Gauge* (Chicago, University of Chicago Press, 2009).

Raitz von Frentz, C, *Lesson Forgotten: Minority Protection Under the League of Nations: The Case of the German Minority in Poland, 1920–1934* (Münster, Lit-Verlag, 1999).

Rajagopal, B, *International Law from Below: Development, Social Movements, and Third World Resistance* (Cambridge, Cambridge University Press, 2003).

Rana, A, *The Constitutional Bind: How Americans Came to Idolize a Document That Fails Them* (Chicago, Chicago University Press, 2024).

RB Larson, *Just Add Water: Solving the World's Problems Using its Most Precious Resource* (Oxford, Oxford University Press, 2020).

Reinhart, CM and Rogoff, KS, *This Time Is Different: Eight Centuries of Financial Folly* (Princeton, Princeton University Press, 2009).

Reisman, WM and Willard, AR (eds), *International Incidents: The Law That Counts in World Politics* (Princeton, Princeton University Press, 1988).

Reisman, WM, *Law in Brief Encounters* (New Haven, Yale University Press, 1999).
Reisman, WM, *Nullity and Revision: The Review and Enforcement of International Judgments and Awards* (New Haven, Yale University Press, 1971).
Renault, L, *Introduction à l'étude du droit international* (Paris, Larose, 1879).
Roberts, A et al (eds), *Comparative International Law* (Oxford, Oxford University Press, 2018).
Roberts, A, *Is International Law International?* (Oxford, Oxford University Press, 2017).
Robertson, C, *The Passport in America: The History of a Document* (Oxford, Oxford University Press, 2010).
Roos, J, *Why Not Default? The Political Economy of Sovereign Debt* (Princeton, Princeton University Press, 2019).
Rosen, G, *A History of Public Health*, revised and expanded edn (Baltimore, John Hopkins University Press, 2015).
Ross, A, *On Law and Justice* (Berkeley, University of California Press, 1959).
Ruger, JP, *Global Health Justice and Governance* (Oxford, Oxford University Press, 2018).
Ruys, T, Corten, O, and Hofer, A (eds), *The Use of Force in International Law: A Case-Based Approach* (Oxford, Oxford University Press, 2018).
Sallinen, H, *Intergovernmental Advocates of Refugees: The Refugee Policy of the League of Nations and the International Labour Organization in the 1920s and 1930s* (Dissertation, University of Helsinki, 2013).
Salter, MB, *Rights of Passage: The Passport in International Relations* (Boulder, Lynne Rienner Publishers, 2003).
Sandholtz, W, *Prohibiting Plunder: How Norms Change* (Oxford, Oxford University Press, 2007).
Sarat, A and Kearns, TR (eds), *Law in Everyday Life* (Ann Arbor, University of Michigan Press, 1995).
Schauer, F, *Thinking Like a Lawyer: A New Introduction to Legal Reasoning* (Cambridge, Harvard University Press, 2009).
Schenk, J, *The Rhine and European Security in the Long Nineteenth Century: Making Lifelines from Frontlines* (Abingdon, Routledge, 2021).
Schladebach, M, *Lufthoheit: Kontinuität und Wandel* (Tübingen, Mohr Siebeck, 2014).
Scholte, JA (ed), *Building Global Democracy: Civil Society and Accountable Global Governance* (Cambridge, Cambridge University Press, 2011).
Schulthess, K, *Das internationale Wasserrecht* (Zurich, Rascher, 1915).
Schwarztrauber, SA, *The Three-mile Limit of Territorial Seas* (Annapolis, Naval Institute Press, 1972).
Scott, JB (ed), *The Proceedings of the Hague Peace Conferences: Translation of the Official Texts, The Conference of 1907, Volume III* (New York, Oxford University Press, 1921).
Scott, JC, *Two Cheers for Anarchism: Six Easy Pieces on Autonomy, Dignity, and Meaningful Work and Play* (Princeton, Princeton University Press, 2012).
Sekalala, S, *Soft Law and Global Health: Problems Lessons from Responses to HIV/AIDS, Malaria and Tuberculosis* (Cambridge, Cambridge University Press, 2017).
Shapiro, SJ, *Legality* (Cambridge, Belknap Press, 2011).
Shelton, D, *International Law and Domestic Legal Systems: Incorporation, Transformation, and Persuasion* (Oxford, Oxford University Press, 2011).
Shiller, RJ, *Narrative Economics: How Stories Go Viral and Drive Major Economic Events* (Princeton, Princeton University Press, 2019).
Shiner, RA, *Legal Institutions and the Sources of Law, Volume 3 of the Treatise of Legal Philosophy and General Jurisprudence* (Dordrecht, Springer, 2005).
Siddiqui, IH, *Hydro Politics & Water Wars in South Asia* (Lahore, Vanguard Books, 2010).
Simma, B, *Das Reziprozitätselement in der Entstehung des Völkergewohnheitsrechts* (Berlin, Duncker & Humblot, 1970).
Simmel, G, *The Sociology of Georg Simmel* (translated, edited, and with an introduction by KH Wolff) (Glencoe, The Free Press, 1950).
Singer, P, *Ethics in the Real World: 82 Brief Essays on Things That Matter* (Princeton, Princeton University Press, 2017).

Sinha, SP, *Legal Polycentricity and International Law* (Durham, Carolina Academic Press, 1996).
Skocpol, T, *States and Social Revolutions: A Comparative Analysis of France, Russia and China* (Cambridge, Cambridge University Press, 1979).
Skran, CM, *Refugees in Inter-War Europe: The Emergence of a Regime* (Oxford, Clarendon Press, 1995).
Slotemaker, LH, *Freedom of Passage for International Air Services* (Leiden, Sijthoff, 1932).
Smil, V, *Energy and Civilization: A History* (Cambridge, MIT Press, 2017).
Snyder, T, *Bloodlands: Europe between Hitler and Stalin* (New York, Basic Books, 2010).
Spaight, JM, *Air Power and War Rights,* 2nd edn (London, Longmans Green & Co, 1933).
Spierman, O, *International Legal Argument in the Permanent Court of International Justice: The Rise of the International Judiciary* (Cambridge, Cambridge University Press, 2005).
Springer, AL, *Cases of Conflict: Transboundary Disputes and the Development of International Environmental Law* (Toronto, University of Toronto Press, 2016).
Štanzel, A, *Wasserträume und Wasserräume im Staatssozialismus: Ein umwelthistorischer Vergleich anhand der tschechoslowakischen und rumänischen Wasserwirtschaft, 1948–1989* (Göttingen, Vandenhoeck & Ruprecht, 2017).
Stasavage, D, *The Decline and Rise of Democracy: A Global History from Antiquity to Today* (Princeton, Princeton University Press, 2020).
Stephen, NC, *Justice Among Nations* (Cambridge, Harvard University Press, 2014).
Stolleis, M, *A History of Public Law in Germany, 1914–1945* (translated by T Dunlap) (Oxford, Oxford University Press, 2004).
Stuurman, S, *The Invention of Humanity* (Cambridge, Harvard University Press, 2017).
Summers, WC, *The Great Manchurian Plague of 1910–1911: The Geopolitics of an Epidemic Disease* (New Haven, Yale University Press, 2012).
Sunstein, CR, *After the Rights Revolution: Reconceiving the Regulatory State* (Cambridge, Harvard University Press, 1993).
Tamanaha, BZ, *A General Jurisprudence of Law and Society* (Cambridge, Cambridge University Press, 2001).
Tamanaha, BZ, *A Realistic Theory of Law* (Cambridge, Cambridge University Press, 2017).
Tamanaha, BZ, *Sociological Approaches to Theories of Law, Cambridge Elements in Philosophy of Law* (Cambridge, Cambridge University Press, 2022).
Tams, CJ and Sloan, J (eds), *The Development of International Law by the International Court of Justice* (Oxford, Oxford University Press 2013).
Teclaff, LA, *The River Basin in History and Law* (The Hague, Martinus Nijhoff, 1967).
Thomas, W, *The Ethics of Destruction: Norms and Force in International Relations* (Ithaca, Cornell University Press, 2014).
Tilly, C, *Democracy* (Cambridge, Cambridge University Press, 2007).
Timasheff, NS, *An Introduction to the Sociology of Law* (Cambridge, Harvard University Committee on Research in the Social Sciences, 1939).
Toman, J and Schindler, D, *The Laws of Armed Conflicts: A Collection of Conventions, Resolutions, and Other Documents,* 3rd edn (Leiden, A.W. Sijthoff, 1973).
Tomz, M, *Reputation and International Cooperation: Sovereign Debt Across Three Centuries* (Princeton, Princeton University Press, 2012).
Torpey, JC, *The Invention of the Passport: Surveillance, Citizenship and the State* (Cambridge, Cambridge University Press, 2018).
Trachtman, JP, *The Economic Structure of International Law* (Cambridge, Harvard University Press, 2008).
Tully, S, *Corporations and International Lawmaking* (Leiden, Martinus Nijhoff, 2007).
Tuori, K, *Ratio and Voluntas: The Tension Between Reason and Will in Law* (Farnham, Ashgate, 2013).
Turack, DC, *The Passport in International Law* (Toronto, Lexington Books, 1972).

Turner, A, *Between Debt and the Devil: Money, Credit, and Fixing Global Finance* (Princeton, Princeton University Press, 2017).
Tvedt, T, McIntyre, O, and Woldetsadik, TK (eds), *A History of Water, Series III, Volume 2: Sovereignty and International Water Law* (London, IB Tauris, 2015).
Twining, W, *General Jurisprudence: Understanding Law from a Global Perspective* (Cambridge, Cambridge University Press, 2009).
Tyler, TR, *Why People Obey the Law* (Princeton, Princeton University Press, 1990).
Ullmann-Margalit, E, *The Emergence of Norms* (Oxford, Clarendon Press, 1977).
Ullrich, G, *The Law of the International Civil Service: Institutional Law and Practice in International Organisations* (Berlin, Duncker & Humblot, 2018).
UNEP, *Global Climate Litigation Report: 2023 Status Review* (Nairobi, UNEP, 2023).
United Nations, *The International Law Commission Fifty Years After: An Evaluation, Proceedings of the Seminar Held to Commemorate the Fiftieth Anniversary of the International Law Commission, 21–22 April 1998* (United Nations, 2000).
van Gestel, R, Micklitz, HW, and Rubin, EL (eds), *Rethinking Legal Scholarship: A Transatlantic Dialogue* (Cambridge, Cambridge University Press, 2017).
Verdross, A, *Die Verfassung der Völkerrechtsgemeinschaft* (Vienna, Springer Verlag, 1926).
von Bernstorff, J, *The Public International Law Theory of Hans Kelsen: Believing in Universal Law* (Cambridge, Cambridge University Press, 2010).
von Bismarck, O, *Die Politischen Reden des Fürsten Bismarck, Vierter Band 1868–1870* (critical edition by H Kohl) (Stuttgart, Cotta, 1893).
von Liszt, F and Fleischmann, M, *Das Völkerrecht: Systematisch Dargestellt von Franz von Liszt*, 12th edn (Berlin, Springer, 1925).
von Liszt, F, *Das Völkerrecht: Systematisch Dargestellt* (Berlin, Haering, 1898).
Waibel, M, *Sovereign Defaults before International Courts and Tribunals* (Cambridge, Cambridge University Press, 2011).
Waldron, J, *The Law* (New York, Routledge, 1990).
Walters, FP, *A History of the League of Nations* (2 Volumes) (New York, Oxford University Press, 1952).
Watson, A, *The Evolution of Western Private Law* (Baltimore, Johns Hopkins University Press, 1985).
Watts, A, *The International Law Commission 1949–1998, Volume I: The Treaties* (Oxford, Oxford University Press, 2000).
Weiler, JHH, *The Constitution of Europe: 'Do the New Clothes Have an Emperor?' and Other Essays on European Integration* (Cambridge, Cambridge University Press, 1999).
Weitz, ED, *A World Divided: The Global Struggle for Human Rights in the Age of Nation-States* (Princeton, Princeton University Press, 2019).
Wempe, SA, *Chronic Disparities: Public Health in Historical Perspective* (Oxford, Oxford University Press, 2020).
Wheatley, N, *The Life and Death of States: Central Europe and the Transformation of Modern Sovereignty* (Princeton, Princeton University Press, 2023).
Wheatley, S, *The Democratic Legitimacy of International Law* (Oxford, Oxford University Press, 2010).
White, AD, *The First Hague Conference* (Boston, World Peace Foundation, 1905 (1912 reprint)).
Whitman, JQ, *The Verdict of Battle: The Law of Victory and the Making of Modern War* (Cambridge, Harvard University Press, 2012).
Wiessner, S (ed), *General Theory of International Law, Volume 1, American Classics of International Law* (Leiden, Martinus Nijhoff, 2017).
Wilf, S, *The Law Before the Law* (Lanham, Lexington Books, 2008).
Witt, JF, *Lincoln's Code: The Laws of War in American History* (New York, Free Press, 2012).
Wood, M and Sender, O, *Identification of Customary International Law* (Oxford, Oxford University Press, 2024).
Woodward, BK, *Global Civil Society in International Lawmaking and Global Governance: Theory and Practice* (Leiden, Martinus Nijhoff, 2010).

World Health Organization, *The First Ten Years of the World Health Organization* (Geneva, World Health Organization, 1958).

Wu, LT, *A Treatise on Pneumonic Plague* (Geneva, League of Nations, 1926).

Yamin, F and Depledge, J, *The International Climate Change Regime: A Guide to Rules, Institutions and Procedures* (Cambridge, Cambridge University Press, 2004).

Yao, J, *The Ideal River: How Control of Nature Shaped the International Order* (Manchester, Manchester University Press, 2022).

Yasuaki, O, *International Law in a Transcivilizational World* (Cambridge, Cambridge University Press, 2017).

Zaring, D, *The Globalized Governance of Finance* (Cambridge, Cambridge University Press, 2019).

ARTICLES

Achiume, ET, 'Migration as Decolonization' (2019) 71 *Stanford Law Review* 1509.

Ahmad, J, 'The Indus Waters Kishenganga Arbitration and State-to-State Disputes' (2013) 29(3) *Arbitration International* 507.

Akhter, M, 'The Hydropolitical Cold War: The Indus Waters Treaty and State Formation in Pakistan' (2015) 46 *Political Geography* 65.

Allott, P, 'State Responsibility and the Unmaking of International Law' (1988) *Harvard International Law Journal* 1.

Anghie, A, 'Finding the Peripheries: Soveriegnty and Colonialism in Nineteenth-Century International Law' (1999) 40 *Harvard International Law Journal* 1.

Baker, RB, 'Customary International Law in the 21st Century: Old Challenges and New Debates' (2010) 21(1) *European Journal of International Law* 173.

Bakker, C, 'The Paris Agreement on Climate Change: Balancing "Legal Force" and "Geographical Scope"' (2016) 25(1) *The Italian Yearbook of International Law* 299.

Balkin, JM and Siegel, RB 'Principles, Practices, and Social Movements' (2005) 154 *University of Pennsylvania Law Review* 927.

Baycroft, T and Wilkin, B, 'The Balloon Post during the Siege of Paris, 1870–71' (2023) 42(3) *War & Society* 215.

Beard, JM, 'Soft Law's Failure on the Horizon: The International Code of Conduct for Outer Space Activities' (2016) *University of Pennsylvania Journal of International Law* 38.

Bederman, DJ, 'Constructivism, Positivism, and Empiricism in International Law' (2001) 89(2) *Georgetown Law Journal* 469.

Benvenisti, E and Lustig, D, 'Monopolizing War: Codifying the Laws of War to Reassert Governmental Authority, 1856–1874' (2020) 31(1) *European Journal of International Law* 127.

Besson, S and Ammann, O, 'La pratique suisse relative à la détermination du droit international coutumier' (2016) 21 *Cahiers fribourgeois de droit européen* 1.

Birn, AE, 'The Stages of International (Global) Health: Histories of Success or Successes of History?' (2009) 4(1) *Global Public Health* 50.

Blankenburg, S and Kozul-Wright, R, 'Preface: Sovereign Debt Restructurings in the Contemporary Global Economy: The UNCTAD Approach' (2016) 41(2) *The Yale Journal of International Law Online* 1.

Blukacz-Louisfert, B, 'The Nansen Archival Collection at the Library of the United Nations Office at Geneva' (2003) 22(1) *Refugee Survey Quarterly* 52.

Bodansky, D, 'Customary (and Not So Customary) International Environmental Law' (1995) 3(1) *Indiana Journal of Global Legal Studies* 105.

Bodansky, D, 'The Paris Climate Change Agreement: A New Hope?' (2016) 110 *American Journal of International Law* 288.

Bodansky, D, 'The United Nations Climate Change Regime Thirty Years on – A Retrospective and Assessment' (2022) 62 *Washburn Law Journal* 1.

Bodansky, D, 'The United Nations Framework Convention on Climate Change: A Commentary' (1993) 18 *Yale Journal of International Law* 451.

Bode, RG, 'Cholera in Haiti: United Nations Immunity and Accountability' (2016) 47 *Georgtown Journal of International Law* 759.

Boisson de Chazournes, L, 'The Notion of Environmental Flows and the Law Applicable to International Watercourses' (2014) 108 *Proceedings of the Annual Meeting (American Society of International Law)* 295.

Bolton, P, Gulati, M, and Panizza, U, 'Sovereign Debt Puzzles' (2023) 15 *Annual Review of Financial Economics* 239.

Bordin, FL and Odermatt, J, 'International Law of Regional Organizations: A Comparative Perspective' (2024) 19 *International Organizations Law Review* 36.

Bordin, FL, 'Reflections of Customary International Law: The Authority of Codification Conventions and ILC Draft Articles in International Law' (2014) 63 *International and Comparative Law Quarterly* 535.

Boyle, AE, 'State Responsibility and International Liability for Injurious Consequences of Acts not Prohibited by International Law: A Necessary Distinction?' (1990) 39 *International and Comparative Law Quarterly* 1.

Brown-Nagin, T, 'Elites, Social Movements, and the Law: The Case of Affirmative Action' (2005) 105(5) *Columbia Law Review* 1436.

Brunnée, J and Toope, S, 'Interactional International Law: An Introduction' (2011) 3(2) *International Theory* 307.

Bubb, R, Kremer, M, and Levine, D, 'The Economics of International Refugee Law' (2011) 40 *Journal of Legal Studies* 367.

Caflisch, L, 'Emerging Rules on International Waterways: The Contribution of the United Nations' (1996) 15 *Political Geography* 273.

Caron, DD, 'The ILC Articles on State Responsibility: The Paradoxical Relationship between Form and Authority' (2002) 96 *American Journal of International Law* 857.

Cass, DZ, 'Navigating the Newstream: Recent Critical Scholarship in International Law' (1996) 65 *Nordic Journal of International Law* 341.

Chatterjee, P, 'Legality of Anti-Satellites Under the Space Law Regime' (2014) 12 *Astropolitics* 27.

Chetail, V, 'Fridtjof Nansen and the International Protection of Refugees: An Introduction' (2003) 22 *Refugee Survey Quarterly* 1.

Chimni, BS, 'Customary International Law: A Third World Perspective' (2018) 112 *American Journal of International Law* 1.

Cohen, HG, 'Finding International Law, Part II: Our Fragmenting Legal Community' (2012) 44(4) *New York University Journal of International Law and Politics* 1049.

Cohen, HG, 'Finding International Law: Rethinking the Doctrine of Sources' (2007) 93 *Iowa Law Review* 65.

Cooper, JC, 'High Altitude Flight and National Sovereignty' (1951) 4 *The International Law Quarterly* 411

Cooper, JC, 'The Chicago Convention – After Twenty Years' (1965) 19(3) *University of Miami Law Review* 333.

Cooper, JC, 'The International Air Navigation Conference, Paris 1910' (1952) 19 *Journal of Air Law and Commerce* 127.

Cover, RM, 'The Origins of Judicial Activism in the Protection of Minorities' (1982) 91(7) *The Yale Law Journal* 1287.

Craven, M, '"Other Spaces": Constructing the Legal Architecture of a Cold War Commons and the Scientific-Technical Imaginary of Outer Space' (2019) 30(2) *European Journal of International Law* 547.

Crawford, J, 'Continuity and Discontinuity in International Dispute Settlement: An Inaugural Lecture' (2010) 1(1) *Journal of International Dispute Settlement* 3.

Cushman, F, 'Rationalization is Rational' (2020) 43(e28) *Behavioral and Brain Sciences.*

d'Aspremont, J, 'The Four Lives of Customary International Law' (2019) *International Community Law Review* 229.

Dahn, F, 'Der Deutsch-Französische Krieg und das Völkerrecht' (1871) 1 *Jahrbücher für die Deutsche Armee und Marine* 79.

Darby, WE, 'The Peril of the Air (concluded from the November issue)' (1912) 74(11) *The Advocate of Peace* 263.

Darby, WE, 'The Peril of the Air' (1912) 74(10) *The Advocate of Peace* 244.

Daugirdas, K, 'International Organizations and the Creation of Customary International Law' 31 (1) *European Journal of International Law* 201.

De Baere, G and Mills, A, 'T.M.C. Asser and Public and Private International Law: The Life and Legacy of "a Practical Legal Statesman"' (2011) 42 *Netherlands Yearbook of International Law* 3.

Deplano, R, 'The Artemis Accords: Evolution or Revolution in International Space Law' (2021) 70 *International & Comparative Law Quarterly* 799.

Dowdeswell, TL, 'The Brussels Peace Conference of 1874 and the Modern Laws of Belligerent Qualification' (2017) 54(3) *Osgoode Hall Law Journal* 805.

Durrani, HA, 'Interpreting "Space Resources Obtained": Historical and Postcolonial Interventions in the Law of Commercial Space Mining' (2019) 57 *Columbia Journal of Transnational Law* 403.

Edgington, R, 'An "All-Seeing Flying Eye": V-2 Rockets and the Promises of Earth Photography' (2012) 28(3) *History and Technology* 363.

Ellickson, RC, 'A Critique of Economic and Sociological Theories of Social Control' (January 1987) XVI *Journal of Legal Studies* 67.

Eskridge, WN, 'Some Effects of Identity-Based Social Movements on Constitutional Law in the Twentieth Century' (2002) 100 *Michigan Law Review* 2062.

Fidler, DP, '"Geographical Morality" Revisited: International Relations, International Law, and the Controversy over Placebo-Controlled HIV Clinical Trials in Developing Countries' (2001) 42(2) *Harvard International Law Journal* 299.

Fidler, DP, 'Bioterrorism, Public Health, and International Law' (2002) 3(1) *Chicago Journal of International Law* 7.

Fidler, DP, 'Challenging the Classical Concept of Custom: Perspectives on the Future of Customary International Law' (1996) 39 *German Yearbook of International Law* 198.

Fidler, DP, 'From International Sanitary Conventions to Global Health Security: The New International Health Regulations' (2005) 4(2) *Chinese Journal of International Law* 325.

Fidler, DP, 'Microbialpolitik: Infectious Diseases and International Relations' (1998) 14(1) *American University International Law Review* 1.

Fischman, JB and Law, DS, 'What Is Judicial Ideology, and How Should We Measure It?' (2009) 29 *Washington University Journal of Law & Policy* 133.

Fleischer, T, 'Jaws on the Danube: Water Management, Regime Change and the Movement Against the Middle Danube Hydroelectric Dam' (1993) 17 *International Journal of Urban and Regional Research* 429.

Freedman, R and Lemay-Hebert, N, 'Towards an Alternative Interpretation of UN Immunity: A Human Rights-Based Approach to the Haiti Cholera Case' (2015) *Questions of International Law* 5.

Freedman, T, 'UN Immunity or Impunity? A Human Rights Based Challenge' (2014) 25 *European Journal of International Law* 239.

Fuller, LL, 'Human Interaction and the Law' (1969) 14(1) *American Journal of Jurisprudence* 1.

Gaja, G, 'Interpreting Articles Adopted by the International Law Commission' (2015) 85(1) *British Yearbook of International Law* 10.

Gathii, JT, 'Review Essay: International Law and Eurocentricity' (1998) 9 *European Journal of International Law* 184.

Gervais, A, 'L'affaire du lac Lanoux, étude critique de la sentence arbitrale du Tribunal arbitral' (1960) 6 *Annuaire Français de Droit International* 372.

Gibbons, AO, 'Sir George Gibbons and the Boundary Waters Treaty of 1909' (1953) 34 *Canadian Historical Review* 124.

Glenn, HP, 'The Grounding of Codification' (1998) 31 *UC Davis Law Review* 765.

Goldsmith, J and Levinson, D, 'Law for States: International Law, Constitutional Law, Public Law' (2009) 122 *Harvard Law Review* 1791.

Goldsmith, JL and Posner, EA, 'A Theory of Customary International Law' (1999) 66 *University of Chicago Law Review* 1113.

Goodwin-Gill, GA, 'International Refugee Law: Where it Comes From, and Where It's Going …' (2017) 45 *International Journal of Legal Information* 24.

Goodwin-Gill, GS, 'The Office of the United Nations High Commissioner for Refugees and the Sources of International Refugee Law' (2020) 69 *International and Comparative Law Quarterly* 1.

Grahl-Madsen, A, 'The European Tradition of Asylum and the Development of Refugee Law' (1966) 3(3) *Journal of Peace Research* 278.

Graybiel, AM, 'Habits, Rituals, and the Evaluative Brain' (2008) 31 *Annual Review of Neuroscience* 359.

Green, JA, 'The Persistent Objector Rule in the Work of the International Law Commission: On the Identification of Customary International Law' (2017) 27(1) *Italian Yearbook of International Law* 175.

Griffiths, J, 'What is Sociology of Law? (On law, rules, social control and sociology)' (2017) 49(2) *The Journal of Legal Pluralism and Unofficial Law* 93.

Gross, A, 'The Past, Present, and Future of Global Health Law Beyond Crisis' (2021) 115(4) *The American Journal of International Law* 754.

Gupta, V, 'Critique of the International Law on Protection of the Outer Space Environment' (2016) 14(1) *Astropolitics* 20.

Haggenmacher, P, 'An Archaeological Look at "International Custom as Evidence of a General Practice Accepted as Law" and Article 38 of the World Court's Statute' (2021) 34(3) *Leiden Journal of International Law* 1.

Haines, D, '(Inter)Nationalist Rivers? Cooperative Development in David Lilienthal's Plan for the Indus Basin, 1951' (2014) 6 *Water History* 133.

Hakimi, M, 'Making Sense of Customary International Law' (2020) 118 *Michigan Law Review* 1487.

Hathaway, JC, 'The Evolution of Refugee Status in International Law: 1920–1950' (1984) 33(2) *The International and Comparative Law Quarterly* 348.

Hathaway, O and Shapiro, SJ, 'Outcasting: Enforcement in Domestic and International Law' (2011) 121 *Yale Law Journal* 252.

Hathaway, OA, 'Path Dependence in the Law: The Course and Pattern of Legal Change in a Common Law System' (2001) 86 *Iowa Law Review* 104.

Hatton, TJ, 'Asylum Migration to the Developed World: Persecution, Incentives, and Policy' (2020) 34(1) *The Journal of Economic Perspectives* 75.

Hawkins, RXD, Goodman, ND, and Goldstone, RL, 'The Emergence of Social Norms and Conventions' (2019) 23(2) *Trends in Cognitive Sciences* 158.

Hébert, B and Schreger, J, 'The Costs of Sovereign Default: Evidence from Argentina' (2017) 107(10) *American Economic Review* 3119.

Heffes, E, 'Some Reflections on the Theory of Sources of International Law: Re-examining Customary International Law' (2018) 51(3) *Israel Law Review* 485.

Heller, KJ, 'Specially-Affected States and the Formation of Custom' (2018) 112 *American Journal of International Law* 191.

Henrich-Franke, C and Tölle, I, 'Competition for European Competence: The Central Commission for Navigation on the Rhine and the European Economic Community in the 1960s' (2011) 27(3) *History and Technology* 331.

Heyking, B, 'The International Protection of Minorities. The Achilles' Heel of the League of Nations' (1927) 13 *Transactions of the Grotius Society* 31.

Hieronymi, O, 'The Nansen Passport: A Tool of Freedom of Movement and of Protection' (2003) 22(1) *Refugee Survey Quarterly* 36.
Hirobe, I, 'American Attitudes toward the Japanese Immigration Question, 1924–1931' (1993) 2(3) *The Journal of American-East Asian Relations* 275.
Holborn, LW, 'The League of Nations and the Refugee Problem' (1939) 203 *The Annals of the American Academy of Political and Social Science* 124.
Hollenberg, S, 'Immunity of the UN in the Case of Haitian Cholera Victims' (2015) 19 *Journal of International Peacekeeping* 118.
Howse, R and Teitel, R 'Beyond Compliance: Rethinking Why International Law Really Matters' (2010) 1(2) *Global Policy* 127.
Huber, M, 'Ein Beitrag zur Lehre von der Gebietshoheit an Grenzflüssen' (1907) 1 *Zeitschrift für Völkerrecht und Bundesstaatsrecht* 29.
Hudson, MO, 'The Progressive Codification of International Law' (1926) 20(4) *The American Journal of International Law* 655.
Jackson, IC, 'Dr. Fridtjof Nansen a Pioneer in the International Protection of Refugees' (2003) 22(1) *Refugee Survey Quarterly* 7.
Jaeger, G, 'On the History of the International Protection of Refugees' (2001) 83(843) *RICR/IRRC* 727.
Johnston, KA, 'Identifying the *jus cogens* Norm in the *jus ad bellum*' (2021) 70 *International and Comparative Law Quarterly* 29.
Joyner, DH, 'Why I Stopped Believing in Customary International Law' (2019) 9(1) *Asian Journal of International Law* 31.
Kahn, PW, 'Reason and Will in the Origins of American Constitutionalism' (1989) 98(2) *Yale Law Journal* 449.
Kalm, S, 'Standardizing Movements: The International Passport Conferences of the 1920s' (2017) 8 *STANCE Working Papers Series* 1.
Kelly, JP, 'The Twilight of Customary International Law' (2000) 40 *Virginia Journal of Intenrational Law* 449
Keohane, RO, 'The International Climate Regime without American Leadership' (2017) 15(3) *Chinese Journal of Population Resources and Environment* 184.
Kersch, KI, 'Constitutive Stories about the Common Law in Modern American Conservativism' (2016) 56 *Nomos* 211.
Kessedjian, C, 'Le tiers impartial et indépendant en droit international: juge, arbitre, médiateur, conciliateur: cours général de droit international' (2019) 403 *Collected Courses of the Hague Academy of International Law* 49.
Kim, MSH, 'Customary Law and Colonial Jurisprudence in Korea' (2009) 57 *American Journal of Comparative Law* 205.
Kingsbury, B, 'The Concept of Compliance as a Function of Competing Conceptions of International Law' (1998) 19 *Michigan Journal of International Law* 345
Klabbers, J, 'The Bridge Crack'd: A Critical Look at Interdisciplinary Relations' (2009) 23(1) *International Relations* 119.
Klabbers, J, 'The Relative Autonomy of International Law or the Forgotten Politics of Interdisciplinary' (2004) 1 *Journal of International Law & International Relations* 35.
Knox, JH, 'The Boundary Waters Treaty: Ahead of Its Time, and Ours' (2008) 54 *Wayne Law Review* 1591.
Kocse, R, 'Final Detonation: How Customary International Law Can Trigger the End of Landmines' (2014) 103 *Georgetown Law Review* 749.
Koh, HH, 'Review Essay: Why Do Nations Obey International Law?' (1997) 106(8) *Yale Law Journal* 2599.
Koh, HH, 'The 1994 Roscoe Pound Lecture: Transnational Legal Process' (1996) 75 *Nebraska Law Review* 181.
Koh, HH, 'The 1998 Frankel Lecture: Bringing International Law Home' (1998) 35 *Houston Law Review* 623.

Kolb, R, 'Selected Problems in the Theory of Customary International Law' (2003) 50(2) *Netherlands International Law Review* 119.

Koplow, DA, 'ASAT-isfaction: Customary International Law and the Regulation of Anti-Satellite Weapons' (2008) 30 *Michigan Journal of International Law* 1187.

Krehbiel, E, 'The European Commission of the Danube: An Experiment in International Administration' (1918) 33(1) *Political Science Quarterly* 38.

Krisch, N, 'The Dynamics of International Law Redux' (2021) 74 *Current Legal Problems* 269.

Kronman, AT, 'The Value of Moral Philosophy' (1998) 111(7) *Harvard Law Review* 1751.

Kuhn, AK, 'The Beginnings of an Aerial Law' (1910) 4(1) *American Journal of International Law* 109.

Kurzban, I, Lindstrom, B, and Jonsson, S, 'UN Accountability for Haiti's Cholera Epidemic' (2014–15) 108 *AJIL Unbound* 17.

Larson, RB, 'Law in the Time of Cholera' (2017) 92 *Notre Dame Law Review* 1271.

Lautze, J and Giordano, M, 'Transboundary Water Law in Africa: Development, Nature, and Geography' (2005) 45(4) *Natural Resources Journal* 1053.

Laylin, JG and Bianchi, RL, 'The Role of Adjudication in International River Disputes: The Lake Lanoux Case' (1959) 53 *The American Journal of International Law* 30.

Ludington, S and Gulati, M, 'A Convenient Untruth: Fact and Fantasy in the Doctrine of Odious Debts' (2008) 48 *Virginia Journal of International Law* 595.

Lycklama à Nijeholt, JF, 'La souveraineté aérienne' (1910) 1 *Revue juridique internationale de la locomotion aérienne* 229.

MacChesney, B, 'Lake Lanoux Case (France-Spain)' (1959) 53 *The American Journal of International Law* 156.

Mamlyuk, BN and Mattei, U, 'Comparative International Law' (2011) 36 *Brooklyn Journal of International Law* 385.

Martini, M et al, 'The Spanish Influenza Pandemic: A Lesson from History 100 Years after 1918' (2019) 60(1) *Journal of Preventive Medicine and Hygiene* E64.

McDougal, MS, 'Emerging Customary Law of Space' (1963) 58 *Northwestern University Law Review* 618.

Mendelson, M, 'The Formation of Customary International Law' (1998) 272 *Collected Courses of the Hague Academy of International Law* 155.

Meron, T, 'International Law in the Age of Human Rights: General Course on Public International Law' (2004) 301 *Collected Courses of The Hague Academy of International Law* 9.

Meyer, TL, 'Towards a Communicative Theory of International Law' (2012) 13 *Melbourne Journal of International Law* 1.

Mills, A, 'The Private History of International Law' (2006) 55(1) *The International and Comparative Law Quarterly* 1.

Moussa, J, 'Implications of the Indus Water Kishenganga Arbitration for the International Law of Watercourses and the Environment' 64 *International and Comparative Law Quarterly* 697.

Murray, KA, 'The Trail Smelter Case: International Air Pollution in the Columbia Valley' (1972) *BC Studies: The British Columbian Quarterly* 68.

Novak, G, 'Reading the Waves: Continuity and Change in Ocean Lawmaking' (2022) 47(2) *Columbia Journal of Environmental Law* 359.

Odermatt, J, 'The Development of Customary International Law by International Organziations' (2017) 66(2) *International & Comparative Law Quarterly* 491, 510–1.

Ordway III, FI et al, 'A Memoir: From Peenemünde to USA: A Classic Case of Technology Transfer' (2007) 60(1) *Acta Astronautica* 24.

Otto, D, 'Subalternity and International Law: The Problems of Global Community and the Incommensurability of Difference' (1996) 5(3) *Social & Legal Studies* 337.

Pacholska, M, 'New Kids on the Block International Organizations as Customary Rules Creators' (2019) 21(3–4) *International Community Law Review* 325.

Penkower, MN, 'Honorable Failures Against Nazi Germany: McDonald's Letter of Resignation and the Petition in its Support' (2010) 30(3) *Modern Judaism* 247.

Petersen, N, 'The International Court of Justice and the Judicial Politics of Identifying Customary International Law' (2017) 28(2) *European Journal of International Law* 357.

Posner, EA, 'International Law and the Disaggregated State' (2005) 32 *Florida State University Law Review* 797.

Posner, EA, and Sykes, AO, 'Efficient Breach of International Law: Optimal Remedies, "Legalized Noncompliance," and Related Issues' (2011) 110(2) *Michigan Law Review* 243.

Postema, GJ, 'Custom, Normative Practice, and the Law' (2012) 62 *Duke Law Journal* 707.

Prado, M and Trebilcock, M, 'Path Dependence, Development, and the Dynamics of Institutional Reform' (2009) 59(3) *The University of Toronto Law Journal* 341.

Puffert, DJ, 'Path Dependence in Spatial Networks: The Standardization of Railway Track Gauge' (2002) 39(3) *Explorations in Economic History* 282.

Ratner, SR and Slaughter, AM, 'Appraising the Methods of International Law: A Prospectus for Readers' (1999) 93(2) *The American Journal of International Law* 291.

Read, JE, 'The Trail Smelter Dispute' (1963) 1 *Canadian Yearbook of International Law/Annuaire canadien de droit international* 213.

Reisman, WM, 'Canute Confronts the Tide: States vs. Tribunals and the Evolution of the Minimum Standard in Customary International Law' (2015) 30(3) *ICSID Review – Foreign Investment Law Journal* 616.

Reisman, WM, 'International Incidents: Introduction to a New Genre in the Study of International Law' (1984) 10 *Yale Journal of International Law* 1.

Reisman, WM, 'The Breakdown of the Control Mechanism in ICSID Arbitration' (1989) 1989(4) *Duke Law Journal* 739.

Reisman, WM, 'The Cult of Custom in the late 20th Century' (1987) 17 *California Western International Law Journal* 142.

Reisman, WM, 'The Quest for World Order and Human Dignity in the Twenty-First Century: Constitutive Process and Individual Commitment: General Course on Public International Law' (2013) 135 *Collected Courses of the Hague Academy of International Law* 9.

Reisman, WM, 'The Shadows Looming over International Law' (2006) 6(1) *Baltic Yearbook of International Law* 19.

Rhode, DL, 'Legal Scholarship' (2002) 115 (5) *Harvard Law Review* 1327.

Riesch, E, 'L'aéronautique militaire au service de l'espionnage en temps de guerre' (1932) *1 Revue générale de droit aérien* 813.

Roberts, A, Stephan, PB, Verdier, PH, and Versteeg, M, 'Comparative International Law: Framing the Field' (2015) 109(3) *The American Journal of International Law* 467.

Roberts, AE, 'Traditional and Modern Approaches to Customary International Law: A Reconciliation' (2001) 95(4) *American Journal of International Law* 757.

Root, E, 'The Need of Popular Understanding of International Law' (1907) 1 *The American Journal of International Law* 1.

Rosenne, S, 'Codification Revisited After 50 Years' (1998) 2(1) *Max Planck Yearbook of United Nations Law Online* 1.

Roucek, JS, 'Procedure in Minorities Complaints' (1929) 23(3) *The American Journal of International Law* 538.

Sand, PH, Lyon, JT, and Pratt, GN, 'An Historical Survey of International Air Law before the Second World War' (1960) 7 *McGill Law Journal* 24.

Sands, P, 'Of Refugees and Resignation' (2017) 6(2) *UCL Journal of Law and Jurisprudence* 1.

Saul, M, 'The Normative Status of Self-Determination in International Law: A Formula for Uncertainty in the Scope and Content of the Right?' (2011) 11(4) *Human Rights Law Review* 609.

Sehdev, PS, 'Arcanum: The Origin of Quarantine' (1 November 2002) 35 *Clinical Infectious Diseases* 1071.

Shirky, C, 'The Political Power of Social Media: Technology, the Public Sphere, and Political Change' (January/February 2011) *Foreign Affairs*.

Slaughter, AM, Tulumello, AS, and Wood, S, 'International Law and International Relations Theory: A New Generation of Interdisciplinary Scholarship' (1998) 92(3) *The American Journal of International Law* 367.
Sohn, LB, 'The New International Law: Protection of the Rights of Individuals Rather Than States' (1982) 32 *American University Law Review* 1.
Spaulding, RM, 'Revolutionary France and the Transformation of the Rhine' (2011) 44(2) *Central European History* 203.
Stokes, H et al, 'Evolution of ISO's Space Debris Mitigation Standards' (2020) 7(3) *Journal of Space Safety Engineering* 325.
Talmon, S, 'Determining Customary International Law: The ICJ's Methodology between Induction, Deduction and Assertion' (2015) 26(2) *European Journal of International Law* 417.
Tan, D, 'Towards a New Regime for the Protection of Outer Space as the Province of All Mankind' (2000) 25 *Yale Journal of International Law* 145.
Tannenwald, N, 'Stigmatizing the Bomb: Origins of the Nuclear Taboo' (2005) 29(4) *International Security* 5.
Tignino, M and Irmakkesen, Ö, 'Water in Peace Operations: The Case of Haiti' (2020) 29(1) *Review of European, Comparative and International Environmental Law* 33.
Tognotti, E, 'Lessons from the History of Quarantine, From Plague to Influenza A' (2013) 19(2) *Emerging Infectious Diseases* 254.
Topol, T, 'A History of Passports and their Design: Passport Function and Feature Changes through the Centuries' (June 2018) *Keesing Journal of Documents & Identity* 12.
Trilla, A et al, 'The 1918 "Spanish Flu" in Spain' (2008) 47 *Clinical Infectious Diseases* 668.
Turack, DC, 'Freedom of Movement and the International Regime of Passports' (1968) 6 *Osgoode Hall Law Journal* 230.
Tyler, TR, 'Whither Legitimacy? Legal Authority in the Twenty-First Century' (2023) 19 *Annual Review of Law and Social Science* 1.
van Aaken, A, 'Behavioral International Law and Economics' (2014) 55 *Harvard International Law Journal* 421.
Verdier, PH and Voeten, E, 'How Does Customary International Law Change? The Case of State Immunity' (2015) 59(2) *International Studies Quarterly* 209.
Verdier, PH and Voeten, E, 'Precedent, Compliance, and Change in Customary International Law: An Explanatory Theory' (2014) 108(3) *The American Journal of International Law* 389.
Verdross, A, 'Entstehungsweisen und Geltungsgrund des universellen völkerrechtlichen Gewohnheitsrechts' (1969) 29 *Zeitschrift für ausländisches öffentliches Recht und Völkerrecht* 635.
Voigt, C and Ferreira, F, 'Differentiation in the Paris Agreement' (2016) 6 *Climate Law* 58.
Weber, M, 'Die „Objektivität" sozialwissenschaftlicher und sozialpolitischer Erkenntnis (1904) 19 *Archiv für Sozialwissenschaft und Sozialpolitik* 22.
Wegerich, K and Olsson, O, 'Late Developers and the Inequity of "Equitable Utilization" and the Harm of "Do no Harm"' (2010) 35 *Water International* 707.
Weinzierl, MC, 'Space, the Final Economic Frontier' (2018) 32(2) *Journal of Economic Perspectives* 173.
Weiss, EB, 'The Evolution of International Environmental Law' (2011) 54 *Japanese Yearbook of International Law* 1.
Welly, ND, 'Enlightened State-Interest – A Legal Framework for Protecting the "Common Interest of All Mankind" from Hardinian Tragedy' (2010) 36(1) *Journal of Space Law* 273.
Wentz, FK, 'Book Review: So It Was True: The American Proestant Press and the Nazi Persecution of the Jews. By Robert W. Ross (1980)' (2009) 51 *Church History* 364.
Wheatley, S, 'A Democratic Rule of International Law' (2011) 22(2) *European Journal of International Law* 525.
Williams, RF, 'Developments in Aerial Law' (1926) 75 *University of Pennsylvania Law Review* 139.
Wirth, JD, 'The Trail Smelter Dispute: Canadians and Americans Confront Transboundary Pollution, 1927–41' (1996) 1(2) *Environmental History* 34.

CONTRIBUTIONS TO EDITED VOLUMES

Adler-Nissen, R, 'Conclusion: Relationalism or Why Diplomats Find International Relations Theory Strange' in OJ Sending, V Pouliot, and IB Neumann (eds), *Diplomacy and the Making of World Politics* (Cambridge, Cambridge University Press, 2015) 284–308.

Alexy, R, 'The Ideal Dimension of Law' in G Duke and RP George, *The Cambridge Companion to Natural Law Jurisdprudence* (Cambridge, Cambridge University Press, 2017) 314–341.

Allum, JR, '"An Outcrop of Hell": History, Environment, and the Politics of the Trail Smelter Dispute' in RM Bratspies and RA Miller (eds), *Transboundary Harm in International Law: Lessons from the Trail Smelter Arbitration* (Cambridge, Cambridge University Press, 2006) 13–26.

Bannelier, K, 'Foundational Judgment or Constructive Myth? The Court's Decision as a Precursor to International Environmental Law' in K Bannelier, T Christakis, and S Heathcote (eds), *The ICJ and the Evolution of International Law: The Enduring Impact of the Corfu Channel Case* (Abingdon, Routledge, 2012) 242–255.

Bantekas, I, 'The Right to Unilateral Repudiation of Odious, Illegal, and Illegitimate Sovereign Debt as a Human Rights Defence' in I Bantekas and C Lumina (eds), *Sovereign Debt and Human Rights* (Oxford, Oxford University Press, 2018) 536–554.

Barnett, MN, 'Refugees and Humanitarianism' in E Fiddian-Qasmiyeh et al (eds), *The Oxford Handbook of Refugee and Forced Migration Studies* (Oxford, Oxford University Press, 2014) 241–252.

Becker, P, 'Remaking Mobility: International Conferences and the Emergence of the Modern Passport System' in P Becker and N Wheatley, *Remaking Central Europe the League of Nations and the Former Habsburg Lands* (Oxford, Oxford University Press, 2020) 193–212.

Benton, L and Clulow, A, 'Legal Encounters and the Origins of Global Law' in JH Bentley et al (eds), *The Cambridge World History: Volume 6: The Construction of a Global World, 1400–1800 CE, Part 2* (Cambridge, Cambridge University Press, 2015) 80–100.

Besson, S, 'Moral Philosophy and International Law' in A Orford and F Hoffmann (eds), *The Oxford Handbook of the Theory of International Law* (Oxford, Oxford University Press, 2016) 385–406.

Betts, A, 'International Relations and Forced Migration' in E Fiddian-Qasmiyeh et al (eds), *The Oxford Handbook of Refugee and Forced Migration Studies* (Oxford, Oxford University Press, 2014) 60–73.

Bodansky, D, 'Prologue to a Theory of Non-Treaty Norms' in MH Arsanjani et al (eds), *Looking to the Future: Essays on International Law in Honor of W. Michael Reisman* (Leiden, Martinus Nijhoff, 2010) 119–134.

Bolton, P and Skeel Jr, DA, 'Odious Debts or Odious Regimes?' in RW Kolb (ed), *Sovereign Debt: From Safety to Default* (Hoboken, Wiley, 2011) 253–260.

Breckman, WW and Gordon, P, 'Introduction' in WW Breckman and P Gordon (eds), *The Cambridge History of Modern European Thought, Volume I (Cambridge, Cambridge University Press, 2019)* 1–16.

Buchheit, L, et al, 'The Restructuring Process' in SA Abbas et al (eds), *Sovereign Debt: A Guide for Economists and Practitioners* (Oxford, Oxford University Press, 2019) 328–364.

Carazo, MP and Klein, D, 'Implications for Public International Law: Initial Considerations' in D Klein et al (eds), *The Paris Agreement on Climate Change Analysis and Commentary* (Oxford, Oxford University Press, 2017) 389–412.

Caron, DD, 'Foreword' in RM Bratspies and RA Miller (eds), *Transboundary Harm in International Law: Lessons from the Trail Smelter Arbitration* (Cambridge, Cambridge University Press, 2006) xix–xxii.

Carty, A, 'The Practice of International Law' in D Armstrong (ed), *Routledge Handbook of International Law* (London, Routledge, 2009) 81–100.

Castellanos-Jankiewicz, L, 'Negotiating Equality: Minority Protection in the Versailles Settlement' in M Erpelding, B Hess, and H Ruiz Fabri (eds), *Peace Through Law: The Versailles Peace Treaty and Dispute Settlement After World War I* (Baden Baden, Nomos, 2019) 123–155.

Chakrabarti, P and Worboys, M, 'Science and Imperialism since 1870' in *The Cambridge History of Science, Volume 8* (Cambridge, Cambridge University Press, 2020) 9–31.

Chinkin, C, 'Monism and Dualism: The Impact of Private Authority on the Dichotomy Between National and International Law' in JE Nijman and A Nollkaemper (eds), *New Perspectives on the Divide Between National and International Law* (Oxford, Oxford University Press, 2007) 134–162.

Choi, SJ and Gulati, M, 'Customary International Law: How do Courts Do It?' in CA Bradely (ed), *Custom's Future: International Law in a Changing World* (Cambridge, Cambridge University Press, 2016) 117–147.

Chriss, JJ, 'Social Control: History of the Concept' in M Deflem (ed), *The Handbook of Social Control* (Oxford, Wiley, 2019) 9–22.

Cueto, M, 'The History of International Health: Medicine, Politics, and Two Socio-Medical Perspectives, 1851 to 2000' in C McInnes, K Lee, and J Youde (eds), *The Oxford Handbook of Global Health Politics* (Oxford, Oxford University Press, 2020) 18–36.

Dempsey, PS, 'Introduction: Multilateral Conventions and Customary International Law' in PS Dempsey and RS Jakhu (eds), *Routledge Handbook of Public Aviation Law* (New York, Routledge, 2016) 1–8.

Dickerson, AM, 'Insolvency Principles: The Missing Link in the Odious Debt Debate' in RW Kolb (ed), *Sovereign Debt: From Safety to Default* (Hoboken, Wiley, 2011) 261–266.

Dubin, MD, 'The League of Nations Health Organisation' in P Weindling (ed), *International Health Organisations and Movements, 1918–1939* (Cambridge, Cambridge University Press, 2009) 56–80.

Dubin, MD, 'Toward the Bruce Report: The Economic and Social Programs of the League of Nations in the Avenol Era' in United Nations Library (ed), *The League of Nations in Retrospect / La Société des Nations: rétrospective* (Berlin, Walter de Gruyter, 1983) 42–72.

Dunoff, JL and Pollack, MA, 'International Law and International Relations' in JL Dunoff and MA Pollack (eds), *Interdisciplinary Perspectives on International Law and International Relations: The State of the Art* (Cambridge, Cambridge University Press, 2012) 3–32.

Dupret, B, 'Legal Traditions and State-Centered Law: Drawing from Tribal and Customary Law Cases of Yemen and Egypt' in D Chatty (ed), *Nomadic Societies in the Middle East and North Africa: Entering the 21st Century* (Leiden, Brill, 2006) 280–301.

Elster, J, 'Introduction' in J Elster (ed), *Deliberative Democracy* (Cambridge, Cambridge University Press, 1998) 1–18.

Feliciano, FP, 'Report of the Director of Studies of the English-speaking Section of the Centre' in D Carreau and MN Shaw (eds), *La dette extérieure/The External Debt* (Dordrecht, Martinus Nijhoff, 1995) 25–52.

Fitzmaurice, MA, 'The Corfu Channel Case and the Development of International Law' in N Ando et al (eds) *Liber Amicorum Judge Shigeru Oda*, Volume I (The Hague, Kluwer, 2002) 119–145.

Fitzmaurice, P, 'Between the Wars – The Refugee Convention of 1933: A Contemporary Analysis' in D Keane and Y McDermott (eds), *The Challenge of Human Rights Past, Present and Future* (Cheltenham, Edward Elgar, 2012) 236–255.

Forteau, M, 'Comparative International Law Within, Not Against, International Law: Lessons from the Intenrational Law Commission' in A Roberts et al (eds), *Comparative International Law* (Oxford, Oxford University Press, 2018) 161–179.

French, D, 'Trail Smelter (United States of America/Canada) (1938 and 1941)' in E Bjorge and C Miles (eds), *Landmark Cases in Public International Law* (Oxford, Hart Publishing, 2017) 159–188.

Gazzini, T, 'The Protection of Minorities at the Origins of the Notion of Erga Omnes Obligations' in A Ziegler and J Küffer (eds), *Les minorités et le Droit / Minorities and the Law: Mélanges en l'honneur du Professeur Barbara Wilson* (Zurich, Schulthess Verlag, 2016) 13–22.

Genin, V, 'The Institute of International Law's Crisis in the Wake of the Franco-Prussian War (1873–1899)' in I Van Hulle and RCH Lesaffer, *International Law in the Long Nineteenth Century (1776–1914) From the Public Law of Europe to Global International Law?* (Leiden, Brill Nijhoff, 2019) 214–232.

Goodin, RE, 'Institutions and Their Design' in RE Goodin (ed), *The Theory of Institutional Design* (Cambridge, Cambridge University Press, 1996) 1–53.

Grahl-Madsen, A, 'The League of Nations and the Refugees' in United Nations Library (ed), *The League of Nations in Retrospect / La Société des Nations: rétrospective* (Berlin, Walter de Gruyter, 1983) 358–368.

Grant, JP and Barker, JC, 'The Harvard Research: Genesis to Exodus and Beyond' in JP Grant and JC Barker (eds), *The Harvard Research in International Law: Contemporary Analysis and Appraisal* (Buffalo, Hein, 2007) 1–40.

Grmek, MD, 'Les débuts de la quarantaine maritime' in C Buchet (ed), *L'Homme, La Santé et La Mer* (Paris, H. Champion, 1997) 39–59.

Hafner, G and Novak, G, 'State Sucession in Respect of Treaty Relationships' in DB Hollis, *The Oxford Guide to Treaties*, 2nd edn (Oxford, Oxford University Press, 2020) 383–413.

Handl, G, 'Trail Smelter in Contemporary International Environmental Law: Its Relevance in the Nuclear Energy Context' in Bratspies, RM and Miller, RA (eds), *Transboundary Harm in International Law: Lessons from the Trail Smelter Arbitration* (Cambridge, Cambridge University Press, 2006) 125–139.

Henckaerts, JM and Debuf, E, 'The ICRC and the Clarification of Customary International Humanitarian Law' in BD Lepard (ed), *Reexamining Customary International Law* (Cambridge, Cambridge University Press, 2017) 161–188.

Houston, AR, 'Applying Lessons from the Past in Haiti: Cholera, Scientific Knowledge, and the Longest-Standing Principle of International Health Law' in M Eccleston-Turner and I Brassington (eds), *Infectious Diseases in the New Millennium Legal and Ethical Challenges* (Cham, Springer, 2020) 13–41.

Kammerhofer, J, 'Between Pragmatism and Disenchantment: The Theory of Customary International Law after the ILC Project' in P Merkouris, J Kammerhofer, and N Arajärvi, *The Theory, Practice, and Interpretation of Customary International Law* (Cambridge, Cambridge University Press, 2022) 3–28.

Karavias, M, 'Corporations and Responsibility under International Law' in P Pazartzis and P Merkouris (eds), *Permutations of Responsibility in International Law* (Leiden, Brill Nijhoff, 2019) 43–65.

Kelly, M, 'The Role of the Military in Globalizing the Rule of Law' in S Zifcak (ed), *Globalisation and the Rule of Law* (New York, Routledge, 2004) 184–203.

Kennedy, D, 'The Mystery of Global Governance' in J Dunoff and J Trachtman (eds), *Ruling the World? Constitutionalism, International Law, and Global Governance* (Cambridge, Cambridge University Press, 2009) 37–68.

Kennedy, D, 'Three Globalizations of Law and Legal Thought: 1850–2000' in DM Trubek and A Santos, *The New Law and Economic Development: A Critical Appraisal* (Cambridge, Cambridge University Press, 2006) 19–73.

Kolb, RW, 'Sovereign Debt: Theory, Defaults, and Sanctions' in RW Kolb (ed), *Sovereign Debt: From Safety to Default* (Hoboken, Wiley, 2011) 3–14.

Kolb, RW, 'The Economics of Sovereign Debt' in *Elgar Research Reviews in Economics* (9 December 2016).

Koskenniemi, M, 'Between Commitment and Cynicism: Outline for a Theory of International Law as Practice' in d'Aspremont, J et al (eds), *International Law as a Profession* (Cambridge, Cambridge University Press, 2017) 38–66.

Kovács, P, 'The Protection of Minorities under the Auspices of the League of Nations' in D Shelton (ed), *The Oxford Handbook of International Human Rights Law* (Oxford, Oxford University Press, 2013) 325–341.

Leiter, B, 'Holmes, Economics, and Classical Realism' in SJ Burton (ed), *The Path of the Law and its Influence: The Legacy of Oliver Wendell Holmes, Jr* (Cambridge, Cambridge University Press, 2000) 285–325.

Lesaffer, R, 'Siege Warfare in the Early Modern Age: A Study on the Customary Laws of War' in A Perreau-Saussine and JB Murphy (eds), *The Nature of Customary Law* (Cambridge, Cambridge University Press, 2007) 176–202.

Lienau, O, 'Sovereignty, Legitimacy, and Creditworthiness' in RW Kolb (ed), *Sovereign Debt: From Safety to Default* (Hoboken, Wiley, 2011) 245–253.

Lowe, V, 'The Politics of Law-Making: Are the Method and Character of Norm Creation Changing?' in M Byers, *The Role of Law in International Politics: Essays in International Relations and International Law* 223 (Oxford, Oxford University Press, 2001) 207–226.

MacCormick, N, 'Four quadrants of jurisprudence' in W Krawietz et al (eds), *Prescriptive Formality and Normative Rationality in Modern Legal Systems: Festschrift for Robert S. Summers* (Berlin, Duncker & Humblot, 1994) 53–70.

Maccormick, N, 'Natural Law and the Separation of Law and Morals' in RP George (ed), *Natural Law Theory: Contemporary Essays* (Oxford, Oxford University Press, 1994) 105–133.

Maier, CS, 'Leviathan 2.0' in ES Rosenberg (ed), *A World Connecting*, Volume 5 of A Iriye and J Osterhammel (general editors), *A History of the World* (Cambridge, Belknap Press, 2013) 29–282.

Maier, CS, 'The World Economy and the Cold War in the Middle of the Twentieth Century' in MP Leffler and OA Westad (eds), *The Cambridge History of the Cold War*, Volume I (Cambridge, Cambridge University Press, 2010) 44–66.

Manicas, P, 'The Social Sciences Since World War II: The Rise and Fall of Scientism' in W Outhwaite and S Turner (eds), *The SAGE Handbook of Social Science Methodology* (Thousand Oaks, Sage Publishing, 2007) 7–31.

McCaffrey, SC, 'Introduction: The Path to the UN Watercourses Convention and Beyond' in L Boisson de Chazournes et al (eds), *The UN Convention on the Law of the Non-Navigational Uses of International Watercourses: A Commentary* (Oxford, Oxford University Press, 2018) 1–18.

Meijers, H, 'On International Customary Law in the Netherlands' in HHG Post (eds), *On the Foundations and Sources of International Law* (The Hague, T.M.C. Asser Press, 2003) 77–128.

Michaelides-Mateou, S, 'Customary International Law in Aviation' in B Lepard (ed), *Reexamining Customary International Law* (Cambridge, Cambridge University Press, 2017) 309–345.

Ørebech, P and Chanock, M, 'Towards Sustainability: The Basis in International Law' in P Ørebech et al (eds), *The Role of Customary Law in Sustainable Development* (Cambridge, Cambridge University Press, 2009) 385–410.

Pénet, P and Zendejas, JF, 'Introduction' in P Pénet and JF Zendejas (eds), *Sovereign Debt Diplomacies: Rethinking Sovereign Debt from Colonial Empires to Hegemony* (Oxford, Oxford University Press, 2021) 1–14.

Reimann, M, 'Historical Jurisprudence' in MD Dubber and C Tomlins (eds), *The Oxford Handbook of Legal History* (Oxford, Oxford University Press, 2018) 397–414.

Roberts, AE and Sivakumaran, S, 'The Theory and Reality of the Sources of International Law' in MD Evans (ed), *International Law*, 5th edn (Oxford, Oxford University Press, 2014) 89–118.

Rosenau, JN, 'Governance, Order, and Change in World Politics' in JN Rosenau and EO Czempiel (eds), *Governance without Government: Order and Change in World Politics* (Cambridge, Cambridge University Press, 1992) 1–29.

Salman, SMA, 'Misconceptions regarding the Interpretation of the UN Watercourses Convention' in FR Loures and A Rieu-Clarke (eds), *The UN Watercourses Convention in Force: Strengthening International Law for Transboundary Water Management* (London, Earthscan, 2013) 28–35.

Schenk, J, 'The Central Commission for the Navigation of the Rhine: A First Step towards European Economic Security?' in B de Graaf, I de Haan, and B Vick (eds), *Securing Europe after Napoleon: 1815 and the New European Security Culture* (Cambridge, Cambridge University Press, 2019) 75–94.

Skran, CM and Easton-Calabria, E, 'Historical Development of Refugee Law' in A Zimmermann et al (eds), *The 1951 Convention Relating to the Status of Refugees and its 1967 Protocol: A Commentary*, 2nd edn (Oxford, Oxford University Press, 2024) 3–38.

Smil, V, 'A New World of Energy' in JR McNeill and K Pomeranz (eds), *The Cambridge World History*, Volume VII (Cambridge, Cambridge University Press, 2015) 164–184.

Thirlway, H, 'Reflections on Multiculturalism and International Law' in S Yee and JY Morin (eds), *Multiculturalism and International Law: Essays in Honor of Edward McWhinney* (Leiden, Martinus Nijhoff, 2009) 95–112.

Toope, SJ, 'Emerging Patterns of Governance and International Law' in M Byers (ed), *The Role of Law in International Politics: Essays in International Relations and International Law* (Oxford, Oxford University Press, 2001) 91–108.

Tyler, TR, 'Procedural Justice' in A Sarat (ed), *The Blackwell Companion to Law and Society* (2004) 435–453.

Veatch, R, 'Minorities and the League of Nations' in United Nations Library (ed), *The League of Nations in Retrospect / La Société des Nations: rétrospective* (Berlin, Walter de Gruyter, 1983) 369–383.

Venzke, I, 'Contemporary Theories and International Lawmaking' in C Brölmann and Y Radi (eds), *Research Handbook on the Theory and Practice of International Lawmaking* (Cheltenham, Edward Elgar, 2016) 66–84.

Verdier, PH and Versteeg, M, 'International Law in National Legal Systems: An Empirical Investigation' in A Roberts et al (eds), *Comparative International Law* (Oxford, Oxford University Press, 2018) 209–230.

Walker, N, 'Europe's Constitutional Overture' in N Barber, M Cahill, and R Ekins (eds), *The Rise and Fall of the European Constitution* (Oxford, Hart Publishing, 2018) 177–196.

Weber, H, 'Der Minderheitenschutz des Völkerbundes' in M Mohr (ed), *Friedenssichernde Aspekte des Minderheitenschutzes in der Ära des Völkerbundes und der Vereinten Nationen in Europa* (Berlin, Springer, 1996) 3–22.

Weindling, P, 'Introduction: Constructing International Health Between the Wars' in P Weindling (ed), *International Health Organisations and Movements, 1918–1939* (Cambridge, Cambridge University Press, 2009) 1–16.

Weiss, EB, 'The Five International Treaties: A Living History' in EB Weiss and HK Jacobson (eds), *Engaging Countries: Strengthening Compliance with International Environmental Accords* (Cambridge, MIT Press, 1998) 89–172.

Zekoll, J, 'Comparative Civil Procedure' in M Reimann and R Zimmermann (eds), *The Oxford Handbook of Comparative Law*, 2nd edn (Oxford, Oxford University Press, 2019) 1306–1338.

Index

www.ingramcontent.com/pod-product-compliance
Ingram Content Group UK Ltd.
Pitfield, Milton Keynes, MK11 3LW, UK
UKHW020844290926
15470UKWH00004B/1540

9 781509 968497